Anglo-Saxon Studies 54

OLD ENGLISH BIBLICAL PROSE

Anglo-Saxon Studies
ISSN 1475-2468

General Editors
Catherine Cubitt
John Hines
David Petts
Andrew Rabin

'Anglo-Saxon Studies' aims to provide a forum for the best scholarship on the Anglo-Saxon peoples in the period from the end of Roman Britain to the Norman Conquest, including comparative studies involving adjacent populations and periods; both new research and major re-assessments of central topics are welcomed.

Books in the series may be based in any one of the principal disciplines of archaeology, art history, history, language and literature, and inter- or multi-disciplinary studies are encouraged.

Proposals or enquiries may be sent directly to the editors or the publisher at the addresses given below; all submissions will receive prompt and informed consideration.

Professor Catherine Cubitt, katy.cubitt@uea.ac.uk

Professor Emeritus John Hines, hines@cardiff.ac.uk

Doctor David Petts, d.a.petts@durham.ac.uk

Professor Andrew Rabin, andrew.rabin@louisville.edu

Boydell & Brewer, editorial@boydellandbrewer.com

Recently published volumes in the series are listed at the back of this book

OLD ENGLISH BIBLICAL PROSE

TRANSLATION, ADAPTATION, INTERPRETATION

Francis Leneghan

D. S. BREWER

© Francis Leneghan 2026

Some Rights Reserved. Without limiting the rights under copyright reserved above, any part of this book may be reproduced, stored in or introduced into a retrieval system, or transmitted, in any form or by any means (electronic, mechanical, photocopying, recording or otherwise)

The right of Francis Leneghan to be identified as
the author of this work has been asserted in accordance with
sections 77 and 78 of the Copyright, Designs and Patents Act 1988

First published 2026
D. S. Brewer, Cambridge

ISBN 978-1-84384-760-1 (Hardback)
ISBN 978-1-84384-761-8 (Paperback)

D. S. Brewer is an imprint of Boydell & Brewer Ltd
and of Boydell & Brewer Inc.
website: www.boydellandbrewer.com

Our Authorised Representative for product safety in the EU is Easy Access System Europe – Mustamäe tee 50, 10621 Tallinn, Estonia,
gpsr.requests@easproject.com

A CIP catalogue record for this book is available
from the British Library

Open Access Licence: CC–BY–NC–ND
Funding Body: Leverhulme Trust [grant number RF-2023-040\1] and the Arts and Humanities Research Council [grant number AH/Y003276/1]

The publisher has no responsibility for the continued existence or accuracy of URLs for external or third-party internet websites referred to in this book, and does not guarantee that any content on such websites is, or will remain, accurate or appropriate

In memory of my father

Contents

List of Illustrations	viii
Acknowledgements	x
Abbreviations	xi
Prefatory Note on Methodology and Translation Theory	xiii
Introduction	1
1 Translating the Psalms for the Clergy and the Laity	24
2 From the Old Law to the New: The Mosaic Prologue to King Alfred's *Domboc*	54
3 Studying, Reading and Preaching the Gospels	78
4 A Perilous Task: Making the Old English Heptateuch	145
5 A Book for Many: Ælfric's *Treatise on the Old and New Testaments*	216
Conclusion	244
Bibliography	254
Index	282

Illustrations

Figures

1. London, British Library, Cotton MS Vespasian A. I, fol. 12^r, 'Vespasian Psalter: Psalms 2–3'. Reproduced by permission of the British Library. — 29
2. London, British Library, Cotton MS Vespasian A. I, fol. 12^v, 'Vespasian Psalter: Psalm 3.' Reproduced by permission of the British Library. — 30
3. Cambridge, University Library, MS Ff. 1, 23, fol. 7^r, 'Cambridge Psalter: Psalm 3.1–3.7'. Reproduced by kind permission of the Syndics of Cambridge University Library. — 37
4. Bibliothèque nationale de France, MS Latin 8824, fol. 2^r, 'Paris Psalter: *Prose Psalms* 2–3'. Reproduced by permission of BnF. — 43
5. London, British Library, Cotton MS Nero D. IV, fol. 29^r, 'Lindisfarne Gospels: Mt. 1.18, with Old English gloss'. Reproduced by permission of the British Library. — 83
6. Oxford, Bodleian Library, MS Auct. D. 2. 19, fol. 2^v, 'Farman's gloss on Rushworth Gospels: Mt. 1.18–19'. Reproduced by permission of the Bodleian Libraries. Open Access Licence CC BY-NC 4.0. — 87
7. Cambridge Corpus Christi College MS 140, fols 2^v–3^r, '*Wessex Gospels*: opening of Gospel of Matthew with Latin headings in red'. Reproduced by permission of The Parker Library, Corpus Christi College, Cambridge. — 104–5
8. Oxford, Bodleian Library, MS Bodley 441, fol. 11^v, '*Wessex Gospels*: Mt. 7–8 with Old English rubric and Latin pericope marker'. Reproduced by permission of the Bodleian Libraries. Open Access Licence CC BY-NC 4.0. — 107
9. London, British Library, Cotton MS Claudius B. IV, fol. 59^v, 'Old English Illustrated Hexateuch: Pharaoh has his baker hanged (Gen. 40.22)'. Reproduced by permission of the British Library. — 154

Illustrations

10. Oxford, Bodleian Library, MS Laud Misc. 509, fol. 1ʳ, 'Ælfric's *Preface to Genesis*'. Reproduced by permission of the Bodleian Libraries. Open Access Licence CC BY-NC 4.0.   156
11. Oxford, Bodleian Library, MS Laud Misc. 509, fol. 3ʳ, 'Old English Heptateuch: End of Ælfric's *Preface to Genesis*/opening of Ælfric's translation of Genesis'. Reproduced by permission of the Bodleian Libraries. Open Access Licence CC BY-NC 4.0.   163
12. Oxford, Bodleian Library, MS Laud Misc. 509, fol. 72ʳ, 'Old English Heptateuch: end of *Leviticus*, opening of *Numbers*'. Reproduced by permission of the Bodleian Libraries. Open Access Licence CC BY-NC 4.0.   184
13. Oxford, Bodleian Library, MS Laud Misc. 509, fol. 120ᵛ, 'Opening of Ælfric's *Treatise on the Old and New Testaments*'. Reproduced by permission of the Bodleian Libraries. Open Access Licence CC BY-NC 4.0.   217

Tables

1. Comparison of Luke 23.34–40 in Vulgate, *Wessex Gospels*, Lindisfarne and Rushworth glosses   95
2. Comparison of Matthew 27.35–42 in Vulgate, *Wessex Gospels* and HomS18   133
3. Comparison of Matthew 27.39–42 in Vulgate, *Wessex Gospels* and Ælfric's Palm Sunday Homily   140
4. Comparison of Genesis 19.1–3 in Vulgate and Ælfric's *Genesis*   167
5. Comparison of Joshua 10.5–10 in Vulgate and Ælfric's *Joshua*   200

Acknowledgements

I am very grateful for the support and encouragement of many colleagues and friends who have read or discussed with me various parts of this book, in particular Daniel Anlezark, Helen Appleton, Mark Atherton, John Barton, Rachel Burns, Ed Clarke, Amy Faulkner, Sarah Foot, Cosima Gillhammer, Niamh Kehoe, Samira Lindstedt, Hugh Magennis, Richard North, Elizabeth Solopova, Rebecca Stephenson and Elaine Treharne. I also warmly thank the anonymous reviewer for Boydell & Brewer for their insightful comments and helpful suggestions. Thanks also to Tamara Atkin, Marilina Cesario, Marina MacKay, Annie Sutherland, Marion Turner, Dan Wakelin and Abigail Williams for being such excellent colleagues. I am thankful to Mikael Males and Alice Jorgensen for facilitating productive and enjoyable visiting fellowships at the University of Oslo and Trinity College Dublin Long Room Hub respectively. For assistance with images, I am grateful to Stewart J. Brookes. I am pleased to acknowledge the generous financial support of the Leverhulme Trust [grant number RF-2023-040\1] and the Arts and Humanities Research Council [grant number AH/Y003276/1], which allowed me to bring this book to completion. Thanks also to Caroline Palmer at Boydell for her sage counsel.

Abbreviations

ASE	*Anglo-Saxon England*
CCSL	Corpus Christianorum Series Latina
CH I	Roy M. Liuzza, ed. and trans., *The Old English Catholic Homilies: The First Series: Ælfric*, DOML 86 (Cambridge, MA: Harvard University Press, 2024)
CH II	Malcolm Godden, ed., *Ælfric's Catholic Homilies: The Second Series: Text*, EETS s.s. 5 (Oxford: Oxford University Press, 1979)
Clayton and Mullins	Mary Clayton and Juliet Mullins, eds and trans., *Old English Lives of the Saints: Ælfric*, 3 vols, DOML 58, 59, 60 (Harvard MA: Harvard University Press, 2019)
CPL	Clauis Patrum Latinorum
CSASE	Cambridge Studies in Anglo-Saxon England
CSEL	Corpus Scriptorum Ecclesiasticorum Latinorum
DOE	*Dictionary of Old English: A to L* online, ed. Angus Cameron, Ashley Crandell Amos, Antonette diPaolo Healey *et al.* (Toronto: Dictionary of Old English Project, 2024), https://doe.artsci.utoronto.ca/
DOE	*Corpus Dictionary of Old English Corpus* (Toronto: Dictionary of Old English Project, 2025), https://corpus-doe-utoronto-ca
DOML	Dumbarton Oaks Medieval Library
EETS, o.s./e.s./s.s.	Early English Texts Society, Original/Extra/Supplementary Series
ES	*English Studies*
fontes	*Fontes Anglo-Saxonici: World Wide Web Register*, https://arts.st-andrews.ac.uk/fontes/
JEGP	*The Journal of English and Germanic Philology*

Abbreviations

Ker	Neil R. Ker, *Catalogue of Manuscripts Containing Anglo-Saxon* (Oxford: Clarendon Press, 1957)[1]
MÆ	*Medium Ævum*
MGH	*Monumenta Germaniae Historica*
MP	*Modern Philology*
N&Q	*Notes & Queries*
PMLA	*Proceedings of the Modern Languages Association of America*
PQ	*Philological Quarterly*
RES	*The Review of English Studies*
SELIM	*Journal of the Spanish Society for Medieval English Language and Literature*
SEM	Studies in the Early Middle Ages
SOEL	Studies in Old English Literature
SP	*Studies in Philology*

[1] References to items described in this work are cited by catalogue number indicated by the siglum §.

Prefatory Note on Methodology and Translation Theory

In his recent study of biblical translation, John Barton observes: 'The translatability of the Bible has been a normal perception for Christians almost from the beginning.'[1] This book follows Barton in drawing on several influential models of translation theory. Jan de Waard and Eugene Nida distinguish between 'formal equivalence', which aims to convey the form, syntax or style of the source text, and 'functional equivalence', wherein a translator's goal is to bring over the meaning rather than the form of the source.[2] Lawrence Venuti categorises translations as either 'foreignising' or 'domesticating' in approach: a foreignising translation is one in which a translator seeks to highlight the foreignness of the source text in the target language (i.e. the translation), for example through the use of archaic, non-standard or 'foreign' syntax or vocabulary carried over from the source text; in a domesticating translation, by contrast, a translator will strive to convey the meaning of the source text in the target language in as natural a manner as is possible, thereby minimising the sense of historical, cultural and linguistic difference.[3] Katherine Reiss and Hans Vermeer identify five categories of translation: an 'interlinear' translation presents a word-for-word rendering of the source text which is 'often incomprehensible for a reader who is not familiar with the source language'; a 'literal' translation, 'unlike the interlinear version, observes the norms and rules of the target language'; a 'philological' translation is one in which 'the syntactic, semantic and pragmatic dimensions of the source-text linguistic signs are "imitated" to such an extent that the target language may seem completely unnatural to the target audience'; in a 'communicative' translation, 'the target text does not feel like a translation, at least not with regard to the language it uses; rather, it is [...] an equivalent of the original text with regard to all of its dimensions'; and finally, a 'creative' translation is 'a separate type where certain concepts, ways of thinking, ideas, objects, etc. do not exist in the target culture so that the translator has to

---

[1] John Barton, *The Word: On the Translation of the Bible* (London: Penguin, 2022), p. 74.
[2] Jan de Waard and Eugene Nida, *From One Language to Another: Functional Equivalence in Bible Translating* (Nashville: Nelson, 1986).
[3] Lawrence Venuti, *The Translator's Invisibility* (New York: Routledge, 1995).

create new terms with which to refer to them'.[4] Reiss and Vermeer further emphasise that the form of every 'translational act' is determined by its purpose (for which they use the Greek term *skopos*), which may differ from that of the source text.[5] Finally, George Steiner outlines four stages of translation which he refers to collectively as the 'hermeneutic motion': first comes 'affirmation', an 'initiative trust, an investment of belief [...] in the meaningfulness' of the source text; the next stage is 'aggression' or 'plundering', whereby the 'translator invades, extracts and brings home' elements of the source text; the third stage, 'incorporation' or 'embodiment', involves the adaptation of the source text into the target language and the decision to retain or omit certain elements; the fourth and final stage is 'compensation' or 'restitution', whereby the translator attempts to redress that which has been lost in the act of translation.[6] These theoretical approaches inform the methodology of the case studies presented in this book, allowing for comparison of the translation strategies adopted by the authors of Old English biblical prose.

All quotations from the Vulgate are taken from *Biblia Sacra Vulgata*, fifth edn, ed. Robert Weber and Roger Gryson (Stuttgart: Württembergische Bibelanstalt, 2007). Unless otherwise stated, all modern English translations of the Vulgate are from *The Holy Bible: Douay-Rheims Version, revised by the servant of God Bishop Richard Challoner A.D. 1749–1752* (London: Baronius Press, 2007), though I have modified punctuation, capitalisation and spelling (e.g. thou > you; thy > your; hath > has; shalt > shall) throughout. I have also consulted the various versions of the Vulgate with Douay-Rheims translations freely available online.

---

[4] Katherine Reiss and Hans J. Vermeer, *Towards a General Theory of Translational Action: Skopos Theory Explained*, trans. by Christiane Nord and Marina Dudenhöfer (London: Routledge Taylor & Francis Group, 2014), pp. 124–5.
[5] Reiss and Vermeer, pp. 85–93.
[6] George Steiner, *After Babel: Aspects of Language and Translation*, 3rd edn (Oxford: Oxford University Press, 1998), pp. 312–19.

Introduction

THE TRANSLATION of the Bible into English does not begin, as is sometimes supposed, with the King James Version of 1611, or with Tyndale in the sixteenth century or Wycliffe in the late fourteenth century.[1] Rather, for the first English translations of Scripture, we must look to the earliest written phase of the language, the Old English period (*c.* 600–1100), which saw a remarkable proliferation of vernacular biblical prose and verse. While Old English biblical poetry continues to be the subject of intense scholarly interest,[2] the much larger corpus of Old English biblical prose remains relatively

---

[1] For example, Oliver Dy and Wim François begin their recent survey of 'Vernacular Translations of the Latin Bible' in the late Middle Ages, making no mention of Old English translations of Scripture: 'Vernacular Translations of the Latin Bible', in *The Oxford Handbook of the Latin Bible*, ed. H. A. G. Houghton (Oxford: Oxford University Press, 2023), pp. 392–405. David Norton acknowledges in passing the verse paraphrase of Cædmon as an example of pre-Wycliffite translation but asserts that 'the main line of English translations starts with the literal, as exemplified by the Psalter of the hermit of Hampole, Richard Rolle (d. 1349)': *A History of the English Bible as Literature* (Cambridge: Cambridge University Press, 2000), p. 5. On myths about the absence of vernacular translations of Scripture in the medieval period and their origin in Protestant Reformation, see Frans van Liere, *An Introduction to the Medieval Bible* (Cambridge: Cambridge University Press, 2014), pp. 177–80. For a recent study that emphasises the continuity of English 'vernacular theology' from Old English through to the late medieval period, with attention to the contribution of Old English prose, see Nicholas Watson, *Balaam's Ass: Vernacular Theology Before the English Reformation, Volume 1: Frameworks, Arguments, English to 1250* (Philadelphia: University of Pennsylvania Press, 2022).

[2] Scholarship on Old English biblical poetry is vast. For a recent study of the most important manuscript witness, see Carl Kears, *MS Junius 11 and its Poetry* (York: York Medieval Press, 2023). See also Roy M. Liuzza, ed. *The Poems of MS Junius 11* (New York: Routledge, 2002); Samantha Zacher, *Rewriting the Old Testament in Anglo-Saxon Verse: Becoming the Chosen People* (London: Bloomsbury, 2013). The heavy preference for biblical verse over prose in scholarship is illustrated by *Old English Literature and the Old Testament*, ed. Michael Fox and Manish Sharma (Toronto: University of Toronto Press, 2012), which contains seven chapters devoted to biblical and hagiographic verse, one which considers both prose and verse (Samantha Zacher, 'Circumscribing the Text: Views on Circumcision in Old English Literature', pp. 89–118) and only two which take Old English prose works as their main focus (Michael Fox, 'Ælfric's *Interrogationes Sigewulfi*', pp. 25–63; Paul E. Szarmach, 'Ælfric's *Judith*', pp. 64–88).

unexplored, a missing chapter in the history of scriptural translation.[3] This book presents the first in-depth study of the earliest attempts to make the sacred words of the Bible available to English readers, clerical and lay, in prose writing. Under consideration are not only translations in the strict sense but also homilies, paraphrases and summaries which together reveal the range of options open to authors of Old English biblical prose.

Arundel vs Alfred

In the early fifteenth century, Archbishop Arundel issued his famous decree prohibiting the translation of the Bible into English without official approval:

> Statuimus igitur et ordinamus, ut nemo deinceps aliquem textum sacrae scripturae auctoritate sua in linguam Anglicanam, vel aliam transferat, per viam libri, libelli, aut tractatus [...] quousque per loci dioecesanum, seu, si res exegerit, per concilium provinciale ipsa translatio fuerit approbata: qui contra fecerit, ut fautor haeresis et erroris similiter puniatur.[4]

---

[3] Geoffrey Shepherd provided a brief account of Ælfric's biblical works and the *Wessex Gospels*, though he is strangely dismissive of attempts to render biblical material into English prior to the sixteenth century: 'English Versions of the Scriptures before Wyclif', in *The Cambridge History of the Bible, Volume 2*, ed. Lampe, pp. 362–87, at 366, 375–7. A notable exception is Richard Marsden, 'The Bible in English', in *The New Cambridge History of the Bible, Volume 2: From 600 to 1450*, ed. Richard Marsden and E. Ann Matter (Cambridge: Cambridge University Press, 2012), pp. 217–38, at 221–6. Barton acknowledges the significance of Old English biblical prose, briefly mentioning Bede's lost Gospel of John, the Alfredian *Prose Psalms*, Ælfric's paraphrases and the Lindisfarne Gospel gloss (*The Word*, p. 15). Old English biblical translations, both in prose and verse, are surveyed in van Liere, *Introduction to the Medieval Bible*, pp. 182–90. Robert Stanton devotes a chapter of his monograph to Old English biblical prose and verse: *The Culture of Translation in Anglo-Saxon England* (Cambridge: D. S. Brewer, 2002), pp. 101–43. Minnie Cate Morrell provides a sample of the sheer range of scriptural translations produced in prose and verse this period: *Manual of Old English Biblical Materials* (Knoxville, TN: University of Tennessee Press, 1965). Substantial work has also been done on Old English homilies and the biblical translations they contain and, in some cases, interpret: see, for example, Paul E. Szarmach and Bernard F. Huppé, eds, *The Old English Homily and its Background* (Albany, NY: State University of New York Press, 1978); and Thomas N. Hall and Winfried Rudolf, eds, *Sermons, Saints, and Sources: Studies in the Homiletic and Hagiographic Literature of Early Medieval England*, SOEL 6 (Turnhout: Brepols, 2025).

[4] David Wilkins, ed., *Concilia Magnae Britanniae et Hiberniae, ab Anno MCCCL ad Annum MDXLV. Volumen Tertium* (London: Davis, 1737), p. 317.

[We decree and we command that from now on no one may by his own authority translate any text of Holy Scripture into the English language, or another, in the form of a book, booklet or tract […] until the same translation will have been approved by the diocesan of the place or, if the subject demands, through the provincial council. Let whoever does the contrary be similarly punished like a supporter of heresy and error.]

Though stopping short of banning English biblical translations outright, Arundel's decree gave voice to anxieties over the association of the vernacular with Lollardy and heresy in late medieval England.[5] At the opposite end of the medieval period, in the late ninth century, King Alfred wrote a letter to his bishops – known as the Prose Preface to the Old English *Pastoral Care* – reflecting a very different attitude to the practice of translating the Bible into English:

Ða gemunde ic hu sio æ wæs ærest on Ebrisc geðiode funden, ond eft, ða hie Creacas geliornodon, ða wendon hie hie on hiora agen geðiode ealle, ond eac ealle oðre bec. Ond eft Lædenware swæ same, siððan hie hie geliornodon, hie hie wendon ealla ðurh wise wealhstodas on hiora agen geðiode. Ond eac ealla oðra Cristna ðioda sumne dæl hiora on hiora agen geðiode wendon.

Forðy me ðyncð betre, gif iow swæ ðyncð, ðæt we eac suma bec – ða ðe niedbeðearfosta sien eallum monnum to wiotonne – ðæt we ða on ðæt geðiode wenden ðe we ealle gecnawan mægen […].

[Then I remembered how the Law was first disclosed in the Hebrew tongue, and, in turn, when the Greeks had studied it, they translated all of it into their own tongue, and all other books, as well. And in turn those of the Latin nations likewise, after they studied it, through wise translators turned it all into their own language. And also all other Christian nations turned a certain portion of it into their own language.

Therefore it seems to me better, if it seems so to you, that we turn certain books – those most necessary for all people to know – into that language that we can all comprehend […].][6]

---

[5] See further Nicholas Watson, 'Censorship and Cultural Change in Late-Medieval England: Vernacular Theology, the Oxford Translation Debate, and Arundel's Constitutions of 1409', *Speculum* 70 (1995), 822–64; Vincent Gillespie and Kantik Ghosh, eds, *After Arundel: Religious Writing in Fifteenth-Century England* (Turnhout: Brepols, 2011); Maureen Jurkowski, 'The Selective Censorship of the Wycliffite Bible', in *The Wycliffite Bible: Origin, History and Interpretation*, ed. Elizabeth Solopova (Leiden: Brill, 2016), pp. 371–88.

[6] Text and translation (with modifications) from R. D. Fulk, ed. and trans., *The Old English Pastoral Care*, DOML 72 (Cambridge, MA: Harvard University Press, 2021), pp. 6–9.

Significantly, whereas Arundel writes in Latin, the official language of Church and state, Alfred writes in *Englisc* (Old English) at a time when knowledge of Latin was in decline among the *Angelcynn* (English people). Alfred justifies his proposal to have certain 'essential' books rendered into English by reminding his readers that the Latin Bible (i.e. the Vulgate) itself is a translation of a translation.[7] In Alfred's letter, *Englisc* therefore sits comfortably alongside Hebrew, Greek and Latin (the three so-called 'sacred languages') and the other vernaculars of Christian peoples as a suitable vehicle for the dissemination of Scripture and other serious writing.[8] Indeed, the availability of biblical writings in the English language (*geðiod*) appears to be central to Alfred's vision of the *Angelcynn* ('English people') as a Christian nation (*ðiod*).[9]

It has long been assumed that 'the books most necessary for all people to know' to which Alfred refers are those same Latin classics which the

---

[7] The first major biblical translation was the Greek translation of the Hebrew Scriptures commissioned by Ptolemy II Philadelphus (r. 309–246 B.C.), known as the Septuagint because it was said to have been made by seventy (or seventy-two) elders of the tribe of Israel. Jerome's dissatisfaction with the Septuagint saw him return to the Hebrew sources in preparing the Latin Vulgate (383–404 A.D.). For the debates surrounding early biblical translation leading to Jerome's Vulgate, see Stanton, *Culture of Translation*, pp. 107–15; Barton, *The Word*, pp. 9–27. On the medieval Bible more generally, see van Liere, *Introduction to the Medieval Bible*.

[8] As Tristan Major has recently pointed out, references to Hebrew, Greek and Latin in Old English and Anglo-Latin sources lack any use of the adjective 'sacred' traditionally applied to these languages, suggesting 'an understanding of the practical function of language for communicating the message of salvation, which extends to the vernacular': '*Awriten on þreo geþeode*: The Concept of Hebrew, Greek, and Latin in Old English and Anglo-Latin Literature', *JEGP* 120 (2021), 141–76, at 176. See also Tristan Major, 'Rebuilding the Tower of Babel: Ælfric and Bible Translation', *Florilegium* 23 (2006), 47–60; and Roberta Frank, 'Some Uses of Paronomasia in Old English Scriptural Verse', *Speculum* 47 (1972), 207–26, at 223. However, a colophon in the earliest manuscript copy of the Old English *Pastoral Care* (Oxford Bodleian Library, MS Hatton 20) demonstrates some limited re-engagement with the three sacred languages in the early tenth century: see Daniel Anlezark, 'The Trilingual *titulus crucis* Tradition in Oxford, Bodleian Library, Hatton 20', in *The Embroidered Bible: Studies in Biblical Apocrypha and Pseudepigrapha in Honour of Michael E. Stone*, ed. Lorenzo DiTommaso, Matthias Henze and William Adler, Studia in Veteris Testamenti Pseudepigrapha 26 (Leiden: Brill, 2017), pp. 64–78.

[9] On connections between language and national identity in Alfredian writing, see esp. Sarah Foot, 'The Making of the *Angelcynn*: English Identity Before the Norman Conquest', *Transactions of the Royal Historical Society* 6 (1996), 25–49. See further below, pp. 20–1, 150, 244–53.

Introduction

twelfth-century Anglo-Norman historian William of Malmesbury claims were translated by the king himself:

> Denique plurimam partem Romanae bibliothecae Anglorum auribus dedit, opimam predam peregrinarum mertium ciuium usibus conuectans; cuius precipui sunt libri Orosius, Pastoralis Gregorii, Gesta Anglorum Bedae, Boetius De Consolatione Philosophiae, liber proprius quem patria lingua Enchiridion, id est Manualem librum appellauit. Quin et prouintialibus grandem amorem studiorum infudit, hos premiis illos iniuriis hortando, neminem illiteratum ad quamlibet curiae dignitatem aspirare permittens. Psalterium transferre aggressus, uix prima parte explicata uiuendi finem fecit.

> [He made a great part of Latin literature accessible to English ears, bringing together a rich cargo of foreign merchandise for the benefit of his countrymen. The chief titles are Orosius, Gregory's *Pastoral Care*, Bede's *History of the English*, Boethius *On the Consolation of Philosophy*, and a book of his own which he called in his native tongue *Enchiridion*, that is *Hand-book*. He also inspired his subjects with a great love of study, encouraging some by rewards and some by penalties, for he allowed no uneducated person to hope for any position at his court. He began to translate the Psalter, but reached the end of his life when he had barely completed the first part.][10]

William's list of Alfred's works is dominated by patristic and late antique authors, with the sole biblical book – the partial translation of the Psalms – appearing at the end. However, with the attribution of this corpus to Alfred no longer certain,[11] Daniel Anlezark has argued that the king had in fact envisaged a project of ecclesiastical and national reform

---

[10] William of Malmesbury, *Gesta Regum Anglorum*, ed. R. A. B. Mynors, R. M. Thomson and M. Winterbottom, Oxford Medieval Texts, 2 vols (Oxford, 1998–99), I, Book II.123, pp. 192–4.

[11] Malcolm Godden cast doubt on Alfred's personal involvement in – and even knowledge of – the translation project beyond the versions of Gregory's *Dialogues* and *Pastoral Care*: 'Did King Alfred Write Anything?', *MÆ* 76 (2007), 1–23; and 'The Alfredian Project and its Aftermath: Rethinking the Literary History of the Ninth and Tenth Centuries', *Proceedings of the British Academy* 162 (2009), 93–12. For a restatement of the traditional view that Alfred was the author of the translations of the *Pastoral Care*, *Boethius*, *Soliloquies* and *Prose Psalms*, but not (as William claims) the *Orosius* and *Bede*, see Janet M. Bately, 'Did Alfred Actually Translate Anything? The Integrity of the Alfredian Canon Revisited', *MÆ* 78 (2009), 189–215. See further Janet M. Bately, 'Alfred as Author and Translator', in *A Companion to Alfred the Great*, ed. Nicole Discenza and Paul E. Szarmach, Brill Companions to the Christian Tradition 58 (Leiden: Brill, 2015), pp. 113–42.

centred on scriptural translation.[12] Indeed, the two earliest extant major Old English biblical translations were produced during Alfred's reign: the *Prose Psalms*, comprising only Psalms 1–50 and therefore matching William's description, and the Mosaic Prologue to Alfred's law code, known as the *Domboc*, which William does not mention.[13] Perhaps as early as the ninth century, gospel excerpts (pericopes) were being translated in vernacular homilies, making the core teachings of the Bible accessible to all levels of English society through liturgical preaching.[14] During the tenth and eleventh centuries, the practice of translating biblical material into Old English prose extended to include renderings of all four gospels (the *Wessex Gospels*) and the first seven books of the Old Testament (Heptateuch).[15] Whereas Arundel's constitutions censored the practice of English Bible translation, Alfred's letter gave it the imprimatur of royal authority. This royal backing for biblical translation was a key factor in the success of Old English biblical prose. However, as we shall see, at least one Old English writer, Ælfric of Eynsham, had serious reservations about the idea of making Scripture accessible to a wide audience in the vernacular without clerical supervision.

Early biblical translation among 'other Christian nations'

What evidence is there to support Alfred's claim that 'all the other Christian nations' (*ealla oðra Cristna ðioda*) had already translated 'a certain portion' (*sumne dæl*) of the Bible from Latin into their own languages? Bede records that King Oswald of Northumbria (r. 634–42) first encountered 'the heavenly word' (*uerbi* [...] *caelestis*) of the Gospels through the Irish-language preaching of Bishop Aidan; having spent part of his youth in Ireland as an exile, Oswald was able to translate Aidan's words into English for the benefit of his ealdormen and thegns (*HE* III.3).[16] An Irish verse paraphrase of Genesis, other parts of the Old Testament and the life of Christ was produced in the late tenth or early eleventh century.[17] Parts of a prose redaction

---

[12] Daniel Anlezark, 'Which Books are "Most Necessary" to Know? The Old English *Pastoral Care* Preface and King Alfred's Educational Reform', *ES* 98 (2017), 759–80.

[13] For the possibility that the Old English translation of the Saxon Genesis known as *Genesis B* was made during Alfred's reign, see below, pp. 12–13 n. 43. On the *Prose Psalms*, see Chapter One, pp. 38–53; for the Mosaic Prologue, see Chapter Two.

[14] See Chapter Three, pp. 80, 130–43.

[15] On the *Wessex Gospels*, see Chapter Three, pp. 91–109; on the Old English Heptateuch, see Chapter Four.

[16] Bertram Colgrave and R. A. B. Mynors, ed. and trans., *Bede's Ecclesiastical History of the English People*, rev. edn (Oxford: Clarendon Press, 1992), pp. 220–1.

[17] See Brian Murdoch, 'An Early Irish Adam and Eve: *Saltair na Rann* and the Traditions of the Fall', *Mediaeval Studies* 35 (1973), 146–77.

of this work are extant in the late fourteenth-century Book of Uí Maine and the early fifteenth-century Leabhar Breac.[18] However, while Irish glosses were added to Latin biblical books as early as the seventh century, no substantial written translations of Scripture into Irish survive from the early medieval period.[19] The earliest extant translation of Scripture into a medieval European vernacular is the Gothic Bible produced in the fourth century by Bishop Ulfilas (Wulfila). Ulfilas played a key role in the conversion of the Goths following their migration into former Roman territory north of the Danube in the mid-fourth century, and his translation was designed to make Scripture accessible to these newly converted people. Ulfilas is said to have translated the entire Bible except for the Books of Kings from the Greek of the Septuagint into Gothic, though only the Gospels and parts of the Pauline epistles now survive.[20] Unlike most other early Germanic translations of Scripture, Ulfilas wrote in prose rather than verse, sticking very closely to the wording and syntax of his Greek source, while making some 'domesticating' concessions to Gothic idiom.[21] Ulfilas employs some rhetorical and literary techniques such as *variatio* – the technique of varying an element of a repeated referent – and there are occasional instances of alliteration, though it is unclear whether this is intentional or accidental.[22] This largely word-for-word, formal-equivalence approach is evident in his

---

[18] See Myles Dillon, 'Scél saltrach na rann', *Celtica* 4 (1958), 1–43.

[19] Fearghus Ó Fearghail comments: 'there is little evidence of an interest in a vernacular Bible in Ireland before the mid-sixteenth century': 'Translating the Bible into Irish 1565–1850', in *Ireland and the Reception of the Bible: Social and Cultural Perspectives*, ed. Bradford A. Anderson and Jonathan Kearney (London: T. & T. Clark, 2018), pp. 59–78, at 59. On biblical allusions in Irish bardic poetry from the thirteenth to seventeenth centuries, as well as biblical influence on early Irish saints' lives and other texts, see Salvador Ryan, 'The Bible and "the People" in Ireland, ca. 1100–ca. 1650', in *Ireland and the Reception of the Bible*, ed. Anderson and Kearney, pp. 43–58. For biblical influences on early Irish literature, see Elizabeth Boyle, *History and Salvation in Early Ireland* (Abingdon: Routledge, 2021). For early Irish biblical glossing, commentary and exegesis, see Martin McNamara, *The Bible in the Early Irish Church 550–850* (Leiden: Brill, 2022). I am grateful to Prof. Máire Ní Mhaonaigh for these references.

[20] The text was edited in 1908 by Wilhelm Streitberg, *Die Gotische Bibel*, 7th edn (Heidelberg: Universitätsverlag C. Winter, 2000). For a detailed study, see Carla Falluomini, *The Gothic Version of the Gospels and Pauline Epistles: Cultural Background, Transmission and Character* (Berlin: de Gruyter, 2015).

[21] On domesticating vs foreignising translations, see above p. xii. For Ulfilas' approach to translation, see Hans Stolzenburg, *Zur Übersetzungstechnik des Wulfila* (Halle a S.: Buchdruckerei des Waisenhauses, 1905).

[22] Falluomini cites the examples of Mt 7.15: *wulfos wilwandans*; Col 2.16: *in draggka aiþþau in dailai dagis dulþuis* (pp. 87–8). See further J. M. N. Kapteijn, 'Die Übersetzungstechnik der gotischen Bibel in den Paulinischen Briefen', *Indogermanische Forschungen* 29 (1911–12), 260–367.

rendering of the opening words of the Gospel of Mark (with Greek text and modern English translation supplied underneath the Gothic): [23]

Mark 1.1:

Anastodeins	aiwaggeljons	Iesuis	Xristaus	sunaus	gudis.
ἀρχὴ τοῦ	εὐαγγελίου	ἰησοῦ	χριστοῦ	υἱοῦ	τοῦ θεοῦ
The beginning of	(the) gospel	of Jesus	Christ,	(the) Son	of God;

Mark 1.2:

swe	gameliþ	ist	in		Esaïin	praufetau
καθὼς	γέγραπτα		ἐν τῷ		ἠσαΐα	τῷ προφήτῃ
As	written	it is	in (the)		Isaiah	(the) prophet

sai,	ik insandja	aggilu	meinana	faura	þus,
ἰδοὺ	ἐγὼ ἀποστέλλω	τὸν ἄγγελόν	μου	πρὸ	προσώπου σου
Behold	I send	(the) messenger	mine	before	you (Got.)/ your face (Gk)

On the whole, Ulfilas sticks so closely to the syntax and lexis of the Greek source that his translation method can be said to be 'interlinear'. The Gothic Bible is therefore not a substitute for the Greek source, but a supplement which guides the reader to its meaning.[24]

The ninth century was a period of major innovation in scriptural translation among the Germanic-speaking peoples of continental Europe, and it is against this background that the remarkable burst of English biblical prose in the long tenth century can best be understood.[25] One genre that would prove especially popular was the 'gospel harmony', in which all four gospels were condensed into a single text. All medieval gospel harmonies ultimately derive from Tatian's second-century Syriac

---

[23] On the distinction between formal and functional equivalence, see above, p. xii.
[24] For Reiss and Vermeer's definition of 'interlinear' translation, see above, p. xii.
[25] See W. B. Lockwood, 'Vernacular Scriptures in Germany and the Low Countries before 1500', in *The Cambridge History of the Bible, vol. 2: The West from the Fathers to the Reformation*, ed. G. W. H. Lampe (Cambridge: Cambridge University Press, 1969), pp. 428–34; Andrew Colin Gow, 'The Bible in Germanic', in *The New Cambridge History of the Bible, vol. 2: From 600 to 1450*, ed. Richard Marsden and E. Ann Matter (Cambridge: Cambridge University Press, 2012), pp. 198–216, at 202–4.

Diatessaron ('made from four'), which was translated into Latin and then gradually modified to bring its readings into line with the text of the Vulgate by the sixth century.[26] A manuscript containing this Latin gospel harmony, together with other parts of the New Testament, was acquired by the English missionary St Boniface, who donated it to the newly founded East Frankish monastery at Fulda in 745. This manuscript, the Codex Fuldensis, served as the immediate source for two early continental gospel harmonies: a poetic version known as the *Heliand*, composed in Old Saxon alliterative verse *c.* 830–840;[27] and a prose version, the Old High German Tatian, written in the East Franconian dialect of Old High German *c.* 830. While the *Heliand* takes an expansive and free approach to the Latin source, employing heroic diction in the manner of the Old English biblical verse epics, the prose version presents a close, word-for-word translation of the Latin *Diatessaron*. Hence, whereas the verse *Heliand* opens with a lengthy proem in praise of the Evangelists, those *thuru craft godas gecorona uurðun* [...] *settian endi singan endi seggian forð / that sea fan Cristes crafte them mikilon / gisâhun endi gehôrdun* ('who were picked by the power of God [...] to compose, sing and proclaim what they had seen and heard of Christ's powerful strength') (ll. 17, 33–5a),[28] the prose Old High German Tatian begins with a close translation of the Vulgate opening of the Gospel of John (1.1–4). Below I print the Vulgate text above the Old High German, with the Douay-Rheims translation provided in the footnote:

1.1. In principio erat verbum et verbum erat apud Deum et Deus erat verbum.[29]
      In anaginne uuas uuort inti thaz uuort uuas mit Gote inti Got selbo uuas thaz uuort.

---

[26] See James William Barker, *Tatian's 'Diatessaron': Composition, Redaction, Recension, and Reception* (Oxford: Oxford University Press, 2021).

[27] The heroic verse style of the *Heliand* resembles that of the *Saxon Genesis*, a free adaptation of Genesis (*c.* 840–50), which seems to have been composed for the edification of the Carolingian court. For the text, see Alger N. Doane, ed., *The Saxon Genesis: An Edition of the West Saxon 'Genesis B' and the Old Saxon Vatican 'Genesis'* (Madison, WI: University of Wisconsin, 1991). For connections with the Old English *Genesis B*, see below, n. 43.

[28] Text cited from *Hêliand: Text and Commentary*, ed. James A. Cathey, Medieval European Studies II (Morgantown, WV: West Virginia University Press, 2002); alliteration is marked in bold. Translation cited from G. Ronald Murphy, trans., *The Heliand: The Saxon Gospel: A Translation and Commentary* (Oxford: Oxford University Press, 1992), pp. 3–4.

[29] *In the beginning was the Word, and the Word was with God, and the Word was God.*

1.2. Hoc erat in principio apud Deum.[30]
Thaz uuas in anaginne mit Gote.

1.3. Omnia per ipsum facta sunt et sine ipso factum est nihil quod factum est.[31]
Alliu thuruh thaz vvurdun gitân inti ûzzan sîn ni uuas uuiht gitânes thaz thâr gitân uuas;

1.4. In ipso vita erat et vita erat lux hominum.[32]
Thaz uuas in imo lîb inti thaz lîb uuas lioht mannô.

1.5. Et lux in tenebris lucet et tenebrae eam non comprehenderunt.[33]
Inti thaz lioht in finstarnessin liuhta inti finstarnessi thaz ni bigriffun.[34]

The translation method of the Old High German Tatian is akin to that of an interlinear gloss, with the author sticking closely to the syntax and wording of the source and making only the occasional allowance for vernacular prose idiom, such as the regular insertion of the definite article *thaz*, 'the/that', and the position of the main verb *uuas* ('was') in 1.4.

A third continental gospel harmony, Otfrid's *Evangelienbuch* (c. 863–71), was produced in rhyming couplets in the South Rhine Franconian dialect of Old High German.[35] In a dedicatory letter to Archbishop Liutbert of Mainz, Otfrid explains that he undertook this work at the behest of his fellow monks, whose ears were disturbed by 'the offensive chanting of laymen' (*laicorum cantus* [...] *obscenu*), and for Judith, a local noblewoman. These patrons asked Otfrid to provide them with a selection of the Gospels *Theotisce* ('in German'):

> ut aliquantulum huius cantus lectionis ludum secularium vocum deleret et in Evangeliorum propria lingua occupati dulcedine sonum inutilium rerum noverint declinare.
>
> [so that a little of the text of this poem might somewhat erase the trivial merriment of worldly voices and, engrossed in the Gospels in their own

---

[30] *The same was in the beginning with God.*
[31] *All things were made by him: and without him was made nothing that was made.*
[32] *In him was life, and the life was the light of men.*
[33] *And the light shines in darkness, and the darkness did not comprehend it.*
[34] *Tatian: Lateinisch und altdeutsch mit ausführlichem Glossar*, ed. Eduard Sievers (Paderborn: Schöningh, 1872), p. 67.
[35] For discussion of these works, see J. Knight Bostock, *A Handbook on Old High German Literature*, 2nd edn (Oxford: Clarendon Press, 1976), pp. 157–83, 190–212. For the text, see Oskar Erdmann, ed., *Otfrids Evangelienbuch*, Altdeutsche Textbibliothek 49 (Tübingen: Max Niemeyer, 1957).

language, they might learn to turn away the noise of futile things with sweetness.]³⁶

It is a source of shame for Otfrid's patrons that while pagan poets such as Virgil, Lucan and Ovid had celebrated the deeds of their people in their own language, and early Christian poets such as Juvencus, Arator and Prudentius had already turned the Bible into Latin verse, the Franks are yet to produce any scriptural translations of their own:³⁷

> nos vero, quamvis eadem fide eademque gratia instructi, divinorum verborum splendorem clarissimum proferre propria lingua dicebant pigrescere.
>
> [But they said that we, though learned in the same faith and the same grace, were sluggardly in setting forth the very brilliant splendour of the divine words in our own language.]³⁸

As is the case with Alfred's preface cited above, there is nothing in this letter to suggest that Otfrid regarded his vernacular as inferior to Latin or unsuitable for the translation of Scripture. Indeed, Otfrid not only translates the Gospels, but he also confidently interprets them for his readers under sections labelled 'Spiritaliter', 'Mystice' and 'Moraliter'.³⁹ Otfrid's *Evangelienbuch* is therefore what we might call a functional equivalence translation, which aims to bring across the meaning of the source text rather than imitating its form. This communicative approach is determined by the work's purpose: a dedicatory poem to King Louis the German (r. 843–76), together with other prefatory and epistolary addresses to various churchmen, indicates that Otfrid intended for his work to reach a mixed audience of lay and clerical readers.⁴⁰

Alfred may have learnt about other vernacular translations of the Bible, such as those discussed above, through the continental scholars whom he

---

³⁶ Latin text and translation taken (with modifications) from Francis P. Magoun Jr, 'Otfrid's Ad Liutbertum', *PMLA* 58 (1943), 869–90, at 873.
³⁷ On the Latin biblical verse epics, see Michael Lapidge, 'Versifying the Bible in the Middle Ages', in *The Text in the Community: Essays on Medieval Works, Manuscripts, Authors, and Readers*, ed. Jill Mann and Maura Nolan (Notre Dame: University of Notre Dame Press, 2005), pp. 11–40; Patrick McBrine, *Biblical Epics in Late Antiquity and Anglo-Saxon England: Divina in Laude Voluntas* (Toronto: University of Toronto Press, 2017).
³⁸ Magoun, 873.
³⁹ The classic study of medieval biblical exegesis is Beryl Smalley, *The Study of the Bible in the Middle Ages* (Oxford: Blackwell, 1952). See further van Liere, *Introduction to the Medieval Bible*, pp. 110–40.
⁴⁰ See Rosamond McKitterick, *The Carolingians and the Written Word* (Cambridge: Cambridge University Press, 2008), pp. 227–35.

recruited to his court in the 890s, such as John the Saxon and Grimbald of St Bertin, or even during his own visit to the court of Charles the Bald as a child.[41] The English ruler's enthusiasm for biblical and patristic learning was matched by his devotion to vernacular verse,[42] and he may therefore have known something of the early Old English biblical paraphrases preserved in MS Junius 11 or the many biblically-inspired poems contained in the Exeter Book.[43] Indeed, prior to the rise of Old English prose in the ninth

[41] Alfred's recruitment of continental scholars is recorded by Asser in his *Life of Alfred*, ch. 78 (*Asser's Life of King Alfred*, ed. William H. Stevenson, with an article by Dorothy Whitelock [Oxford: Clarendon Press, 1957], p. 63; *Alfred the Great: Asser's 'Life of King Alfred' and Other Contemporary Sources*, ed. and trans. Simon Keynes and Michael Lapidge [Harmondsworth: Penguin, 1983], p. 93), while his visit to Charles the Bald's court is mentioned in ASC MS A 853. According to Asser (*Life of Alfred*, ch. 2), Alfred's maternal grandmother was of Gothic origin, though scholars have generally assumed that this is a result of his confusion of Jutes and Goths: see Keynes and Lapidge, pp. 68, 295–96. On the importance of the Goths in Alfredian literature and culture, see Malcolm Godden, 'The Anglo-Saxons and the Goths: Rewriting the Sack of Rome', *ASE* 31 (2002), 47–68; Craig. R. Davis, 'Gothic *Beowulf*: King Alfred and the Northern Ethnography of the Nowell Codex', *Viator* 50 (2019), 99–129. On the influence of Gothic legend on Old English literature more generally, see Roberta Frank, 'Germanic Legend in Old English Literature', in *The Cambridge Companion to Old English Literature*, 2nd edn, ed. Malcolm Godden and Michael Lapidge (Cambridge: Cambridge University Press, 2013), pp. 82–100. For the possibility that Alfred knew a vernacular poetic anthology resembling the Exeter Book, see Mercedes Salvador-Bello, 'Educating King and Court: The Exeter Book and the Transmission of Poetic Anthologies in the (Post-)Alfredian Period', *SELIM* 29, special edition on *New Readings in Alfredian Literature*, ed. Francis Leneghan (2024), 71–94.

[42] Asser, *Life of Alfred*, chs 22, 23; Keynes and Lapidge, pp. 74–5.

[43] Further possible evidence for the influence of continental biblical translations on English literature in this period is provided by *Genesis B*, an adaptation of the *Saxon Genesis* into Old English verse which has been approximately dated to the late ninth century. See Thomas A. Bredehoft, *Authors, Audiences and Old English Verse* (Toronto: University of Toronto Press, 2009), pp. 65–93. For the suggestion that the wedding of Alfred's father, King Æthelwulf of Wessex (r. 839–858) and Judith, daughter of the Frankish emperor Charles the Bald (r. 843–877), in 856 provides a plausible context for the transmission of the Saxon Genesis and *Heliand* to England, see Alger N. Doane, 'The Transmission of *Genesis B*', in *Anglo-Saxon England and the Continent*, ed. Hans Sauer and Joanna Story, with the assistance of Gaby Waxenberger (Tempe, AZ: Arizona Center for Medieval and Renaissance Studies, 2011), pp. 63–81, at 66–7; and Barbara Raw, 'The Probable Derivation of Most of the Illustrations in Junius 11 from an Illustrated Old Saxon Genesis', *ASE* 5 (1976), 133–48, at 148. However, Daniel Thomas notes that the West Saxon dynasty had close ties with the Carolingians during the reign of Æthelwulf's father, King Ecgberht of Wessex (r. 802–39), opening up the possibility for the earlier transmission of these Saxon poems

Introduction

century, it was more common to translate the Bible into alliterative verse. It will therefore be helpful to provide a brief sketch of the beginnings of Old English biblical poetry.

The origins of Old English biblical verse

The earliest reference to the composition of Old English biblical poetry is Bede's famous account of Cædmon, preserved in his *Historia Ecclesiastica gentis Anglorum* (*Ecclesiastical History of the English People*) completed in 731. According to Bede, Cædmon was a lay brother at the Northumbrian double-monastery of Streanæshalch (modern-day Whitby) during the abbacy of Hild (657–680) (*HE* IV.24). Not knowing the songs that were routinely sung in the monastery during feasts, Cædmon went out to tend to the cows and fell asleep, whereupon he received a vision in which a man instructed him to sing of Creation. Thus inspired, Cædmon began to sing *in laudem Dei Conditoris uersus quos numquam audierat* ('verses which he had never heard before in praise of God the Creator').[44] Although Bede provides only a Latin summary of the song, a short Old English poem now known as *Cædmon's Hymn* is preserved in multiple manuscripts of the *Historia* in both the original Northumbrian dialect and a later West Saxon recension, which reads as follows:

> Nu sculon herigean heofon-rices weard,
> meotodes meahte and his mod-geþanc
> weorc wuldor-fæder, swa he wundra gehwæs
> ece drihten, *or onstealde.*
> He *ærest sceop* eorðan bearnum
> heofon to hrofe, halig *scyppend;*
> þa middangeard moncynnes weard
> ece drihten, æfter *teode*
> firum foldan, frea ælmihtig.[45]

[Now we must praise the Guardian of the Kingdom of Heaven, the might of the Measurer, and his great intention, the work of the Glory-Father, thus *he created* each wonder *in the beginning*, Eternal

---

to the English: 'Revolt in Heaven: Lucifer's Treason in *Genesis B*', in *Treason: Medieval and Early Modern Adultery, Betrayal, and Shame*, ed. Larissa Tracy, Explorations in Medieval Culture 10 (Leiden: Brill, 2019), pp. 147–69, at 165–6.

[44] Colgrave and Mynors, pp. 416–17.

[45] Cited from Daniel Paul O'Donnell, *Cædmon's Hymn: A Multimedia Study, Edition and Archive* (Cambridge: D. S. Brewer, 2005). The Northumbrian version is printed with translation in *Old English Shorter Poems: Volume I: Religious and Didactic*, ed. and trans. Christopher A. Jones, DOML 15 (Cambridge, MA: Harvard University Press, 2012), pp. 100–1.

Lord. *First he shaped* the earth for men, heaven as a roof, Holy *Shaper*;
then the Guardian of Mankind, Eternal Lord, afterwards *fashioned*
the earth for men, Lord Almighty.] (Emphases added).

In this short poem, the traditional techniques of Germanic alliterative verse which had formerly been used to praise secular heroes are now (*Nu*) repurposed for the praise of the Christian God.[46] For example, the poem features structural alliteration (e.g. *Nu sculon herigean heofon-rices weard/ meotodes meahte and his mod-geþanc*), variation (e.g. *heofon-rices weard,/meotodes meahte* [...] *moncynnes weard*) and compound diction (e.g. *heofon-rices, mod-geþanc, wuldor-fæder*), while the proximity of the verb *sceop* ('created') and the noun *Scyppend* ('Shaper/Creator') suggests that the song sung by the poet (Old English *scop*) Cædmon is itself divinely inspired.

In Bede's account, Abbess Hild was so impressed by Cædmon's newly acquired skill that she instructed him to take monastic orders. Following his ordination, Cædmon went on to compose many more Old English poems on biblical themes.[47] Although it may have some basis in fact, Bede's story of Cædmon's miraculous poetic inspiration has parallels in many cultures and is now usually read as a largely mythic account of the origins of English Christian verse.[48] The method of paraphrasing Latin Scripture into English verse that may have developed at the time is implied by Bede's statement that *quicquid ex diuinis litteris per interpretes discere t, hoc ipse post pusillum uerbis poeticis maxima suauitate et conpunctione conpositis in sua, id est Anglorum, lingua proferret* ('whatever he learned from the holy Scriptures by means of interpreters, he quickly turned into extremely delightful and moving poetry in English, which was his own tongue').[49] Bede goes on to explain that other poets soon followed in Cædmon's footsteps, though none possessed his skill.[50]

---

[46] See E. G. Stanley, 'New Formulas for Old: *Cædmon's Hymn*', in *Pagans and Christians: The Interplay between Christian Latin and Traditional Germanic Cultures in Early Medieval Europe*, ed. Tette Hofstra, L. A. J. R. Houwen and Alasdair A. MacDonald, Medievalia Groningana 16 (Groningen: Egbert Forsten, 1995), pp. 131–48.

[47] Colgrave and Mynors, pp. 418–19.

[48] See, for example, John D. Niles, 'The Myth of the Anglo-Saxon Oral Poet', *Western Folklore* 62 (2003), 7–61; Andy Orchard, 'The Word Made Flesh: Christianity and Oral Culture in Anglo-Saxon Verse', *Oral Tradition* 24 (2009), 293–318. Stanton characterises Cædmon as a 'prophetic' or 'miraculous' translator of the Bible (*Culture of Translation*, pp. 110–17), contrasting his approach with that of more pragmatic translators such as Alfred and Ælfric (pp. 121–43).

[49] *HE* IV.24; Colgrave and Mynors, pp. 414–15.

[50] *HE* IV.24: *Et quidem et alii post illum in gente Anglorum religiosa poemata facere temtabant, sed nullus eum aequiperare potuit* ('It is true that after him other Englishmen attempted to compose religious poems, but none could compare with him') (Colgrave and Mynors, pp. 414–15).

Introduction

A remarkably rich and diverse corpus of Old English biblical and liturgical verse has indeed survived, much of it dating from roughly the first two centuries after the conversion (*c.* 600–*c.* 825). Notable examples include the Old Testament epics *Genesis A*, *Exodus* and *Daniel*, as well as shorter poems on New Testament themes such as the *Advent Lyrics* and the celebrated *Dream of the Rood*.[51] It was not the aim of the earliest English biblical poets to provide a word-for-word or formal-equivalence translation of their scriptural sources. Rather, they sought to produce a living version of the biblical narrative in the form of traditional alliterative verse, a medium that would appeal to English-speaking audiences, lay and clerical alike. To this end, the versifiers exercised a great deal of freedom in their approach to their biblical source, be it the *Vetus Latina* (Old Latin) or Vulgate text, routinely omitting episodes and scenes, compressing and rearranging narrative elements and sometimes even introducing new ones. This independent approach to translation – known as 'functional' or 'dynamic equivalence'[52] – is evident even in the nine verse lines of *Cædmon's Hymn* cited above, which loosely paraphrase various parts of the Creation narrative from Genesis 1.1 and 2.1 while also appearing to draw on other sources such as the Preface to the Canon of the Mass.[53] Turning to the longer biblical verse paraphrases, *Genesis A* does not begin as we might expect, with an account of the Creation of the World (Gen. 1), but with an invocation to praise God which itself echoes *Cædmon's Hymn* (ll. 1–14) followed by an extended and dramatic account of the Fall of the Angels (ll. 15–102) derived from apocryphal and patristic sources. The rest of the poem focuses on the stories of the Fall of Man, Noah and the Great Flood and Cain and Abel before ending with the story of Abraham and Isaac (Gen. 22), omitting a large chunk of the biblical narrative (Gen. 23–50). The two other Old Testament verse epics preserved in MS Junius 11, *Exodus* and *Daniel*, similarly focus on isolated episodes from their own respective biblical books, namely the Crossing of the Red Sea (Ex. 13.20–14.31) and the captivity of the Israelites in Babylon (Dan. 1–5).[54] The imaginative freedom with which these poets adapted scriptural sources continues to attract admirers.

---

[51] For the dating of these poems, see R. D. Fulk, *A History of Old English Meter* (Philadelphia: University of Pennsylvania Press, 1992), p. 392.

[52] See above, p. xii.

[53] For connections between the opening of *Genesis A*, *Cædmon's Hymn* and the Preface to the Canon of the Mass, see Laurence Michel, '*Genesis A* and the *Praefatio*', *Modern Language Notes* 62 (1947), 545–50.

[54] See further Malcolm Godden, 'Biblical Literature: The Old Testament', in *Cambridge Companion to Old English Literature*, 2nd edn, ed. Godden and Lapidge, pp. 214–33, at 223–4.

That Cædmon and his followers should have chosen alliterative verse as their preferred medium for rendering Scripture into the vernacular should not surprise us, given that this was the literary form most familiar to English speakers in the centuries following their migration from the continent in the fifth century. A century or so after Cædmon, Alcuin would famously complain of the singing of songs about pagan Germanic heroes in the monastic refectory where lives of saints would be more appropriate.[55] Vernacular biblical verse – as well as the model of verse hagiography popularised by Cynewulf – provided an edifying alternative to such material and was therefore actively embraced by the Church. Indeed, there is even a possibility that Bede himself may have followed Cædmon in composing his own vernacular biblical verse.

Bede's lost translation of the Gospel of John: poem, prose or gloss?

At the end of his *Historia Ecclesiastica*, Bede tells us that from the age of seven, when he entered monastic orders at Wearmouth-Jarrow, he applied himself *omnem meditandis Scripturis operam* ('entirely to the contemplation of the Scriptures').[56] Bede's monastery was responsible for the production of the earliest extant complete Bible (pandect) containing the Latin text of the Old and New Testaments – the Codex Amiatinus[57] – and the majority of his own writings took the form of Latin scriptural commentaries and exegesis.[58] However, as André Crépin notes, Bede was not ideologically opposed to the use of the vernacular for scriptural translation and preaching.[59] Hence, Bede states in his Letter to Ecgbert that he made his own English versions of the Creed and the Lord's Prayer (Matthew 6.9–13) for the benefit of ignorant priests who did not know Latin.[60] It is not known

---

[55] *Epistolae Karolini Aevi* II, ed. Ernst Dümmler, MGH Epistolae 4 (Berlin: Weidmann, 1895), 183 (no. 124).
[56] *HE* V.24; Colgrave and Mynors, pp. 566–7.
[57] See Celia Chazelle, *The Codex Amiatinus and Its Sister Bibles: Scripture, Liturgy, and Art in the Milieu of the Venerable Bede* (Leiden: Brill, 2019).
[58] On the celebration of Bede's career as biblical exegete and translator in the thirteenth-century *First Worcester Fragment*, see Conclusion, pp. 244–6.
[59] André Crépin, 'Bede and the Vernacular', in *Famulus Christi: Essays in Commemoration of the Thirteenth Centenary of the Birth of the Venerable Bede*, ed. Gerald Bonner (London: S.P.C.K., 1976), pp. 170–92, at 182.
[60] For Ælfric's criticism of unlearned priests in his *Preface to Genesis*, and the possibility that such figures were among the intended audience of the Old English Heptateuch, see Chapter Four below. The tenth capitulary at the second Council of Clofesho in 747 similarly decreed that priests should learn how to construe and explain the Creed and Lord's Prayer in their own tongue, as well as the words used in the sacraments of mass and baptism: for the text, see Arthur West Haddan and William Stubbs, eds, *Councils and ecclesiastical*

Introduction

if Bede's translations of the Creed and Lord's Prayer were done in Old English verse or prose.

The nature of Bede's other biblical translation, a rendering of the first part of the Gospel of John, is equally obscure. In his account of Bede's last days appended to several manuscripts of the *Historia Ecclesiastica*, the monk Cuthbert writes that his teacher was working on *duo opuscula multum memoria digna* ('two pieces of work very worthy of remembering') at the time of his death:

> a capite euangelii sancti Iohannis usque ad eum locum in quo dicitur 'Sed haec quid sunt inter tantos?' in nostram linguam ad utilitatem ecclesiae Dei conuertit, et de libris Rotarum Ysidori episcopi exceptiones quasdam, dicens 'Nolo ut pueri mei mendacium legant, et in hoc post meum obitum sine fructu laborent.'[61]

> [He translated from the beginning of the gospel of St John up to the place where it says, 'But what are they among so many?' (John 6.9), into our language for the benefit of the Church of God, and a selection from Bishop Isidore's book *On the Wonders of Nature*, saying, 'I don't want my children to read lies and to labour in vain in this after my death.']

No trace of either work survives. The Isidorean work may have taken the form of a series of excerpts in the manner of the popular genre of the *florilegium*. As for Bede's translation of John, scholars are divided as to whether this was done in verse or prose. Bede was familiar with the Latin biblical verse epics, such as Juvencus' *Euangelia* and Sedulius' *Carmen paschale*,[62] while Cuthbert reports that he knew *nostris carminibus* ('our [Old English] poems'). Indeed, immediately prior to his description of Bede's translation of John, Cuthbert quotes a five-line Old English alliterative poem, now known as *Bede's Death Song*, which he says Bede composed *in nostra [...] lingua* ('in our own language') in preparation for death.[63] It is certainly possible, then, that Bede translated the opening of John into

---

documents relating to Great Britain and Ireland, 3 vols (Oxford: Clarendon Press, 1869–78), III, pp. 362–76, at 366; for a translation, see John Johnson, trans. *A collection of the laws and canons of the Church of England from its first foundation to the conquest, and from the conquest to the reign of King Henry VIII*, 2 vols (Oxford: John Henry Parker, 1850), I, pp. 242–63, at 247; for discussion, see Simon Keynes, *The Councils of 'Clofesho'* (Leicester: Leicester University Press, 1994); Catherine Cubitt, *Anglo-Saxon Church Councils, 650–850* (Leicester: Leicester University Press, 1995), pp. 91–152.

[61] Colgrave and Mynors, p. 582; translation my own.
[62] For citations from these two works in Bede, see Michael Lapidge, *The Anglo-Saxon Library* (Oxford: Oxford University Press, 2006), pp. 219, 224.
[63] Colgrave and Mynors, pp. 582–3.

Old English verse in the Cædmonian style.[64] Indeed, given the fashion for adapting Scripture into vernacular poetry at the time, Cuthbert may have assumed that any biblical translation Bede made would be done in verse.[65] A verse translation or paraphrase of the Gospel of John might have proved a useful impetus to prayer and meditation for Bede himself as well as his fellow monks and nuns, comparable with his Latin verse *Life of Cuthbert*.[66]

Alternatively, it has sometimes been suggested that Bede's partial translation of John was among the earliest examples of Old English prose.[67] Such a work, had it ever existed, would however be truly exceptional: it is not until the ninth century that we find substantial evidence for Old English prose being used for purposes other than the writing of law and the occasional charter. Scholars have therefore generally preferred to take the view that Bede was working on a word-for-word gloss rather than a continuous prose translation.[68] Cuthbert tells us that Bede was taken ill about a fortnight 'before Easter' and that he died on the eve of Ascension Day, that is May 26th 735, and readings from John 1–6 are used as lections

---

[64] See Godden, 'Why did the Anglo-Saxons switch from Verse to Prose?', pp. 567–8.

[65] See Christine Rauer, 'The Earliest English Prose', *Journal of Medieval History* 47 (2021), 485–56, at 489–91.

[66] Michael Lapidge argues that this work serves as a 'meditation on the spiritual significance of the events described prosaically by the [anonymous] Lindisfarne author': *Anglo-Latin Literature, 600–899* (London: Hambledon Press, 1996), p. 333. On the suitability of Bede's verse *Life of Cuthbert* for monastic *ruminatio*, see Britton Elliott Brooks, *Restoring Creation: The Natural World in the Anglo-Saxon Saints' Lives of Cuthbert and Guthlac*, Nature and Environment in the Middle Ages 3 (Cambridge: D. S. Brewer, 2019), pp. 67–122.

[67] For example, Janet M. Bately describes Bede's lost John and Isidore translations as works which were 'arguably in prose': 'Old English Prose Before and During the Reign of Alfred', *ASE* 17 (1988), 93–138, at 96 n. 18.

[68] As suggested by Alan S. C. Ross, 'A Connection between Bede and the Anglo-Saxon Gloss to the Lindisfarne Gospels', *Journal of Theological Studies* 20 (1969), 482–94, at 492–93. See also Christine Rauer, Review of Michelle P. Brown, *Bede and the Theory of Everything*, *SELIM* 29 (2024), 142–5, who suggests Bede was glossing the Gospel of John 'as a study tool underpinning live class-room teaching and study of Latin' (144). It has even been proposed that such a gloss lies behind part of the tenth-century Old English gloss added to the Lindisfarne Gospels: see Ross, 'Bede and the Anglo-Saxon Gloss to the Lindisfarne Gospels'; Alan S. C. Ross, 'Supplementary Note to "A Connection between Bede and the Anglo-Saxon Gloss to the Lindisfarne Gospels?"', *Journal of Theological Studies* 24 (1973), 519–21; Constance O. Elliott and Alan S. C. Ross, 'Aldrediana XXIV: The Linguistic Peculiarities of the Gloss to St John's Gospel', *English Philological Studies* 13 (1972), 49–72; Michelle P. Brown, *Bede and the Theory of Everything* (London: Reaktion Books, 2023), pp. 141–51. On the Lindisfarne Gospel gloss, see below pp. 81–91.

Introduction

in the liturgy between Christmas and Easter. Cuthbert's statement that the project was intended *ad utilitatem ecclesiae Dei* ('for the benefit of the Church of God') might suggest then that Bede's translation (or indeed gloss) of John was limited to those short passages read in the liturgy during his illness.[69] While the question must remain open, then, it seems most likely that Bede's lost translation of the Gospel of John either took the form of a verse paraphrase or an interlinear gloss, perhaps restricted to those sections used as liturgical readings.

The rise of Old English prose

One of the most remarkable features of the literary culture of pre-Conquest England is the unusual prestige attached to the written form of the vernacular and the concomitant rise of lay literacy from the time of Alfred.[70] English laws had been written out in vernacular prose since the seventh century, but by the turn of the tenth century charters, wills, letters and other administrative documents previously composed in Latin were now increasingly done in the vernacular. In the wake of Alfred's educational reforms, and building on earlier developments in the kingdom of Mercia, major Latin works of history, science, philosophy and theol-

---

[69] Colgrave and Mynors translate this phrase as 'to the great profit of the Church'. See Richard Marsden, 'Cain's Face, and Other Problems: The Legacy of the Earliest English Bible Translations', *Reformation* 1 (1996), 29–51, at 31–2.

[70] See esp. Patrick Wormald, 'Anglo-Saxon Society and its Literature', in *The Cambridge Companion to Old English Literature*, ed. Malcolm Godden and Michael Lapidge (Cambridge: Cambridge University Press, 1991), pp. 1–22, at 16–19. In an earlier article, Wormald had downplayed the importance of lay literacy: see 'The Uses of Literacy in Anglo-Saxon England and Its Neighbours', *Transactions of the Royal Historical Society*, 5th series, 27 (1977), 95–114. For further discussion of the importance of the vernacular in the late Old English period, see Susan Kelly, 'Anglo-Saxon Lay Society and the Written Word', and Simon Keynes, 'Royal Government and the Written Word in Late Anglo-Saxon England', both in *The Uses of Literacy in Early Medieval Europe*, ed. Rosamond McKitterick (Cambridge: Cambridge University Press, 1990), pp. 36–62 and 226–57; Mechthild Gretsch, *The Intellectual Foundations of the English Benedictine Reform*, CSASE 25 (Cambridge: Cambridge University Press, 1999); Elaine Treharne, 'The Authority of English, 900–1150', in *The Cambridge History of Early Medieval English Literature*, ed. Clare A. Lees (Cambridge: University of Cambridge Press, 2013), pp. 554–78; Helen Gittos, 'The Audience for Old English Texts: Ælfric, Rhetoric and "The Edification of the Simple"', *ASE* 43 (2014), 231–66; Mark Atherton, *The Making of England: A New Literary History of the Anglo-Saxon World* (London: I. B. Tauris, 2017), pp. 59–74. See also more generally, Stanton, *Culture of Translation*.

ogy were translated into Old English prose.[71] Moreover, whereas in the centuries after the conversion Latin saints' lives and homilies had been routinely adapted into Old English verse, by the tenth century it had become more fashionable to turn them into vernacular prose.[72] The same switch from verse to prose that seems to have taken place in the ninth century would determine the shape of Old English biblical translations. Where Old English verse had been the preferred medium for biblical adaptation in the age of Bede, during Alfred's reign prose translations of the Psalms and parts of Exodus and Acts were made, while the tenth and eleventh centuries saw the production of prose translations of all four gospels and the first seven books of the Old Testament, as well as a proliferation of vernacular prose homilies and biblical summaries.[73]

The rise of Old English biblical prose from the ninth to the eleventh centuries coincides with the emergence of the nation of *Engla-land* from the various ethnicities which comprised the *Angelcynn*.[74] Countering the view taken by some historians that national identity cannot be traced earlier than the nineteenth century, Adrian Hastings has argued that 'ethnicities naturally turn into nations or integral elements within nations at the point when their specific vernacular moves from an oral to written usage to the extent that it is being regularly employed for the production of a literature, and particularly for the translation of the Bible.'[75] As Hastings

---

[71] For a recent overview, see Amy Faulkner and Francis Leneghan, 'Introduction: Rethinking English Literary Culture *c.* 850–950', in *The Age of Alfred: Rethinking English Literary Culture, c. 850–950*, ed. Amy Faulkner and Francis Leneghan, SOEL 3 (Turnhout: Brepols, 2024), pp. 17–48.

[72] See Malcolm Godden, 'Why did the Anglo-Saxons switch from Verse to Prose?', in *Age of Alfred*, ed. Faulkner and Leneghan, pp. 565–91.

[73] Although dwarfed by the corpus of Old English biblical prose, vernacular biblical poetry continued to be produced in the later period: for example, *Judith* and the *Metrical Psalms* were both composed in the late ninth or tenth centuries. Other biblical poems such as *Christ and Satan* and *Christ III* (*Christ in Judgment*) are of unknown date. For the possibility that *Genesis B* was composed in or around the Alfredian period, see above, pp. 12–13 n. 43.

[74] On the emergence of the English nation in this period, see Foot, 'The Making of the *Angelcynn*'; Patrick Wormald, '*Engla lond*: The Making of an Allegiance', *Journal of Historical Sociology* 1 (1994), 1–24; James Campbell, *The Anglo-Saxon State* (London-New York: Hambledon and London, 2000); Patrick Wormald, 'Germanic Power Structures: The Early English Experience', in *Power and the Nation in European History*, ed. Len Scales and Oliver Zimmer (Cambridge: Cambridge University Press, 2005), pp. 105–24; Sarah Foot, 'The Historiography of the Anglo-Saxon "Nation-State"', in *Power and the Nation*, ed. Scales and Zimmer, pp. 125–42; George Molyneaux, *The Formation of the English Kingdom in the Tenth Century* (Oxford: Oxford University Press, 2015); Atherton, *Making of England*.

[75] Adrian Hastings, *The Construction of Nationhood: Ethnicity, Religion and*

notes, the Bible's presentation of Israel as a nation – 'a unity of people, language, religion, territory and government' – provided medieval peoples with a 'mirror for national self-imagining'.[76] This book will argue that the production of Old English biblical prose from the ninth to the eleventh centuries played an important role in the emergence of England as a nation. By widening access to Scripture to members of the English laity, from kings and ealdormen to minor gentry and other churchgoers, Old English biblical prose provided the *Angelcynn* with the textual foundations for imagining themselves as members of a Christian nation.

The argument and structure of this book

Chapter One focuses on the vibrant culture of Psalm translation during the Old English period (*c.* 600–1100). The strict word-for-word approach taken in the interlinear glosses is contrasted with the much more free-flowing, idiomatic literary style of the Alfredian *Prose Psalms*. Chapter Two considers another Alfredian work, the selective prose translation of legal sections of Exodus, the Gospels and Acts of the Apostles that comprises the so-called Mosaic Prologue to Alfred's law code (the *Domboc*). This important but little-studied biblical translation was designed to provide the king's poorly-educated judges with a grounding in the history of Judeo-Christian law. Together with the *Prose Psalms*, the Mosaic Prologue is a key component of Alfred's efforts to restore wealth and wisdom to the *Angelcynn*.[77]

Chapters Three and Four demonstrate how the growing demand for biblical translations in the tenth century was met by the production of a series of ambitious prose translations of large parts of the Old and New Testaments. Chapter Three explores three different approaches to the translation of the gospels in the tenth century. Serving a monastic readership engaged in intense study of the Bible, the Old English glosses added to the Lindisfarne and Rushworth Gospels take a scholarly approach to

---

Nationalism (Cambridge: Cambridge University Press, 1997), p. 12. For the argument that the development of national identity was not possible until the nineteenth century with the spread of vernacular literacy, the decline of monarchy and the spread of 'print capitalism', see Benedict Anderson, *Imagined Communities: Reflections on the Origin and Spread of Nationalism* (New York: Verso, 1983; revised 1991). A range of perspectives on the origins of nationhood are presented in Scales and Zimmer, eds, *Power and the Nation*.

[76] Hastings, *Construction of Nationhood*, p. 18.

[77] For a similar approach, see now Jay Paul Gates, 'The Alfredian Prose Psalms and a Legal English Identity', in *Law, Literature, and Social Regulation in Early Medieval England*, ed. Andrew Rabin and Anya Adair, Anglo-Saxon Studies 47 (Cambridge: D. S. Brewer, 2023), pp. 31–53.

the scriptural source, though at times there are passages that read as if they are derived from another free-standing prose translation.[78] The *Wessex Gospels*, by contrast, provide a fluent and confident translation of all four gospels. This major but frequently overlooked prose translation was probably produced in the second half of the tenth century, perhaps for private reading by laity and priests before being repurposed as a liturgical aid. Towards the end of the tenth century, Ælfric responded to the circulation of gospel translations lacking an exegetical framework by composing his own two series of *Catholic Homilies*. Finally, this chapter highlights the popularity of two apocryphal gospels, the Gospels of Nic(h)odemus[79] and Pseudo-Matthew, both of which were translated into fluent Old English prose in this period despite their exclusion from the orthodox canon of the Bible. Chapter Four then turns to the Old English Heptateuch, an ambitious translation of the first seven books of the Old Testament made for noble lay readers *c.* 1000. This chapter focuses on the involvement of Ælfric in this project, despite his reservations about the wisdom of making the Old Testament available to the laity, as well as analysing the translation strategies of the various anonymous contributors, all of whom strove to make these biblical narratives accessible and meaningful to contemporary readers.

In Chapter Five, I argue that Ælfric found a solution to the problem of translating the Bible for the laity in his *Treatise on the Old and New Testaments* (also known as the *Letter to Sigeweard*), another largely neglected work which represents the culmination of his career as a biblical translator and exegete. The Bible (from Greek *biblia*, 'books') was rarely presented as a single book in the medieval period: more typically, copies were made of individual biblical books, most frequently the Psalms and Gospels.[80] In Ælfric's *Treatise*, we see the first move towards the creation of an English Bible, though here conceived as a library of sanctioned books containing a mixture of reliable vernacular translation and authoritative commentary on Scripture. Taken together, Chapters Three to Five highlight the tension between, on the one hand, the increasing demand for scriptural translations among the laity in the decades following Alfred's reforms, and on the other, Ælfric's ongoing reservations about making the Bible available

---

[78] Julia Fernández Cuesta and Sara M. Pons-Sanz, eds, *The Old English Gloss to the Lindisfarne Gospels: Language, Author and Context*, Anglia Book Series 51 (Berlin: De Gruyter, 2016).

[79] The most common modern English spelling is *Nicodemus*, and this is therefore the one I have used throughout, though the edition by J. E. Cross cited below (pp. 110–15) favours *Nichodemus* as this is the form used in the Old English text.

[80] For debates about the unity of the Bible in the medieval period, and the rarity of complete Bibles, see van Liere, *Introduction to the Medieval Bible*, pp. 20–52.

Introduction

to such readers without a robust exegetical framework. The Conclusion considers the lasting impact of Old English biblical prose on conceptions of the English nation, Church and language, its continuing use in the centuries following the Norman Conquest and its influence on later medieval and early modern translations of the Bible.

1

Translating the Psalms for the Clergy and the Laity

THE BOOK of Psalms was by far the most influential biblical book in the Middle Ages. The Psalter's intense, often lyrical prayers served as the textual bedrock of the monastic office, while exegetes read this Old Testament book as a microcosm of the essential teachings of the entire Bible.[1] The Psalms were therefore translated more frequently than any other part of the Bible. Old English psalm translation took three main forms: gloss, continuous prose and verse paraphrase.[2] This chapter will be concerned with the first two categories.[3]

Complete Old English glosses survive in no less than fifteen extant psalters, ranging from what Jane Roberts calls 'opportunistic' additions to existing Latin manuscripts to 'integral glosses' which involve 'the thoughtful interaction of Latin psalms and English words'.[4] Old English glosses are usually inserted above or sometimes alongside each individual Latin word to aid the reader in understanding its meaning. Alderik Blom identifies three main forms of psalter gloss: (1) 'substitution glosses', which 'replace a lemma from the principal text with another term, in order to provide more or less exact lexical equivalents or perceived equivalents';

---

[1] See *The Psalms and Medieval English Literature: From the Conversion to the Reformation*, ed. Tamara Atkin and Francis Leneghan (Cambridge: D. S. Brewer, 2017).

[2] The major study is M. J. Toswell, *The Anglo-Saxon Psalter* (Turnhout: Brepols, 2014). For a helpful overview of the range of Psalm translations, glosses and paraphrases in Old English prose and verse, see Morrell, *Manual of Old English Biblical Materials*, pp. 45–155.

[3] The main verse paraphrases are the *Kentish Psalm* (a free rendering of Psalm 50) and the *Metrical Psalms*, a translation of the entire psalter of which Psalms 51–150 are preserved along with the *Prose Psalms* in the Paris Psalter, while excerpts of Psalms 1–50 appear in other manuscripts. For discussion, see Francis Leneghan, 'Making the Psalter Sing: The Old English *Metrical Psalms*, Rhythm and *Ruminatio*', in *Psalms and Medieval English*, ed. Atkin and Leneghan, pp. 173–97.

[4] Jane Roberts, 'Some Anglo-Saxon Psalters and their Glosses', in *Psalms and Medieval English*, ed. Atkin and Leneghan, pp. 37–71 (at pp. 40–2). On the interpretative dimension to these glosses, see Stanton, *Culture of Translation*, pp. 9–54, 117–20.

(2) 'supplement glosses', which 'elucidate the morphology and syntax of the principal text by supplying additional clarifying word forms, often repeated, or otherwise deduced, from context'; and (3) 'commentary glosses', which 'provide new information to elucidate a given lemma, but without substituting or supplementing the principal text'.[5] The majority of the glosses under consideration in this chapter fall into the first category, though in some cases the gloss serves to supplement and even offer interpretive commentary on the Latin source text. On some occasions when the scribe was uncertain of the meaning of a Latin word or wanted to convey more than one meaning, multiple English equivalents – or 'substitution glosses' – are provided. The result is that the interlinear psalter glosses are usually not readable as free-standing Old English prose without reference to the Latin text they accompany. Robert Stanton has therefore described the Old English psalter glosses as 'a hybrid language, unique to the glosses, which is neither wholly subservient to the Latin text nor a fully independent English rendering'.[6] As an example of the 'opportunistic' glossing tradition, this chapter begins with a discussion of the Vespasian Psalter, in which an Old English gloss was inserted above the Latin text some considerable time after the first phase of the book's production. The chapter will then consider the case of the Cambridge Psalter, which by contrast features an 'integral' gloss conceived as part of the original design of the codex. For a genuinely independent Old English prose translation of the Latin psalter, the chapter then turns to the *Prose Psalms*, a free rendering of Psalms 1–50 made in the late ninth or early tenth century and closely linked with other works associated with King Alfred. Through these three case studies, we will witness the emergence of Old English prose as a flexible and highly effective medium for the transmission of the sacred word of Scripture.

Glossed Psalters

The Vespasian Psalter

The Vespasian Psalter is the earliest extant witness to the Romanum Psalter, the first of the three Latin translations of the Psalms produced by Jerome in the late fourth century.[7] The Latin text of the Romanum, accom-

---

[5] Alderik Blom, *Glossing the Psalms: The Emergence of the Written Vernaculars in Western Europe from the Seventh to the Twelfth Centuries* (Berlin: De Gruyter, 2017), pp. 29–34.
[6] Stanton, *Culture of Translation*, p. 45.
[7] While the Romanum would remain popular in England beyond the Norman Conquest, it was superseded in Ireland and on the continent by Jerome's

panied by a full-page illustration of King David surrounded by his court musicians (now fol. 30ᵛ), was executed in majuscule uncial script with beautifully decorated initials in the mid-eighth century in the kingdom of Kent, probably at Canterbury, where Augustine had first established his church in 597. In the mid-ninth century, an interlinear Old English gloss in the Mercian dialect was added in insular cursive minuscule script.[8] The original plan of this Psalter manuscript clearly did not extend to the inclusion of a vernacular gloss, which is squeezed in above the Latin text. The text's editor, Sherman M. Kuhn, has maintained that the gloss is original to the Vespasian Psalter, but others have argued for its derivation from an earlier, perhaps eighth-century, archetype.[9] It seems safest to concur with Phillip Pulsiano that 'other psalters, perhaps fully glossed psalters, most likely existed, and we should not presume, without clear evidence to the contrary, that the *Vespasian* gloss stands as an original and independent production'.[10] Indeed, one earlier glossed psalter does in fact survive, the Blickling Psalter, a Latin psalter produced in the mid-eighth century to which a partial gloss of twenty-six Old English words was added in red ink in the late eighth or early ninth century.[11] While the Vespasian Psalter

---

revised version, the Gallicanum, and this is the version printed in all editions of the Vulgate Bible and therefore translated in the Douay-Rheims edition. Both the Romanum and Gallicanum are translated from the Greek. For the third and final revision, the Hebraicum, Jerome went back to the Hebrew source that lies behind the Greek. The Hebraicum was known to some scholars in early medieval England but did not have anything like the impact of the Romanum, which remained the standard text for liturgical use and study. See Sarah Larratt Keefer and David R. Burrows, 'Hebrew and the Hebraicum in late Anglo-Saxon England', *ASE* 19 (1990), 67–80.

[8] The manuscript is London, British Library, Cotton MS Vespasian A. I; Ker §203. The standard edition is *The Vespasian Psalter*, ed. Sherman M. Kuhn (Ann Arbor: University of Michigan Press, 1967). For a facsimile, see D. H. Wright, ed. *Early English Manuscripts in Facsimile, XIV: The Vespasian Psalter, British Museum Cotton Vespasian A. I* (Copenhagen and London: Rosenkilde and Bagger, 1967).

[9] Kenneth Sisam, *Studies in the History of Old English Literature* (Oxford: Clarendon Press, 1953), p. 4 n. 2; Sherman M. Kuhn, 'The Vespasian Psalter Gloss: Original or Copy?', *PMLA* 74 (1959), 161–77. For the argument that the Vespasian gloss is a copy, see esp. Kenneth Sisam, 'Canterbury, Lichfield, and the Vespasian Psalter', *RES* 7 (1956), 1–10 and 113–31; and Phillip Pulsiano, 'The Originality of the Old English Gloss of the *Vespasian Psalter* and its Relation to the Gloss of the *Junius Psalter*', *ASE* 25 (1996), 37–62. See further Blom, *Glossing the Psalms*, pp. 161–4.

[10] Pulsiano, 'Old English Gloss', 39.

[11] Pierpoint Morgan Library MS M.776; Ker §287. See further Joseph P. McGowen, 'On the "Red" Blickling Psalter Glosses', *N&Q* 54 (2007), 205–7; Roberts, 'Some Anglo-Saxon Psalters and their Glosses', pp. 43–5. Roberts suggests that the Blickling gloss was not part of the original plan for the psalter, but that 'some early reader added a few translations of words and phrases that had given

gloss may not have been the first such Old English biblical translation produced, it nevertheless remains the earliest substantial witness we have to the vibrant tradition of continuous glossing of the entire psalter in early medieval England.[12] It was long believed that the Vespasian Psalter gloss served as a source for all the later Old English psalter glosses, hence its labelling as an 'A-type' gloss.[13] However, Pulsiano has cautioned against assuming a direct relationship between any of the individual psalter glosses, emphasising that all are copies and that lost intermediaries must have existed.[14] Nevertheless, the fifteen extant glossed psalters, ranging in date from the ninth to the twelfth centuries, are remarkably consistent in their vocabulary, pointing to a standardised approach to Psalter glossing in this period.[15]

The interlinear Vespasian Psalter gloss is a good example of what Roberts terms 'opportunistic' glossing, whereby a vernacular translation was added to a manuscript which was originally ruled solely for the Latin text. The glossator takes a formal-equivalence or word-for-word approach, carefully following the syntax and wording of the source text and making no attempt to produce readable Old English sentences. As

---

him pause, using red as a natural means of differentiating his additions from the surrounding text' (p. 43). Roberts notes that even earlier Old English – and Old Irish – psalm glosses are included in the exegetical catena on Pss 39–151 in Vatican City, MS Pal. lat. 68, fols 1–46 ('Some Anglo-Saxon Psalters and their Glosses', p. 43 n. 15); Ker §388.

[12] For overviews of the glossed psalters, see Toswell, *Anglo-Saxon Psalter*, pp. 221–82; and Roberts, 'Some Anglo-Saxon Psalters and their Glosses'. The Sisams surmised that hundreds of similar glossed psalters were produced in the period: Celia and Kenneth Sisam, eds, *The Salisbury Psalter*, EETS o.s. 242 (London: Oxford University Press, 1959), p. 75.

[13] The theory that the Vespasian Psalter was the source for all subsequent glosses was first advanced by Albert S. Cook (*Biblical Quotations in Old English Prose Writers* [London: MacMillan and Co., 1898], p. xxvi). Uno Lindelöf argued that the Junius Psalter gloss (B-type), dating from the early tenth century, is a direct copy of the Vespasian gloss, while the Cambridge Psalter (C) is an eleventh-century copy of the Vespasian Gloss; the tenth-century Regius Psalter gloss (D) served as the source for the twelfth-century Eadwine (or Canterbury) Psalter (E) gloss, as well as the glosses in the Stow (F), Vitellius (G), Tiberius (H), Arundel (J) and Salisbury (K) psalters: *Studien zu altenglischen Psalterglossen*, Bonner Beiträge zur Anglistik, Heft XIII (Bonn: P. Hanstein, 1904).

[14] Pulsiano, 'Old English Gloss'.

[15] Toswell demonstrates that this uniformity of vocabulary extends even to the *Metrical Psalms*, which frequently employ the same words as the glossed psalters (*Anglo-Saxon Psalter*, pp. 242–50). On the recent discovery of fragments of another Old English glossed psalter connected with the D-type gloss (Regius), see Thijs Porck, 'Newly Discovered Pieces of an Old English Glossed Psalter: The Alkmaar Fragments of the N-Psalter', *ASE* 49 (2024), 1–66.

an example of the glossator's approach, I present below the text of Psalm 3 (fols 12ʳ–12ᵛ), the first complete Psalm in the manuscript. This short lament psalm comprises eight verses plus the traditional heading associating the psalm with David's flight from his son Absalom, which is not glossed in the Vespasian Psalter. Although there are traces of patristic influence elsewhere in the Vespasian gloss, in translating Psalm 3, the glossator does not appear to have made use of any of the major interpretations, such as Augustine, for example, who identified this psalm with Christ's Passion and associated the figure of Absalom with Judas Iscariot.[16] Instead, the translator carefully engages with the wording and grammar of the Romanum Psalter in isolation from such interpretative aids. Whenever a Latin word's meaning was self-evident – as in the case of personal and place names – the gloss was deemed superfluous and no Old English text supplied.[17] First it will be helpful to have the text of the Psalm from the Romanum Psalter, with a modified version of the Douay-Rheims translation of the Vulgate:[18]

Romanum (from Vespasian Psalter):

III. ⁽¹⁾ PSALMUS DAVID CUM FUGERET A FACIE ABESSALON FILII SUI.

¹ ⁽²⁾ Domine, quid multiplicati sunt qui tribulant me? Multi insurgunt adversum me.
² ⁽³⁾ Multi dicunt animae meae, 'Non est salus illi (Gal.: ipsi) in Deo eius.'
³ ⁽⁴⁾ Tu autem, Domine, susceptor meus es, gloria mea et exaltans caput meum.
⁴ ⁽⁵⁾ Voce mea ad Dominum clamavi, et exaudivit me de monte sancto suo.
⁵ ⁽⁶⁾ Ego dormivi et somnum cepi (Gal.: et soporatus sum), et resurrexi (Gal.: exsurrexi) quoniam (Gal.: quia) Dominus, suscepit me.
⁶ ⁽⁷⁾ Non timebo milia populi circumdantis me. Exsurge, Domine,

---

[16] *Expositions on the Book of Psalms by Saint Augustine of Hippo*, ed. and trans. by A. Cleveland Coxe, Nicene and Post-Nicene Fathers: First Series, Volume VIII (New York: 1888), pp. 4–8. Augustine's Christological reading of the psalm is echoed by Bede: see Gillingham, *A Reception History Commentary on Psalms 1–72*, p. 48. On the influence of commentaries on the Vespasian gloss more generally, see Blom, *Glossing the Psalms*, p. 166.
[17] As noted by Roberts, 'Some Anglo-Saxon Psalters and their Glosses', p. 43.
[18] The standard edition of the Romanum Psalter is *Collectanea Biblica Latina x, Le Psautier Romain et les autres anciens psautiers latins*, ed. Dom Robert Weber (Rome: Libreria Vaticana, 1953), which uses the Vespasian Psalter as its base text; variant readings in the Gallican Psalter (i.e. the text printed in the Vulgate Bible) are indicated in brackets. For the history of Psalm 3 and its reception, see Susan Gillingham, *Psalms Through the Centuries: A Reception History Commentary on Psalms 1–72* (Chichester: Wiley-Blackwell, 2018), pp. 47–53.

salvum me fac, Deus meus,

⁷⁽⁸⁾ quoniam tu percussisti omnes adversantes mihi sine causa; dentes peccatorum contervisti (Gal.: contrivisti).

⁸⁽⁹⁾ Domini est salus, et super populum tuum benedictio tua.

[III. ⁰⁽¹⁾ [*titulus*] THE PSALM OF DAVID WHEN HE FLED FROM THE FACE OF HIS SON ABSALOM.

¹⁽²⁾ Why, O Lord, are they multiplied that afflict me? Many are they who rise up against me.

²⁽³⁾ Many say to my soul: 'There is no salvation for him in his God.'

³⁽⁴⁾ But you, O Lord, are my protector, my glory, and the lifter up of my head.

⁴⁽⁵⁾ I have cried to the Lord with my voice: and he has heard me from his holy hill.

⁵⁽⁶⁾ I have slept and taken my rest: and I have risen up, because the Lord has protected me.

⁶⁽⁷⁾ I will not fear thousands of the people surrounding me: arise, O Lord; save me, O my God.

⁷⁽⁸⁾ For you have struck all of them who are my adversaries without cause: you have broken the teeth of sinners.

⁸⁽⁹⁾ Salvation is of the Lord: and your blessing is upon your people.]

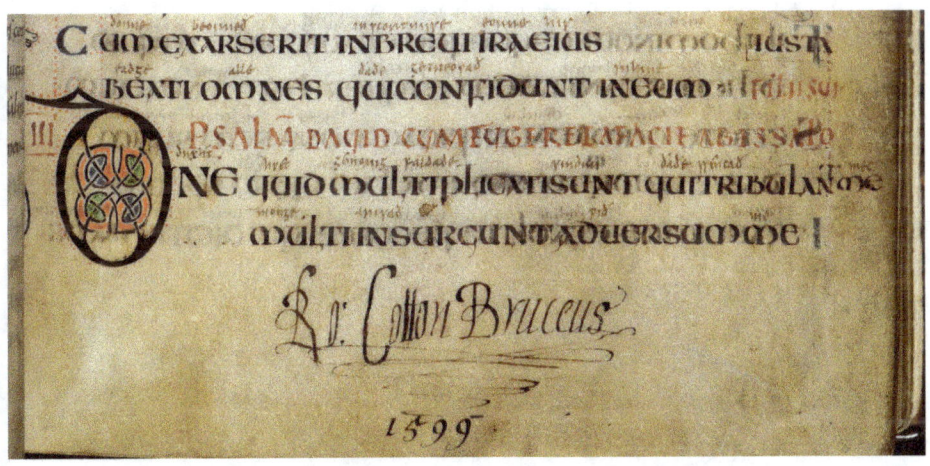

Figure 1. London, British Library, Cotton MS Vespasian A. I, fol. 12ʳ, 'Vespasian Psalter: Psalms 2–3'.

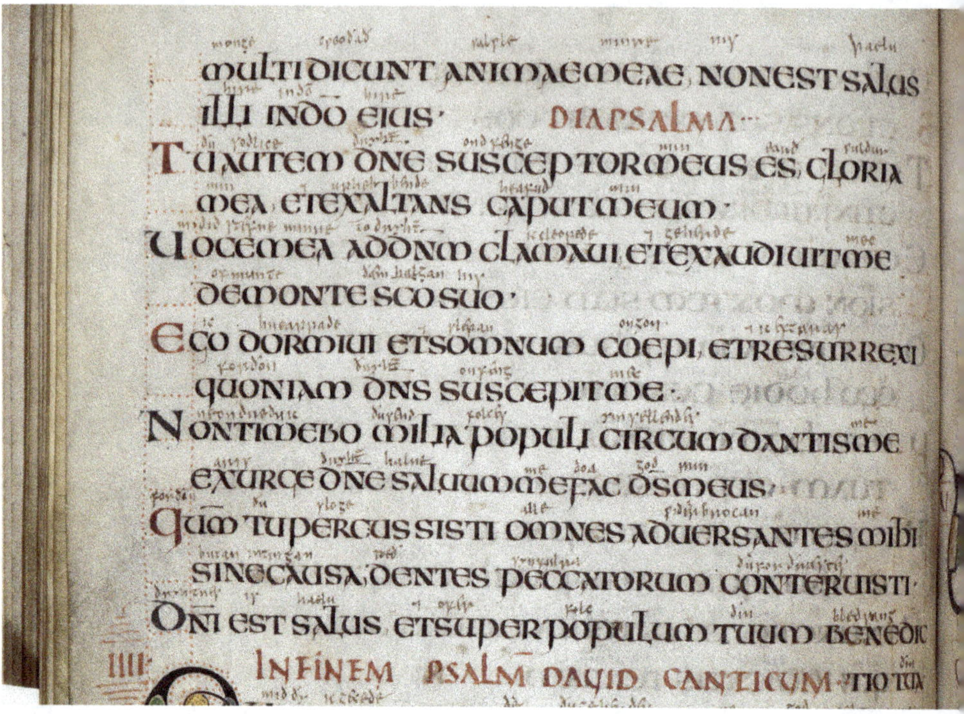

Figure 2. London, British Library, Cotton MS Vespasian A. I, fol. 12ᵛ, 'Vespasian Psalter: Psalm 3'

The diplomatic transcription supplied below shows how the Old English gloss sits above each individual Latin word in the Vespasian Psalter; abbreviations in the manuscript are retained and discussed below:

Ps. 3: (1) **PSALM̄ DAVID CUM FUGERET A FACIE ABESSALON FILII SUI**

Ps. 3.1 (2)

dryhtē̄	hwet	gemonigfaldade	sindun	ða ðe	swencað	mec
DÑE	QUID	MULTIPLICATI	SUNT	QUI	TRIBULANT	ME

3.2 (3)

monge	arisað	wið	me
MULTI	INSURGUNT	ADUERSUM	ME

30

Translating the Psalms for the Clergy and the Laity

monge	cweoðað	salwle	minre	nis	haelu
MULTI	DICUNT	ANIMAE	MEAE	NON EST	SALUS

hire	in	dō	hire
ILLI	IN	DŌ	EIUS

3.3 (4)

ðu	soðlice	dryhf	ondfenge	min	earð	wuldur
TU	AUTEM	DÑE	SUSCEPTOR	MEUS	ES,	GLORIA

min	7	uphebbende	heafud	min
MEA	ET	EXALTANS	CAPUT	MEUM

3.4 (5)

mid id stefne	minre	to	dryhf	ic cleopede	7	geherde	mec
UOCE	MEA	AD	DÑM	CLAMAUI	ET	EXAUDIUIT	ME

of	munte	ðæm halgan	his
DE	MONTE	SCŌ	SUO

3.5 (6)

ic	hneappade	7	slepan	ongon	7	ic eft aras
EGO	DORMIUI	ET	SOMNUM	COEPI,	ET	RESURREXI

forðon	dryhī	onfeng	mec
QUONIAM	DÑS	SUSCEPIT	ME

3.6 (7)

ne	ondredu ic	ðusend	folces	ymsellendes	me
NON	TIMEBO	MILIA	POPULI	CIRCUMDANTIS	ME

aris	dryhī	halne	me	doa	god	min
EXURGE	DÑE	SALUUM	ME	FAC	DŠ	MEUS

3.7 (8)

forðon	ðu	sloge	alle	widerbrocan	me
QŪM	TU	PERCUSSISTI	OMNES	ADUERSANTES	MIHI

butan	intingan	toeð	synfulra		ðu forðræstes			
SINE	CAUSA,	DENTES	PECCATORUM		CONTERUISTI.			

3.8 (9)

dryhtnes	is	haelu	7	ofer	folc	ðin	bledsung	ðin
DŃI	EST	SALUS,	ET	SUPER	POPULUM	TUUM	BENEDICTIO	TUA

The majority of these glosses are substitution glosses in which a single vernacular equivalent lexeme is supplied, though there are some supplement glosses where Latin verbs are expanded through the insertion of a personal pronoun (3.4: CLAMAUI > *ic cleopode*; 3.5: RESURREXI > *ic eft aras*; 3.6: TIMEBO > *ondredu ic*; 3.7: CONTERUISTI > *ðu forðræstes*).[19] The glossator made numerous copying errors throughout the project, including the misspelling of familiar Old English words, repetitions and omissions, and this passage is no exception.[20] One common type of error, noted by Kuhn, occurs when the scribe accidentally began copying out the Latin word before realising the mistake and then switching to Old English midway through the word, thereby producing a garbled linguistic hybrid.[21] Hence, for example, in Psalm 3.8 the glossator initially wrote the meaningless *sælu* above the Latin word *SALUS* (perhaps thinking of the Old English word *gesælig*, 'blessed'), before correcting it to *hælu* (see fig. 2). An example of dittography (the accidental repetition of letters) occurs in the gloss to Ps. 3.4, where the Latin *UOCE* is translated as *mid id stefne* (fig. 2).[22] While glossing Ps. 3.6 *CIRCUMDANTIS*, the scribe omitted a medial letter *b*, writing the otherwise unattested *ymsellendes* (fig. 2), where the Junius and Cambridge Psalters have the common form *ymbsellendes/ymbsyllyndys*.[23]

Reflecting the practical, pedagogic function of the Vespasian gloss, all poetic or ambiguous diction is strictly avoided. For example, the Latin

---

[19] For further examples, see Blom, *Glossing the Psalms*, pp. 164–73.

[20] Kuhn attributes these errors to fatigue, rather than ignorance ('The Vespasian Psalter', 162). Pulsiano provides a list of errors, including the omission of medial letters, incomplete glosses, dittography, alterations of original readings and false starts, and letter confusion ('Old English Gloss', 44–7).

[21] Kuhn notes twenty-two examples of this type of copying error ('The Vespasian Psalter', 175).

[22] Pulsiano notes that other Old English glossed psalters translate the same Latin word as *mid stefne* (Junius Psalter) or simply *stefne* (Cambridge Psalter) ('Old English Gloss', 45).

[23] Pulsiano includes this example in his list of omissions of medial letters in psalter glosses: 'Old English Gloss', 44.

term *Dominus* is rendered consistently with the substitution gloss *drihten* in verses 1, 3, 4, 5 and 7, while *Deus* is translated as *God* in verse 3.5, though in one instance the glossator mistakenly reproduces the abbreviated form of the Latin word, writing *dō* above *DŌ* (*deo*) (Ps. 3.3). Poetic epithets for the deity which occur frequently in the biblical verse paraphrases discussed above, such as 'Metod', 'Frea', 'Scyppend' or 'heofonrices weard', are never used.[24] The extent to which the gloss is dependent on its 'host text' is perhaps best indicated by the fact that some abbreviated words in the Latin text are also abbreviated in the gloss. So, for example, abbreviated forms of the Latin noun *Domine*, *DÑE* (3.1, 3.6), *DÑUM* (3.4) *DÑUS* (3.5) are routinely abbreviated as Old English *dryhť*, though in Ps. 3.8 the scribe had space to write the entire Old English word *dryhtnes* above *DÑI*.

The gloss is similarly subservient to the Latin source in terms of syntax, resulting in non-standard Old English word order.[25] This syntactical mirroring is most apparent in the replication of Latin possessive constructions that follow the pattern NOUN + PERSONAL PRONOUN: hence Ps. 3.1: IN DEO EIUS > *in deo hire*; 3.3: CAPUT MEUM > *heafud min*; 3.4: SANCTO SUO > *ðæm halgan his*; 3.6: DEUS MEUS > *god min*.[26] In his *Letter to Pammachius*, Jerome himself had maintained that the word order of the Hebrew Bible was a spiritual 'mystery' which should not be altered in a translation.[27] However, as Barton notes, Jerome did not stick to this principle in producing the Vulgate, instead rendering the Hebrew and Greek texts of the Old and New Testament into the word order of contemporary Latin prose.[28] In making no attempt to produce natural English prose and

---

[24] See above, pp. 13–16.
[25] As Roberts puts it, the Vespasian glosses 'cling to the order of the Latin ones' ('Some Anglo-Saxon Psalters and their Glosses', p. 43). The classic study of the subject is Bruce Mitchell, *Old English Syntax* (Oxford: Clarendon Press, 1985).
[26] Kuhn cites examples from the *Lorica Prayer* (Henry Sweet, ed., *The Oldest English Texts*, EETS o.s. 83 [London: Trübner and Co., 1885], p. 174) as evidence that the GENITIVE + NOUN construction was preferred in Mercian prose ('The Vespasian Psalter Gloss', 163).
[27] *Jerome: Epistulae*, ed. Isidor Hilberg, CSEL 54 (Turnhout: Brepols, 2010), Letter 57.5, p. 508: *in interpretatione graecorum absque scripturis sanctis, ubi et uerborum ordo mysterium est, non uerbum e uerbo, sed sensum exprimere de sensu* ('in translation from the Greek – except in the case of Sacred Scripture where the very order of the words is a mystery – I render not word for word, but sense for sense'). For a translation, see Lawrence Venuti, ed., *The Translation Studies Reader* (London: Routledge, 2012), pp. 21–30, at 23.
[28] Barton, *The Word*, pp. 58, 231. For Ælfric's views on the necessity of changing the syntax of Latin sources when translating into Old English, see below, Chapter Four, pp. 161–4. Stanton traces this idea of 'literalism' back to Philo Judaeus, who in the first century B.C. equated the accuracy of the translators of the Septuagint with divine inspiration (*Culture of Translation*, pp. 107–13).

instead replicating the word order of the Latin source, the Vespasian gloss can be termed a foreignising translation rather than a domesticating one, opting for formal rather than functional equivalence.[29]

For what purpose, then, was the Old English gloss added to the Latin text of the Vespasian Psalter? It will be clear from the examples above that the glossator's goal was to provide readers of the psalter with a crib to the Latin text rather than a free-standing 'prose' translation. The Vespasian Psalter gloss is thus representative of the type of translation which, in Schleiermacher's phrase, 'move[s] the reader towards the text rather than the text towards the reader'.[30] Given the limited evidence for lay literacy prior to Alfred's educational reforms in the late ninth century, the implied reader of the Vespasian Psalter and its gloss was probably either a monk or nun, who recited the Latin psalter as the core of the Divine Office. In the Prose Preface to the *Pastoral Care*, Alfred offered a damning assessment of the poor state of Latinity in the English Church at the time when he assumed the throne in 871:

> Swæ clæne hio wæs oðfeallenu on Angelcynne ðæt swiðe feawa wæron behionan Humbre ðe hiora ðeninga cuðen understondan on Englisc, oððe furðum an ærenendgewrit of Lædene on Englisc areccean; ond ic wene ðætte noht monige begiondan Humbre næren. Swæ feawa hiora wæron ðæt ic furðum anne anlepne ne mæg geðencean be suðan Temese ða ða ic to rice feng.

> [So entirely were they (i.e. the religious orders) decayed among the English that there were very few on this side of the Humber who could make sense in English of their services, or translate even one missive from Latin into English; and I expect that there were by no means many beyond the Humber. There were so few of them that I cannot think of even a single one south of the Thames when I came to the throne.][31]

Although Alfred is probably referring specifically here to poorly educated priests who are unable to explain the meaning of the Latin liturgy (*hiora ðeninga*, 'their services') in English, in such straitened circumstances monastic readers may also have felt the need to add glosses to the text around which their spiritual lives revolved.[32] The practice of glossing

---

[29] On formal and functional equivalence, and domesticating and foreignising translation, see Prefatory Note above, pp. xii–xiii.

[30] F. D. E. Schleiermacher, 'Über die verschiedenen Methoden des Übersetzens', transl. Susan Bernovsky as 'On the Different Methods of Translating', in *The Translation Studies Reader*, ed. Lawrence Venuti (London: Routledge, 2004), pp. 43–63; cf. Barton, *The Word*, p. 57.

[31] Fulk, ed. and trans., *Pastoral Care*, pp. 4–5.

[32] See Helmut Gneuss, 'King Alfred and the History of Anglo-Saxon Libraries',

psalters in the ninth century may thus have originated from the practical needs of the English Church during a time of existential crisis.

The Cambridge Psalter

In contrast to the 'opportunistic' glosses added to existing Latin psalters such as the Vespasian Psalter are the 'integral' glosses preserved in manuscripts originally 'ruled for' an Old English gloss as well as the Latin text.[33] In these more 'competent' glosses, the translator typically engages thoughtfully with the Latin source rather than translating mechanically, as in the manner of the Vespasian gloss.[34] Examples include the Royal (Regius) Psalter, in which the D-type gloss is written in the same hand as the Latin text, perhaps for use as a class-book for teaching Latin, and the Lambeth Psalter, which features double I-type glosses that offer the reader alternative translations of a single Latin word, inviting them to reflect on the interpretative possibilities of either translation.[35] In some of these later psalters the gloss attains a degree of independence from the Latin source text: Jane Roberts notes, for example, that the scribe responsible for glossing the Regius Psalter 'sometimes thinks in phrases' rather than translating word-by-word.[36] Toswell goes a step further in referring to these manuscripts as 'bilingual psalters' rather than 'glossed psalters', on

---

in *Modes of Interpretation in Old English Literature: Essays in Honour of Stanley B. Greenfield*, ed. Phyllis Rugg Brown, Georgina Ronan Crampton and Fred C. Robinson (Toronto: University of Toronto Press, 1986), pp. 29–49. For the argument that Alfred is exaggerating the poor state of learning for rhetorical effect, see Jennifer Morrish, 'King Alfred's Letter as a Source on Learning in England', in *Studies in Earlier Old English Prose: Sixteen Original Contributions*, ed. Paul E. Szarmach (Albany, NY: State University of New York Press, 1986), pp. 87–108.

[33] Roberts, 'Some Anglo-Saxon Psalters and their Glosses', p. 40.

[34] Evert Wiesenekker, 'The Vespasian and Junius Psalters Compared: Glossary or Translation?', *Amsterdamer Beiträge zur älteren Germanistik* 40 (1994), 21–39, at 23.

[35] Evert Wiesenekker, *Word be Worde, Andgit of Andgite: Translation Performance in the Old English Interlinear Glosses of the Vespasian, Regius and Lambeth Psalters* (Huizen: Bout, 1991). On connections between the Regius Psalter and the Winchester school of Bishop Æthelwold, see Gretsch, *Intellectual Foundations*. On the Regius and Lambeth Psalters, see Blom, *Glossing the Psalms*, pp. 189–204, 209–30. On the Lambeth Psalter, see Samira Lindstedt, 'Prayer as Performance, c. 1050–1250' (unpublished doctoral dissertation, University of Oxford, 2021), pp. 76–124.

[36] Roberts, 'Some Anglo-Saxon Psalters and their Glosses', p. 49. See further Joseph Crowley, 'Anglicized Word Order in Old English Continuous Interlinear Glosses in British Library, Royal 2.A.XX', *ASE* 29 (2000), 123–51; Mechthild Gretsch, 'The Junius Psalter Gloss: Tradition and Innovation', in *Edward the Elder 899–924*, ed. N. J. Higham and David Hill (London: Routledge, 2001), pp. 280–91.

the grounds that the Old English text has equal status with the Latin on the page, suggesting that in some cases the gloss may even have been read independently as free-standing prose.[37]

To test this theory, let us consider another striking example of an integral gloss: the C-type gloss contained in the mid-eleventh-century Cambridge (or Winchcombe) Psalter. In this manuscript, the Old English text, written in red ink and insular minuscule, stands out against the black ink and Caroline minuscule used for the Latin psalm verses (again from the Romanum Psalter) (fig. 3).[38]

Arguing that Old English rather than Latin was 'the primary text in this manuscript', Toswell describes the Cambridge Psalter as 'a bilingual psalter in every way, almost a kind of double psalter if that were possible with alternate-line texts'.[39] Certainly, the gloss takes up just as much space on the page as the Latin text. However, despite the visual prominence afforded to the gloss, the Old English text in the Cambridge Psalter nevertheless follows the syntax of the Latin, even when this results in unidiomatic constructions akin to those that we observed in the Vespasian gloss (e.g. 3.3: CAPUT MEUM > *heafud min*; 3.4: UOCE MEA > *stefne minre*). Again, each Old English word is carefully placed above its corresponding Latin source to serve as a substitution gloss, and there are often large gaps where the vernacular text requires less space. Moreover, whereas the Latin always fits within the allocated ruled space, on several occasions, such as on fol. 7ʳ, the Old English translation outruns the space allocated for the Latin, with the result that the scribe had to squeeze the text into the right-hand margin. It is thus the Latin text, rather than the Old English gloss, which determines the layout of the manuscript page.

In terms of the vocabulary, the only major difference between the Cambridge and Vespasian glosses is dialectal. For example, the Vespasian gloss translates Latin *me* in Ps. 3.1 with the Mercian form *mec*, whereas the Cambridge has the late West Saxon *me*. Occasionally, words are added to the gloss for the clarification of sense. For example, where Vespasian translates the vocative *Domine* in the opening word of Ps. 3.1 as simply *dryht(en)* (abbreviated), the Cambridge glossator has the exclamatory *eala*

---

[37] Toswell, *Anglo-Saxon Psalter*, pp. 250–82.

[38] The Cambridge Psalter is preserved in Cambridge, University Library, MS Ff. 1, 23; Ker §13. Images are viewable online at: https://cudl.lib.cam.ac.uk/view/MS-FF-00001-00023/1. The text is edited by Karl Wildhagen, *Der Cambridger Psalter (Hs. Ff. 1.23 University Libr. Cambridge) zum ersten Male hrsg., mit besonderer Berücksichtigung des lateinischen Textes, von Karl Wildhagen: I. Text mit Erklärungen*, Bibliothek der angelsächsischen Prosa vol. 7 (Hamburg: H. Grand, 1910). For discussion, see Toswell, *Anglo-Saxon Psalter*, pp. 268–74; Roberts, 'Some Anglo-Saxon Psalters and their Glosses', pp. 57–60.

[39] Toswell, *Anglo-Saxon Psalter*, pp. 273–4.

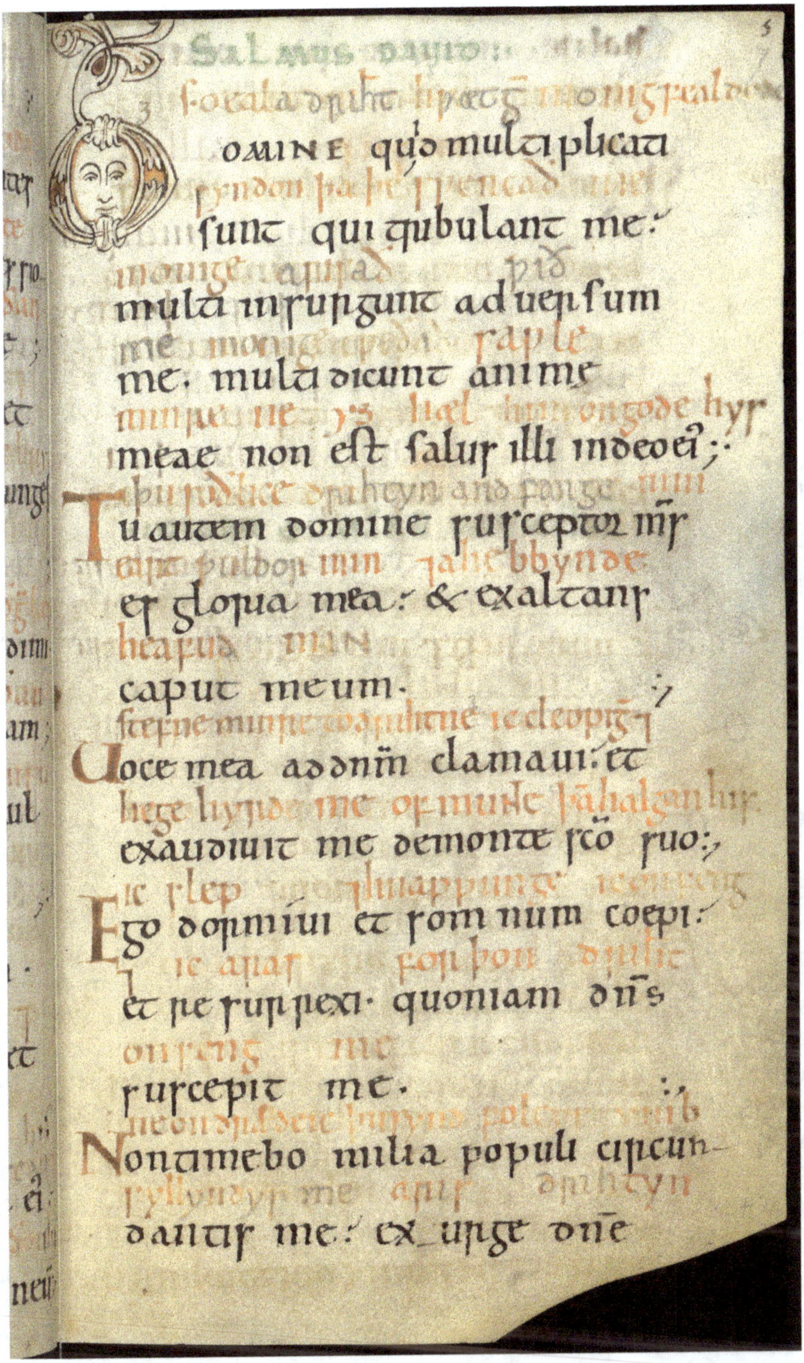

omine quo multiplicati
sunt qui tribulant me:
multi insurgunt aduersum
me. multi dicunt anime
meae non est salus illi indeo eius;
Tu autem domine susceptor m̄s
et gloria mea: & exaltans
caput meum.
Uoce mea ad d̄n̄m clamaui: et
exaudiuit me demonte s̄c̄o suo;
Ego dormiui et som̄num coepi:
et resurrexi. quoniam d̄n̄s
suscepit me.
Non timebo milia populi circun-
dantis me: ex urge d̄n̄e

Figure 3. Cambridge, University Library, MS Ff. 1, 23, fol. 7ʳ, 'Cambridge Psalter: Psalm 3.1–3.7'.

driht(en) ('O Lord'); as we shall see below, the author of the *Prose Psalms* makes the same choice.[40] In translating Psalm 3.5, *Ego dormiui et somnum coepi*, the Cambridge gloss has *ic slep 7 hnappunge ic onfeng* where the Vespasian version glosses the two synonyms for 'sleep' the other way round: *ic hneappade 7 slepan ongon*.

Like the gloss added to the Vespasian Psalter, the Cambridge Psalter gloss does not function as an independent prose translation but rather serves to 'guide the reader back to the source text'. These psalter glosses are therefore best viewed not as independent prose texts but rather as what Stanton describes as 'facsimiles' of the Latin psalter, 'the ultimate literal renderings' of Scripture.[41] Considered together as a group, the interlinear glosses provide important evidence for how English monks and nuns engaged carefully with each individual word of the Latin Psalter. The increasing space allocated to the Old English text in later psalters, and the occasional syntactical independence of gloss from source text, reflect the growing prestige of the vernacular as a language of Scripture in the post-Alfredian period. However, during the Alfredian period an altogether more ambitious, literary prose translation of the Psalms was composed for a very different readership.

The Prose Psalms

Together with the Mosaic Prologue to Alfred's *Domboc* discussed in the next chapter, the *Prose Psalms* constitute the first major extant continuous prose translation of the Bible into the English language. Adopting a sense-for-sense or functional equivalence approach, the anonymous author translated Psalms 1–50 of the Romanum Psalter into fluent and at times even stylish Old English prose. By contrast with the interlinear glossed psalters, which sought to 'move the reader to the text', the *Prose Psalms* are a 'communicative translation' which aims to 'move the text to the reader'. While the glosses serve as an adjunct to the Latin text for monastic readers, the *Prose Psalms* effectively displace the source text by presenting an authoritative English version of the first fifty Psalms for readers who are untrained in Latin. With these (largely) monolingual readers in mind, the translator domesticates the biblical source, smoothing out cultural and linguistic differences. The *Prose Psalms* are also an interpretative translation, drawing on a range of exegetical materials, including the *Argumenta* of Pseudo-Bede and a Latin translation and epitome of Theodore of Mopsuestia's commentary

---

[40] Cf. MS F (Stowe Psalter): *eala ðu driht(en)*.
[41] Stanton, *Culture of Translation*, p. 118.

made by Julian of Eclanum, as well, perhaps, as Cassiodorus' *Expositio Psalmorum*.⁴² Like Otfrid, the author of the *Prose Psalms* confidently uses the vernacular to convey not only the literal but also the spiritual meaning of the biblical source.⁴³

King Alfred and the Psalm Introductions

Linguistic, stylistic and thematic affinities between the *Prose Psalms* and the Old English *Pastoral Care*, *Boethius* and *Soliloquies* have encouraged the view that this work was part of the body of translations commissioned by King Alfred as part of his educational programme.⁴⁴ Unlike

---

⁴² For full discussion of the sources, see Patrick P. O'Neill, *King Alfred's Old English Prose Translation of the First Fifty Psalms*, Medieval Academy Books 104 (Cambridge, MA: Medieval Academy of America, 2001), pp. 31–44. All quotations are from this edition. O'Neill's text of the *Prose Psalms* is reprinted together with that of the *Metrical Psalms* and facing-page translation in his *Old English Psalms*, DOML 42 (Cambridge, MA: Harvard University Press, 2016). Other possible sources identified by O'Neill include the Pseudo-Jerome *Breviarum in Psalmos* and the *Glossa Psalmorum ex tradtione seniorum*. O'Neill suggests that all of these sources except for the Romanum Psalter itself may have been available to the author via a single Irish glossed psalter, given the popularity of these works in early medieval Ireland: 'The Prose Translation of Psalms 1–50', in *Companion to Alfred the Great*, ed. Discenza and Szarmach, pp. 256–81, at 276. For the Irish background, see Martin McNamara, 'Psalter Text and Psalter Study in the Early Irish Church (A.D. 600–1200)', in his *The Psalms in the Early Irish Church*, Journal for the Study of the Old Testament Supplement Series 165 (Sheffield: Sheffield Academic Press, 2000), pp. 19–142.

⁴³ On Otfrid's *Evangelienbuch*, see above, pp. 10–11.

⁴⁴ The connection between the *Prose Psalms* and the Alfredian corpus was first noticed by John I'A Bromwich, 'Who Was the Translator of the Prose Portion of the Paris Psalter', in *The Early Cultures of North-West Europe*, ed. Cyril Fox and Bruce Dickins (Cambridge: Cambridge University Press, 1950), pp. 289–304. See further Janet Bately, 'Lexical Evidence for the Authorship of the *Prose Psalms* in the Paris Psalter', *ASE* 10 (1982), 69–95. For a more sceptical view of the relationship between the *Prose Psalms* and the Alfredian corpus, see Michael Treschow, Paramjit S. Gill and Tim B. Swartz, 'King Alfred's Scholarly Writings and the Authorship of the First Fifty Prose Psalms', *Heroic Age* 12 (2009). For a recent discussion, which sets the *Prose Psalms* within a broader context of burgeoning European interest in the psalter in this period, see M. J. Toswell, 'The Ninth-Century Psalter in England', in *Age of Alfred*, ed. Faulkner and Leneghan, pp. 389–408. Stanton treats the Alfredian *Prose Psalms* as a development from the tradition of psalter glossing (*Culture of Translation*, pp. 121–9). Noting the translator's eclectic method, 'which insouciantly blends the allegorical interpretations of the Alexandrian school with the literal/historical of the Antiochene', O'Neill envisages a 'secular author – no doubt assisted by clerical exegetes – composing for a lay audience', and concludes that this author might well have been Alfred himself ('The Prose Translation of Psalms

these works, however, the sole manuscript copy of the *Prose Psalms* in the Paris Psalter does not feature a preface, epilogue or colophon attributing the translation to the king himself. Such an attribution, if it ever existed, might have become detached during the transmission of the text. However, each individual Old English prose psalm (except for Ps. 1) is preceded by its own Introduction which attributes its composition to King David or other kings of Israel, notably Hezekiah. After foregrounding the 'historical' interpretation, the Introductions then provide readers with a 'moral' and 'Christological' context for understanding each psalm.[45] This prioritising of the literal level of interpretation aligns the Introductions to the *Prose Psalms* with a tradition of psalm commentary ultimately derived from the writing of the Greek scholar Theodore of Mopsuestia (d. 428) which treats David as a prophet and the author of all the Psalms. This tradition proved popular in early medieval Ireland and it is therefore possible that the author had access to Irish sources. These Introductions reveal the author's special interest in the way the Psalms give voice to the physical and mental suffering of a pious king and the tribulations of his people, surrounded by enemies.[46] For

---

1–50', pp. 280–1). Amy Faulkner has recently highlighted affinities between the sustained exploration of the workings of the mind (*mod*) in the *Prose Psalms* and the *Boethius*: 'The Mind in the Old English *Prose Psalms*', *RES* 70 (2019), 597–617. On Alfred's evocation of the translation of Pentateuch from Hebrew to Greek to Latin and then into vernaculars of all Christian peoples in the Prose Preface to the *Pastoral Care*, see above, pp. 3–4.

[45] The *Argumenta* are printed with each *Prose Psalm* in *Liber Psalmorum: The West-Saxon Psalms, Being the Prose Portion, or the 'First Fifty', of the so-called Paris Psalter*, ed. James W. Bright and Robert L. Ramsay (Boston: D. C. Heath & Co., 1907). For discussion, see esp. Emily Butler, 'Alfred and the Children of Israel in the Prose Psalms', *N&Q* 57 (2010), 10–17; Emily Butler, '"And Thus Did Hezekiah": Perspectives on Judaism in the Old English Prose Psalms', *RES* 67 (2016), 617–35. O'Neill notes that the placement of the moral interpretation before the Christological violates the normal fourfold method of Irish exegesis as well as the chronology of Scripture, suggesting that the translator, whom he refers to as the 'paraphrast', 'regarded the moral interpretation as more important' ('The Prose Translation of Psalms 1–50', p. 279). For connections between Alfred and David, see Allen J. Frantzen, *King Alfred* (Boston: Twayne Publishers, 1986), pp. 89–105; Keynes and Lapidge, *Alfred the Great*, pp. 31–2; Pratt, *Political Thought*, pp. 242–63; Michael Treschow, '*Godes Word* for *Vox Domini* in Psalm 28 of the Paris Psalter: Biblical Translation and Alfredian Politics', *Florilegium* 31 (2014), 165–80; Daniel Orton, 'Royal Piety and Davidic Imitation: Cultivating Political Capital in the Alfredian Psalms', *Neophilologus* 98 (2014), 477–92; Toswell, *Anglo-Saxon Psalter*, pp. 75–82; Gates, 'Alfredian Prose Psalms'.

[46] Emily Butler has recently argued, 'Although some psalms are clearly focused on praise, the apparatus surrounding the *Prose Psalms* seems most often to

example, the Introduction to Psalm 2 explains how David *seofode on þæm sealme and mænde to Drihtne be his feondum, ægðer ge inlendum ge utlendum, and be eallum his earfoðum* ('lamented in the psalm and complained to the Lord about his enemies, domestic and foreign, and about all his difficulties'),[47] while the Introduction to Psalm 5 states that Hezekiah sang this psalm *þa he alysed wæs of his mettrumnesse* ('when he had been freed from his illness').[48] Although this focus on royal suffering could resonate with the predicament of almost any English king in this period, Alfred's wars with the Vikings and his physical illnesses present a particularly compelling context for these Psalm Introductions.[49] Indeed, the image of David lamenting *þæt on his dagum sceolde rihtwisnes and wisdom beon swa swiðe alegen* ('that in his time justice and wisdom should be brought so very low') in the Introduction to Psalm 11 presents a striking biblical counterpart to Alfred's famous lament on the decline of learning among the *Angelcynn* in the Prose Preface to the *Pastoral Care*.[50] Asser records Alfred's personal devotion to the Psalter,[51] while as we have seen, William of Malmesbury states that the West Saxon ruler 'began to translate the Psalter, but reached the end of his life when he had barely completed the first part'.[52] Although it is possible that the author's plan was only to translate the first fifty psalms,[53] William's portrait of Alfred translating the Bible at the moment of his death echoes the monk Cuthbert's account of Bede's unfinished translation of the Gospel of John.[54] The Psalter was almost certainly high on the list of essential books that the king requested be translated in the Prose Preface to the *Pastoral Care*. Although Alfred's personal authorship of the *Prose Psalms*

---

reflect a sense of threat or precarity': 'Examining Dualities in the Old English Prose Psalms', in *Age of Alfred*, ed. Faulkner and Leneghan, pp. 409–28, at 409.

[47] O'Neill, ed. and trans., *Old English Psalms*, pp. 4–5 (O'Neill translates *Drihtne* as 'God'). David's enemies are further mentioned in the Introductions to Psalms 4, 9, 12, 16, 17, 21, 27, 29, 40, 42, 46 and 47.

[48] O'Neill, ed. and trans., *Old English Psalms*, pp. 12–13. For further references to Hezekiah's illness, see the Introductions to Psalms 6, 15, 27, 28, 29 and 31.

[49] On Alfred's illnesses, see Asser, *Life of Alfred*, chs 74, 76 and 91 (Stevenson, *Asser's Life of Alfred*, pp. 54–9, 76–9; Keynes and Lapidge, *Alfred the Great*, pp. 88–91, 101–2). See further David Pratt, 'The Illnesses of King Alfred the Great', *ASE* 30 (2001), 31–90.

[50] O'Neill, ed. and trans., *Old English Psalms*, pp. 32–3. On the Prose Preface to the *Pastoral Care*, see pp. 3–4, 34–5

[51] *Life of Alfred*, chs 24 and 76; Stevenson, pp. 21, 59; Keynes and Lapidge, *Alfred the Great*, pp. 75, 91. See further David Pratt, *The Political Thought of King Alfred the Great* (Cambridge: Cambridge University Press, 2007), pp. 242–5.

[52] Mynors, Thomson and Winterbottom, eds, I, Book II.123, p. 194.

[53] Since the time of Cassiodorus (d. c. 585), it had become conventional to divide the Psalter into three groups of fifty.

[54] See above, pp. 16–19.

cannot be proved, it seems probable that this work – with its pronounced interest in royal wisdom and suffering – was composed in response to the king's call for a renewal of education among the *Angelcynn*.

The Paris Psalter

The sole extant copy of the *Prose Psalms* is preserved in the Paris Psalter, an eleventh-century codex, where it is presented alongside the Latin text of the Romanum Psalter in parallel columns.[55] The compiler completed the English section of this bilingual Psalter by including verse translations of Psalms 51–150 from a mid-tenth-century verse paraphrase known as the *Metrical Psalms*.[56] The book is highly unusual in shape and design: it is long and narrow, as though intended to be kept in a box and carried around, but at the same time its appearance is aesthetically pleasing, and the attractive pen-and-ink illustrations in the margins of the first few psalms draw the reader into the text (fig. 4).[57] These features suggest that the codex was a presentation copy, perhaps designed as a gift for a wealthy patron who wanted to read the Psalms in both Latin and Old English. The Old English prose and verse in the right-hand column of the Paris Psalter is not provided to guide the reader in understanding the Latin in the manner of the glossed psalters. Rather, the layout of this codex reflects the remarkable prestige of written English in eleventh-century England.

---

[55] Paris, Bibliothèque nationale de France, MS Lat. 8824; Ker §367. Images of the Paris Psalter are viewable online at: https://gallica.bnf.fr/ark:/12148/btv1b8451636f. For an overview of scholarship, see O'Neill, 'The Prose Translation of Psalms 1–50'.

[56] Excerpts from *Metrical Psalms* 1–50 missing from the Paris Psalter appear in another manuscript of this period, Junius 121, indicating that this work originally constituted a translation of the entire Psalter; for discussion of the *Metrical Psalms*, see Anlezark, 'Old English Benedictine Office'; Leneghan, 'Making the Psalter Sing'.

[57] As suggested by Toswell, *Anglo-Saxon Psalter*, pp. 128–9.

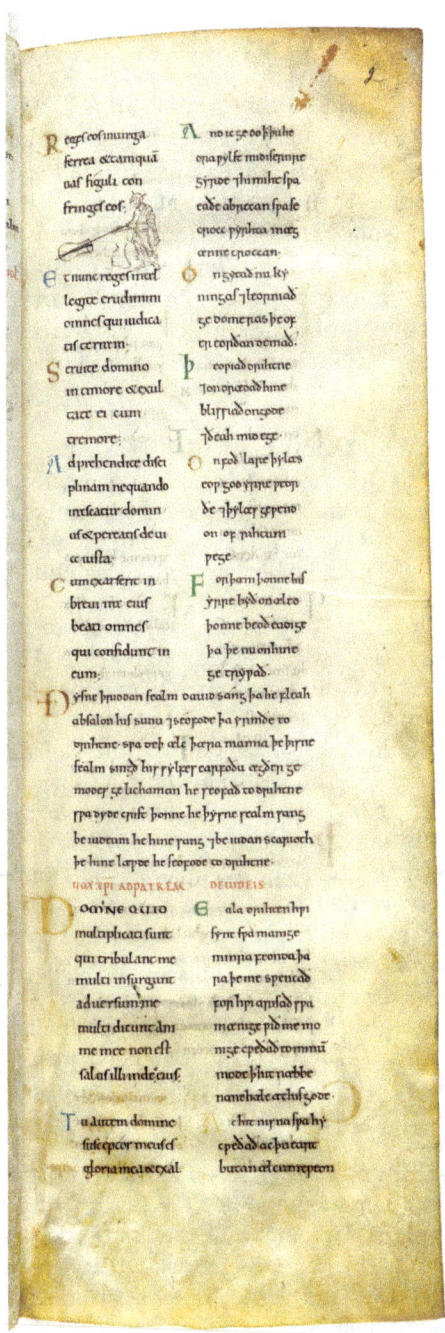

Reges eos in uirga
ferrea & tamqua
uas figuli con
fringes eos.

Et nunc reges intel
legite erudimini
omnes qui iudica
tis terram

Seruite domino
in timore & exul
tate ei cum
tremore

Adprehendite disci
plinam nequando
irascatur domin
us & pereatis de ui
a iusta

Cum exarserit in
breui ira eius
beati omnes
qui confidunt in
eum.

Ano ꞅe gōd ꞅſahte
ona pyſſe moiſeṇṇe
ſyṅoe ꝥ hıṁ hıſ ſpa
eaꝺe abṅecan ſpaſe
enoce pyṫḣra metꞅ
oenne onocean
ning gread nu key
ningaſ ꝥ teopniad
ge dommaſ þeoꝛ
on eoꝛdan oemad.
eopıað ꝺruhtne
ꝺonopoaꝺð hım
blıſſıað on gooe
ꝺeah mıᵭ ege
on peað laꞇe þyſaꞇ
ꞇop god þýnne peoꝛ
ꝺe ꝥ þy læꞅ gepenꝺ
on oꝛ op pıhcum
pege
on þam honne hiſ
ýrre byð onæleð
honne beoð eaꞅıge
þa þe nu on hıne
ge tryſpað

Dyꞅne þunðan ꞅealm daue ꞅang, þa he flea̋h
abſalon hıſ ſunu, ꝫ ſcopoꝺe þa ꝅyṅde ꝼo
ꝺe þıḣhe, ſpa ꝺeþ ælc ꝼṅa manna þe þyrṅe
ſealm ꞅıṅgð ḃıꞅ ꝝyłtæꞅ canꞅtoðu ꝯðen ge
moꝺeꞅ ge lıchaman he ꞅeopað to ꝺrıhtne
ꞅpa ꝺyꝺe crıꞅt þonne he þyṙne ſealm ꞅang
be ıuðun he hıne ſang, ꝫ be ıudan ꞅcarıoth
þe hıne laſde he ſcopoꝺe to ꝺrıhtne.

uox xpi ad patrem   **de iudeis**

Domıne quid
multiplicati sunt
qui tribulant me
multi insurgunt
aduersum me
multi dicunt ani
me mee non est
salus illi in deo eius

Tu autem domine
susceptor meus es
gloria mea & exal

eala ðrıhten hpı
ſyṅd ſpa manige
mıṅṅa ꝼeonoa, þa
na þe me ſpencað
ꝼoꞇ hpı apſæꝺ ꞅpa
mænıge plð me mo
nıge geðeað to mıṅṅ
moðe þþı nabbe
nane hale ætcluſ goðe
elne nıꝫ na ꞅpa hý
epeðað ac þu eaꝛt
butan æle anꞇepteon

Figure 4. Bibliothèque nationale de France,
MS Latin 8824, fol. 2ʳ, 'Paris Psalter: *Prose
Psalms 2–3*'.

Translation style

The presentation of the Old English text of Psalms 1–50 in the Paris Psalter is probably unrepresentative, however, of the original purpose for which the *Prose Psalms* were designed. Indeed, as we shall see below, the translation strategies adopted by the author indicate that this translation was meant to be read in isolation from – and indeed instead of – its Latin source text. The *Prose Psalms* are a biblical translation which displaces the source text rather than supplementing it in the manner of the psalter glosses discussed above. I therefore present below the Old English text of Psalm 3 from the *Prose Psalms* without the Latin that accompanies it in the Paris Psalter:

> Ðysne þriddan sealm Dauid sang þa he fleah Absalon his sunu, and seofode þa yrmðe to Drihtne; swa deþ ælc þæra manna þe þisne sealm singð: his sylfes earfoðu, ægðer ge modes ge lichaman, he seofað to Drihtne; swa dyde Crist þonne he þysne sealm sang: be Iudeum he hine sang and be Iudan Scarioth þe hine læwde. He seofode to Drihtne:
>
> 3.1 (2) Eala, Drihten, hwi synt swa manige minra feonda, þara þe me swencað; for hwi arisað swa mænige wið me?
> 3.2 (3) Monige cweðað to minum mode þæt hit næbbe nane hæle æt his Gode.
> 3.3 (4) Ac hit nis na swa hy cweðað, ac þu eart butan ælcum tweon min fultum and min wuldor, and þu ahefst upp min heafod.
> 3.4 (5) Mid minre stemne ic cleopode to Drihtne, and he me gehyrde of his þam halgan munte.
> 3.5 (6) Þa ongan ic slapan, and slep, and eft aras, for ðam þe Drihten me awehte and me upp arærde.
> 3.6 (7) For ðam ic me nu na ondræde þusendu folces, þeah hi me utan ymbþringen; ac ðu, Drihten, aris and gedo me halne, for þam þu eart min[58] God.
> 3.7 (8) For ðam þu ofsloge ealle þa ðe me wiðerwearde wæron butan gewyrhton, and þara synfulra mægen þu gebryttest,
> 3.8 (9) for ðam on ðe ys eall ure hæl and ure tohopa; and ofer þin folc sy þin bletsuncg.

[David sang this third psalm when he fled from his son, Absalom, and lamented that distressing situation to the Lord; so too does everyone who sings this psalm, lamenting to the Lord their own sufferings, spiritual and physical; likewise did Christ, when he recited this psalm, singing about the Jews, and about Judas Iscariot who betrayed him. David complained to the Lord:

---

[58] The MS reads *mid* here, but most editors, including O'Neill, emend to *min*.

3.1 (2) O Lord, why are my enemies who oppress me so numerous; why do so many rise up against me?

3.2 (3) Many say to my soul that it gets no security from its God.

3.3 (4) But it is not as they say, for you are certainly my help and glory, and you raise up my head.

3.4 (5) I invoked the Lord with my appeal, and he heard me from his holy mountain.

3.5 (6) Then I began to sleep, and slept, and afterward arose, because the Lord awoke me and raised me up.

3.6 (7) Because of that, I do not now fear even if thousands of people throng about me; but arise, Lord, and keep me safe, because you are my God.

3.7 (8) Because you have struck down all those who were hostile to me without good reason, and have broken the power of sinners,

3.8 (9) so all of our salvation and our hope is in you; and may your blessing rest on your people.][59]

Although many of the introductions to the *Prose Psalms* feature two historical interpretations, Ps. 3 has only one,[60] followed by the usual brief moral and Christological interpretation. The opening of the Introduction is derived from the *titulus* that normally accompanies this psalm in the Romanum Psalter but which is absent from the Paris Psalter: *Psalmus David cum fugeret a facie Abessalon filii sui* ('The psalm of David when he fled from the face of his son Absalom'). The final clause of the Introduction, *and seofode þa yrmðe to Drihtne* ('and lamented that distressing situation to the Lord'), is derived from the other main source for the Introductions, the Pseudo-Bedan *Argumenta*, which attributes this Psalm to Hezekiah, *qui circumdatus Assyrio exercitu Dominum inuocauerit. Aliter, uox Christi ad Patrem de Iudaeis* ('who, surrounded by the Assyrian army, called upon the Lord. Alternatively, the voice of Christ calling to the Father concerning the Jews').[61] As is the case in many of the Introductions, the phrase *seofode/seofað to Drihtne* ('lamented/laments to the Lord') serves as a rhetorical frame, linking the lamenting voices of David, *ælc þæra manna þe þisne sealm singð* ('everyone who sings this psalm'), and Christ. Stylistic flourishes of this nature signal that we are dealing with a confident author of vernacular prose.

---

[59] Text and translation (with some modifications) from O'Neill, *Old English Psalms*, pp. 6–9. Psalms are numbered to match the Vespasian Psalter, with O'Neill's numbering (which includes that of the missing *titulus* for each psalm) in brackets.

[60] For commentary, see O'Neill, *King Alfred's Old English Prose Translation of the First Fifty Psalms*, pp. 169–70.

[61] Bright and Ramsay, p. 4. O'Neill notes that the substitution of David for Hezekiah occurs throughout the Introductions (*King Alfred's Old English Prose Translation of the First Fifty Psalms*, p. 169).

In striking contrast to the glosses discussed above, the translation of the psalm itself that follows is entirely independent of the word order of the Latin. For example, unlike the glossators, the author reverses the syntax of the Latin NOUN + GENITIVE PERSONAL PRONOUN construction to reflect the natural word order of Old English:[62]

3.2. Romanum: in deo eius
Vespasian: in deo[63] hire
Cambridge: on gode his
Prose Psalms: his Gode

3.3. Romanum: caput meum
Vespasian: heafud min
Cambridge: heafud min
Prose Psalms: min heafod

3.4. Romanum: sancto suo
Vespasian: ðæm halgan his
Cambridge: þam halgan his
Prose Psalms: his þam halgan

3.6. Romanum: deus meus
Vespasian: god min
Cambridge: god min
Prose Psalms: min God.

In transforming this Latin psalm into smooth Old English prose, the translator appears to have been influenced by Cassiodorus' *Expositio Psalmorum*, which focuses on the structural organisation of each psalm.[64] Cassiodorus divides Ps. 3 into two sections, each reflecting different aspects of the person of Christ. In the first part (verses 1 (2)–4(5)), Christ addresses God the Father and chides those who have persecuted him; in the second (verses 5(6)–8(9)), Christ consoles the faithful with the hope of resurrection.[65] This sectional division is reflected in the *Prose*

---

[62] Henry Hargreaves notes a similar distinction between the Early and Late Versions of the Wycliffite Bible, whereby the former tends to reproduce Latinate syntax with forms such as *forgete thou not*, whereas the latter renders this phrase *ne forget*: 'From Bede to Wyclif: Medieval English Bible Translations', *Bulletin of the John Rylands University Library* 48 (1965), 118–40, at 121. See further Solopova, ed. *The Wycliffite Bible*. For connections between Old and Middle English Bible translations, see Conclusion, pp. 247–50.

[63] The glossator has (presumably accidentally) carried over the Latin noun *deo* into the gloss here.

[64] O'Neill, 'The Prose Translation of Psalms 1–50', pp. 275–7.

[65] *Cassiodorus: Explanation of the Psalms, Vol. 1*, trans. P. G. Walsh (New York:

Psalms by the insertion of the temporal adverb *Þa* ('then') at the beginning of 3.5(6), *Þa ongan ic slapan, and slep*.[66] This phrase reverses the variations of the Latin, which has *ego dormiui et somnum cepi* (literally 'I slept and began [the/my] sleep'), resulting in a more natural and logical word order in the Old English. In addition, the transition from the first, plaintive section to the second, more consolatory section is underscored by a shift from a simple, paratactic style, in which clauses and verses are linked by coordinating conjunctions such as *ac* ('but') or *and* (e.g. Ps. 3.3(4)): *Ac hit nis na swa hy cweðað, ac þu eart butan ælcum tweon min fultum and min wuldor, and þu ahefst upp min heafod*), to a more complex, hypotactic mode in which subordinating conjunctions (*for þam*, literally 'for that', i.e. 'because'; *þeah*, 'although') and dependent clauses make causation more apparent. For example, where the Latin source features the subordinating conjunction *quoniam* ('because, so') only twice in Pss 3.5(6)–7(8), the Old English has the equivalent term *forþam* five times and *þeah* once in the same verses:

3.5 Ego dormiui et somnum cepi, et resurrexi **quoniam** Dominus suscepit me
3.6 Non timebo milia populi circumdantis me. Exsurge, Domine, salvum me fac, Deus meus,
3.7 **quoniam** tu percussisti omnes adversantes mihi sine causa; dentes peccatorum contervisti.
3.8 Domini est salus, et super populum tuum benedictio tua.

[3.5 I have slept and taken my rest: and I have risen up, **because** the Lord has protected me.
3.6 I will not fear thousands of the people, surrounding me: arise, O Lord; save me, O my God.
3.7 **For** you have struck all of them who are my adversaries without cause: you have broken the teeth of sinners.
3.8 Salvation is of the Lord: and your blessing is upon your people.]

3.5 Þa ongan ic slapan, and slep, and eft aras, **for ðam** þe Drihten me awehte and me upp arærde.
3.6 **For ðam** ic me nu na ondræde þusendu folces, **þeah** hi me utan ymbþringen; ac ðu, Drihten, aris and gedo me halne, **for þam** þu eart min God.
3.7 **For ðam** þu ofsloge ealle þa ðe me wiðerwearde wæron butan gewyrhton, and þara synfulra mægen þu gebryttest,

---

Paulist Press, 1990), p. 69.
[66] O'Neill notes that the placement of *for ðam* at the beginning of Ps. 9.4(5) has a similar effect, making this and the next verse 'the explanation for the preceding two verses' (*King Alfred's Prose Translation of the First Fifty Psalms*, p. 46).

³·⁸ **for ðam** on ðe ys eall ure hæl and ure tohopa; and ofer þin folc sy þin bletsuncg.

[³·⁵ Then I began to sleep, and slept, and afterward arose, **because** the Lord awoke me and raised me up.

³·⁶ **Because of that**, I do not now fear **even if** thousands of people throng about me; but arise, Lord, and keep me safe, **because** you are my God.

³·⁷ **Because** you have struck down all those who were hostile to me without good reason, and have broken the power of sinners,

³·⁸ **so** all of our salvation and our hope is in you; and may your blessing rest on your people.]

This shift into hypotaxis is well suited to the exposition of the second part of the psalm, which in Cassiodorus' interpretation traces a series of steps from Christ's death and resurrection (3.5(6)) to the salvation of the faithful.

The confident literary style of the *Prose Psalms* is further on display in the regular but unobtrusive use of a range of rhetorical devices, which cumulatively enhance the aural quality – and hence memorability – of the biblical text.[67] For example, in Ps. 3.1 where the Latin text has the single question, *Domine, **quid** multiplicati sunt qui tribulant me? Multi insurgunt adversum me* ('**Why**, O Lord, are they multiplied that afflict me? Many are they who rise up against me'), the Old English attains a more plaintive tone through the inclusion of two rhetorical questions: *Eala, Drihten, **hwi** synt swa manige minra feonda, þara þe me swencað; **for hwi** arisað swa mænige wið me?* ('O Lord, **why** are my enemies who oppress me so numerous; **why** do so many rise up against me?'). The translator also makes extensive use of alliteration to emphasise certain points and make the psalm more memorable for its readers.[68] For example, in the Introduction, *s*- alliteration is used to link the key concepts of 'psalm', 'singing' and 'suffering/lamenting':

Ðysne þriddan **s**ealm Dauid **s**ang þa he fleah Ab**s**alon his **s**unu, and **s**eofode þa yrmðe to Drihtne; swa deþ ælc þæra manna þe þisne **s**ealm **s**ingð, his **s**ylfes earfoðu, ægðer ge modes ge lichaman, he **s**eofað to Drihtne; **s**wa dyde Crist þonne he þysne **s**ealm **s**ang: be Iudeum he hine **s**ang and be Iudan **S**carioth þe hine læwde. He **s**eofode to Drihtne:

Alliteration is also used for ornamental effect in the translation of the psalm itself:

---

[67] On techniques for memorising the Psalter in this period, see Leneghan, 'Making the Psalter Sing'.

[68] O'Neill, *King Alfred's Prose Translation of the First Fifty Psalms*, p. 51, compares the *Prose Psalms* author's sense of rhythm and use of alliteration with that on display in the Old English *Orosius* and Ælfric's early prose. For alliteration in Ælfric see below, p. 169.

3.1 (2) **hwi** synt **swa** **m**anige **m**inra feonda, þara þe **me** swencað; for **hwi** arisað **swa** mænige wið **me**? [...]

3.4 (5) **he me** gehyrde of **h**is þam **h**algan munte. [...]

3.5 (6) Þa ongan ic **s**lapan, and **s**lep, and eft aras, for ðam þe Drihten me awehte and me upp arærde [...]

3.7 (8) **wi**ðerwearde wæron butan gewyrhton [...]

3.8 (9) **e**all **u**re hæl and **u**re tohopa [...].

By comparison, the Latin source does not feature any identifiable pattern of alliteration, save for the repeated use of forms of the personal pronoun *me*, the threefold repetition of *multi-* in verses 1(2)–2(3), and the phrase *sancto suo* in verse 4(5). The introduction of alliteration in the *Prose Psalms* can therefore be safely regarded as a conscious stylistic choice on the part of the Old English translator. Further stylistic flourishes include the use of polyptoton (the repetition of words with different inflections), such as in Ps. 3.5: *dormiui et somnum coepi* > *slapan/slep*, and doublets, as in Ps. 3.3: *gloria mea* > *min fultum and min wuldor*;[69] Ps. 3.5: *resurrexi* > *me awehte and me upparærde*; Ps. 3.8: *salus* > *ure hæl and ure tohopa*.

The translator almost doubles the number of personal pronouns (from eighteen to thirty-one), in keeping with the moral interpretation of the Introduction, which explains how this psalm serves as a vehicle not only for David and Christ in their respective lamentations but also for *ælc þæra manna þe þisne sealm singð, his sylfes earfoðu, ægðer ge modes ge lichaman, he seofað to Drihtne* ('everyone who sings this psalm, lamenting to the Lord their own sufferings, spiritual and physical'). This increase in personal pronouns is particularly prominent in the final verse, 3.8, in which the psalmist's invocation of the covenant between God and his chosen people is now directly addressed to God:

Romanum: Domini est salus, et super populum **tuum** benedictio **tua**

[Salvation is of the Lord: and **your** blessing is upon **your** people.]

Prose Psalms: for ðam on **ðe** ys **eall ure** hæl and **ure** tohopa; and ofer **þin** folc **sy þin** bletsuncg.

[so in **you** is **all** of **our** salvation and **our** hope; and on **your** people may **your** blessing rest.]

---

[69] In his discussion of these very verses, Cassiodorus draws attention to the use of this same rhetorical device in the Latin text, commenting: 'We have here the splendid figure called by the Greeks *auxesis*, which increases and redoubles by appending words in individual phrases' (Walsh, p. 69). The Latin style thus partly influences the Old English prose style.

The addition of the intensifier *eall* ('all') provides further alliteration with the twofold repetition of the added personal pronoun *ure*, further heightening the plaintive tone of this moving vernacular version of the lament psalm.

Audience and Purpose

For what sort of readership was this confident, stylish and communicative prose translation of the Psalms made? We have seen how, by contrast to the Old English psalter glosses which were intended to assist monastic readers in language acquisition and prayer, the *Prose Psalms* were probably designed to be read as an independent vernacular biblical translation for an audience with little or no Latin. In his Prose Preface to the *Pastoral Care*, Alfred himself called for the basic education of all young English free men:[70]

> Forðy me ðyncð betre, gif iow swæ ðyncð, ðæt we eac suma bec – ða ðe niedbeðearfosta sien eallum monnum to wiotonne – ðæt we ða on ðæt geðiode wenden ðe we ealle gecnawan mægen, ond gedon swæ we swiðe eaðe magon mid Godes fultume, gif we ða stilnesse habbað, ðætte *eall sio gioguð ðe nu is on Angelcynne friora monna*, ðara ðe ða speda hæbben ðæt hie ðæm befeolan mægen, sien to liornunga oðfæste, ða hwile ðe hie to nanre oðerre note ne mægen, oð ðone first ðe hie wel cunnen Englisc gewrit arædan; lære mon siððan furður on Lædengeðiode ða ðe mon furður læran wille ond to hieran hade don wille.

> [Therefore it seems to me better, if it seems so to you, that we turn certain books – those most necessary for all people to know – into that tongue that we can all comprehend, and arrange, as we very readily can with God's aid, if we have cessation of hostilities, that *all the present English youth of the class of freeborn persons* who have the wherewithal to commit to it, be applied to learning for as long as they cannot be put to any other employment, until such time as they can well read English writing; let those be instructed further in the Latin tongue whom it is desirable to instruct further and to appoint to higher office.][71] (Emphases added).

Regardless as to whether the phrase *to hieran hade* ('to higher office') refers to those who are being ordained into the clergy or to members of the laity who wish to continue their studies, Alfred's letter implies that vernacular translations of essential books will suffice for most of the lay nobility.[72]

---

[70] *Life of Alfred*, chs 75 and 102 (Stevenson, *Asser's Life of Alfred*, pp. 58, 88–9; Keynes and Lapidge, *Alfred the Great*, pp. 90, 107).
[71] Fulk, ed. and trans., *Pastoral Care*, pp. 8–9; transl. adapted with modifications.
[72] For the argument that *to hieran hade* denotes those being ordained, see Dorothy Whitelock, 'The Prose of Alfred's Reign', in *Continuations and Beginnings:*

The Introductions to the *Prose Psalms* might have been designed to educate such lay readers in key facts of biblical history while also providing them with clear instruction in how to apply each psalm's spiritual meaning to their own lives.[73] Similarly, the subtle stylistic touches highlighted above in the translations themselves serve to enhance the work's readability, bringing the biblical source's meaning over to an audience unable to access the Psalms via the Latin text.[74]

The central role of the Psalter in the basic education of the lay aristocracy in this period is hinted at in Asser's description of how Alfred's children, Edward and Ælfthryth, were schooled in the liberal arts:

> nam et psalmos et Saxonicos libros et maxime Saxonica carmina studiose didicere, et frequentissime libris utuntur.[75]

> [for they have attentively learned the Psalms, and books in English, and especially English poems, and they very frequently make use of books.][76]

As the most widely read and studied book of the Bible, the Psalms present a strong case for inclusion in Alfred's list of 'books most necessary for all people to know'.[77] Indeed, together with the translations of parts of Exodus and Acts contained in the Mosaic Prologue to Alfred's *Domboc*, the *Prose Psalms* may have served as the cornerstone of the royal project of lay education and ecclesiastical revival. As we shall see in Chapters Three and

---

Studies in Old English Literature, ed. Eric G. Stanley (London: Nelson, 1966), pp. 67–103, at 68–9. For an alternative reading allowing for the possibility of a higher stratum of lay education, see Godden, 'King Alfred's Preface'. Some lay people were educated in both Old English and Latin, among them – according to Asser – Alfred's own son, Æthelweard (*Life of Alfred*, ch. 75). In his discussion of Alfred's frustration with the poor education of his judges, Asser implies that even some slaves could read books in English at this time (*Life of Alfred*, ch. 106); see further below, p. 57.

[73] O'Neill, 'The Prose Translation of Psalms 1–50', notes that the historical Introductions 'could act as cues for expanding on the narratives of David's (and Ezechias') life as related in the Book of Kings or Paralipomenon (Chronicles) and thus serve an educational purpose' (p. 277). Noting the focus on Christ's suffering in the Introductions, O'Neill suggests the *Prose Psalms* may also have served a devotional purpose, reminding readers of their debt to Christ (p. 278).

[74] As O'Neill notes, the case for a secular readership of the *Prose Psalms* is further strengthened by the 'consistent theme of release from all present tribulations – rather than temptations or vices, as one finds for this interpretation in commentaries of monastic provenance' ('The Prose Translation of Psalms 1–50', pp. 279–80).

[75] *Life of Alfred*, ch. 75; Stevenson, *Asser's Life of Alfred*, p. 59.

[76] Keynes and Lapidge, *Alfred the Great*, p. 91.

[77] See Anlezark, 'Which books are "most necessary" to know?'

Four, lay demand for access to books otherwise only available to those in religious orders would increase in the tenth and eleventh centuries, driving the practice of biblical translation to new heights.

Conclusion

This chapter has demonstrated how ninth- and tenth-century English prose authors took by turns conservative and free approaches to psalm translation depending on the needs of their respective audiences. The glossed psalters provide a window onto the world of the monastic scriptorium, in which scribes carefully studied and weighed up the meaning of each individual word of the Latin Psalter. In these interlinear translations, the Old English text is normally subservient to the Latin, largely replicating its word order, with no further guide to interpretation save the wording of the gloss itself. Such word-for-word, formal-equivalence translations were probably made by and for monastic readers as an aid to prayer and as a tool for the acquisition of the Latin language. By contrast, in the *Prose Psalms* the vernacular 'displaces the source text' to the extent that lay readers could also access the meaning of the Psalter without needing to learn Latin at all.[78] In both of these approaches we can observe a willingness to use the vernacular to make the Bible accessible and meaningful to a specific group of readers in whatever form was most practical. None of the biblical translations analysed in this chapter betray any concern with the status of English in relation to the 'three sacred languages', Hebrew, Greek and Latin.[79]

In Steiner's terminology, the initial decision to translate the Psalms into English corresponds to the first stage of translation: 'affirmation'.[80] For the monks and nuns engaged in glossing the Psalms, this decision was determined by the centrality of the Psalter in the Divine Office; for the lay elite from the late ninth century onwards, the Psalms were probably among those 'books most necessary for all people to know' which Alfred and his scholars selected for translation. The two principal approaches to translating the Psalms considered above begin to diverge when considered in the light of Steiner's second stage: 'aggression' (or 'plundering').

---

[78] I borrow these terms from Robert Stanton, 'The (M)other Tongue: Translation Theory and Old English', in *Translation Theory and Practice in the Middle Ages*, ed. Jeanette Beer (Kalamazoo, MI: Medieval Institute Publications, 1997), pp. 33–46, at 39; cited in O'Neill, *King Alfred's Prose Translation of the First Fifty Psalms*, p. 46 n. 5.

[79] On familiarity with the idea of the three sacred languages in this period, see above, p. 4.

[80] For Steiner's theory of translation, see above, p. xiii.

Whereas the glosses attempt to convey the meaning of every individual word of the Latin psalter for monks and nuns who required a complete translation, the *Prose Psalms* are much more selective in plundering the source, resulting in a version of the psalter that would better serve the needs of lay readers. Further variance occurs during Steiner's third stage: the process of 'incorporation', or adaptation into the target language. The glosses achieve this via a foreignising, word-for-word formal-equivalence approach which guides monastic readers to the meaning of the Latin text, whereas the *Prose Psalms* thoroughly domesticate the Romanum psalter into flowing Old English prose suitable for readers unskilled in Latin. It is at Steiner's fourth stage of translation, 'compensation', that the most significant differences in approach become evident: while the glossed psalters offer no significant compensatory measures save for the occasional double gloss, the *Prose Psalms* compensate for the cultural gap between the source text and its English lay readership in a number of ways, including rearranging the syntax and providing explanatory passages. Short Introductions also explain the historical and spiritual context of each psalm and guide the reader in its interpretation, while stylistic flourishes such as the use of doublets, parallelism and alliteration make the text more readable and memorable. While the glosses bring the monastic reader to the Latin psalter, the *Prose Psalms* thus bring the words of David, Hezekiah and Christ to English lay readers who cannot access them in Latin. The *Prose Psalms* thus provide important evidence for the growing need for translations of Scripture among lay readers in the wake of Alfred's educational reforms. In striking contrast to the conservative, scholarly approach of the glossators, the author of the *Prose Psalms* had no hesitation in freely altering not only the syntax but the wording of his Latin source to convey the meaning of the Bible to readers who did not otherwise have the educational tools to unlock its complexities. The next chapter will highlight the remarkable freedom which the author of the Mosaic Prologue to Alfred's law code (the *Domboc*) exercised in adapting the laws of the Old and New Testament for lay readers.

2

From the Old Law to the New: The Mosaic Prologue to King Alfred's *Domboc*

IN THE early 890s, King Alfred justified his plan to produce translations of 'the books most necessary for all people to know' by drawing his bishops' attention to the fact that the Law (æ) was first composed in Hebrew before it was turned into Greek, Latin and the languages of all Christian peoples.[1] In referring to the Law, Alfred probably had in mind the Laws of Moses contained in the Pentateuch, the first five books of the Christian Old Testament: Genesis, Exodus, Leviticus, Numbers and Deuteronomy. It would not be until a century later that an Old English prose translation of the Pentateuch was produced.[2] Yet, during Alfred's own reign, translations of the legal sections of Exodus (Ex. 20–23.13) together with the 'Apostolic Letter' from the New Testament Book of Acts (Acts 15.23–9) were incorporated into the so-called 'Mosaic Prologue' to the king's law code or *Domboc*.[3] The Mosaic Prologue has mainly attracted attention from legal historians on account of its unusual treatment of the Decalogue and its relationship to various putative sources. In addition to the base text of the Vulgate,[4] it has been proposed that the author was influenced by works such as the *Liber ex Lege Moysi*, a seventh-century Breton composition containing legal excerpts from

---

[1] See above, Introduction, pp. 3–4
[2] See Chapter Three.
[3] The *Domboc* is preserved in the mid-tenth-century manuscript Cambridge Corpus Christi College 173 fols 33–52ᵛ; Ker §39. A later copy survives in the twelfth-century *Textus Roffensis*, in addition to several fragments in other manuscripts. The text of the *Domboc* together with the Mosaic Prologue was recently edited and translated in full by Stefan Jurasinski and Lisi Oliver, *The Laws of Alfred: The Domboc and the Making of English Law* (Cambridge: Cambridge University Press, 2021). All citations and translations are from this edition; section numbers marked § are those originally assigned by Liebermann and replicated in all subsequent editions. For succinct discussion of the manuscript history, see also Frantzen, *King Alfred*, 11–12. For an overview of scholarship on the *Domboc*, see Mary P. Richards, 'The Laws of Alfred and Ine', in *Companion to Alfred the Great*, ed. Discenza and Szarmach, pp. 282–309.
[4] See Richard Marsden, *The Text of the Old Testament in Anglo-Saxon England*, CSASE 15 (Cambridge: Cambridge University Press, 1995), pp. 401–2.

Exodus, Leviticus, Numbers and Deuteronomy,[5] and the *Collatio legum Mosaicarum et Romanorum*, a late antique work which aligns excerpts from the Pentateuch with Roman law.[6] More broadly, Patrick Wormald has highlighted affinities with the political thought of the great Carolingian theologian Hincmar of Rheims (d. 882), who traced the development of written law from the period before Moses, when humankind lived under Natural Law, through the *lex litterae* ('law of the letter') given by God to Moses and the *lex Evangelii* ('law of the Gospel') preached by Christ and the Apostles, up to the writings of contemporary secular lawgivers.[7] Less attention, however, has been paid to the Mosaic Prologue as a literary work in its own right or as a major Old English biblical translation.[8] This chapter will therefore concentrate on how the author confidently and at times creatively translated, adapted and interpreted various biblical sources to cater for the needs of a specific readership.

---

[5] The text is edited in Sven Meeder, 'The *Liber ex lege Moysi*: Notes and Text', *The Journal of Medieval Latin* 19 (2009), 173–218. For connections with the *Domboc*, see Felix Liebermann, 'King Alfred and Mosaic Law', *Transactions of the Jewish Historical Society* 6 (1912), 21–31; Bryan Carella, 'The Source of the Prologue to the Laws of Alfred', *Peritia* 19 (2005), 91–118; Bryan Carella, 'Evidence for Hiberno-Latin Thought in the Prologue to the Laws of Alfred', *SP* 108 (2011), 1–26; Bryan Carella, 'Asser's Bible and the Prologue to the Laws of Alfred', *Anglia* 130 (2012), 195–206; Pratt, *Political Thought*, p. 230. However, Anya Adair has recently stressed the independence of the Mosaic Prologue from earlier legal works such as the *Liber ex Lege Moysi*, highlighting how its author displayed 'a freedom in the omission or inclusion of the laws themselves, a willingness to intervene substantially in the biblical text on doctrinal grounds, and an interest in the legal logic that sequences and links the biblical clauses': 'A Troublesome Source: The *Liber Ex Lege Moysi* and the Mosaic Prologue to King Alfred's *Domboc*', *American Notes & Queries* 35 (2022), 212–17, at 215.

[6] Wormald, *Making of English Law*, p. 418.

[7] Wormald, *Making of English Law*, pp. 423–5. See further Pratt, *Political Thought*, pp. 223–9; and Jurasinski and Oliver, *The Laws of Alfred*, pp. 61–9.

[8] Marsden describes the Mosaic Prologue as 'the earliest surviving example of continuous biblical prose translation in Old English' (*Text of the Old Testament*, p. 401). Jurasinski and Oliver similarly describe the Mosaic Prologue as 'a lengthy translation into English of biblical material – the earliest extant since we have no trace of Bede's rendering of the Fourth Gospel' (*The Laws of Alfred*, p. xiv). For studies which focus on the *Domboc* and its prologue as literature, see esp. Frantzen, *King Alfred*, pp. 11–21; Pratt, *Political Thought*, pp. 214–41; and Wormald, *Making of English Law*, pp. 416–29. As Frantzen points out, the division of the laws into 120 chapters 'reflects a literary tradition rather than a logical necessity' (*King Alfred*, p. 13), seeing as Moses was said to have lived for 120 years; for further discussion of this division, see further Wormald, *Making of English Law*, pp. 417–18. For a recent discussion of the prologue and its literary contexts, see Irvine, *Alfredian Prologues and Epilogues*, pp. 143–50.

Alfred's 'Domboc' and its background

The laws of English kings had been written out in vernacular prose since the conversion of Æthelberht of Kent in 597, making law, as Stefan Jurasinski and Lisi Oliver point out, 'the most ancient of the Old English prose genres'.[9] Each English law code features some prefatory or introductory material, which usually provides an authorising frame by referring to the king in whose name the laws were issued, as well as an appeal to Christian authority. The issuing of Alfred's *Domboc* at some point in the 880s or 890s, however, marks a major development in English law. In asserting its incorporation of elements from earlier laws issued by the kings of Kent, Mercia, and Wessex, the *Domboc* mirrors the new political reality of what Simon Keynes has called Alfred's 'Kingdom of the Anglo-Saxons,' which united these once-independent realms under a single West Saxon ruler.[10] Furthermore, the *Domboc* portrays Alfred himself as a wise guardian and enforcer of Christian justice.[11] Key to what David Pratt calls the *Domboc*'s 'reorientation of royal law' is its elaborate and lengthy prologue, which positions Alfred's laws within the long history of Judeo-Christian legislation stretching back to the moment when God issued the Ten Commandments to Moses on Mount Sinai.[12]

Alfred's personal involvement in the administration of law is described in detail by Asser in the closing chapter of the *Life of Alfred* (ch. 106). Echoing the biblical story of the Judgement of Solomon (I Kings 16.3–28), Asser relates how Alfred 'used also to sit at judicial hearings for the benefit both of his nobles and of the common people', looking carefully into all judgements passed in his absence throughout his realm.[13] If any judge-

---

[9] Jurasinski and Oliver, *The Laws of Alfred*, p. 3.

[10] See Simon Keynes, 'Alfred the Great and the Kingdom of the Anglo-Saxons', in *Companion to Alfred the Great*, ed. Discenza and Szarmach, pp. 13–46.

[11] For discussion of new laws protecting the king's authority and prohibiting rebellion in the *Domboc*, see below, pp. 72–4. Patrick Wormald places the *Domboc*'s composition after 893 (*The Making of English Law: King Alfred to the Twelfth Century, Vol. 1: Legislation and its Limits* [Oxford: Blackwell, 1999], pp. 281, 286), but Pratt dates it to 'between Fulk's letter (886) and 893 (Asser's *Life*)' (*Political Thought*, p. 219).

[12] Pratt, *Political Thought*, pp. 214–41. Patrick Wormald notes that the Mosaic Prologue 'occupies over a fifth of the total book', making it unparalleled in length among the prefatory materials attached to 'any other medieval law text' (*Making of English Law*, p. 418).

[13] Stevenson, *Asser's Life of Alfred*, p. 92: *Studebat is quoque in iudiciis etiam propter nobelium et ignobilium suorum utilitatem*. Asser compares Alfred to Solomon in his love of wisdom in *Life of Alfred*, ch. 75. This image of Alfred's active involvement in adjudication is confirmed by the early tenth-century Fonthill Letter, which depicts the king washing his hands as he listens to an arbitration hearing concerning land ownership before passing judgement.

ment were found to be unjust in the king's view, Alfred would admonish his judges for neglecting 'the study and application of wisdom', commanding them either to relinquish their office 'or else to apply yourselves much more attentively to the pursuit of wisdom'.[14] In Asser's account, the king's threat to remove his judges from office appears to have had its desired effect, inspiring them to acquire the basic reading skills that they had neglected in their youth:

> ita ut mirum in modum illiterati ab infantia comites pene omnes, praepositi ac ministri literatoriae arti studerent, malentes insuetam disciplinam quam laboriose discere, quam potestatum ministeria dimittere. Sed si aliquis litteralibus studiis aut pro senio vel etiam pro nimia inusitati ingenii tarditate proficere non valeret, suum, si haberet, filium, aut etiam aliquem propinquum hominem, liberum vel servum, quem ad lectionem longe ante promoverat, libros ante se die nocteque, quandocunque unquam ullam haberet licentiam, Saxonicos imperabat recitare.[15]

> [As a result, nearly all the ealdormen and reeves and thegns (who were illiterate from childhood) applied themselves in an amazing way to learning how to read, preferring rather to learn this unfamiliar discipline (no matter how laboriously) than to relinquish their offices of power. But if one of them – either because of his age or because of the unresponsive nature of his unpractised intelligence – was unable to make progress in learning to read, the king commanded the man's son (if he had one) or some relative of his, or even (if he had no one else) a man of his own – whether freeman or slave – whom he had caused to be taught to read long before, to read out books in English to him by day and night, or whenever he had the opportunity.][16]

Asser's reference to the reading of books in English (*Saxonicos*) suggests that to be literate in this context meant the ability to understand the written form of the vernacular rather than Latin – as we have seen, this accords with the limited education which Alfred recommends for the lay nobility in the Prose Preface to the *Pastoral Care*. Asser presents the judges whom Alfred chastises as men of an older generation who had missed out on the benefits of his newly founded *scholae* on account of their advanced years:

> Et suspirantes nimium intima mente dolebant, eo quod in iuventute sua talibus studiis non studuerant, felices arbitrantes huius temporis iuvenes, qui liberalibus artibus feliciter erudiri poterant, se vero

---

[14] Stevenson, *Asser's Life of Alfred*, p. 93: *sapientiae autem studium et operam neglexistis. [...] aut sapitentiae studiis multo devotius docere ut studeatis, impero.*
[15] Stevenson, *Asser's Life of Alfred*, p. 94.
[16] Keynes and Lapidge, p. 110 (with modifications).

infelices existimantes, qui nec hoc in iuventute didicerant, nec etiam in senectute, quamvis inhianter desiderarent, poterant discere. Sed hanc senum iuvenumque in discendis literis solertiam ad praefati regis notitiam explicavimus.[17]

[Sighing greatly from the bottom of their hearts, these men regretted that they had not applied themselves to such pursuits in their youth, and considered the youth of the present day to be fortunate, who had the luck to be instructed in the liberal arts, but counted themselves unfortunate because they had not learned such things in their youth nor even in their old age, even though they ardently wished that they had been able to do so. But I have explained this concern for learning how to read among the young and old in order to give some idea of the character of King Alfred.][18]

Alfred's frustration with these same men's ignorance in legal matters seems to have led to the production of the Mosaic Prologue to the *Domboc*, which provides them with an accessible and succinct primer in the evolution of written Judeo-Christian law.[19] Hence, for example, in describing how the apostles responded to the initial lack of success of their mission, the Mosaic Prologue states that they then set down their teaching in the form of an *ærendgewrit* ('written document'), whereas the biblical source, Acts 15.22–3, simply records that the apostles and ancients wrote *per manus* ('by their hands').[20] Through this emphasis on the written form of the apostles' teaching, the Mosaic Prologue instructs Alfred's judges that writing, rather than oral custom, is the proper medium for the Christian laws which they are charged with upholding.

---

[17] Stevenson, *Asser's Life of Alfred*, pp. 94–95.
[18] Keynes and Lapidge, p. 110.
[19] See Treschow, 'Spirit of Mercy', 82; Jurasinski and Oliver, *The Laws of Alfred*, pp. 53–61. On the value attached to written law more generally, see Wormald, *Making of English Law*; and Pratt *Political Thought*, pp. 214–18. Felix Liebermann, whose edition remained the standard text until that of Jurasinski and Oliver, had earlier argued that Alfred's main aim was, 'through a *Humanitätsideal*, first to raise the consciousness of his judges, and ultimately the *Rechskultur* of the nation': *Die Gesetze der Angelsachsen*, 3 vols (Halle: Max Niemeyer, 1903–16), III, p. 36, trans. by Wormald, *Making of English Law*, p. 422.
[20] Jurasinski and Oliver, *The Laws of Alfred*, p. 60. For the text, see Jurasinski and Oliver, *The Laws of Alfred*, pp. 266–7.

Contents and Structure

The Mosaic Prologue opens with a translation of Exodus 20–23.13, comprising the Decalogue (MP §1–10; Ex. 20.1–23) and a long section of Old Testament laws (MP §11–48; Ex. 21–23.9).[21] The second section is an abbreviated paraphrase of the Apostolic Letter (MP §49.2–49.5; Acts 15.23–9), which explains how the Old Law's emphasis on retributive justice was modified in the New Law preached by Christ and the Apostles through the new doctrine of mercy (OE *mildheortnesse*).[22] The Mosaic Prologue concludes with a paraphrase of the Golden Rule, that is the principle that one should treat others as one would expect to be treated by them (§49.5). There follows a 'second prologue' (MP §49.7–8) which explains the *Domboc*'s relationship to preceding English law codes, before the long list of Alfred's laws themselves begins.

Hearing the Voice of the Lord

The most immediately striking stylistic feature of the opening of the prologue is the author's decision to render the past simple verb in the opening clause of the Vulgate (Ex. 20.1: **Locutusque est** *Dominus cunctos sermones hos*, 'And the Lord **spoke** all these words') in the past continuous tense (*Dryhten **wæs sprecende** ðas word to Moyse and þus cwæð*, 'The Lord **was speaking** these words to Moses and said as follows').[23] By contrast, the Old English Heptateuch follows the grammar of the Vulgate here in using the past indicative: *God spræc þus* ('God spoke thus').[24] Indeed, the passive continuous form of the Old English verb *sprecan* ('to speak, say') is used only once to translate the past indicative Latin form *locutus est* in the Old English Heptateuch, in the account of how the Lord instructed Moses to go and die on Mount Nebo (Deuteronomy 32.48):

Vulgate: **locutus**que est Dominus ad Mosen in eadem die dicens

[And the Lord **spoke** to Moses the same day, saying]

---

[21] These laws include: instructions on the treatment of slaves and homicides; compensation for physical injury and cursing; punishments for theft, breaking and entering, damage to property and the seduction of virgins; prohibitions against the receiving of enchanters, magicians and witches, bestiality and idolatry, the harming of widows and orphans, the abusive lending of property, blasphemy, the eating of unclean meat, bribery, the mistreatment of foreigners and the invocation of heathen gods.

[22] See Michael Treschow, 'The Prologue to Alfred's Law Code: Instruction in the Spirit of Mercy', *Florilegium* 13 (1994), 79–110.

[23] This opening verse is omitted in the *Liber ex lege Moysi*, which begins instead with Ex 20.2: *Ego sum dominus deus tuus, qui eduxit te de terra aegypti, de domo seruitulis*.

[24] On the prose *Exodus*, see pp. 177–81.

OE Heptateuch: Drihten wæs ða sprecende to Moyse, ðus cweðende[25]

[The Lord **was speaking** then to Moses, saying thus.] (Emphases added)

The collocation of the noun *Dryhten* with the verb phrase *wæs sprecende* occurs once elsewhere in Alfredian prose for *locutus est* and once for the gerund *loquens*,[26] while Ælfric uses the construction once to translate the imperfect form *loquebatur* and once in a passage with no direct Latin source.[27] The rarity of the construction suggests that the use of the past continuous translation here was a deliberate stylistic choice designed to place the reader *in medias res* on Mount Sinai where the law was first delivered by God to Moses.[28]

---

[25] Richard Marsden, ed., *The Old English Heptateuch and Ælfric's 'Libellus de veteri testament et novo'*, 2 vols, EETS o.s. 330 (Oxford: Oxford University Press, 2008), I, p. 175. Volume II of this edition, containing commentary and glossary, remains unpublished at the time of writing.

[26] Romanum Psalter: *Deus deorum Dominus **locutus est*** > Prose Psalm 49.1: *Dryhtna Dryhten **wæs sprecende*** ('The Lord of lords **was speaking**') (O'Neill, ed. and trans., *Old English Psalms*, pp. 182–3; O'Neill translates *wæs sprecende* as 'said'). Cf. *Cura Pastoralis* III.34: *Ecce de caelo dominus **loquens** persecutoris sui facta corripuit, nec tamen ilico quae essent facienda monstrauit* > *Pastoral Care* 58: *Loca nu, hu Dryhten **wæs sprecende** of hefonum to his ehtere, and hine ðreade for his ærgedonan weorcum* ('See, now, how the Lord **was speaking** from heaven to his persecutor and upbraided him for his previous accusations' (Fulk, ed. and trans., *Pastoral Care*, pp. 494–95).

[27] CH I.35 (pp. 630–1): *Loquebatur Iesus cum discipulis suis in parabolis, dicens, et reliqua*. **Drihten** *wæs sprecende on sumere tide to his apostolum mid bigspellum, þus cweþende* ('*Jesus was speaking to his disciples in parables, saying, etc*. The Lord **was speaking** at a certain time to his apostles in parables, saying'); CH I.40 (pp. 734–5): *Se godspellere lucas awrat on þysum dægiþerlicum godspelle þæt* **ure drihten wæs sprecende** *þysum wordum to his leorningcnihtum* ('The Evangelist Luke wrote in this day's gospel that **our Lord was speaking** in these words to his disciples'). All citations from the *Catholic Homilies* are from *CH* I and *CH* II, with some modifications of punctuation and orthography.

[28] Treschow notes that this grammatical choice 'adds dramatic immediacy to the narrative' ('Spirit of Mercy', 82). Stefan Jurasinski (personal communication) notes that the Sermon on the Mount, a text that is typically read in conjunction with the Ten Commandments, opens with a series of present participles: Mt. 5. 1–2: **videns** *autem turbas ascendit in montem et cum sedisset accesserunt ad eum discipuli eius et* **aperiens** *os suum docebat eos* **dicens** ('And **seeing** the multitudes, he went up into a mountain, and when he was set down, his disciples came unto him. And **opening** his mouth he taught them, **saying**'). The opening words of the Mosaic Prologue might therefore be said to be preparing the reader for the Christological interpretation of Mosaic Law that appears in the prologue more generally from the outset. For the use of Mt. 5 in the Mosaic Prologue §49, see below. The translation of this passage in the *Wessex Gospels* renders each of these present continuous verbs in the past simple: *Soðlice þa se Hælend* **geseh** *þa*

The likelihood that the use of the past continuous was a conscious artistic decision increases when we consider that the same construction appears, with some variation, in a passage for which there is no known Latin source which rounds off the Mosaic Prologue's summary of Exodus:

> §49 Þis sindan ða domas þe se ælmihtega God self **sprecende wæs** to Moyse and him bebead to healdanne
>
> [These are the judgments that the almighty God himself **was speaking** to Moses and bade him keep.][29] (Emphases added).

The additions of the epithet *se ælmihtega* ('the almighty') and the reflexive personal pronoun *self* ('himself') underline God's real physical presence on Mount Sinai, reminding Alfred's judges of the sacred origin of Christian law.

The foregrounding of God's voice in the opening sentence of the Mosaic Prologue is sustained in the translation of Ex. 20.7, presented here as the second commandment due to the omission of Ex. 20.4–6.[30] Here the translator substitutes the accusative Latin clause *nomen Domini Dei tui/sui* ('the name of the Lord your/his God') for the Old English genitive phrase *minne noman* ('my name'), as well as translating *Dominus* ('the Lord') as *me*, thereby reminding the reader or listener that it is the Lord himself who is speaking these words:

> Ex. 20.7. Non assumes **nomen Domini Dei tui** in vanum, nec enim habebit insontem **Dominus** eum qui assumpserit **nomen Domini Dei sui** frustra
>
> [You shall not take **the name of the Lord your God** in vain, for **the Lord** will not hold him guiltless that shall take **the name of the Lord his God** in vain.]
>
> §2. Ne **minne noman** ne cig ðu on idelnesse; forðon þe ðu ne bist unscyldig wið **me**, gif ðu on idelnesse cigst **minne noman**.

---

*menigu, he astah on þone munt; and þa he sæt, þa genealæhton his leorningcnihtas to him. And he **ontynde** his muð and lærde hi, and **cwæð*** ('Truly when the Saviour **saw** the multitude, he went up onto that mountain; and when he sat, then his disciples drew to him. And he **opened** his mouth and taught them, and **said**'). A similar stylistic choice is made in the opening section of the prose preface to another Alfredian text, the *Soliloquies*, the sole twelfth-century copy of which begins with a woodsman already engaged in the act of gathering building materials: *Gaderode me þonne kigclas and stuþansceaftas and lohsceaftas* ('Then for myself I gathered sturdy sticks and supporting beams and wall posts'): Leslie Lockett, ed. and trans., *Augustine's 'Soliloquies' in Old English and in Latin*, DOML 76 (Cambridge, MA: Harvard University Press, 2022), pp. 182–3.

[29] Jurasinski and Oliver, *The Laws of Alfred*, pp. 162–3 (translation modified).
[30] See below, p. 63–4.

[You will not invoke **my name** idly: for you will not be guiltless with **me**, if you take **my name** idly.] (Emphases added).

An interest in the literary possibilities of voice, and what David Lawton – writing about the later medieval period – has described as 'revoicing', provides a further link between the Mosaic Prologue and the wider corpus of Alfredian texts.[31] In works such as the *Prose Psalms, Dialogues, Pastoral Care, Boethius, Soliloquies,* and *Orosius* as well as their respective prefaces and epilogues, the voices of various biblical and patristic authorities are ventriloquised, reinforcing and at times merging with an 'Alfredian' voice of contemporary royal and episcopal authority.[32] In the Mosaic Prologue, however, it is the voices of Moses and the Lord (*Dryhten*) himself that are revoiced, lending supreme authority to Alfred's laws. As we shall see below, this process of biblical revoicing is taken to new heights in the second prologue, where the voice of Christ temporarily merges with that of Alfred.

Omissions and Substitutions

So often does the Mosaic Prologue diverge from its various scriptural sources that the work's most recent editors describe it as 'a remarkably *unfaithful* translation of the laws of Moses [...] and the Apostolic "Council of Jerusalem"' (emphasis mine).[33] The translator's highly selective, domesticating approach to the scriptural source is evident in the rendering of the Decalogue which opens the work (MP §1–10; Ex. 20.1–17, with an extra verse included from Ex. 20.23):

> Dryhten wæs sprecende ðas word to Moyse and þus cwæð:
> Ic eom Dryhten ðin God. Ic ðe utgelædde of Egipta londe and of hiora
>   ðeowdome.

---

[31] David Lawton, *Voice in Later Medieval English Literature: Public Interiorities* (Oxford: Oxford University Press, 2016).

[32] The question of voice in Alfredian literature has yet to be explored extensively: studies include Mary Kate Hurley, 'Alfredian Temporalities: Time and Translation in the Old English *Orosius*', *JEGP* 112 (2013), 405–32; Amy Faulkner, 'Royal Authority in the Biblical Quotations of the Old English *Pastoral Care*'; Tatyana Solomonik-Pankrashova, 'Giving Voice to the Psalms in the Alfredian Metre 4 of Boethius', *Logos: A Journal, of Religion, Philosophy Comparative Cultural Studies & Art* 115 (2023), 140–9. See also Mark Atherton, 'Quoting and Requoting: How the Use of Sources Affects Stylistic Choice in Old English Prose', *Studia Neophilologica* 72 (2000), 6–17.

[33] Jurasinski and Oliver, *The Laws of Alfred*, p. 9. Wormald places the translation style somewhere between the freedom of the *Boethius* and *Soliloquies* and the more faithful approach to sources taken in the *Prose Psalms* and *Pastoral Care* (*Making of English Law*, p. 419).

The Mosaic Prologue to King Alfred's Domboc

§1 Ne lufa ðu oðre fremde godas ofer me.
§2 Ne minne noman ne cig ðu on idelnesse; forðon þe ðu ne bist unscyldig wið me, gif ðu on idelnesse cigst minne noman.
§3 Gemyne þæt ðu gehalgige þone ræstedæg; wyrceað eow VI dagas and on þam siofoðan restað eow: forðam on VI dagum Crist geworhte heofonas and eorðan, sæs and ealle gesceafta þe on him sint, and hine gereste on þone siofoðan dæg, and forðon Dryhten hine gehalgode.
§4 Ara ðinum fæder and þinre medder, ða þe Dryhten sealde, þæt ðu sie þy leng libbende on eorþan.
§5 Ne sleah ðu.
§6 Ne lige ðu dearnenga.
§7 Ne stala ðu.
§8 Ne sæge ðu lease gewitnesse.
§9 Ne wilna ðu þines nehstan ierfes mid unryhte.
§10 Ne wyrc ðe gyldne godas oððe sylfrene.

[The Lord was speaking these words to Moses and said as follows:
I am the Lord your God. I led you out from the land of the Egyptians and from slavery to them.
§1 You will not love other strange gods in place of me.
§2 You will not invoke my name idly: for you will not be guiltless with me, if you take my name idly.
§3 Remember to keep holy the day of rest; you will work six days and on the seventh you shall rest; because Christ made the heavens and the earth in six days, the seas and all the creatures that are in them, and he rested on the seventh day, and therefore the Lord made it holy.
§4 Honour your father and mother, they whom the Lord gave you, so that you may live long on the earth.
§5 Do not kill.
§6 Do not fornicate.
§7 Do not steal.
§8 Do not give deceitful testimony.
§9 Do not wrongfully covet the possessions of your neighbour.
§10 Do not make for yourself gods of gold or silver.][34]

The omission of the commandment on not making graven images (Ex. 20.4–6) and insertion of the prohibition against making golden or silver idols (Ex. 20.23) at the end of the Decalogue effectively creates a new tenth commandment. While this might appear a radical rewriting of Scripture,

---

[34] Text and translation cited with modifications from *The Laws of Alfred*, ed. Jurasinksi and Oliver, pp. 224–31; I have silently emended the Tironian sign to 'and'.

scholars have noted that the omission of the second commandment follows Western ecclesiastical custom after the iconoclasm controversy with Byzantium of the eighth century had subsided, while the inclusion of the prohibition against idols might reflect an attempt to suppress pagan practices reintroduced to Britain by the Vikings.[35]

Elsewhere, the translator streamlines the Vulgate source, omitting details deemed irrelevant to the lives of the *Domboc*'s readers. Hence, for example, the commandment against coveting one's neighbour's possessions (Ex. 20.17; MP §9) is substantially abbreviated:[36]

[20.17] Non concupisces domum proximi tui, nec desiderabis uxorem eius, non servum, non ancillam, non bovem, non asinum, nec omnia quae illius sunt.	§9 Ne wilna ðu þines nehstan ierfes mid unryhte.
[You shall not covet your neighbour's house: neither shall you desire his wife, nor his servant, nor his handmaid, nor his ox, nor his ass, nor any thing that is his.]	[Do not wrongfully covet the possessions of your neighbour.]

Similarly, the prohibition against working on the Sabbath is curtailed through the omission of the instruction: *non facies omne opus in eo, tu, et filius tuus et filia tua, servus tuus et ancilla tua, iumentum tuum, et advena qui est intra portas tuas* ('you shall do no work on it, you, nor your son, nor your daughter, nor your manservant, nor your maidservant, nor your beast, nor the stranger that is within your gates') (Ex. 20.10).[37] More telling, however, is the replacement of Latin *Dominus* with Old English

---

[35] Liebermann, 'King Alfred and Mosaic Law', 25–6; Jurasinski and Oliver, *The Laws of Alfred*, p. 225 n. 11.

[36] Jurasinski and Oliver, *The Laws of Alfred*, p. 231 n. 17, comment that the omission of the reference to coveting one's neighbour's wife is probably due 'to the influence of patristic tradition', in which this prohibition was considered part of the same commandment as coveting one's neighbour's property. Liebermann notes that all eight references to the donkey or ass (Lat. *asino*) in the sections of Exodus translated in the prologue are omitted, doubtless reflecting the low standing this animal had in the English economy at the time ('King Alfred and Mosaic Law', 31); see further Treschow, 'Spirit of Mercy', 98.

[37] Jurasinski and Oliver note that Ælfric also omits this list in his sermon for Mid-Lent, suggesting that 'one or both instances may be attributable to the uncertain (and disputed) nature of Sunday observance in pre-Conquest England' (*The Laws of Alfred*, p. 227 n. 13).

Crist in the reference to the Creator of the world in the fourth commandment on observing the sabbath (Ex. 20.11; MP §3). As Treschow notes, this small but significant translation choice anticipates the movement from the justice of the Old Mosaic Law to the mercy of the New Law of Christ that is the subject of the later sections of the prologue (§49–49.8).[38] We saw in the previous chapter how the Introductions to the *Prose Psalms* establish how each psalm was sung first by David or Hezekiah and then by Christ. The following chapters will highlight how the difficulty of explaining the complex relationship between the Old and New Testaments to the laity was to become a recurring concern for Ælfric in his own biblical translations, ultimately pushing him away from word-for-word translation and towards homiletic exegesis. With the Alfredian *Prose Psalms* and Mosaic Prologue, the practical necessity of providing the laity with basic biblical education in the vernacular outweighs any such theological scruples.

Following the translation of the Decalogue, the Alfredian author omits all of Exodus 20.19–26, except for a single verse, Ex. 20.23, which as we have seen was promoted into the preceding version of the Decalogue as a new 'tenth commandment' in place of the second commandment against making graven images (Ex. 20.4). The excised verses describe the fear of the Israelites as Moses returns from the mountain and God's instruction to Moses to speak to them. By skipping over this narrative section, the translator keeps the focus squarely on the written laws themselves.[39] It is in this selective treatment of the Vulgate source, as well as the occasional reframing of biblical material to reflect contemporary concerns, that the creativity and freedom of the author of the Mosaic Prologue is most evident.[40]

The translation of Exodus 21–23.9 (§11–48) that follows sticks fairly closely to the biblical source, though the author frequently makes small but cumulatively significant alterations in order to bring Mosaic law into line with contemporary English practice.[41] This section contains injunctions against theft, idolatry, murder, the mistreatment of foreigners, extortionate lending of money to the poor, the eating of unclean meat and many other offences. Certain injunctions are excised as they would have had no relevance to contemporary readers, such as God's instruction to Moses to tell the Israelites to give him their first-born sons (Ex. 22.28).

---

[38] Treschow, 'Spirit of Mercy', 90–91.
[39] Wormald notes that the Mosaic Prologue is far more selective in its approach to Exodus than proposed sources such as the *Liber ex Lege Moysi*, which are more comprehensive in their listing of the laws of the Pentateuch, including, for example, a long list of curses from Deuteronomy (*Making of English Law*, p. 421).
[40] As we shall see in Chapter Four of this volume, the translators of the Heptateuch similarly abbreviated large and small sections of their Latin sources whenever they deemed material to be otiose.
[41] See Treschow, 'Spirit of Mercy', 91–102.

Some details of the Old Law which the translator considered extraneous are omitted, such as the statement that a man shall go out with his raiment in Ex. 21.4, while others are updated to make them meaningful and intelligible – if not directly applicable – to contemporary readers. Hence, for example, the Hebrew slave (*servum Hebraeum*) of Ex. 21.2 is now cast as a Christian slave (*Cristenne þeow*) in §11, just as the shekels (*siclos*) of Ex. 21.32 are now shillings (*scil*) (MP §21).[42] Through these and many other small alterations, as well as the translator's highly selective, functional equivalence approach to Exodus more generally, the Mosaic Prologue comprehensively 'domesticates' the Latin biblical source, making the unfamiliar terminology of the Old Testament intelligible and meaningful to Alfred's judges.

Occasionally in the course of this long section, the translator saw fit to expand on the biblical source to clarify the full meaning of a law. For example, the biblical prohibition against sorcerers (Ex. 22.18: *Maleficos non patieris vivere*, 'Wizards you shall not suffer to live') is emended in MP §30 to read: *Ða fæmnan þe gewuniað onfon gealdorcræftigan and scinlæcan and wiccan, ne læt þu ða libban* ('Those women who are accustomed to receive enchanters and magicians and witches – do not permit them to live'). This expansion may have resulted from confusion with the preceding verse (Ex. 22.17), which contains the phrase *quam virgines accipere* ('which virgins are wont to receive'),[43] or it may reflect contemporary concerns about the involvement of women in witchcraft as expressed in penitentials.[44] Another expansion occurs in the translator's treatment of the opening clause of the law concerning 'an eye for an eye, tooth for a tooth':

> Ex. 21.24–5: oculum pro oculo, dentem pro dente, manum pro manu, pedem pro pede, adiustonem pro adiustone, vulnus pro vulnere, livorem pro livore
>
> [Eye for eye, tooth for tooth, hand for hand, foot for foot, burning for burning, wound for wound, stripe for stripe.]
>
> MP §19: Gif hwa oðrum his eage oðdo, selle his agen fore: toð fore teð, honda wið honda, fet fore fet, bærning for bærninge, wund wið wunde, læl wið læle.

---

[42] Pratt, *Political Thought*, p. 231: 'There can be no question of the Mosaic excerpts actually applying to Alfred's kingdom. The effect was rather to supply a convincing impression of what law would look like without the benefits of Christian augmentation.'

[43] As suggested by M. H. Turk, ed. *The Legal Code of Ælfred the Great* (Boston: Ginn and Company, 1893), p. 37.

[44] Liebermann, 'King Alfred and Mosaic Law', 26. See further Jurasinski and Oliver, *Laws of Alfred*, p. 253 n. 60.

[If someone should put out another's eye, let him give his own for it: tooth for tooth, hand for hand, feet for feet, burning for burning, wound for wound, bruise for bruise].[45]

The *Gif X [...] selle Y* construction used here appears frequently elsewhere in English laws, explaining the circumstances resulting in this particular injury.

Contemporary notions of sacral kingship are hinted at in the remarkable translation of Ex. 22.28, *Diis non detrahes, et principi populi tui non maledices* ('You shall not speak ill of the gods, and the prince of your people you shall not curse'), as *Ne tæl ðu ðinne Dryhten, ne ðone hlaford þæs folces ne werge þu* ('Do not blaspheme your Lord, nor may you curse the lord of the people') (MP §38). Jurasinski and Oliver state that *hlaford* here 'should be taken to mean "king"'.[46] The king's special status as the Lord's anointed (Latin: *christus*) is foregrounded in other Alfredian texts such as the *Prose Psalms* as well as the earliest English Coronation *ordines*, while the genealogy provided for Alfred's father, Æthelwulf, in the long Anglo-Saxon Chronicle entry for the year 853, stretches back to Christ.[47] As we shall see below, in the second prologue to the *Domboc* the words of Christ are manipulated in support of the argument that the king's life was sacrosanct.

From the Old Law to the New

The transition from the justice of the Old Law to the mercy of the New heralded by the birth of Christ occurs in MP §49, a section which has no known direct source:

§49. Þis sindan ða domas þe se ælmihtega God self sprecende wæs to Moyse and him bebead to healdanne; and siððan se ancenneda Dryhtnes sunu, ure God, þæt is hælend Crist, on middangeard cwom, he cwæð ðæt he ne come no ðas bebodu to brecanne ne to forbeodanne,

---

[45] Jurasinski and Oliver, *The Laws of Alfred*, pp. 242–3.
[46] Jurasinski and Oliver, *The Laws of Alfred*, p. 257 n. 64.
[47] For example, Ps. 2.1: *And ic eam, þeah, cincg geset fram Gode ofer his ðone halgan munt Syon, to þam þæt ic lære his willan and his æ* (cf. **Romanum:** *ego autem constitutus sum rex ab eo super Sion montem sanctum eius praedicans praeceptum Domini*); Ps. 17.51: *Gemycla nu and gemonigfealda þa hælo þæs cynges ðe ðu gesettest ofer folcum, and do mildheortnesse þinum gesmyredan Davide and his cynne on ecnesse* (cf. **Romanum:** *magnificans salutare regis ipsius et faciens misericordiam christo suo David et semini eius usque in saeculum*). See further Stanton, *Culture of Translation*, p. 125. On Coronation *Ordines*, see Pratt, *Political Thought*, pp. 72–8, 232. On the West Saxon genealogy, see Daniel Anlezark, 'Sceaf, Japheth and the Origins of the Anglo-Saxons', *ASE* 31 (2006), 13–46. On this genealogy's claim that Noah had a fourth son named Sceaf, see Chapter Five, p. 219.

ac mid eallum godum **to ecanne**; and mildheortnesse and eaðmodnesse he lærde.

[These are the judgments that almighty God was speaking himself to Moses and bade him keep; and after the only begotten son of the Lord our God, that is the saviour Christ, came into the world, he declared, that he did not come in any way to break or forbid these commandments, but rather **to increase** them with all good [laws]; and he taught mercy and humility.] (Emphasis added).[48]

As noted above, this passage echoes the opening of the Mosaic Prologue in its use of the past continuous form of the verb *sprecan* to describe how God – now referred to more empathically as *se ælmihtega God self* rather than simply *Dryhten* – was 'speaking' to Moses on Mount Sinai. Having reintroduced the figure of God the Father as the ultimate source of Christian law, the translator now adopts a more homiletic style to explain the mystery of Christ's nature in simple terms (*Dryhtnes sunu, ure God, þæt is hælend Crist*). This exegetical mode is suitable for an audience who were relatively unfamiliar with – or needed regular reminders of – the basic tenets of Christian doctrine.[49] Again, there is an emphasis on speech: just as God the Father 'was speaking' to Moses on Mount Sinai, so Christ 'declared' that He had not come to overthrow the Old Law. The author probably had in mind here the words of Christ in the Sermon on the Mount in Matthew 5.17: *nolite putare quoniam veni solvere legem, aut prophetas. Non veni solver, sed adimplere* ('Do not think that I am come to destroy the law, or the prophets. I am not come to destroy, but to fulfil').[50] However, as Jurasinski and Oliver observe, the verb *eacan* ('to increase') which here translates *adimplere* ('to fulfil') is used in earlier law codes to describe the process whereby a king supplements, rather than fulfils, the laws of his predecessors. Indeed, as Treschow notes, it is chiefly through the new emphasis on mercy that Christ is shown to 'increase' the Old Law.[51] The Mosaic Prologue thus teaches Alfred's judges that the Old Law was not simply overturned by the New but rather that it was extended or

---

[48] Jurasinski and Oliver, *The Laws of Alfred*, pp. 262–3.

[49] Treschow comments that this passage 'has a credal tone that invites the readers' assent' ('Spirit of Mercy', 86).

[50] Wormald, *Making of English Law*, p. 425, notes that Hincmar similarly emphasises mercy as the key element that distinguishes the New Law of Christ from the Old Law of Moses. Pratt comments that the statement that Christ *ne come no ðas bebodu to brecanne ne to forbeodanne ac mid eallum godum to ecanne* ('did not come in any way to break or forbid these commandments, but rather to increase them') is 'a loose adaptation' of Mt. 5.17, a verse which Hincmar cites in a similar context (*Political Thought*, p. 227).

[51] Treschow, 'Spirit of Mercy', 87–7.

improved upon through Christ's teaching of mercy. It is for this reason that Alfred wanted his lawmakers to learn about both the laws of Moses and Christ, so they could see for themselves the transformative impact of the Incarnation on salvation history. Whereas the passages discussed above, which are closely modelled on the biblical sources, generally lack stylistic flourishes, the author's more creative treatment of this pivotal moment in legal history is marked by a move into a heightened prose style evident in consistent and selective use of alliteration (*on middangeard cwom, he cwæð ðæt he ne come no ðas bebodu to brecanne ne to forbeodanne*) as well as doublets (*mildheortnesse and eaðmodnesse*) and balanced phrasing and homeoteleuton (*to healdanne* [...] *to brecanne ne to forbeodanne* [...] *to ecanne*). The author of the Mosaic Prologue reserves this sophisticated literary prose style for especially significant moments in biblical legal history.

The next section of the prologue comprises a highly condensed paraphrase of Acts 15.23–9, the 'Apostolic Letter'.[52] This paraphrase is itself prefaced by another bridging passage which again has no direct biblical source, summarising how the apostles began their evangelising work after Christ's passion:

> §49.1. Ða æfter his ðrowunge, ærþam þe his apostolas tofarene wæron geond ealle eorðan to læranne, and þa giet ða hie ætgædere wæron, monega hæðena ðeoda hie to Gode gecerdon. Þa hie ealle ætsomne wæron, hie sendan ærendwrecan to Antiohhia and to Syrie, Cristes æ to læranne.
>
> [Then after his passion, before his apostles went through all the world to teach, and were still together, they turned many heathen peoples to God. When they all were assembled, they sent messengers to Antioch and to Syria, to teach the law of Christ.][53]

Again, a sense of literary style is on display in this seemingly original passage. Notably the use of parallelism (*his apostolas tofarene wæron* [...] *hie ætgædere wæron* [...] *hie to Gode gecerdon* [...] *hie ealle ætsomne wæron; ealle eorðan to læranne* [...] *Cristes æ to læranne*) underscores the dedication of the apostles as a group to the dissemination of Christ's law.

---

[52] Jurasinski and Oliver note that while in the scriptural account the Apostolic Letter is concerned with the clarification of moral and ritual obligations to the newly converted Christian communities of Antioch, Syria and Cilicia, the Mosaic Prologue 'instead presents the letter as a response to the earlier failure of spoken admonitions', an alteration which complements the overall 'effort throughout the Prologue to diminish the importance of the oral over the written in matters of law' (*The Laws of Alfred*, p. 265 n. 72).

[53] Jurasinski and Oliver, *The Laws of Alfred*, pp. 263–4.

At the end of the paraphrase of the Apostolic Letter (Acts 15.29), the author inserts a highly idiosyncratic version of the Golden Rule:

> §49.5 [...] and þæt ge willen, þæt oðre men eow ne don, ne doð ge ðæt oþrum monnum.

> ["[...] and what you wish that other men not do to you, do not to other men."]

The Alfredian author's negative version of the Golden Rule differs from the two iterations of this precept in the Gospels:

> Lk. 6.31: et prout vultis ut faciant vobis homines et vos facite illis similiter

> [And as you would that men should do to you, do you also to them in like manner.]

> Mt. 7.12: omnia ergo quaecumque vultis ut faciant vobis homines et vos facite eis haec. Est enim lex et prophetae.

> [All things therefore whatsoever you would that men should do to you, do you also to them. For this is the law and the prophets.]

Liebermann identified a closer match for the Mosaic Prologue's negative rendering of the Golden Rule (*ne deme* [...] *nolde*) in Tobit 4.16, *quod ab alio odis fieri tibi, vide ne alteri tu aliquando facias* ('What you would hate to have done to you by another, see you never do to another'),[54] while Wormald notes that the negative version of the Golden Rule occurs in some Old Latin readings of the Bible, including the late ninth-century Book of Armagh, in which it also comes at the end of the Apostolic Letter.[55] It appears, then, that the Alfredian author is not so much translating as freely adapting various biblical sources in this passage for a specific, educational purpose.

A similarly creative approach to scriptural translation appears to have produced the passage that follows, which seemingly takes its inspiration from Luke 6.37, *Nolite judicare, et non judicabimini* ('Judge not, and you shall not be judged'):

> §49.6 Of ðissum anum dome mon mæg geðencean, þæt he æghwelcne on ryht gedemeð; ne ðearf he nanra domboca oþerra. Geðence he, þæt he nanum men ne deme þæt he nolde ðæt he him demde, gif he ðone dom ofer hine sohte.

---

[54] Liebermann, *Gesetze*, III, p. 48. Cf. Jurasinksi and Oliver, *The Laws of Alfred*, p. 269 n. 77, for further references.

[55] Wormald, *Making of English Law*, p. 423.

[§49.6 From this one judgment one may reason in such a way that he judge each man rightly; he requires no other book of laws. Let him think that he judge no man in a manner that he would not be judged by him, if he sought judgement over him.]

In this stylised passage, the Alfredian author underlines the Mosaic Prologue's central theme of just (*on ryht*) judgement through extensive polyptoton and alliteration (*dom, gedemeð, domboca, deme, demde, dom*).[56] As we have seen above, it was probably Alfred's concern with the justness of legal judgements issued in his own kingdom that provided the impetus for the composition of the *Domboc* and its elaborate biblical prologue.[57]

From the Apostles to the 'Angelcynn'

Echoing the Prose Preface to the *Pastoral Care*, the Mosaic Prologue then briefly summarises the development of Church synods in the post-Apostolic era among the various Christian peoples, including the English:[58]

§49.7: Siððan ðæt þa gelamp, þæt monega ðeoda Cristes geleafan onfengon, þa wurdon monega seonoðas geond ealne middangeard gegaderode, and eac swa geond Angelcyn, siððan hie Cristes geleafan onfengon, halegra biscepa and eac oðerra geðungenra witena; hie ða gesetton, for ðære mildheortnesse þe Crist lærde, æt mæstra hwelcre misdæde þætte ða weoruldhlafordas moston mid hiora leafan buton synne æt þam forman gylte þære fiohbote onfon, þe hie ða gesettan; [...]

[After it happened that many peoples received the faith of Christ, then many synods were gathered through all the world, and also among the English, after they received the faith of Christ, of holy bishops and also of other distinguished counsellors; they then established, because of the mercy that Christ taught, that worldly lords might with their leave [and] without sin receive the monetary payment that they [the bishops] established at the first offence for most of those misdeeds; [...].]

While this passage has no direct biblical source, Wormald notes that it closely resembles and may have been directly inspired by Archbishop Fulk of Rheims' Letter to Alfred written *c.* 886, which lamented the poor state to which the English Church had fallen since the Augustinian mission and similarly traced the history of Christian law from the time

---

[56] As Treschow notes, the use of the word *deman* in this passage 'indicates that the Golden Rule, and so the whole prologue, is addressed to magistrates in particular' ('Spirit of Mercy', 81).
[57] See above, pp. 56–8.
[58] On the Prose Preface to the *Pastoral Care*, see above, pp. 3–4, 34–5.

of the Apostles to the early synods of the Church.[59] The reference to *weoruldhlafordas* ('worldly lords') receiving monetary payment for misdeeds positions Alfred's judges operating at a local level – the primary audience of the *Domboc* – within the long history of Judeo-Christian law, reminding them of their duty to exercise mercy (*mildheortnesse*) in the manner exemplified by Christ.

The closing words of the Mosaic Prologue refine the claim that these worldly lords were initially merciful toward most offenders, culminating in the work's most striking 'revoicing' of Scripture:

> §49.7 [...] buton æt hlafordsearwe hie nane mildheortnesse ne dorston gecweðan, forþam ðe God ælmihtig þam nane ne gedemde þe hine oferhogdon, ne Crist Godes sunu þam nane ne gedemde þe hine to deaðe sealde, and he bebead þone hlaford lufian swa hine.
>
> [[...] but for betrayal of one's lord they dared not proclaim any mercy, for God almighty judged none for those who despised him, nor did Christ, God's son, grant any [mercy] to those who gave him to death, and he laid down [that one should] love one's lord just as oneself.][60]

In order to enshrine the sanctity of the life of an earthly lord (*hlaford*) in English law, the Mosaic Prologue here flatly contradicts Luke 23.34, *Iesus autem dicebat: 'Pater, dimitte illis, non enim sciunt quid faciunt'* ('And Jesus said: "Father, forgive them, for they know not what they do"'), while conflating Christ's first and second great commandments, Mt. 22.37, *Diliges Dominum Deum tuum ex toto corde tuo, et in tota anima tua, et in tota mente tua* ('You shall love the Lord your God with your whole heart and with your whole soul and with your whole mind') and Mt. 22.39, *Diliges proximum tuum, sicut teipsum* ('You shall love your neighbour as yourself'). This exceptionally bold rewriting of the Gospels effectively places new words in Christ's mouth in order to buttress the authority of earthly lords such as Alfred himself.[61] Jurasinski and Oliver suggest that the author 'probably

---

[59] Wormald, *Making of English Law*, pp. 425–6. See further Pratt, *Political Thought*, p. 223. For the text, see *Councils and Synods with other Documents relating to the English Church I*, ed. Dorothy Whitelock, M. Brett and C. N. L. Brooke, 2 vols (Oxford, 1981), I, no. 4, pp. 6–12. The letter is also translated in Keynes and Lapidge, *Alfred the Great*, pp. 183–4. For discussion of the letter and its background, see Janet L. Nelson, '"... *sicut olim gens Francorum ... nunc gens Anglorum*": Fulk's Letter to Alfred Revisited', in *Alfred the Wise: Studies in Honour of Janet Bately on the Occasion of Her Sixty-Fifth Birthday*, ed. Jane Roberts and Janet L. Nelson, with Malcolm Godden (Cambridge: D. S. Brewer, 1997), pp. 135–44.

[60] Jurasinski and Oliver, *The Laws of Alfred*, pp. 270–1.

[61] Wormald notes that this statement 'spectacularly distort[s]' Christ's second commandment (*Making of English Law*, p. 423).

alludes here' to Psalm 68.22, *Et dederunt in escam meam fel, et in siti mea potaverunt me aceto* ('And they gave me gall for food, and in my thirst, they gave me vinegar to drink'), noting that Peter quotes the same verse from Ps. 68.25, *Effunde super eos iram tuam, et furor irae tuae comprehendat eos* ('Pour out your indignation upon them, and let the heat of your wrath take hold of them') in reference to the traitor Judas (Acts 1.20): [62]

> Scriptum est enim in libro Psalmorum: 'Fiat commoratio eorum deserta, et non sit qui inhabitet in ea: et episcopatum eius accipiat alter.'
>
> [For it is written in the book of Psalms: 'Let their habitation become desolate, and let there be none to dwell therein. And his bishopric let another take.']

Another possible biblical inspiration which emphasises the authority of the Lord God rather than an earthly lord is Leviticus 19.18: *non quaeres ultionem, nec memor eris iniuriae civium tuorum. Diliges amicum tuum sicut temet ipsum. Ego Dominus* ('Seek not revenge, nor be mindful of the injury of your citizens. You shall love your friend as yourself. I am the Lord'). An even closer match is found in the Second Epistle of James, in which the observance of God's law is explicitly connected to royal authority and mercy is shown to balance judgement:

> [2.8] Si tamen legem perficitis regalem, secundum Scripturas, 'Diliges proximum tuum sicut te ipsum', bene facitis. [9] Si autem personas accipitis, peccatum operamini redarguti a lege quasi transgressores. [10] Quicumque autem totam legem servaverit offendat autem in uno factus est omnium reus. [11] Qui enim dixit: 'Non moechaberis', dixit et: 'Non occides'. Quod si non moechaberis, occides autem, factus es transgressor legis. [12] Sic loquimini et sic facite sicut per legem libertatis incipientes iudicari. [13] Iudicium enim sine misericordia illi qui non fecit misericordiam. Superexultat autem misericordia iudicio.
>
> [[2.8] If then you fulfil the royal law, according to the Scriptures, 'You shall love your neighbour as yourself', you do well. [9] But if you have respect to persons, you commit sin, being reproved by the law as transgressors. [10] And whosoever shall keep the whole law, but offend in one point, is become guilty of all. [11] For he that said: 'You shall not commit adultery', said also: 'You shall not kill.' Now if you do not commit adultery, but shall kill, you are become a transgressor of the law. [12] So speak you and so do, as being to be judged by the law of liberty. [13] For judgment

---

[62] Jurasinski and Oliver, *The Laws of Alfred*, p. 271 n. 80. Pratt points to parallels with Exodus 22.20 (*qui immolat diis occidetur praeter Domino soli*, 'He who sacrifices to gods, shall be put to death, save only to the Lord') (*Political Thought*, p. 233).

without mercy to him that has not done mercy. And mercy exalts itself above judgment.]

The author of the Mosaic Prologue may have drawn on some or perhaps all of these biblical passages, and others besides, in composing this injunction against *hlafordsearwe* ('betrayal of one's lord').

The political motivation behind this pseudo-biblical defence of earthly lordship is made clear in Alfred's law code itself, which contains the following injunction:

> V.4: Gif hwa ymb cyninges feorh sierwe, ðurh hine oððe ðurh wreccena feormunge oððe his manna, sie he his feores scyldig and ealles þæs ðe he age.
>
> [If someone plots against the king's life, either by his own actions, or by the harbouring of those who have been banished or of his men, let him be liable for his life and all that he owns.][63]

No such injunction against treason had featured in the laws issued by earlier English kings, though it does form part of the statutes issued by the Papal Legates to English kings in 786:[64]

> XII. [...] In necem regis nemo communicare audeat, quia christus Domini est: et si quis tali sceleri adhæserit, si Episcopus est, aut ullus ex Sacerdotali gradu, ex ipso detrudatur, et a sancta hæreditate dejiciatur.[65]
>
> [12. [...] Let no one dare to conspire to kill a king, for he is the Lord's anointed, and if anyone take part in such a crime, if he be a bishop or anyone of the priestly order, let him be expelled from it and cast out from the holy heritage.][66]

The Mosaic Prologue's positioning of Alfred in a chain of legal authority stretching from God to Moses, and from Christ to the Apostles, and its designation of the crime of *hlafordsearwe* ('plotting against a lord') as a breach of *Cristes æ* ('Christ's law') punishable by death, forcefully reminds all of Alfred's subjects of the divine source of his earthly authority.

---

[63] Jurasinski and Oliver, *The Laws of Alfred*, pp. 292–93. For discussion of *hlafordsearwe* (lord-treachery) in the *Domboc*, see Pratt, *Political Thought*, pp. 232–8.

[64] Wormald has suggested that the legates' statutes may in fact be the laws of Offa of Mercia which Alfred refers to as a source for his *Domboc* (*Making of English Law*, pp. 107, 280–1). See further Pratt, *Political Thought*, pp. 220–1, 232–8; Jurasinski and Oliver, *The Laws of Alfred*, pp. 276–9.

[65] *Epistolae Karolini Aevi* II, ed. Dümmler, 19–29, at 21–4 (no. 3).

[66] *English Historical Documents, c. 500–1042*, English Historical Documents 1, 2nd edn, ed. and trans. Dorothy Whitelock (London: Routledge, 1979), no. 191, p. 771.

The Second Prologue

Following the conclusion of the Mosaic Prologue, the *Domboc* proper begins with its own prologue (the 'Second Prologue'), in which the figure of Alfred is finally introduced as the agent of Christ's laws.[67] Speaking in the first person, Alfred presents himself as a diligent compiler, who took personal responsibility for gathering, correcting and updating the legal writings of his royal forebears, Æthelberht of Kent (*r. c.* 589–616), Ine of Wessex (*r.* 688–726) and Offa of Mercia (*r.* 757–796):[68]

> *Ic ða Ælfred cyning* þas togædere gegaderode and awritan het, monege þara þe ure foregengan heoldon, ða ðe me licodon; and manege þara þe me ne licodon ic awearp mid minra witena geðeahte, and on oðre wisan bebead to healdanne.
>
> Forðam ic ne dorste geðristlæcan þara minra awuht fela on gewrit settan, forðam me wæs uncuð, hwæt þæs ðam lician wolde ðe æfter us wæren. Ac ða ðe ic gemette awðer oððe on Ines dæge, *mines mæges, oððe on Offan Mercna cyninges, oððe on Æþelbryhtes þe ærest fulluhte onfeng on Angelcynne*, þa ðe me ryhtoste ðuhton, *ic þa heron gegaderode, and þa oðre forlet.*
>
> *Ic ða Ælfred Westseaxna cyning* eallum minum witum þas geeowde, and hie ða cwædon, þæt him þæt licode eallum to healdanne.
>
> [*Then I, Alfred the king*, gathered these [rulings] together and commanded to be written many of them which our ancestors held – those that pleased me. And many of them that did not please me I discarded with the consent of my counsellors, and directed them to be held in a different manner.
>
> Thus I did not dare presume to set many of mine in writing, because it was not known to me, what would please those who came after us. But those that I found either from the time of *Ine, my kinsman, or of Offa, king of the Mercians, or of Æthelberht who first in England received baptism*, those which seemed most just to me, *I gathered herein, and left out the others.*
>
> *I, Alfred, king of the West Saxons*, then presented these (rulings) to all my counsellors, and they then said, that it pleased them all to hold (them).] (Emphases added).[69]

This description of Alfred judiciously selecting elements from the laws of his predecessors and discarding others with the advice of his counsellors

---

[67] Pratt identifies this passage as 'the operative moment' in the *Domboc* as a whole, in which 'Alfred's own modest judgement' is foregrounded (*Political Thought*, p. 218).

[68] The sense that Alfred is updating Ine's laws is underlined by their inclusion after the copy of the *Domboc* in MS CCC 173.

[69] Jurasinski and Oliver, *The Laws of Alfred*, pp. 280–3.

complements the portrait of the king collaborating with his circle of scholars presented in the Prose Preface to the *Pastoral Care*.[70] While the Mosaic Prologue had begun with the Lord speaking in the third person to Moses (*Dryhten wæs sprecende to Moyse; God self sprecende wæs to Moyse*), before proceeding to summarise the core teachings of Christ and the Apostles (*Dryhtnes sunu, ure God, þæt is hælend Crist,* [...], *he cwæð; Crist lærde,* [...] *forþam ðe God ælmihtig þam nane ne gedemde þe hine oferhogdon, ne Crist Godes sunu þam nane ne gedemde*), the *Domboc* now presents Alfred, as the mouthpiece of God's laws, speaking directly to his judges in the first person (*Ic ða Ælfred cyning; Ic ða Ælfred Westseaxna cyning*). The emphasis on written law (*awritan het*) and the presentation of Alfred as an extender or increaser of law aligns the earthly ruler with Christ, who as we have seen is said to have extended the laws of Moses. Presented with such a comprehensive and accessible summary of Judeo-Christian law in their own tongue, Alfred's judges could be left in no doubt of their sacred duty to apply themselves to wisdom and administer the law with justice and mercy.

Conclusion

With the production of the Mosaic Prologue and the Second Prologue to the laws, Alfred aimed to rectify the poor standard of education among his judges by equipping them with a streamlined translation of the Laws of Moses and Christ. These prefatory materials also provided Alfred's judges with the tools to understand the dynamic relationship between the Old and the New Law and to administer the law with justice and mercy. The generally communicative approach to biblical translation taken throughout both prologues can be compared with that adopted in the Alfredian *Prose Psalms*. However, at times the author was remarkably creative in translating and adapting Scripture, notably in the revoicing of Christ's second commandment to shore up Alfred's own earthly authority. As Pratt notes, the survival of six manuscript witnesses, as well as frequent references and allusions to the work in subsequent laws and charters, demonstrates that the *Domboc* was something that members of the English aristocracy were expected to know.[71] Moreover, the Mosaic Prologue's summary of biblical law, along with the Second Prologue's reference to the laws of Kent, Mercia and Wessex, establishes the *Domboc* as the sole law code for all the *Angelcynn* – a Christian nation ruled by a single West Saxon king whose authority comes from God.

---

[70] See above, pp. 3–4, 34–5.
[71] Pratt, *Political Thought*, pp. 238–41.

The Mosaic Prologue to King Alfred's Domboc

The Mosaic Prologue deserves recognition as an ambitious biblical translation that combines selective scriptural translation with original passages and even creative adaptation of the words of Christ.[72] In its willingness to freely edit and at times radically alter the wording of Scripture, the Mosaic Prologue reflects a growing confidence in the use of Old English prose as a vehicle for biblical translation in the late ninth century.

---

[72] See Frantzen, *King Alfred*, pp. 19–22.

3

Studying, Reading and Preaching the Gospels

THE GOSPELS are the most important text of the Christian Bible, containing the narrative of Christ's life, ministry, death and resurrection. Gospel readings form the centrepiece of the Mass and are understood by Christians as the fulfilment of the prophecies of the Old Testament – the process known as typology. Between the conversion period (*c.* 600–700) and the eleventh century, the Gospels were continually translated, adapted and interpreted in Old English prose and verse.[1] Vernacular poems based on or inspired by gospel stories proved especially popular in the early Old English period, though in most cases these were not direct translations as such but rather adaptations or paraphrases drawing on intermediary sources as well as the Bible.[2] For example, the *Advent Lyrics* (also known as *Christ I*), are a series of hymns in celebration of Christ's nativity and in praise of the Virgin Mary, mostly based on the Latin 'O antiphons' used in the liturgy, while *Christ in Judgement* (*Christ III*) dramatises the Second Coming and Last Day by combining elements of the biblical narrative with material derived from a sermon by Caesarius of Arles.[3] Drawing on both of these Old English poems, as well as works by Gregory the Great and Sedulius, the (probably) ninth-century Mercian poet Cynewulf composed a bridging work, *Ascension* (*Christ II*), to complete a tripartite narrative of the life of Christ which now stands at the head of the tenth-century anthology of vernacular verse known as the Exeter Book.[4] Christ's Passion, his Harrowing of Hell and his role as judge on the Last

---

[1] For a summary, see Morrell, *Manual of Old English Biblical Materials*, pp. 154–97.
[2] On the origins of Old English biblical poetry, see Introduction, pp. 13–16.
[3] See Jasmine Jones, 'Vernacular Theology in the Old English *Advent Lyrics*: Monastic Devotion to Mary', *RES* 75 (2024), 1–16; Thomas D. Hill, 'Vision and Judgement in the Old English *Christ III*', *SP* 70 (1973), 233–42.
[4] See Colin Chase, 'God's Presence through Grace as the Theme of Cynewulf's *Christ II* and the Relationship of this Theme to *Christ I* and *Christ III*', *ASE* 3 (1974), 87–101; Thomas D. Hill, 'Literary History and Old English Poetry: The Case of *Christ I, II, III*', in *Sources of Anglo-Saxon Culture*, ed. Paul E. Szarmach with the assistance of Virginia Darrow Oggins, Studies in Medieval Culture 20 (Kalamazoo, MI: Medieval Institute Publications, Western Michigan University, 1986), pp. 3–22; Andy Orchard, 'Alcuin and Cynewulf: The Art and Craft of Anglo-Saxon Verse', *Journal of the British Academy* 8 (2020), 295–399.

Day are also the subject of *The Dream of the Rood*, a highly sophisticated poem preserved in the tenth-century Vercelli Book that blends the gospel narrative with accounts of the Passion of St Andrew as well, perhaps, as the hymns of Venantius Fortunatus (d. *c.* 600).[5] The popularity of this particular New Testament poem across the Old English period is attested by inscriptions on the eighth-century Ruthwell Cross and the tenth-century Brussels Cross as well as citations in homilies.[6] Further Old English poems on broadly biblical themes are also preserved in the Vercelli Book, including *Andreas*, a long narrative poem based on the apocryphal Acts of Andrew and Matthew, and Cynewulf's own work, *The Fates of the Apostles*, a short versification of a Latin martyrology, itself derived from the Acts of the Apostles.[7] Other Old English poems on New Testament themes are scattered across various manuscripts, with Judgement Day proving by far the most popular theme.[8] Indeed, Bede himself composed a short Old English poem on Judgement Day, which survives in the monk Cuthbert's account of his dying days, now known as *Bede's Death Song*.[9] Given the popularity of the genre of the gospel harmony on the continent, it is perhaps surprising that no such work survives in the corpus of extant

---

[5] On connections between *The Dream of the Rood* and the martyrdom of St Andrew, see Thomas D. Hill, 'The *Passio Andreae* and *The Dream of the Rood*', *ASE* 38 (2010), 1–10. On the poem's various iterations and connections with medieval Latin poetry, liturgy and art, see Éamonn Ó Carragáin, *Ritual and the Rood: Liturgical Images and the Old English Poems of the Dream of the Rood Tradition* (Toronto: University of Toronto Press, 2005). On the Harrowing of Hell, see p. 111.

[6] For evidence of the influence of *The Dream of the Rood* on Old English homilies, see below, p. 132.

[7] Both poems appear to be influenced by *Beowulf*: see further Andy Orchard, 'Both Style and Substance: The Case for Cynewulf', in *Anglo-Saxon Styles*, ed. Catherine E. Karkov and George Hardin Brown (Binghampton, NY: SUNY Press, 2003), pp. 271–305; *Andreas: An Edition*, ed. Michael D. Bintley and Richard North (Liverpool: Liverpool University Press, 2016).

[8] *Judgement Day I* and *The Descent into Hell* are copied in the Exeter Book; *Judgement Day II*, a poem based on Bede's *De die iudicii*, is in Cambridge Corpus Christi College (CCC) MS 201; *Christ and Satan*, which combines Old Testament stories such as the Fall of the Rebel Angels and Fall of Man with the New Testament accounts of the Temptation in the Desert and Judgement Day, is preserved as the final item in Oxford Bodleian Library MS Junius 11, following a sequence of poems on Old Testament themes, *Genesis A* (and *B*), *Exodus* and *Daniel*. Three poems based on the Lord's Prayer (Mt. 6.9–13; Lk. 11.2–4) are included in the Exeter Book, CCC 201 and Junius 121, respectively. For the impact of the New Testament on Old English literature more generally, see Richard Marsden, 'Biblical Literature: The New Testament', in *Cambridge Companion to Old English Literature*, 2nd edn, ed. Godden and Lapidge, pp. 234–50.

[9] On Cuthbert's account of Bede's death, see above, pp. 16–19.

Old English poetry, though the combination of the three Christ poems preserved in the Exeter Book may reflect an attempt to produce something broadly analogous.[10]

Evidence for the translation and adaptation of the Gospels into Old English prose is, however, harder to trace prior to the tenth century. As discussed in the Introduction, Bede was reportedly working on a translation of the beginning of the Gospel of John 'for the use of the Church' at the time of his death, though what form this now-lost work took is unknown.[11] It appears that gospel pericopes were being translated for inclusion in homilies from at least the ninth century, though the earliest manuscript witnesses date from the tenth century. On occasion, the anonymous authors of these homilies merged passages from different gospels to produce something approaching a gospel harmony in vernacular prose.[12] During the latter part of the tenth century, complete interlinear Old English glosses were added to two of the most splendidly illuminated Latin gospel books produced in eighth-century Northumbria and ninth-century Ireland respectively: the Lindisfarne and Rushworth (or MacRegol) Gospels. Growing demand for biblical translations in the tenth century also saw the production of the first continuous prose rendering of all four gospels into any modern European vernacular, the *Wessex Gospels*. Apocryphal gospels such as the Gospels of Mary and the Gospel of Nicodemus were also rendered into Old English prose at unknown dates, though it is unlikely that they were composed before the tenth century. The first part of this chapter explores how these two contrasting approaches to gospel translation, the one interlinear and mostly formal equivalence, the other communicative and functional equivalence, reflect the needs of differing sets of English readers of the Bible. As we shall see, the glosses were primarily intended for a monastic audience as an aid to study and an impetus to *meditatio*; the *Wessex Gospels*, on the other hand, may have been designed for private reading by lay readers or as an adjunct to the preaching materials used by priests. The final section of this chapter contrasts Ælfric's highly selective and richly exegetical interpretation of gospel pericopes in his *Catholic Homilies* with the often less sophisticated approach of anonymous homilists.[13]

---

[10] On the production of vernacular gospel harmonies in ninth-century Francia, see above, pp. 8–11.

[11] See above, pp. 16–19.

[12] See below, pp. 130–43. For the connection between Old English homilies and the tradition of the gospel harmony, see Christopher A. Jones, 'Early English Homiletic Treatments of Christ's Passion: Generic and Liturgical Influences', in *Sermons, Saints, and Sources*, ed. Hall and Rudolf, pp. 241–63, at 244–9. I am grateful to Prof. Jones for sharing a pre-published version of this article.

[13] On Ælfric's return to the exegetical style in the *Treatise*, see below, Chapter Five.

The Lindisfarne and Rushworth Glosses

During the tenth century, complete interlinear Old English glosses were added to two of the most prestigious Latin gospel books produced in early medieval England. The Lindisfarne Gospels, penned by Eadfrith around 687–698, are among the most magnificent of all the illuminated codices that survive from early medieval Europe and one of the crowning achievements of the so-called 'Golden Age' of Northumbrian art. An Old English gloss was inserted above Eadfrith's Latin text sometime between 950 and 970 by a scribe who identifies himself in a colophon as the priest Aldred. This colophon reveals that Aldred provided the gloss at least partly to establish his credentials on joining the community of St Cuthbert, which by the tenth century had relocated to Chester-le-Street in the wake of Viking raids.[14] Another Old English gloss was added in the late tenth century to the Rushworth (or MacRegol) Gospels, an Irish codex originally made *c.* 800. This gloss was written out by two scribes who made use of Aldred's gloss on the Lindisfarne Gospels: Farman provided the gloss for all of Matthew, Mark 1–2.15 and John 18.1–3, while Owun was responsible for all the other sections.[15] The combined work of these three tenth-century glossators provides important evidence for the ongoing use of Anglian dialects at a time when late West Saxon had come to dominate

---

[14] The Lindisfarne Gospels are preserved in London, British Library, Cotton MS Nero D. IV; Ker §165. Images of this manuscript are available online at: https://iiif.bl.uk/uv/#?manifest=https://bl.digirati.io/manifests/ark:/81055/man_10000006.0x000001. On the production and reception of the codex, see Janet Backhouse, *The Lindisfarne Gospels* (Ithaca, NY: Cornell University Press, 1981). For discussion of Aldred's gloss, see Stanton, *Culture of Translation*, pp. 49–53; Michelle P. Brown, *The Lindisfarne Gospels: Society, Spirituality and the Scribe* (Toronto: University of Toronto Press, 2003), pp. 90–102; Karen Louise Jolly, *The Community of St. Cuthbert in the Late Tenth Century: The Chester-le-Street Additions to Durham Cathedral Library A.IV.19* (Columbus: Ohio State University Press, 2012).

[15] The Rushworth Gospels are preserved in Oxford, Bodleian Library, MS Auct. D. 2. 19 (SC 3946); Ker §292. Manuscript images are available online at: https://digital.bodleian.ox.ac.uk/objects/b708f563-b804-42b5-bd0f-2826dfaeb5cc/surfaces/f0fd9c40-0e3d-45b4-9a1d-19d092474ad4/. For the texts of Lindisfarne and Rushworth glosses, in parallel with two MSS of the *Wessex Gospels*, see Walter W. Skeat, ed., *The Holy Gospels in Anglo-Saxon, Northumbrian, and Old Mercian Versions* (Cambridge: Cambridge University Press, 1871–87). See also Kenichi Tamoto, ed., *The MacRegol Gospels or The Rushworth Gospels: Edition of the Latin Text with the Old English Interlinear Gloss Transcribed from Oxford Bodleian Library, MS Auctarium D. 2. 19* (Amsterdam: John Benjamins, 2013); Tadashi Kotake, ed., *Rushworth One: An Edition of Farman's Old English Interlinear Gloss to the Rushworth Gospels*, Medium Ævum Monographs 44, new series (Oxford: The Society for the Study of Medieval Languages and Literature, 2023).

written documents produced in the south of England:[16] both Aldred and Owun wrote in the Northumbrian dialect, whereas Farman uses Mercian spellings. The addition of Old English glosses to these highly prized and already ancient Latin Gospel books bears witness to the prestige of the vernacular in tenth-century England.

As with the psalter glosses discussed in Chapter One, both the Lindisfarne and Rushworth glosses were designed to serve as guides to the Latin text which they accompany rather than as a substitute. For the most part, the glosses therefore closely follow the syntax of the Latin source-text above which they sit. While interlinear glosses of this nature were often used as teaching aids, it seems highly unlikely that such valuable codices would be used in the schoolroom to teach novices Latin. Nevertheless, the importance of making the meaning of the Gospels as clear as possible evidently exceeded any considerations about the integrity of the manuscript page for these tenth-century glossators and their respective monastic communities. The function of these gospel glosses as linguistic cribs is made clear by the frequent provision of alternative translations indicated by the abbreviation *l* for Old English *oððe*/Latin *vel* ('or'), which appears whenever the scribe was either unsure of the meaning of a Latin term or wished to provide a range of vernacular options.

To illustrate the painstaking, scholarly approach of these glossators, I present below the Vulgate text of the opening of the Gospel of Matthew with the Douay-Rheims translation underneath, followed by a semi-diplomatic transcription of the Latin and Old English text as it appears in the Lindisfarne Gospels (Mt. 1.18–19), Cotton MS Nero D. IV, fols 29^r–29^v. Fig. 5 shows fol. 29^r which contains the opening of Mat. 1.18 up to the word *Iospeh*:[17]

> [18] Christi autem generatio sic erat. Cum esset desponsata mater eius Maria Ioseph, antequam convenirent inventa est in utero habens de Spiritu Sancto. [19] Ioseph autem vir eius cum esset iustus, et nollet eam traducere, voluit occulte dimittere eam.

> [[18] Now the generation of Christ was in this manner. When as his mother Mary was espoused to Joseph, before they came together, she was found with child, of the Holy Ghost. [19] Whereupon Joseph her husband, being a just man, and not willing publicly to expose her, was minded to put her away privately.]

---

[16] On the development of late West Saxon as the standard form of written English, see below, pp. 92–3.

[17] Text cited from Skeat, ed., *Holy Gospels*, pp. 27–9.

Figure 5. London, British Library, Cotton MS Nero D. IV, fol. 29ʳ, 'Lindisfarne Gospels: Mt. 1.18, with Old English gloss'.

Fol. 29r:

onginneð	godspell	æfter	matheus
Incipit	**euangelium**	**secundum**	**mattheu**

cristes
[18]CHRISTI[18]

soðlice
AUTEM GENE-

cynnreccenisse 1 cneuresuu	suæ 1 ðus	wæs	mið ðy
-RATIO	**SIC**	**ERAT**	**CUM**

wæs	biwoedded 1 beboden 1 befæstnad 1 betaht
ESSET	**DESPONSATA**

moder	his		
MATER	**EIUS**	**MARIA**	**IOSEPH**

Fol. 29v:

ær ðon	hia gegeadradon 1 gecuomun
ante quam	**conuenirent**

bigetten 1 infunden	wæs 1 is	in	hrif
inuenta	**est**	**in**	**utero**

hæfde	of	halig	gaast
habens	**de**	**spiritu**	**sancto**

ioseph	cuðlice	uer	hire
[19]IOseph	**autem**	**uir**	**eius**

mið ðy	wæss	soðfæst
cum	**esset**	**iustus**

---

[18] This word is written in the manuscript in the form of a magnificent, illuminated Chi-Rho-Iota, spelling the first three letters of the name *Christi* (fig. 5).

7	nalde	hea
et	**nollet**	**eam**

gebrenge ł gelæda	
traducere	

ah ʰᵉwalde	deiglice
uoluit	**occulte**

forleitta	hea ł ða ilca
dimittere	**eam**

The majority of Aldred's gospel glosses are substitution glosses, with one or more Old English terms supplied above each equivalent Latin word. In verse 18 alone, for example, Aldred supplies two alternative readings for five individual Latin terms: *generatio* > *cynnreccenisse ł cneuresuu*, *sic* > *suæ ł ðus*, *conuenirent* > *hia gegeadradon ł gecuomun*, *inuenta* > *bigetten ł infunden*, and *est* > *wæs ł is*, while he gives no less than four vernacular options for the Latin verb *desponsata* ('betrothed, engaged') > *biwoedded ł beboden ł befæstnad ł betaht*. The provision of such a multiplicity of Old English equivalents may have arisen from Aldred's consultation of a variety of sources. Alternatively, as Stanton suggests, this range of options might reflect a contemporary drive to expand Old English vocabulary and to extend the semantic range of existing terms.[19] While the second of the two glosses given for Latin *generatio*, Old English *cneuresuu*, appears frequently in prose and verse as well as psalter glosses,[20] the first term, *cynnreccenisse*, is confined to the Lindisfarne gloss to Matthew, where it also appears above the words *generationis* (in Jerome's Prologue to Matthew) and *genealogia* (Mt. 1.0).[21] As the editors of the *DOE* note, the range of terms supplied for *desponsata* may reflect Aldred's hesitancy over the carnality of Joseph and Mary's relationship: the first, *biwoedded*, is a common word, while the second, *beboden*, is rare in the sense used here;[22] the third, *befæstnad*, is unique in this sense,[23] and the fourth, *betaht*, is only recorded in this sense in one other instance.[24] As we

---

[19] Stanton, *Culture of Translation*, pp. 51–2.
[20] *DOE* s.v. *cyn-recenes*: 'account of (someone's) lineage, genealogy'.
[21] *DOE* s.v. *cnēoris*: '1.a. progeny, line of descendants, tribe; [...] 2.a. group of individuals born about the same period, generation'.
[22] *DOE* s.v. *be-bēodan*: 'D.3.a.i. to commit, entrust (someone *acc.* to the care or protection of someone, or to the keeping of God *dat.*)'
[23] *DOE* s.v. *be-fæstnian*: '2. to pledge (someone) in marriage, betroth'.
[24] *DOE* s.v. *be-tǣcan*: '2.d. to commit in marriage, betroth', appears in the

shall see below, Ælfric went to considerable lengths in his *Catholic Homilies* to prevent any misunderstanding of the Virgin Birth and to promote its orthodox interpretation throughout the English Church.[25]

In addition to weighing up the various possible translations of each Latin word, Aldred pays careful attention to the grammar of his source-text: for example, the genitive inflection of the opening Latin word *Christ-i* is mirrored in the Old English gloss *christ-es*. Personal names are often left untranslated (e.g. *Maria*, *Ioseph*) when the meaning is obvious to Aldred's tenth-century readers, though *Ioseph* is supplied once in the gloss at the beginning of verse 19 to clarify the referent of the sentence. Inflected Latin verbs are sometimes expanded to form an Old English verb phrase, the process known in linguistics as 'periphrasis', as in the supplement gloss of *uoluit* as *ah he walde*. Despite these small concessions to vernacular idiom, for the most part the Lindisfarne gloss closely adheres to the syntax of the Latin source text that it sits above: for instance, Latin NOUN + GENITIVE DETERMINER constructions are replicated in the vernacular (e.g. *mater eius* > *moder his*), a feature which we also observed in the glossed psalters.[26] There is only one exception in this extract to this general practice of syntactical mirroring, where Latin *de spiritu sancto* is rendered as *on halig gaast*, with the placement of the adjective *halig* before the noun reflecting standard Old English word order.[27]

These features of the Lindisfarne gloss point to its primary purpose as a guide to the Latin, facilitating close study of the meaning of each individual Latin word at the level of grammar and sense. Whenever more information is required to aid understanding, the reader's eye moves upward from the Latin majuscule of the main text to the Old English minuscule of the gloss. The production of the gloss itself might be viewed as an act of prayerful

---

eleventh-century Old English translation of the Rule of Chrodegang. Eric G. Stanley notes that Aldred supplies a marginal gloss to this verse, further clarifying its meaning: *to gemanne nalles to habban for wif* ('to take care of, not at all to possess as a woman'): 'The Lindisfarne Gospels: Aldred's Gloss For God and St Cuthbert and All the Saints Together Who are in the Island', in *The Lindisfarne Gospels: New Perspectives*, ed. Richard Gameson, Library of the Written Word 57 (Leiden: Brill, 2017), pp. 206–17, at 210. In the same article, Stanley also discusses Aldred's 'encyclopaedic' marginal gloss on Mt. 1.18, which confusingly states that the Old Testament priest Abiathar was *forebiscop* ('high bishop') in Jerusalem and *bebeod* ('committed') Mary into Joseph's care (210).

[25] See pp. 125–30.
[26] See p. 46.
[27] This reversal of word-order is noted by Ruta Nagucka, 'Glossal Translation in the Lindisfarne Gospel according to Saint Matthew', *Studia Anglica Posnaniensia* 31 (1997), 179–201, at 181. See further Giuseppe Pagliarulo, 'Word Order in the Lindisfarne Glosses?', *Neophilologus* 94 (2010), 625–35.

study in which we witness Aldred himself meditating on the vocabulary, grammar and syntax of his scriptural source before weighing up its various possible meanings.[28] Aldred's provision of multiple glosses for certain Latin words in turn invites his fellow monastics to ruminate on the full meaning of the scriptural text. As well as assisting in the acquisition of Latin vocabulary essential for a novice, Aldred's rich and variegated gloss could thus also prove useful in the practice of *lectio divina*, the constant prayerful reading of sacred books that lay at the heart of the monastic *opus dei*.[29]

The subsidiary nature of Farman's gloss on the opening section of Matthew in the Rushworth Gospels is evident in his placement of the first word, *kristes*, to the right of the large, illuminated capitals CRI (CHI-RO-IOTA, an abbreviation for *CRISTI*) and partially above the next word *autem* (fig. 6). Again, the Old English gloss is written in Anglo-Saxon square minuscule above the insular majuscule of the Latin:[30]

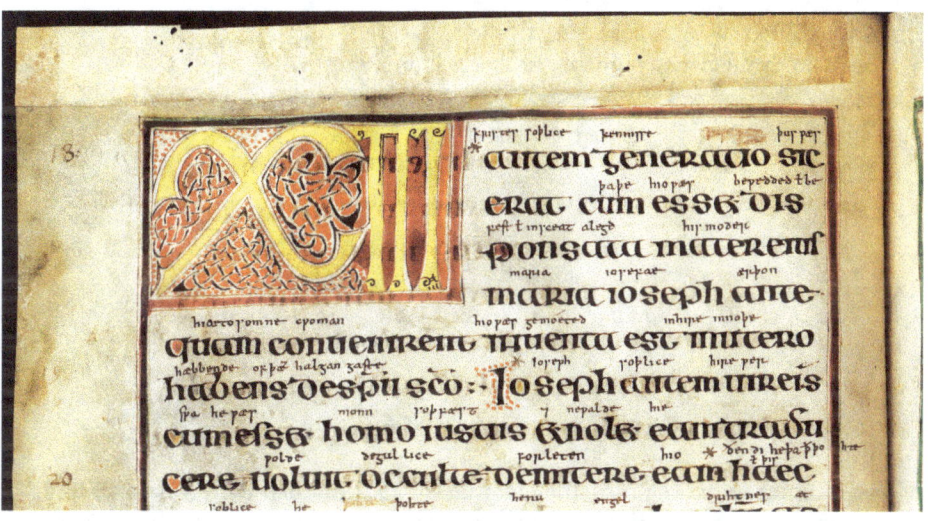

Figure 6. Oxford, Bodleian Library, MS Auct. D. 2. 19, fol. 2ᵛ, 'Farman's gloss on Rushworth Gospels: Mt. 1.18–19'.

---

[28] On monastic reading in this period, see Malcolm Parkes, 'Rædan, areccan, smeagan: How the Anglo-Saxons read', *ASE* 26 (1997), 1–22.

[29] On *lectio divina*, see Jean Leclerq, *The Love of Learning and the Desire for God*, trans. Catherine Misrahi (New York: Fordham University Press, 1961).

[30] Text cited from Kotake, ed., *Rushworth One*, p. 90. The Latin text of the Rushworth Gospels is broadly similar to the Vulgate but contains some readings which are closer to Old Latin, and has therefore been classed as belonging to an 'Insular Vulgate' group: see Tamoto, *The MacRegol Gospels or The Rushworth Gospels*, pp. xlii–xlvii.

kristes	soþlice	kennisse	þus wæs	
¹⁸CR(IST)I	autem	generatio	sic	

	þa þe	hio wæs	bewedded ł be-	
erat	cum	esset	dis-	

-fæst ł in sceat alegd	his moder
-ponsata	mater eius

maria	iosefae	ærþon
maria	ioseph	ante-

hiae tosomne cwoman	hio wæs gemoeted	in hire innoþe
-quam conuenirent	inuenta est	in utero

hæb- bende	of þæ(m)	halgan	gaste	ioseph	soþlice	hire wer
habens	de	sp(irit)u	s(an)c(t)o	¹⁹Ioseph	autem	uir ei(u)s

swa	he wæs	monn	soþfæst	7	ne walde hie	
cum	esset	homo	iustus	et	nolet eam	tradu-

	wolde	degullice	forletten	hio
-cere	uoluit	occulte	demittere	eam

As Kenichi Kotake notes, the fact that the Old English words *þus wæs* have been erased above the last part of *generatio* at the end of the first line of folio 2ᵛ yet placed correctly above the following word *sic* suggests that Farman was copying from an existing gloss rather than translating word by word.[31] While the scribe responsible for the Latin text has indicated the beginning of each biblical verse by encircling the initial letter with a series of red dots, Farman inserts an asterisk (*) before each verse in his gloss to help readers match the Old English text to the Latin.

However, where Farman differs from Aldred is in his provision of far fewer alternative translations, with the result that his gloss comprises a steady flow of vernacular phrases which at times begins to approach the rhythm of Old English prose. Hence, for example, where Aldred

[31] Kotake, ed., *Rushworth One*, p. 199.

provides two translations of *generatio* (*cynnreccenisse ł cneuresuu*), Farman offers only a single Old English term (*kennisse*).³² Moreover, while Aldred follows the syntax of Latin genitive phrases *mater eius* (> *moder his*) and *uir eius* (> *uer hire*), Farman opts for more idiomatic English word order (*his moder*; *hire wer*).³³ Farman's concerted efforts to produce a gloss that is readable on its own can also be seen in his decision to translate even those personal names which Aldred omits (verse 18: *maria, iosefae*). This move towards a more natural prose style is also evident in Farman's expansion of the Latin verb *conuenirent* (translated by Aldred as *hia gegeadradon ł gecuomun*, 'they gathered *or* came') to the phrase *hiae tosomne cwoman* ('they came together'); the insertion of the adverb *tosomne* helps clarify the two senses implied by Aldred's gloss into a single, fluent clause. Similarly, where Aldred follows the Latin closely in translating *in utero* as *in hrif* ('in womb') and *esset* as simply *wæss*, Farman inserts personal pronouns to aid his readers: *in hire innoþe* ('in her womb'), *he wæs* ('he was'). Farman also adds the dative pronoun *þæ(m)* in rendering the Latin *de*, to further clarify the grammar. Indeed, only one Latin word, the infinitive verb *traducere* ('to expose'), is not glossed by Farman. Kotake suggests that Farman may have skipped this word because he took the personal pronoun *hie*, which appears as part of the phrase written above the preceding words, *nolem eam* (> *ne walde hie*), as the accusative object of *ne walde* ('and he did not desire her').³⁴ Overall, Farman supplies supplement glosses more frequently than his predecessor Aldred had done, expanding on the source text whenever it was deemed necessary for the sake of clarity.

Printed in isolation from the Latin source text, Farman's gloss certainly appears a step closer to the smooth, idiomatic vernacular prose style of the *Wessex Gospels* discussed below:

> ¹⁸ kristes soþlice kennisse þus wæs þa þe hio wæs bewedded (oððe befæst oððe in sceat alegd) his moder Maria Iosefae ær þon hiae tosomne cwoman hio wæs gemoeted in hire innoþe hæbbende of þæ(m) halgan gaste.
>
> ¹⁹ Ioseph soþlice hire wer swa he wæs monn soþfæst and ne walde hie […] wolde degullice forletten hio.

Indeed, Farman might have repurposed an earlier, free-standing translation of the Gospels, adapting it into his gloss.³⁵ Alternatively, he may

---

³² *DOE* s.v. *cennes* (1. birth […], 2. childbirth') records 10 occurrences, mostly in prose.
³³ On the relative independence of Farman's syntax compared to other interlinear glosses of the period, see Kotake, ed. *Rushworth One*, pp. 69–75.
³⁴ Kotake, ed., *Rushworth One*, p. 200.
³⁵ Kotake suggests that Farman's exemplar 'could have contained a freer transla-

have intentionally crafted these more idiomatic translations, anticipating that his readers – perhaps still developing their Latin proficiency – would benefit from glosses that aligned more closely with their native language than the Latin source. Farman's gloss thus transforms the Rushworth Gospels into a bilingual gospel book, which like the Paris Psalter could be read either in Latin or English.[36]

The Lindisfarne and Rushworth (MacRegol) glosses provide a window onto the painstaking and intensive study of the Gospels undertaken by tenth-century English monks. In Steiner's terminology, Aldred and Farman (and his co-glossator Owun) affirmed the value of the Gospels themselves by making the initial decision to translate them from Latin into English.[37] As we have observed, in both cases, the priority of understanding the Latin source outweighed concerns about preserving the integrity of the magnificent codices that contained the Vulgate text. In the case of the Lindisfarne Gospels in particular, practical considerations may have also been a factor in the production of the gloss, notably Aldred's desire to establish himself in the monastic community at Chester-le-Street. The addition of these glosses might even be said to enhance the pages of these Latin gospel books with words from the by-now prestigious written Old English of the Kingdom of England. Once the decision had been made to provide an interlinear translation to these Latin gospel books, the glossators 'plundered' each individual lexical item of the Vulgate text, reflecting on various possible meanings before supplying readers with either single or multiple equivalents in the target language. With a few small exceptions, such as personal names where the meaning is obvious in the Latin, the entire text of the Gospels was incorporated into the target language, allowing monastic readers to match up the Latin words with their vernacular equivalents when studying the scriptural text. Finally, while Aldred made little effort to provide compensatory measures, cleaving closely to the word order of the Latin source and supplying mostly substitution glosses, Farman often provided supplement glosses which when read together begin to approximate Old English prose. Both these splendid Latin gospel books were furnished with Old English glosses for the same principal purpose: to facilitate the constant meditation on the words of Scripture (*lectio divina*) that lay at the heart of monastic life. Although it seems highly unlikely that such prestigious manuscripts were ever used in the classroom, these glosses would nev-

---

tion than a word-for-word interlinear version and accordingly that his faithful copying from such an exemplar made his gloss more idiomatic than one would expect to find in an interlinear gloss text' (*Rushworth One*, p. 70).

[36] For Toswell's argument that some of the glossed psalters are similarly bilingual, see above, pp. 35–6.

[37] On Steiner's translation theory, see above, p. xiii.

ertheless provide any monk or nun looking at these beautiful codices with the opportunity to gain a deeper understanding of the Latin gospel text's literal and spiritual meaning. The Old English gospel glosses were thus produced within an enclosed space for highly specialised use by members of monastic communities. For a tenth-century translation of the Gospels into Old English prose intended for readers outside the cloister, we must turn now to the *Wessex Gospels*.

The Wessex Gospels

The earliest extant continuous prose rendering of all four gospels into any medieval European vernacular, the *Wessex Gospels* are attested in six complete manuscripts, four of which date from the eleventh century (MSS A, B, C and Cp) and two from the twelfth (MSS H and R), with several further fragments surviving from the tenth to the twelfth centuries.[38] Like

---

[38] The manuscripts are described in full by Roy M. Liuzza, ed., *The Old English Version of the Gospels*, 2 vols, EETS o.s. 304, 314 (Oxford: Oxford University Press, 1994, 2000), I, pp. xvi–xliii, and the description below is based on his account with Ker numbers supplied; dates are those provided by Ker. The complete text of all four gospels is preserved in the following manuscripts: MS A, Cambridge University Library Ii.2.11 (Ker §20), possibly identical with the volume referred to as *þeos Englisc Cristes bec* in Leofric's donation list to Exeter Cathedral library and also containing the Old English prose translation of the Gospel of Nicodemus and the Avenging of the Saviour (on these texts, see below, pp. 110–15), all copied by the same hand and dated to the second half of the eleventh century with some Latin and Old English headings added (the latter in the same hand as the main text); MS B, Oxford, Bodleian Library, MS Bodley 441 (Ker §312), closely related to MS C, written in a single hand dated to the first half of the eleventh century, with various sixteenth-century additions and emendations including Old English rubrics copied from MS Cp; MS C, London, British Library, Cotton MS Otho C. I, vol. I (Ker §181), copied by a single hand dated to the first half of the eleventh century, whose text of Matthew was lost in the 1731 Cottonian fire (part of Matthew was already missing by then) and Mark badly damaged; MS Cp, Cambridge Corpus Christi College MS 140 (Ker §35), copied by four hands all dating from the first half of the eleventh century, also containing two lists of manumissions and an Old English homily based on the Latin 'Sunday Letter', all written in the second half of the eleventh century, as well as a Latin list of popes, archbishops and bishops and various Latin documents relating to Bath in later hands; MS H, Oxford, Bodleian Library, MS Hatton 38 (Ker §325), twelfth- or thirteenth-century, probably copied from MS R, itself derived from MS B; MS R, London, British Library, MS Royal I.A XIV (Ker §425), second half of the twelfth century, based on MS B. A fragment of the Gospel of John is preserved in the eleventh-century MS L, Oxford, Bodleian Library, MS Eng. Bib. C.2 (Ker §322); two tenth- or eleventh-century fragments of Mark and Matthew are found in MS Y, New

the translation of the Heptateuch discussed in the next chapter, this ambitious project was undertaken by a team of translators working in the south of England at some point in the tenth century. Linguistic and stylistic evidence indicates that the gospels of Mark and Luke were translated by one individual, while one or more others worked on Matthew and John.[39] Although scholars have often assigned a date of composition towards the end of the tenth century, the recent discovery of two fragmentary witnesses in a hand which closely resembles that of the Exeter Book might push the project back to as early as the 960s or 970s.[40] This period saw the expulsion of secular clerks from religious houses in the south and west of England and their replacement by Benedictine monks. The chief instigators of the Benedictine Reform, King Edgar (r. 959–975), Æthelwold Bishop of Winchester (d. 984), Dunstan Archbishop of Canterbury (d. 988) and Oswald Archbishop of York (d. 992), realised the potential of vernacular prose as a medium for disseminating orthodox Christian teaching not only to literate churchmen but also to the laity, among whom literacy had continued to grow since the time of Alfred.[41] The spread of vernacular literacy among both the clergy and laity was facilitated by the development of a standard written form of English in the mid-tenth century by Bishop Æthelwold of Winchester, now known as late West Saxon.[42] Æthelwold also translated the Benedictine Rule into Old English, ensuring that monks and nuns had access to the key text of the reform in

---

Haven, Beinecke Library Beinecke 578 (Ker §1). On the recent discovery of another eleventh-century fragment, see Winfried Rudolf, 'A Fragment of the Old English Version of the Gospel of Mark in the Folger Shakespeare Library, Washington, DC', *The Library* 7 (2017), 405–17. Liuzza's edition, which is cited here, is based on MS Cp, with corrections from B and C. Liuzza's edition is semi-diplomatic, following manuscript punctuation; I have therefore emended some elements of punctuation and spelling.

[39] A change in translation style at Matthew ch. 21 may indicate the work of another contributor; see Liuzza, ed., *Gospels*, II, pp. 102–19.

[40] The two fragments were sold at auction at Sotheby's in London in 2014 to a private collector; see Roy M. Liuzza, 'Reconstructing a Lost Manuscript of the Old English Gospels', in *Medieval English and Dutch Literatures: The European Context: Essays in Honour of David F. Johnson*, ed. Larissa Tracy and Geert H. M. Claassens (Cambridge: D. S. Brewer, 2022), pp. 15–28.

[41] See Rebecca Stephenson, *The Politics of Language: Byrhtferth, Ælfric, and the Multilingual Identity of the Benedictine Reform* (Toronto: University of Toronto Press, 2015).

[42] See Helmut Gneuss, 'The Origin of Standard Old English and Æthelwold's School at Winchester', *ASE* 1 (1972), 63–83; Walter Hofstetter, 'Winchester and the Standardization of Old English Vocabulary', *ASE* 17 (1988), 139–68; and Mechthild Gretsch, 'Winchester Vocabulary and Standard Old English: The Vernacular in Late Anglo-Saxon England', *Bulletin of the John Rylands Library* 83 (2001), 41–87.

their own language.⁴³ However, monastic readers were not the only ones who stood to benefit from this translation: in another Old English work of this period, known as *King Edgar's Establishment of Monasteries*, Æthelwold explains that the king instructed him to translate the Rule for *ungelæredum woroldmonnum* ('unlearned laypeople').⁴⁴ This climate of monastic reform, vernacular book production and increasing lay literacy presents a plausible context for the composition of the *Wessex Gospels*.

Translation Style

Unlike the free and at times even creative approach to the Bible taken by the Alfredian translators, and in marked contrast to the subsequent rendering of the Heptateuch, the team responsible for the *Wessex Gospels* stuck very closely to the wording of the source text, aiming for what Liuzza calls 'literal fidelity'.⁴⁵ However, this reverential approach to the Latin source does not result in a formal-equivalence translation in the manner of the gospel glosses discussed above. On the contrary, these translators worked hard to ensure that the meaning of the gospel story was brought across to the reader as clearly as possible by routinely departing from the syntax and phrasing of the Latin, thereby producing a functional equivalence translation of the Gospels in smoothly idiomatic English prose. Comparison of the treatment of the Golden Rule in the *Wessex Gospels* with that in the Second Prologue to the *Domboc* will serve to illustrate this point. While the Alfredian author creatively reinterpreted the wording of the Gospels, asserting that Christ *ne gedemde þe hine to deaðe sealde, and bebead þone hlaford lufian swa hine* ('did not grant any [mercy] to those who gave him to death, and he laid down [that one should] love one's lord just as oneself'), the translators of the *Wessex Gospels* render the corresponding biblical passages with lexical fidelity to the Vulgate.⁴⁶ In

---

⁴³ For the Old English text of the Benedictine Rule, see Arnold Schröer, ed., *Die angelsächsischen Prosabearbeitungen der Benediktinerregel*, Bibliothek der angelsächsischen Prosa 2 (Kassel: G. H. Wigand, 1885–88); for a translation with introduction, see Jacob Riyeff, trans., *The Old English Rule of Saint Benedict with Related Old English Texts* (Collegeville, MN: Cistercian Publications, 2017). Rohini Jayatilaka argues that the Rule was first translated for monks but subsequently adapted for use by nuns: 'The Old English Benedictine Rule: Writing for Women and Men', *ASE* 32 (2007), 147–87, at 184–5.

⁴⁴ *Councils & Synods with other Documents relating to the English Church, I: A.D. 871–1204*, ed. Dorothy Whitelock, Martin Brett and Christopher N. L. Brooke (Oxford: Clarendon Press, 1981), pp. 150–1. See David Pratt, 'The Voice of the King in "King Edgar's Establishment of Monasteries"', *ASE* 41 (2012), 145–204.

⁴⁵ Liuzza, ed., *Gospels*, II, p. 1.

⁴⁶ See above, pp. 72–4.

terms of vocabulary, the *Wessex Gospels* are therefore more closely aligned with the interlinear glossing tradition exemplified by the Lindisfarne and Rushworth glosses (Table 1).

Nevertheless, in a departure from the glossing style, a number of small syntactical alterations, such as the reversal of genitive constructions (e.g. *Deum tuum* > *þinne god*; *anima tua* > *þinre heortan*; *mente tua* > *þinum mode*), and grammatical modifications (e.g. present tense: *pendet* > present tense + participle: *byþ gefylled*), accommodate the scriptural source into idiomatic English prose. Similarly, the regular translation of the personal name *Iesus* with the epithet *se hælend* ('the Saviour') – common in Old English – makes the Gospel's central doctrinal message abundantly clear to the reader.[47] Lexical changes, notably the omission of the personal pronoun *illi* ('to them') (Mt. 22.37) and the compression of the phrase *universa lex* [...] *et prophetae* to *eall seo æ* (Mt. 22.40), contribute to the overall streamlining of the gospel narrative. We will see similar translation techniques taken to much greater lengths – with far more significant implications for sense – in the subsequent translation of the Heptateuch. This conservative but communicative approach to biblical translation characterises the *Wessex Gospels* as a whole. Indeed, the most striking difference between the *Wessex Gospels* and the other major biblical translations discussed in this book is the translators' consistently faithful approach to the scriptural source.

Those small expansions that do occur in the *Wessex Gospels* are invariably provided to clarify sense. Hence, for example, in translating Matthew 27.46, the Old English expands the Vulgate's adjectival phrase *hoc est* to *þæt is on englisc*:

> et circa horam nonam, clamavit Iesus voce magna, dicens: 'Heli, Heli, lema sabacthani?' *Hoc est*, Deus meus, Deus meus, ut quid dereliquisti me?'

> [And about the ninth hour, Jesus cried with a loud voice, saying: 'Eli, Eli, lamma sabacthani?' *That is*, 'My God, My God, why have you forsaken me?']

---

[47] The use of the term *hælend* for *Iesus* is an etymological translation of the Hebrew *Yəhôšua'*, as Ælfric states in his homily for the Annunciation of St Mary, *His nama wæs 'Hiesus', þæt is "hælend", forðan ðe he gehælð ealle ða þe on hine rihtlice gelyfað* ('His name was *Jesus*, that is "saviour", because he saves all those who rightly believe in him') (*CH* II.13, pp. 238–9), while in his homily on Mid-Lent Sunday, he explains, *Iesus is ebreisc nama, þæt is on leden Saluator, and on englisc Hælend, forðan ðe he gehælð his folc fram heora synnum* ('*Jesus* is a Hebrew name, that is *Salvator* in Latin, that is *Hælend* in English, because he heals his people from their sins') (*CH* II.12, p. 122); cf. the Old Saxon cognate in the poem *Heliand*.

Table 1. Comparison of Luke 23.34–40 in Vulgate, *Wessex Gospels*, Lindisfarne and Rushworth glosses.

Vulgate	Wessex Gospels	Lindisfarne Gloss	Rushworth Gloss
Lk 23.34: Iesus autem dicebat: 'Pater, dimitte illis non enim sciunt quid faciunt.'	Ða cwæð se Hælend: 'Fæder, forgyf him forþam hig nyton hwæt hig doð.'	se hælend ða gecuoeðað fader forgef him ne forðm wuton huæd hia doas	ðe hælend ða cwæð fæder forgef him ne forðon wutun þæt hwæt hie doað
[And Jesus said: 'Father, forgive them, for they know not what they do.']	[Then the Saviour said: 'Father, forgive them for they know not what they do.']	[The Saviour then said: 'Father, forgive them because they know not what they do.']	[The Saviour then said: 'Father, forgive them because they know not what they do.']
Mt. 22.37: Ait illi Iesus diliges: 'Dominum Deum tuum ex toto corde tuo et in tota anima tua et in tota mente tua.'	Ða cwæð se Hælend: 'Lufa drihten þinne God on ealre þinre heortan and on ealre þinre sawle and on eallum þinum mode.'	cuæð him ðe hælend lufa drihten god ðinne of alle hearte ðine 7 of alle sauele ðine 7 in alle ðoht ðine	7 cwæþ him to se hælend lufa dryhten god þinne of alre heortan þines 7 of alre saule þinre 7 of alra mode ðinum
[Jesus said to him: 'You shall love the Lord your God with your whole heart and with your whole soul and with your whole mind.']	[Then the Saviour said: 'Love the Lord your God in all your heart and in all your soul and all your mind.']	[Said to them the Saviour: 'Love (the) Lord your God with all your heart and with all your soul and in all your thought.']	[Said to them the Saviour: 'Love (the) Lord your God with all your heart and with all your soul and in all your thought.']
Mt. 22.38: Hoc est maximum et primum mandatum.	þæt ys þæt maeste and þæt fyrmeste bebod.	þis is forðon maast ł heest 7 ðe forma bod	forþon þe þis bebod þæt maeste 7 þæt aereste
[This is the greatest and the first commandment.]	[This is the greatest and the first commandment.]	[This is therefore the greatest or highest and the first commandment.]	[Therefore is this commandment the greatest and the first.]

Mt. 22.39: Secundum autem simile est: huic diliges proximum tuum sicut te ipsum. [And the second is like to this: You shall love your neighbour as yourself.]	Opyr ys þysum gelic: 'Lufa þinne nehstan swa swa þe sylfne.' [The second is like this: 'Love your neighbour as yourself'.]	ðe æfterra uutedlice gelic is ðisum lufa ðone ðe neesta ðin suæ ðeh seolfne [The second is truly like this: 'Love your neighbour as yourself.]	þæt æftere þonne is gelic þæm lufa þone næhstu þinne swa þec seolfne [The second then is like that: 'Love your neighbour as yourself.]
Mt. 22.40: In his duobus mandatis universa lex pendet et prophetae [...]. [On these two commandments depends the whole law and the prophets.]	On þysum twam bebodum byþ gefylled eall seo æ [...]. [In these two commandments is fulfilled the whole law.]	in ðisum tuæm bodum all æ stondes 1 honges 7 witgo [In these two commandments all (the) law stands *or* depends and (the) prophets.]	in þissum twæm bebodum ealle æ hongað 7 witga [In these two commandments all (the) law depends and (the) prophets.]

And ymbe þa nygoðan tid clypode se Hælend mycelre stefne and þuss cwæð: 'Heli Heli lema zabandi. *Þæt ys on englisc*, 'Min god, min god, to hwi forlete þu me?'[48]

[And about the ninth hour the Saviour cried with a loud voice and said thus: 'Heli Heli lema zabandi.' *That is in English*, 'My God, my God, why have you abandoned me?']
(Emphases added)

A similarly exegetical style, in which clarity of meaning and avoidance of ambiguity are paramount, is adopted in the translation of Matthew 27.33, *et venerunt in locum qui dicitur Golgotha, quod est Calvariae locus* ('And they came to the place that is called Golgotha, which is the place of Calvary'), as *Ða comon hig on þa stowe þe is genemned Golgotha, þæt is heafodpannan stowe* ('Then they came to that place that is called Golgotha, which is the place of the skull').[49] In all these grammatical, syntactical and lexical choices, the translators of the *Wessex Gospels* endeavour to bring the full meaning of the source to the reader in English instead of presenting them with a guide to the wording of the Vulgate Latin.

In Steiner's terminology, this fidelity to the source 'affirms' the pre-eminence of the Gospels among all the books of the Bible.[50] Hence, the rendering of the opening of the Gospel of Matthew retains the fourteen-generation genealogy of Christ (Mt. 1–17) in its entirety – as we shall see, the translators of the Heptateuch would take a much more selective approach to their Old Testament sources, typically omitting long genealogies and lists of names and places deemed irrelevant to the audience.[51] This same close adherence to the content of the source-text is maintained in the opening section of the gospel narrative proper that follows, in which as many elements of the source text as possible are 'plundered' and subsequently 'incorporated' into English. The Latin text from the Vulgate reads:

> Mt. 1.18 Christi autem generatio sic erat. Cum esset desponsata mater eius Maria Ioseph, antequam convenirent inventa est in utero habens de Spiritu Sancto. ¹⁹ Ioseph autem vir eius cum esset iustus et nollet eam traducere voluit occulte dimittere eam. ²⁰ Haec autem eo cogitante, ecce angelus Domini in somnis apparuit ei dicens: 'Ioseph fili David noli timere accipere Mariam coniugem tuam quod enim in ea natum est de

---

[48] Liuzza, ed., *Gospels*, I, p. 60.
[49] The Lindisfarne gloss on Matthew 22.33 has *heafudponnes styd ɫ stowa*; Rushworth has *heafodpanne stouwstede*. The accounts of the crucifixion in Mark 15.22, Luke 23.33 and John 19.17 also have *heafodpannena stow*, as do the glosses, while a Palm Sunday homily in MS Bodley 340 has *heafodbollan stow*.
[50] For Steiner's theory of translation, see above, p. xiii.
[51] See Chapter Four, pp. 164–5.

Spiritu Sancto est. ²¹ Pariet autem filium et vocabis nomen eius Iesum ipse enim salvum faciet populum suum a peccatis eorum.' ²² Hoc autem totum factum est ut adimpleretur id quod dictum est a Domino per prophetam dicentem: ²³ 'Ecce virgo in utero habebit et pariet filium et vocabunt nomen eius Emmanuhel quod est interpretatum: Nobiscum Deus.' ²⁴ Exsurgens autem Ioseph a somno, fecit sicut praecepit ei angelus Domini, et accepit coniugem suam. ²⁵ Et non cognoscebat eam donec peperit filium suum primogenitum: et vocavit nomen eius Iesum.

[¹·¹⁸ Now the generation of Christ was in this manner. When as his mother Mary was espoused to Joseph, before they came together, she was found with child, of the Holy Ghost. ¹⁹ Whereupon Joseph her husband, being a just man, and not willing publicly to expose her, was minded to put her away privately. ²⁰ But while he thought on these things, behold the Angel of the Lord appeared to him in his sleep, saying: 'Joseph, son of David, fear not to take unto you Mary your wife, for that which is conceived in her, is of the Holy Ghost. ²¹ And she shall bring forth a son: and you shall call his name Jesus. For he shall save his people from their sins.' ²² Now all this was done that it might be fulfilled which the Lord spoke by the prophet, saying: ²³ 'Behold a virgin shall be with child, and bring forth a son, and they shall call his name Emmanuel, which being interpreted is, God with us.' ²⁴ And Joseph rising up from sleep, did as the angel of the Lord had commanded him, and took unto him his wife. ²⁵ And he knew her not till she brought forth her first-born son: and he called his name Jesus.]

As is the case throughout the *Wessex Gospels*, each individual biblical verse is carefully rendered into English in full, as the translator sticks very closely to the wording of the Latin source while freely altering the syntax and grammar to produce fluent Old English prose:⁵²

¹·¹⁸ *Soðlice* þus wæs **C**ristes **c**neores: Ða *þæs* **H**ælendes **mo**dor Maria wæs Iosepe beweddod, ær hi tosomne becomun, heo wæs gemet on innoðe hæbbende of þam Halegan Gaste. ¹⁹ *Soðlice* Iosep hyre **w**er, ða he wæs rih**tw**is and nolde hi gewidmærsian, he **w**olde hi dihlice forlætan. ²⁰ Him þa *soðlice* ðas þing *ðencendum* Drihtnes engel on swefnum ætywde, and him to cwæð: 'Iosep, Dauides sunu, nelle þu ondrædan **M**arian þine ge**m**æccean to onfonne; þæt on hire acenned ys, hyt ys of þam Halgan Gaste. ²¹ *Witodlice* heo cenð sunu, and þu **n**emst hys **n**aman **H**ælend; he *soðlice* hys folc **h**al gedeð fram hyra synnum.' ²² *Soþlice* eal þys wæs geworden þæt gefylled wære þæt fram Drihtne gecweden wæs þurh þone **w**itegan. ²³ *Soðlice* seo fæmne hæfð on innoðe, and heo cenð sunu, and hi **n**emnað his **n**aman Emanuhel, þæt ys gereht <u>on ure geþeode</u>:

---

⁵² Alliteration is marked in bold, alterations of the Latin source are in italics, expansions in the Old English underlined.

'God mid us.' ²⁴ Ða aras Iosep of swefene, and **d**yde swa **D**rihtnes engel him bebead, and he onfeng his gemæccean; ²⁵ and he ne grette hi. Heo cende hyre frumcennedan sunu, and **n**emde hys **n**aman *Hælend*.

[¹·¹⁸ *Truly* Christ's generation was in this manner. When as *the Saviour's* mother Mary was wedded to Joseph, before they came together, she became pregnant of the Holy Ghost. ¹⁹ *Truly* Joseph her man, being that he was righteous and did not wish to expose her, he wished to put her away privately. ²⁰ While he *truly* was thinking on these things the Angel of the Lord appeared to him in sleep, and said to him: 'Joseph, David's son, fear not to take unto you Mary your wife; for that which is conceived in her, it is of the Holy Ghost. ²¹ *Certainly* she shall bring forth a son, and you shall call his name *Saviour*; he *truly* shall save his people from their sins.' ²² *Truly* all this was done that it might be fulfilled which was said by the Lord through the prophet. ²³ *Truly* the virgin has become pregnant, and she shall bring forth a son, and they shall call his name Emmanuel, that is interpreted <u>in our language</u>: 'God with us.' ²⁴ Then Joseph arose from sleep, and did just as the Lord's angel commanded him, and he took his wife; ²⁵ and he knew her not. She brought forth her first-born son, and he called his name *Saviour*.]

Minor alterations of wording, such as the omission of the verb of speech, *dicentem*, at the end of verse 22, are driven by the translator's desire to convey the sense of the source as clearly as possible in the target language. However, the omission of the conjunction *donec* ('till') in verse 25 may be, as Liuzza suggests, 'a doctrinally-motivated omission',⁵³ intended to downplay any potentially confusing or controversial elements of the Virgin Birth for readers who might struggle to grasp its full spiritual meaning. As noted above, the translator consistently uses the epithet *Hælend* ('Saviour') to refer to Christ in place of the Latin personal pronoun *eius* (verse 18) and the personal name *Iesum* (verses 21 and 25).⁵⁴ A rare addition to the Latin source appears in verse 23, where the phrase *quod est interpretatum* ('which being interpreted is') is expanded to *þæt ys gereht on ure geþeode* ('that is interpreted in our language'), emphasising the work's own status as a translation; by comparison, the Lindisfarne and Rushworth glosses have simply *ðæt is getræht* and *þæt is gereht* respectively.

Despite the translator's primary concern with conveying the meaning of the source as accurately as possible, their sense of literary style is also on display in this passage. For example, alliteration is used sparingly but effectively to create memorable word pairings (*Crist/acenned*; *modor/Maria*; *forð/faran*; *nemnede/naman*). More striking is the consistent front-placement of the adverb *soðlice* ('truly') at the beginning of many biblical verses to

---

⁵³ Liuzza, ed. *Gospels*, II, p. 61.
⁵⁴ See above, p. 94.

render a variety of Latin terms, most commonly the conjunction *autem* ('but, now, then') in verses 18, 19, 20, 22 and once for the interjection *ecce* ('behold') in verse 23, a term glossed in both Lindisfarne and Rushworth as *he(o)nu*. On one occasion, in verse 21, the translator varies this practice by rendering *autem* as *witodlice* ('certainly, indeed'), before reintroducing *soðlice* for *enim* ('for') in the second cola of the same verse; here the translation is closest to the Lindisfarne gloss which renders *autem* in this verse first as *witodlice* and then as *soðlice*.

This combination of precise, conservative translation and a modest sense of literary style is evident throughout the *Wessex Gospels*. The rendering of Matthew's account of Christ's Passion, the climactic moment in biblical and Christian history, provides a good illustration of this careful but confident approach to scriptural translation. The Vulgate version of Matthew 27.35–54 reads:

> [35] Postquam autem crucifixerunt eum, diviserunt vestimenta eius, sortem mittentes: ut impleretur quod dictum est per prophetam dicentem: 'Diviserunt sibi uestimenta mea, et super uestem meam miserunt sortem.' [36] Et sedentes servabant eum. [37] Et inposuerunt super caput eius causam ipsius scriptam: 'Hic est Iesus rex Iudaeorum.' [38] Tunc crucifixi sunt cum eo duo latrones: unus a dextris, et unus a sinistris. [39] Praetereuntes autem blasphemabant eum moventes capita sua, [40] et dicentes: 'Vah! qui destruis templum Dei, et in triduo illud reaedificas: salva temet ipsum: si Filius Dei es, descende de cruce.' [41] Similiter et principes sacerdotum inludentes cum scribis et senioribus dicebant: [42] 'Alios salvos fecit, se ipsum non potest salvum facere: si rex Israhel est, descendat nunc de cruce, et credemus ei. [43] Confidit in Deo; liberet nunc, si vult, dixit enim quia: "Filius Dei sum".' [44] Id ipsum autem et latrones, qui crucifixi erant cum eo, inproperabant ei. [45] A sexta autem hora tenebrae factae sunt super universam terram usque ad horam nonam. [46] Et circa horam nonam clamavit Iesus voce magna, dicens: 'Heli, Heli, lemma sabacthani?' hoc est: 'Deus meus, Deus meus, ut quid dereliquisti me?' [47] Quidam autem illic stantes, et audientes, dicebant: 'Eliam vocat iste.' [48] Et continuo currens unus ex eis, acceptam spongiam implevit aceto, et inposuit harundini, et dabat ei bibere. [49] Ceteri vero dicebant: 'Sine, videamus an veniat Elias liberans eum.' [50] Iesus autem iterum clamans voce magna, emisit spiritum. [51] Et ecce velum templi scissum est in duas partes a summo usque deorsum: et terra mota est, et petrae scissae sunt, [52] et monumenta aperta sunt: et multa corpora sanctorum, qui dormierant, surrexerunt. [53] Et exeuntes de monumentis post resurrectionem eius, venerunt in sanctam civitatem, et apparuerunt multis. [54] Centurio autem, et qui cum eo erant, custodientes Iesum, viso terraemotu, et his quae fiebant, timuerunt valde, dicentes: 'Vere Dei Filius erat iste.'

[³⁵ And after they had crucified him, they divided his garments, casting lots; that it might be fulfilled which was spoken by the prophet, saying: 'They divided my garments among them; and upon my vesture they cast lots.' ³⁶ And they sat and watched him. ³⁷ And they put over his head his cause written: 'This is Jesus the King of the Jews.' ³⁸ Then were crucified with him two thieves: one on the right hand, and one on the left. ³⁹ And they that passed by, blasphemed him, wagging their heads, ⁴⁰ And saying: 'Look! You who destroyed the temple of God, and in three days rebuilt it: save your own self: if you are the Son of God, come down from the cross.' ⁴¹ In like manner also the chief priests, with the scribes and ancients, mocking, said: ⁴² 'He saved others; himself he cannot save. If he is the king of Israel, let him now come down from the cross, and we will believe him. ⁴³ He trusted in God; let him now deliver him if he will have him; for he said: "I am the Son of God."'⁴⁴ And the selfsame thing the thieves also, that were crucified with him, reproached him. ⁴⁵ Now from the sixth hour there was darkness over the whole earth, until the ninth hour. ⁴⁶ And about the ninth hour Jesus cried with a loud voice, saying: 'Eli, Eli, lamma sabacthani?'; that is, 'My God, my God, why have you forsaken me?' ⁴⁷ And some that stood there and heard, said: 'This man calls Elias.' ⁴⁸ And immediately one of them running took a sponge, and filled it with vinegar; and put it on a reed, and gave him to drink. ⁴⁹ And the others said: 'Let be, let us see whether Elias will come to deliver him.' ⁵⁰ And Jesus again crying with a loud voice, yielded up the ghost. ⁵¹ And behold the veil of the temple was rent in two from the top even to the bottom, and the earth quaked, and the rocks were rent. ⁵² And the graves were opened: and many bodies of the saints that had slept arose, ⁵³ and coming out of the tombs after his resurrection, came into the holy city, and appeared to many. ⁵⁴ Now the centurion and they that were with him watching Jesus, having seen the earthquake, and the things that were done, were sore afraid, saying: 'Indeed, this was the Son of God.']

In keeping with the reverential approach to the source text that characterises the *Wessex Gospels*, the translator sticks very closely to the wording of the Vulgate in this passage, save for the consistent use of *hælynd* for *Iesus* and the reference to the *englisc* language noted above; further alterations are highlighted in italics and expansions are underlined:

³⁵ Soþlice æfter þam þe hig hyne *on rode ahengon* hig todældon hys reaf: and wurpon hlot þærofer þæt wære gefylled þæt ðe gecweden wæs þurh ðone witegan and þus cwæð: 'Hig todældon heom mine reaf, and ofer mine reaf hig wurpon hlot.' ³⁶ And hig beheoldon hyne sittende, ³⁷ and hig asetton ofer hys heafod hys gylt þuss awritene: 'Ðis ys se Hælynd Iudea Cyning.' ³⁸ Ða wæron ahangen mid him twegen sceaþan an on þa swiðran healfe and oðer on þa wynstran. ³⁹ Witodlice þa wegferendan hyne bysmeredon and cwehton heora heafod ⁴⁰ and

cwædon: 'Wa þæt ðes towyrpð godes templ, and on þrim dagum hyt eft getimbrað. Gehæl <u>nu</u> þe sylfne. Gyf þe sy Godes Sunu, ga nyþer of þære rode.' ⁴¹ Eac sacerda ealdras hyne bysmerdon mid þam bocerum and mid þam ealdrum and cwædun: ⁴² 'Oþere he gehælde and hyne sylfne gehælan ne mæg. Gyf he Israhela Cyning sy, ga nu nyþer of þære rode and we gelyfað hym. ⁴³ He gelyfð on God. Alyse he hyne nu gyf he wylle. <u>Witodlice</u> he sæde, "Godes Sunu ic eom."' ⁴⁴ Gelice þa sceaðan þe mid him ahangene wæron, hyne hyspdun. ⁴⁵ Witodlice fram þære sixtan tide wæron gewurden þystru ofer ealle eorðan oþ þa nigoþan tide. ⁴⁶ And ymbe þa nygoðan tid clypode *se Hælend* mycelre stefne and þuss cwæð: 'Heli Heli, lema zabandi.' Þæt is <u>on Englisc,</u> 'Min God, min God to hwi forlete þu me.' ⁴⁷ *Soþlice* sume þa ðe þær stodon and þis gehyrdon cwædon: 'Nu he clypað Heliam.' ⁴⁸ Ða hrædlice *arn* an heora and genam ane spongean and fylde hig mid ecede and asette an hreod þæron and sealde hym drincan. ⁴⁹ Witodlice þa oðre cwædon: 'Læt utun geseon hwæþer Helias cume <u>and wylle</u> hyne alysan.' ⁵⁰ Þa clypode *se Hælynd* eft micelre stefne and asende <u>hys</u> gast. ⁵¹ And þærrihte ðæs temples wahryft wearð tosliten on twegen dælas, fram ufeweardon oð nyþeweard. And seo eorð bifode and stanas toburston, ⁵² and byrgena wurdun geopenode, and manige halige lichaman ðe ær slepon aryson. ⁵³ And þa *hig uteodon* of þam byrgenum æfter hys æryste hig comun on þa haligan ceastre and æteowdon hig manegum. ⁵⁴ Witodlice þæs hundredes ealdor and ða þe mid him wæron healdende *þone Hælynd*, þa hig gesawon þa eorðbifunge and þa ðing ðe þær gewurdon, hig ondredon heom ðearle and cwædon: 'Soðlice Godes Sunu wæs þes [...].'⁵⁵

[³⁵ Truly after they had hanged him on a cross, they divided his garment, and they cast lots thereover that it might be fulfilled that which was spoken by the prophet, and thus said: 'They divided my garments among them, and upon my garments they cast lots. ' ³⁶ And they beheld him sitting. ³⁷ And they put over his head his charge thus written: 'This is the Saviour, King of the Jews.' ³⁸ Then were hanged with him two thieves, one on the right side and the other on the left. ³⁹ Indeed, those that passed by mocked him and shook their heads ⁴⁰ and *they said*, 'Alas! You that destroy God's temple, and in three days afterwards rebuild it, <u>now</u> save yourself: if you are God's son, come down from the cross.' ⁴¹ Also the chief priests mocked him, with the scribes and the ancients, and said: ⁴² 'He saved others, and he cannot save himself. If he is the king of Israel, come down from the cross and we will believe him. ⁴³ He trusted in God; let him now deliver him if he wishes; <u>indeed</u>, he said: "I am God's son."' ⁴⁴ Likewise the thieves that were hanged with him; they mocked him. ⁴⁵ Indeed from the sixth hour there was darkness over all the earth until the ninth hour. ⁴⁶ And about the ninth hour *the Saviour*

---

⁵⁵ Liuzza, ed. *Gospels*, I, p. 60.

called out with a great voice and said thus: 'Heli Heli lema zabandi.' That is <u>in English</u>: 'My God, my God, who have you forsaken me?' ⁴⁷ Truly some of those that stood there and heard this said: 'Now he calls Elias.' ⁴⁸ Then immediately one of them *ran* and took a sponge and filled it with vinegar and put it on a reed thereon and gave him to drink. ⁴⁹ Indeed then the others said: 'Let be, let us see whether Elias will come <u>and wish</u> to deliver him.' ⁵⁰ Then *the Saviour* cried out again with a great voice and sent <u>his</u> ghost. ⁵¹ And straightaway the temple's curtain was rent into two parts, from the top to the bottom. And the earth trembled and stones burst. ⁵² And graves were opened, and many holy bodies that slept there before arose, ⁵³ and then *they came* out of those tombs after his resurrection, they came into the holy city, and appeared to many. ⁵⁴ Indeed, the centurion and those that were with him guarding *the Saviour*, when they saw the earthquake and those things that happened there, they were greatly afraid and said: 'Truly this was God's son.']

In order to incorporate the source-text into the target language and to bring its meaning across as effectively as possible, a number of small alterations of syntax and minor grammatical adjustments are made by the translator. Hence, the tense of a Latin verb is sometimes altered to produce idiomatic English (e.g. verse 48: *currens* > *arn*), while on other occasions a personal pronoun denoted by the inflection of a Latin verb is inserted in the English translation for the sake of clarity (e.g. verse 50: *emisit spiritum* > *asende hys gast*). The cumulative effect of these many small but significant translation choices is the total transformation of the Vulgate source into highly readable, fluent Old English prose. The *Wessex Gospels* can thus be viewed as a step beyond Farman's prose-like gloss on the Rushworth Gospels, accurately conveying the meaning of the entire gospel text to the reader while effectively displacing the Latin source. Unlike most of the other biblical translations considered in this book, remarkably few compensatory measures are taken: alliteration and parallel phrasing, for instance, do not feature in this passage (except in verse 51: *And seo eorð bifode and stanas toburston*), though we saw above that these techniques are occasionally used elsewhere in the translation.

Purpose and readership

The circumstances behind the composition of the *Wessex Gospels* are unknown and can only be guessed at from the evidence of (mostly later) manuscript witnesses and the team's translation strategy. In several manuscripts, gospel passages excerpted for use in the mass (pericopes) are marked up in Latin. Figure 7 shows the opening of the Gospel of Matthew

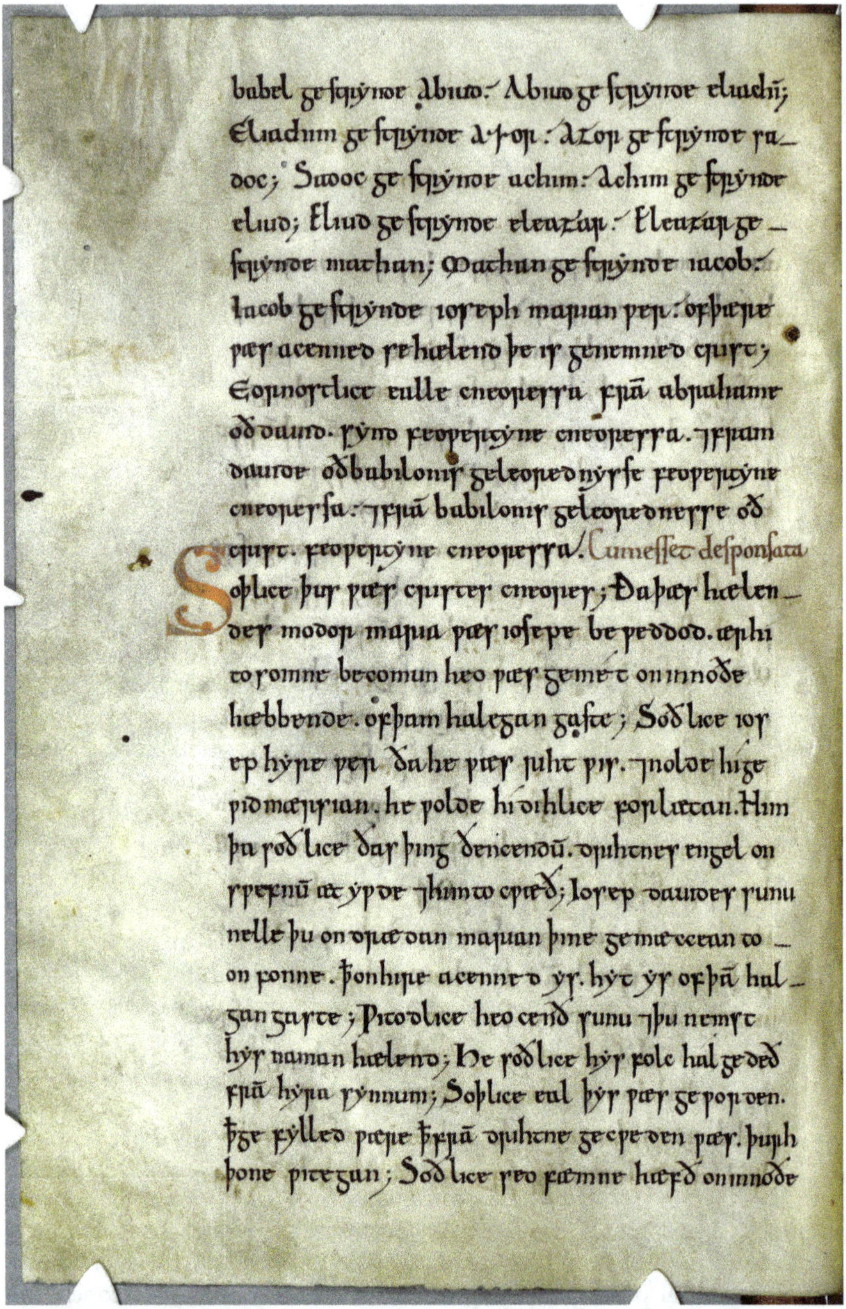

babel gestrynde abiud. Abiud ge strynde eliachim;
Eliachim ge strynde asor. Asor ge strynde sa_
doc; Sadoc ge strynde achim. Achim ge strynde
eliud; Eliud ge strynde eleazar. Eleazar ge_
strynde mathan; Mathan ge strynde iacob;
Iacob ge strynde ioseph marian wer. of þære
wæs acenned se hælend þe is genemned crist;
Eornostlice ealle cneoressa fram abrahame
oð dauid. synd feowertyne cneoressa. ⁊ fram
dauide oð babilonis geleorednysse feowertyne
cneoressa. ⁊ fram babilonis geleorednesse oð
crist. feowertyne cneoressa. Cum esset desponsata
Soþlice þus wæs cristes cneores; Ða þær hælen_
des modor maria wæs iosepe beweddod. ær hi
tosomne becomun heo wæs gemet on innoðe
hæbbende. of þam halgan gaste; Soðlice ios
ep hyre wer ða he wæs riht wis. ⁊ nolde hi ge_
widmærsian. he wolde hi dihlice forlætan. Him
þa soðlice ðas þing ðencendū. oþ hi næs engel on
swefnū æt ywde ⁊ him to cweð; Ioseph dauides sunu
nelle þu on dred an marian þine gemæccean to _
on fonne. Þon hwæt acenned ys. hyt ys of þā hal_
gan gaste; Witodlice heo cend sunu ⁊ þu nemst
hys naman hælend; He soðlice hys folc hal gedeð
fram hyra synnum; Soþlice eal þis wæs geworden.
þt ge fylled wære þt fram drihtne gecweden wæs. þuh
þone witegan; Soðlice seo fæmne hæfð on innoðe

Figure 7. Cambridge Corpus Christi College MS 140, fols 2ᵛ–3ʳ, '*Wessex Gospels*: opening of Gospel of Matthew with Latin headings in red' (above and opposite).

⁊ heo cenð sunu ⁊ hi nemnað his naman. emanuhel.
þꝛt ge þeht on uꝛe geþeode god mid uꝛ; Ða aꝛaꝛ ioseph
of ꝛpefene. ⁊ dyde ꝛpa ꝛpa drihtneꝛ engel him bebead.
⁊ he on feng hiꝛ ge mæccean ⁊ he ne grette hi; Heo
cende hyre frum cenne ðan sunu; ⁊ nemde hyꝛ naman
hælend; Cumnatus esset ðis in bechleem.
Soþlice þa ꝛe hælend acenned pæꝛ on iudeiꝛcum
bethleem. on þæꝛ cyningeꝛ dagum herodeꝛ; þa
comon þa tungol pitegan. fram east dæle to hieru
ꝛalem ⁊ þuꝛ don. hpær yꝛ ꝛe iudea cyning þe acen
ned yꝛ; Soðlice pe ge ꝛapon hyꝛ ꝛteorran on east
dæle. ⁊ pe comon uꝛ him to ge eadmedenne; Ða he
rodeꝛ þæꝛ hyrde ða peaꝛð he ge drefed ⁊ eal
hieroꝛolim paru mid him; ⁊ þa ge gaderode he roðer
ealle ealdoraꝛ þæra ꝛaceroa ⁊ foleꝛ ꝛpꝛiteraꝛ;
⁊ axode hpæꝛ cꝛiꝛt acenned pære; Ða ꝛæ don
hi hiꝛ on iudeiꝛcere bethlem; Þuꝛ olic buꝛh yꝛ
apꝛiten. þuꝛh þone pitegan; And þu bethleem
iudea land. pitoðlice ne eaꝛt þu læꝛt on iuda eal
dꝛum: of ðe forð gæð ꝛe heꝛe toga ꝛe þe peꝛð
min folc iꝛꝛahel; Heꝛodeꝛ þa clypode on ꝛun
dꝛꝛ ꝛprære ða tungel pitegan; ⁊ be fram hi geoꝛne
hpænne ꝛe ꝛteorra him æt eopde; And he aꝛende
hi to bethlem ⁊ þuꝛ cpæð; Faꝛað ⁊ axiað geoꝛn
lice be þam cilde. ⁊ þonne ge hyt gemetað cyþað
eft me: þic cume ⁊ me to him ge bidde; Ða hiꝛ
ge bod ge hyrdon þa feꝛdon hi: ⁊ ꝛoþlice ꝛe ꝛteorra

from an eleventh-century manuscript, Cambridge Corpus Christi College 140 (MS Cp), with the end of Christ's genealogy and the beginning of the narrative of the Nativity (Mt. 1.13–2.9).[56]

The main Old English gospel text is written in a late Anglo-Saxon square minuscule hand of the first half of the eleventh century. The first words of each chapter have been inserted in Latin in red ink (*Cum esset desponsata* above Mt. 1.18 midway down fol. 2ᵛ; *Cum natus esset iesus in bethleem* above Mt. 2.1 a third of the way down fol. 3ʳ) in 'a nearly contemporary hand'.[57] These Latin headings were only supplied for the opening of the Gospel of Matthew (Mt. 1–5). In the right-hand margin of fol. 3ʳ the Latin heading *Ca. 2* ('chapter 2') appears next to the text of Mt. 2.1 (fig. 7), indicating that the pericope begins here. Another manuscript copy of the *Wessex Gospels*, MS Bodley 441 (c. 1000–1050), features Latin pericope markers written in a Caroline minuscule roughly contemporary with that of the main hand as well as Old English rubrics inserted by a sixteenth-century hand copying from Cambridge University Library Ii.2.11 (MS A).[58] The text of Mt. 7.28 begins halfway down fol. 11ᵛ with a large red capital Ð (fig. 8). The Old English rubric squeezed in above Mt. 7.28 reads: *Ðys sceal on þone þryddan sunnan dæg ofer epiphan(us)* ('This is for the third Sunday after Epiphany'), while the Latin heading in the left-hand margin, *Ca. viii* (chapter 8), indicates that the pericope begins here at Mt. 8.1.

In both these manuscript witnesses of the *Wessex Gospels*, the page was not originally ruled to include the Latin pericope markers or the Old English rubrics, all of which are later additions. Indeed, Ursula Lenker has shown how, at some point after the initial translation was made, the 'clean' text of the *Wessex Gospels* was combined with the Roman pericope system, perhaps at Exeter during the episcopacy of Leofric (1050–72).[59] As Lenker notes, the combination of the text of the *Wessex Gospels* with this standard liturgical system could have assisted 'a preacher trying to elucidate the deeper meaning of the gospel text', while 'the text of the West Saxon Gospels may indeed have been read to the congregation during the mass – instead of or as part of a homily'.[60] On the basis of these headings

---

[56] Images of Cambridge Corpus Christi College 140 are available online at: https://parker.stanford.edu/parker/catalog/ks656dq8163.

[57] Ker, p. 47.

[58] Ker, p. 376. Archbishop Parker's scribes used this volume as the base text for the edition presented by John Foxe to Queen Elizabeth I in 1571; on Foxe's edition of the *Wessex Gospels*, see Conclusion, pp. 250–1.

[59] Ursula Lenker, 'The West Saxon Gospels and the Gospel Lectionary in Anglo-Saxon England: Manuscript Evidence and Liturgical Practice', *ASE* 28 (1999), 141–78, at 149.

[60] Lenker, 'The West Saxon Gospels and the Gospel Lectionary in Anglo-Saxon England', 173–4.

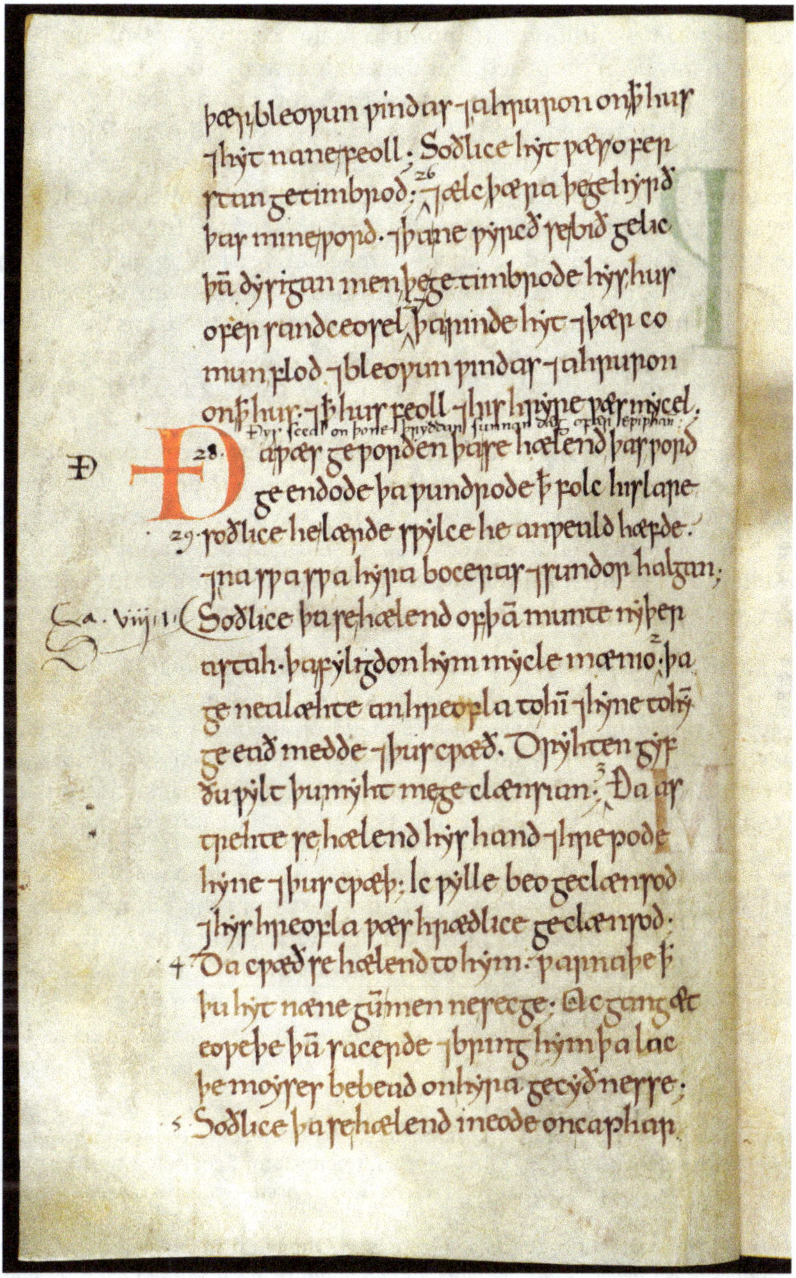

Figure 8. Oxford, Bodleian Library, MS Bodley 441, fol. 11ᵛ, 'Wessex Gospels: Mt. 7–8 with Old English rubric and Latin pericope marker'.

and other Latin additions in multiple manuscript copies of the *Wessex Gospels*, it has been proposed that the original translation itself was made primarily for liturgical usage rather than for private reading.[61] Hence Roy Liuzza has argued that the *Wessex Gospels* were designed 'to aid the secular priest's exposition of the Gospel pericope', serving 'as a gloss on a received Latin liturgical reading rather than as an independent text'.[62] Nevertheless, Liuzza acknowledges that this prose translation of the Gospels 'began as an independent vernacular version' which was 'originally free-standing', to which Latin liturgical headings were subsequently added in stages.[63] Like the *Prose Psalms*, then, and the translation of the Heptateuch considered in the next chapter, the *Wessex Gospels* appear to have been originally conceived as a free-standing biblical translation made for private reading.

Richard Marsden suggests that the *Wessex Gospels* 'were probably used mainly by monks and clerics, to help them in their doctrinal studies or in the learning of Latin, and also by a few devout and wealthy lay people'.[64] Robert Stanton makes a stronger case for lay readership, noting that despite the presence of Latin headings in the late manuscript witnesses, there is no continuous Latin text in the translation itself:

> The English version could certainly be read by someone checking the Latin carefully as he went; but equally, its fullness, accuracy, and readability would have allowed it to be read on its own by someone with deficient Latin. […]. A full prose version is a potential substitute in a way that a gloss is not. […] A complete English prose version was eminently suitable for private reading, perhaps for a wealthy lay patron.[65]

The analysis of translation style presented above, in particular the syntactical independence of the Old English text from the Latin source, and the absence of Latin words in the original Old English text which might serve as cues, substantiates Stanton's suggestion that the *Wessex Gospels* were designed to serve as an independent, free-standing prose translation for private reading. The absence of interpretive passages, such as those

---

[61] See M. Grünberg, ed., *The West-Saxon Gospels: A Study of the Gospel of Saint Matthew with Text of the Four Gospels* (Amsterdam: Scheltema and Holkema, 1967) for the argument that the *Wessex Gospels* are based on an earlier Mercian gloss.

[62] Roy M. Liuzza, 'Who Read the Gospels in Old English?', in *Words and Works: Studies in Medieval English Language and Literature in Honour of Fred C. Robinson*, ed. Peter S. Baker and Nicholas Howe (Toronto: University of Toronto Press, 1998), pp. 3–24, at 14–15.

[63] Liuzza, 'Who Read the Gospels in Old English?', pp. 12–13.

[64] Marsden, 'New Testament', p. 236.

[65] Stanton, *Culture of Translation*, p. 130.

found in the introductions to the *Prose Psalms* or the exegetical passages included especially in the Ælfrician sections of the Heptateuch, indicates that the reader(s) who commissioned the translation wanted a 'clean' text of the Gospels, unencumbered by exegetical tools or liturgical prompts. Such a clean but accurate and readable translation of the Gospels might have appealed to a pious lay reader, perhaps one of the beneficiaries of Alfred's drive to educate the sons of freeborn men in English letters or a secular priest who wished to read the Gospels in private, either as inspiration for composing homilies or for their own spiritual edification. Within an aristocratic household, a chaplain might have read excerpts from such a gospel translation to his noble patron and other family members. Although monastic readers may have used the *Wessex Gospels* in *lectio divina* as a stimulus to prayer, the marked independence of the translation from its Vulgate source suggests that its primary audience lay outside the walls of the monastery.

As a major piece of Old English biblical prose designed to be read independently of the Vulgate source rather than as an aid to the study of Latin, the *Wessex Gospels* sit at a midway point between the Alfredian renderings of the Psalms and Laws and the translation of the Heptateuch made around the turn of the millennium. Together these ambitious Old English prose translations made key parts of Scripture accessible to a wide range of English readers, extending the learning of the monastery into the private houses and spiritual lives of the nobility. This widening of access to scriptural translation did not come without risks: making the Bible available to readers who were untrained in exegesis could lead to misunderstanding and misinterpretation, which in turn could lead Christians into sin. The final section of this chapter will consider how Ælfric produced his *Catholic Homilies* in the late tenth century to provide the laity with the exegetical framework that the *Wessex Gospels* and other anonymous homilies lack. Before turning to Ælfric, however, I will briefly discuss the translation of two apocryphal gospels into Old English prose in this period.

Apocryphal Gospels

Many books on biblical subjects designated as apocryphal on the grounds of their dubious origins or authenticity remained in circulation throughout the Middle Ages.[66] Notably, the influence of the Book of Enoch (or

---

[66] Notably, the Gelasian decree, attributed to Pope Gelasius I (492–96) but now assigned to the sixth century, listed the canonical books of the Bible and condemned a number of other works as apocryphal. See van Liere, *Introduction to the Medieval Bible*, pp. 53–79. See further *Apocryphal Texts and Traditions in*

I Enoch), with its dramatic retelling of the Fall of the Angels, has been detected in a range of early medieval English sources,[67] while the *Visio Sancti Pauli*, though rejected by Aldhelm and Ælfric, was nevertheless translated into anonymous Old English prose and influenced various Old English homilies and poetic works.[68] Ælfric's own writings embody the ambivalent attitude of contemporary commentators towards such apocryphal material: in his *Treatise on the Old and New Testaments*, he restricted the contents of the English *bibliotheca* ('Bible') to those works approved by Jerome, yet he still produced translations of apocryphal works such as the *Letter of Christ to Agbar*.[69] Given this chapter's focus on the translation of the Gospels, I will restrict this brief discussion of apocrypha to two major works: the extended narratives of Christ's Passion in the Old English *Gospel of Nicodemus* and its companion piece *The Avenging of the Saviour*; and the account of the Virgin Mary's nativity in the *Gospel of Pseudo-Matthew*.

'The Gospel of Nicodemus' and 'The Avenging of the Saviour'

Appended to the text of the *Wessex Gospels* in one of its principal manuscripts, Cambridge University Library Ii.2.11, are Old English prose translations of two closely related apocryphal works: the Gospel of Nicodemus

---

Anglo-Saxon England, ed. Kathryn Powell and Donald Scragg, Publications of the Manchester Centre for Anglo-Saxon Studies 2 (Cambridge: D. S. Brewer, 2003); *Sources of Anglo-Saxon Literary Culture: The Apocrypha*, Instrumenta Anglistica Medievalia 1, ed. Frederick M. Biggs (Kalamazoo, MI: Medieval Institute Publications, 2007); Brandon Hawk, *Preaching Apocrypha in Anglo-Saxon England* (Toronto: University of Toronto Press, 2018).

[67] See Elizabeth Coatsworth, 'The Book of Enoch and Anglo-Saxon Art', in *Apocryphal Texts and Traditions*, ed. Powell and Scragg, pp. 135–50; Robert E. Kaske, '*Beowulf* and the Book of Enoch', *Speculum* 46 (1971), 421–31; Francis Leneghan, 'Beowulf, the Wrath of God and the Fall of the Angels', *English Studies* 105 (2024), 383–403.

[68] Antonette diPaolo Healey, ed. *The Old English Vision of St. Paul* (Cambridge, MA: Mediaeval Academy of America, 1978), pp. 41–57. See further Charles D. Wright, *The Irish Tradition in Old English Literature*, CSASE 6 (Cambridge: Cambridge University Press, 1993), pp. 106–74.

[69] Ælfric's translation of the *Letter of Christ to Agbar* is included in his *Lives of the Saints* following the account of the martyrdom of Abdon and Sennes. See Christopher M. Cain, 'The Apocryphal Legend of Abgar in Ælfric's *Lives of Saints*', *PQ* 89 (2010), 383–402; Stephen C. E. Hopkins, 'An Old English Fragment of the *Letter of Christ to Agbar*', *N&Q* 66 (2019), 173–6. On Ælfric's restriction of the biblical canon to those books translated by Jerome, see Chapter Five, pp. 235–38.

and the Avenging of the Saviour.[70] Originally composed in Greek, the Gospel of Nicodemus was translated into Latin by the fifth century and subsequently into many Eastern and Western vernaculars.[71] The Latin version (*Euangelium Nichodemi*) from which the Old English translation is derived combines two originally separate narratives: the *Acta Pilati* (Acts of Pilate) and the *Descensus ad infernos* (Descent into Hell). The *Acta Pilati* considerably expands on the narratives of the trial of Christ in John 18 and Luke 23. New episodes include: the dream of Pilate's wife, Procula, which convinces them both of Christ's innocence; the defence of Christ by Nicodemus, Joseph of Arimathea and the woman who had touched the hem of Christ's garment against the Jewish accusations of witchcraft and sorcery; Joseph's burial of Christ's body and miraculous escape from the Jews; and the subsequent conversion of the Jews. The *Descensus ad infernos* contains an account of the Harrowing of Hell which was related to the Jews after Christ's Resurrection by the two sons of Simeon, Leucius and Carinus. In addition to its incorporation into the Apostles' Creed (*descendit ad infernos*) in the fourth century, the Harrowing would prove immensely popular in medieval preaching and its associated literature, and Old English poems such as *The Descent into Hell* and *The Dream of the Rood* and prose works such as Blickling Homily VII all betray traces of its influence, direct or indirect.[72] The *Vindicta Salvatoris*, composed in Latin *c.* 700 in southern Gaul, is the longest and most complex of a series of subsidiary narratives that expand on various parts of the *Euangelium Nichodemi*, and the two works often therefore travel together in manuscripts. The *Vindicta* relates the stories of Veronica's veil, the healing of the Emperor Titus and his destruction of Jerusalem in 70 A.D., the healing of the Emperor Tiberius, and the condemnation, exile and death of Pilate.

---

[70] For details of this manuscript, see above, p. 91 n. 38. See further the entries by Frederick M. Biggs and James H. Morey ('Gospel of Nicodemus') and Thomas N. Hall ('Vindicta Salvatoris') in Biggs, ed., *Apocrypha*, pp. 29–33.

[71] For discussion of the origins of both traditions and their medieval transmission, see Zbigniew Izydorczyk, 'Introduction', in *The Medieval Gospel of Nicodemus: Texts, Intertexts, and Contexts*, ed. Zbigniew Izydorczyk (Tempe, AZ: Medieval and Renaissance Texts and Studies, 1997), pp. 1–19; and Thomas N. Hall, 'The *Euangelium Nichodemi* and *Vindicta Saluatoris* in Anglo-Saxon England', in *Two Old English Apocrypha and Their Manuscript Source: 'The Gospel of Nichodemus' and 'The Avenging of the Saviour'*, ed. J. E. Cross, CSASE 19 (Cambridge: Cambridge University Press, 1996), pp. 36–81.

[72] It is unclear to what extent any of these works were directly indebted to the Gospel of Nicodemus itself, as opposed to the various traditions contained within it that circulated in the early Church in the form of sermons and other writing. See Jackson J. Campbell, 'To Hell and Back: Latin Tradition and Literary Use of the *Descensus ad Infernos* in Old English', *Viator* 13 (1982), 107–58.

The influence of these apocryphal works in the early Old English period was probably indirect, and it appears that they were not translated until the eleventh century. Remarkably, the Latin source for both the Old English *Gospel of Nicodemus* and the *Avenging of the Saviour* has been traced to a single ninth-century continental manuscript, Saint-Omer, Bibliothèque Municipale, 202. This manuscript appears to have been brought to Exeter in the early eleventh century, perhaps by Bishop Leofric.[73] It was probably at Exeter, then, that the *Euangelium Nichodemi* and *Vindicta Salvatoris* were translated into Old English from this manuscript in the early eleventh century by a single author whose work in turn served as the exemplar for the late eleventh-century manuscript copy which preserves both vernacular apocrypha.

Because both the Old English texts were written out by the same hand responsible for the four preceding, canonical gospels (i.e. the *Wessex Gospels*) in Cambridge University Library Ii.2.11, it has been suggested that the combined *Gospel of Nicodemus* and the *Avenging of the Saviour* were regarded at the time as almost a 'fifth gospel'.[74] However, Thomas N. Hall cautions that it was not uncommon to juxtapose canonical and apocryphal works in medieval Latin Bible manuscripts.[75] Moreover, C. W. Marx notes that while each of the four canonical gospels starts on a new recto page in Cambridge University Library Ii.2.11, the *Gospel of Nicodemus* begins uniquely on a verso (fol. 173^v), while the opening of the *Avenging of the Saviour* on fol. 193^r is not presented as a new text but as a new chapter which follows on immediately from the end of *Nicodemus*. Marx concludes that both apocrypha were included in this manuscript not because the compilers regarded them as of equal status to the canonical gospels but rather 'to supplement and extend the account of the life of Christ up to and including the destruction of Jerusalem'.[76] As we shall see in the next chapter, a similar anthologising tendency may explain the addition of Ælfric's paraphrases of the first two historical books of the Old Testament, Joshua and Judges, to the translation of the Pentateuch in another eleventh-century manuscript, Oxford, Bodleian Library, MS Laud Misc. 509.[77]

---

[73] On this discovery, see J. E. Cross, 'Introduction', in *Two Old English Apocrypha*, ed. Cross, pp. 3–9.

[74] Antonette di Paolo Healey, 'Anglo-Saxon Use of the Apocryphal Gospel', in *The Anglo-Saxons: Synthesis and Achievement*, ed. J. Douglas Woods and David A. E. Pelteret (Waterloo, ON: Wilfrid Laurier University Press, 1986), pp. 93–104, at 98.

[75] Hall, '*Euangelium Nichodemi* and *Vindicta Saluatoris* in Anglo-Saxon England', p. 50.

[76] C. W. Marx, 'The *Gospel of Nicodemus* in Old English and Middle English', in *Medieval Gospel of Nicodemus*, ed. Izydorczyk, pp. 207–59, at 207–8.

[77] See below, pp. 149–50, 198–214.

As Andy Orchard has shown, the author responsible for translating *Nicodemus* and *Avenging* renders most verses of the Latin sources faithfully and accurately, though at times they were forced to supply material missing in the Saint-Omer manuscript, which is often defective and features unusual Latin orthography.[78] Passages which repeat material from the four canonical gospels are often omitted, while an unobtrusive sense of literary style is evident in the translator's use of doublets and frequent insertion of intensifying adverbs, such as *swiðe* ('very, greatly') and *sona* ('suddenly'). For example, the translation of *Nicodemus* XXII.2 expands substantially on the comparatively terse account of Christ's binding of Satan in the Latin source:

> Tunc Rex Gloriae, Dominus, maiestate sua conculcans mortem, conprehendens Satan Principem, tradidit Inferi potestae et adtraxit Adam ad suam claritatem.
>
> [Then the King of Glory, the Lord, trampling down death in his majesty, grabbing hold of Prince Satan gave him the power of Hell and drew Adam to his own brightness.]
>
> Ac se Wuldorfæsta Cyning and ure Heofenlica Hlaford þa nolde þæra deofla gemæðeles mare habban ac he þone deoflican deað feor nyðer atræd and he Satan gegrap and hyne fæste geband and hyne þær helle sealde on angeweald. Ac heo hyne þa underfeng eall swa hyre fram ure Heofonlican Hlaforde gehaten wæs.
>
> [But then the Glorious King and our Heavenly Lord would have no more talk from the devils, but he trod down devilish death far below; and he seized Satan and bound him fast and delivered him to the power of Hell. And it received him, just as it was ordered by our Heavenly Lord.][79]

A number of large- and small-scale expansions make the Old English version of Satan's binding considerably more vivid than the Latin account on which it is based. For example, the insertion of the idiomatic English verb phrase *þa nolde [...] mare habban* ('[he] did not wish to have any more') lends a more personal dimension to God's actions, while Hell itself is now granted agency in receiving Satan (*heo hyne þa underfeng*), echoing the account of Grendel's death in *Beowulf* (*him hel onfeng*, 1. 852b). Parallel phrasing lends structure and rhythm (*and he Satan gegrap and hyne fæste geband and hyne þær helle sealde*), while the addition of adjectives (*Heofenlica*,

---

[78] See Andy Orchard, 'The Style of the Texts and the Translation Strategy', in *Two Old English Apocrypha*, ed. Cross, pp. 105–30.

[79] Latin and Old English texts and translations from *Two Old English Apocrypha*, ed. Cross, pp. 222–3, with modifications.

deoflican) creates alliterative two-stress phrases reminiscent of Ælfric's late, rhythmical style (e.g. *Heofenlica Hlaford, deofla gemæðeles mare habban ac he þone deoflican deað*); further sound-patterning is produced by internal rhyme (*helle sealde on angeweald*). Additional details not present in the Latin source, such as the statement that God *hyne fæste geband* ('bound him fast') and placed him *feor nyðer* ('far below'), lend further intensity to this highly stylised vernacular account of Satan's punishment. The final sentence of the Old English extract quoted above replaces the reference to Adam's salvation in the Latin source with a second mention of the heavenly Lord, thus emphasising God's supreme power over Satan: *eall swa hyre fram ure Heofonlican Hlaforde gehaten wæs* ('just as it was ordered by our Heavenly Lord'). In passages such as this, we observe an Old English prose author confidently adapting a Latin source. Such relatively free handling of the source may reflect the translator's awareness of the work's apocryphal status, or it may simply be a product of an individual author's personal translation style.

The *Vindicta Salvatoris* is translated in much the same manner, with otiose sections omitted and others expanded for the sake of clarity, as in the opening passage:

> In diebus illis Tyberii caesaris tethrarcha sub Puntio Pilato traditus fuit a Iudeis, celatus a Tyberio. In diebus illis erat quidam homo nomine Tyrus, regulus Tyberii in regnum Aquitanie in ciuitatem Libiae, que dicitur Burdigala, et erat insanus in narem dextram habens cancrum faciem delaceratam usque ad oculum.

> [In the days of the emperor Tiberius, tetrarch under Pontius Pilate, he was betrayed by the Jews, and it was kept secret from Tiberius. In those days there was a certain man, Tyrus by name, an underking of Tiberius in the kingdom of Aquitainia in a city of Libia which is called Burdigala, and he was ill, having a cancer on the right nostril, his face being destroyed up to the eye.]

> On Tiberius dagum ðæs miclan caseres hyt gelamp bynnan lytlum fyrste æfterþam þe ure Heofenlica Hlaford ahangen wæs, hyt wæs, þæt sum æðele man wæs, þæs nama wæs Tyrus. And he wæs on Equitania rice cyning under Tyberie þam casere, and he wæs oftost wunigende on þære ceastre, þe wæs genemned Lybie. And he wæs, se ylca Tyrus, þæs ðe bec secgað, swa unhal on hys andwlitan, þæt ðæt adl, þe we hatað 'cancer', hym wæs on þam nebbe fram þam swyðran næsþryle oð hyt com to þam eage.

> [In the days of Tiberius the great emperor, it happened within a short time after our Heavenly Lord was crucified, that there was a certain noble man, whose name was Tyrus. And he was king in the kingdom

of Aquitania under the emperor Tiberius and he usually dwelt in the city called Libya. And, according to books, he, this same Tyrus, was so afflicted in his face, that the disease, which we call cancer, affected his nose from the right nostril until it reached his eye.]⁸⁰

The Latin text's fulsome description of Tiberius' rank (*caesaris tethrarcha sub Puntio Pilato*) is reduced to *ðæs miclan caseres*, while the description of Tyrus as an underking (*regulus*) is periphrastically expanded with the statement that he *was cyning under Tyberie þam casere*, and the detail that Christ's betrayal by the Jews *celatus a Tyberio* ('was kept secret from Tiberius') is cut entirely. Some alterations of the source may be the result of misunderstanding on the part of the translator: where the Latin states that Tyrus dwelt *in ciuitatem Libiae, que dicitur Burdigala* ('in a city of Libia, which is called Burdigala'), the Old English conflates the nation with the city, thereby presenting him as living *on þære ceastre, þe wæs genemned Lybie* ('in the city called Libya'). Other elements of the narrative which the translator considered obscure are either expanded or altered: hence, where the Latin simply states *traditus fuit a Iudeis* ('He was betrayed by the Jews'), the Old English version supplies the identity of the referent and explains the circumstances of his death and its doctrinal significance, employing the same alliterating collocation that we observed in the Nicodemus translation: *ure Heofenlica Hlaford ahangen wæs* ('our Heavenly Lord was crucified'). Cumulatively these alterations result in a more streamlined and succinct narrative, making the story more accessible to readers relatively unfamiliar with Roman and early Church history and clarifying its spiritual meaning.

The Gospel of Pseudo-Matthew

The mystery of the Virgin Birth inspired a series of apocryphal narratives in the early Church concerning Mary's own birth, childhood, nativity, death and assumption into heaven. The most important of these was the Protoevangelium of James, composed in Greek in the second century. Although it was rejected by Jerome and then condemned, first by Pope Innocent I in 405 and then by the Gelasian decree (519–553), the tradition of Mary's infancy remained current in the medieval West thanks to the circulation of a Latin translation of the Protoevangelium of James, the *Pseudo-Matthaei Evangelium*.⁸¹ By the eighth century, if not earlier, the feast of Mary's nativity had entered into the English liturgy.⁸² The common

---

[80] Latin and Old English texts and translations (with modifications) from *Two Old English Apocrypha*, ed. Cross, pp. 248–9.
[81] On the Gelasian Decree, see above, pp. 109 10 n. 66
[82] The tenth-century Old English calendar poem, *The Menologium*, includes Mary's

theme in these apocryphal accounts of Mary's life is her sinlessness, which marks her out from the other virgins in the temple where she lives.[83]

Among the various Old English versions of this narrative are three anonymous homilies for the nativity of Mary, all of which are derived from the *Pseudo-Matthaei Evangelium*.[84] The earliest manuscript witness to the Old English *Gospel of Pseudo-Matthew*, Oxford Bodleian Library MS Hatton 114, contains a translation of Chs I–XII and dates from the late eleventh century.[85] The date of the composition of the Old English *Gospel of Pseudo-Matthew* is unknown: Donald G. Scragg has argued that the work is pre-Ælfrician, but Mary Clayton, the work's most recent editor, places it much nearer to the date of its manuscript, in the early eleventh century.[86] Clayton notes that the translator faithfully renders the first twelve of the thirty-five chapters of the *Pseudo-Matthaei Evangelium*, save for Ch. XII in which Joseph and Mary prove their purity to the bishops and high priests by undergoing a test of the water of the Lord. The translator appears to have judged this detail too obscure for the work's intended readers, and has therefore abbreviated this chapter. While there are some minor expansions which clarify or explain features of the narrative left implicit in the Latin, other small details are omitted or downplayed, including references to sacrifices made to God.[87]

---

nativity among the list of feasts celebrated in the English Church (ll. 167b–69a). See further Mary Clayton, 'Ælfric and the Nativity of the Blessed Virgin Mary', *Anglia* 104 (1986), 286–315.

[83] For a succinct summary of the tradition and its reception in early medieval England, see Mary Clayton, ed., *The Apocryphal Gospels of Mary in Anglo-Saxon England*, CSASE 26 (Cambridge: Cambridge University Press, 1998), pp. 1–5.

[84] See Mary Clayton, *The Cult of the Virgin Mary in Anglo-Saxon England*, CSASE 2 (Cambridge: Cambridge University Press, 1990) esp. pp. 244–53; and the entry by Thomas N. Hall ('Gospel of Pseudo-Matthew') in Biggs, ed., *Apocrypha*, pp. 23–5.

[85] The text is copied on fols 201–12; Ker §331.

[86] Clayton, *Apocryphal Gospels of Mary*, p. 139; Donald G. Scragg, 'The Corpus of Anonymous Lives and Their Manuscript Context', in *Holy Men and Holy Women: Old English Prose Saints' Lives and Their Contexts*, ed. Paul E. Szarmach (Albany, NY: State University of New York Press, 1996), pp. 209–30, at 214–15. See further Donald G. Scragg, 'The Corpus of Vernacular Homilies and Prose Saints' Lives before Ælfric', *ASE* 8 (1979), 223–77, at 253–5. The Old English *Pseudo-Matthew* is preserved in two further manuscripts, both from the twelfth century: Cambridge Corpus Christi College 367, Part II (Ker §63), and Oxford Bodleian Library MS Bodley 343 (Ker §310). An independent translation of a section of *Pseudo-Matthaei Evangelium* is preserved in Vercelli Homily VI (for Christmas Day).

[87] As we shall see in the next chapter, the translators of the Heptateuch took a similar approach to references to sacrifices to God in the Old Testament: see p. 195.

The generally close translation style of the Old English *Gospel of Pseudo-Matthew* is illustrated by the careful treatment of Ch. X.1, in which the sinless nature of Joseph and Mary's relationship is revealed. The *Pseudo-Matthaei Evangelium* relates how the five virgins with whom she lived defended her purity to Joseph after he had returned home to find her pregnant:

> Cum haec agerentur, Ioseph in fabricandis tabernaculis regionum maritimarum erat opere praeoccupatus, erat enim ligni faber. Post vero menses novem, reversus est in domum suam et invenit Mariam praegnantem. Unde totus in angustia positus contremuit et exclamavit, dicens: 'Domine Deus, accipe spiritum meum, quoniam melius est mihi mori quam amplius vivere!' Cui dixerunt virgines, quae cum Maria erant: 'Quid ais, domine Ioseph? Nos scimus quoniam vir non tetigit eam. Nos sumus testes quoniam virginitas et integritas perseverat in ea. Nos custodivimus super eam. Semper in oratione nobiscum permansit, quotidie angeli Dei cum ea loquuntur, quotidie de manu Domini escam accepit. Nescimus quomodo fieri possit, ut sit peccatum aliquod in ea! Nam si suspicionem nostram tibi vis, ut pandamus, istam gravidam nemo fecit, nisi angelus Domini.[88]

> [While these things were happening, Joseph was occupied with his work, building houses in the districts by the seashore, for he was a carpenter. After nine months, he came back to his house and found Mary pregnant, as a result of which, being in the utmost distress, he trembled and cried out, saying: 'O Lord God, receive my spirit, for I would prefer to die than to live any longer!' The virgins who were with Mary said to him: 'Joseph, what are you saying? We know that no man has touched her. We are witnesses that she is still a virgin and untouched. We have watched over her. She has always remained with us in prayer, the angels of God speak with her daily, she receives food from the hand of the Lord daily. We do not know how it might be that there can be any sin in her! But if you wish us to tell you what we suspect, nobody but the angel of the Lord has made her pregnant.'][89]

The translator generally follows the wording of the Latin source while adapting the grammar and syntax to produce idiomatic Old English prose, only occasionally adding clarifying details, such as the fact that Joseph was 'a skilful worker' (*mænigtweawa wyrhta*):

---

[88] Latin text of *Pseudo-Matthaie Evangelium* cited with modifications from Constantin von Tischendorf, ed., *Evangelia Apocrypha* (Leipzig: Hermann Mendelsohn, 1853; 2nd edn, 1876), pp. 52–112, at 69–70.

[89] Translation adapted with modifications from *Apocryphal Gospels, Acts, and Revelations*, trans. Alexander Walker (Edinburgh: T. & T. Clark, 1870), p. 28.

On þa tid þe þis gelamp wæs Iosep on þam lande, þe Carfanaum hatte, ymbe his cræft. He wæs smið and *mænigtweawa wyrhta*. Ða þa he þanon gecyrde to his agenum hame þa gemette he hi bearn hæbbende on hire gehrife. Ða wæs he sona swyðe forht and sorhfull and ðus cwæð: 'Drihten, Drihten min, onfoh minum gaste; me is dead selre þonne lif.' Ða cwædon þa fæmnan him to, þe mid hyre wæron, þæt he geare wiston þæt hyre nan wer ne onhran, ac heo wære onwelges mægðhades and unwemme: 'And we witon þæt heo wæs dæges and nihtes on halgum gebedum wuniende and Godes encgel wið hyre spræc and heo dæghwamlice of ðæs engles handum mete þigde. Hu mæg þæt gewurðan, þæt þæt sy swa, forðan þe we witon þæt hit man ne dyde ac Godes encgel?'

[At the time when this happened Joseph was in the country which is called Capharnaum, at his trade. He was a carpenter and *a skilful worker*. When he returned to his own home from there, he found her with a child in her womb. Then he was immediately very frightened and sorrowful and spoke as follows: 'Lord, my Lord, receive my spirit; death is preferable to me than life.' Then the virgins who were with her said to him that they knew well that no man had touched her, but that she was of perfect and unblemished virginity. 'And we know that she persevered day and night at holy prayers and God's angel spoke with her and she received food daily from the hands of the angel. How can that happen, that it should be so, for we know that a man did not do it but the angel of God?']⁹⁰ (Emphases added).

Further small additions lend immediacy to the Old English narrative: for instance, Joseph's distress at hearing the news of Mary's pregnancy is intensified through the doublet *forht and sorhfull*, while his despairing prayer opens with the repeated, psalm-like invocation of *Drihten, Drihten min* where the Latin has simply *Domine deus* ('O Lord God').⁹¹ The first part of the virgins' speech is related by the narrator before the text shifts into reported speech. Alliteration is used lightly to lend rhythm and emphasis (e.g. *On þa tid þe þis gelamp wæs Iosep on þam lande, þe Carfanaum hatte, ymbe his cræft; bearn hæbbende on hire gehrife; Ða wæs he sona swyðe forht and sorhfull; onwelges mægðhades and unwemme*). Again, it is clear that we are dealing with a confident prose stylist freely adapting a biblical – or rather apocryphal – source.

---

[90] Old English text and translation from Clayton, ed., *Apocryphal Gospels of Mary*, pp. 186–7.

[91] The same construction appears several times in the Alfredian *Prose Psalms* (e.g. Ps. 21.1: *Drihten, Drihten, min God, beseoh to me*; Ps. 34.23: *Drihten, Drihten, min God, dem me æfter þinre mildheortnesse*; Ps. 37.8: *Drihten, Drihten, þu wast nu eall hwæs ic wilnie*).

As is the case with the two other manuscripts containing Marian nativity homilies, MS Hatton 114 is a collection of mainly Ælfrician homilies, supplemented by anonymous homilies such as this one, which is headed with the rubric 'DE NATIUITATE SANCTAE MARIAE' ('For the Nativity of St Mary'). As Clayton observes, Ælfric explained in a short note entitled 'De Sancta Maria' ('On St Mary') at the end of his homily for the sixteenth Sunday after Pentecost that he has not composed a homily on the nativity of Mary despite his evident familiarity with this apocryphal tradition.[92] In place of the detailed narrative of Mary's birth, childhood and nativity found in the *Gospel of Pseudo-Matthew*, Ælfric restricts himself in this note to the simple facts that she was conceived (*gestryned*) through a father and a mother like other people, and was born on the sixth ide of September (i.e. September 8th), and her father was named Joachim and her mother Anna, righteous people under the Old Law, before concluding: *ac we nellað be ðam na swiððor awritan þy læs ðe we on ænigum gedwylde befeallon* ('but we do not wish to write any more about that, lest we should fall into any heresy').[93] Ælfric's reluctance to be drawn on this apocryphal tradition in his *Catholic Homilies* was doubtless influenced by the fact that the Gospel of Pseudo-Matthew had been banned at the Gelasian decree. It is to Ælfric's *Catholic Homilies*, which actively sought to weed out any such heresy (*gewyld*) among English biblical writings and preaching, that we now turn.

Ælfric's 'Catholic Homilies'

In a pastoral letter issued by Bishop Wulfsige of Sherborne in 998, Ælfric instructs English priests to interpret the gospel reading to the people in English on Sundays and massdays, as well as the Pater Noster and Creed:[94]

---

[92] Clayton, ed., *Apocryphal Gospels of Mary*, p. 139. See also Clayton, *Cult of Virgin Mary*, pp. 244–8, 286–94.

[93] *CH* II.31, p. 271. Despite this statement, Ælfric would in fact go on to compose a homily for Mary's nativity (Assmann 3); cf. Bruno Assmann, ed., *Angelsaechsische Homilien und Heiligenleben. Bibliothek der Angelsaechsischen Prosa*, 3 vols (Kassel: Wissenschaftliche Buchgesellschaft, 1889).

[94] Canon XVII of the Council of Tours in 813 instructed priests to translate homilies into *rusticam romanam linguam aut Thiotiscam* ('the rustic Romance language or German'); see Roger Wright, 'Late Latin and early Romance: Alcuin's *De Orthographia* and the Council of Tours (813 A.D.)', *Papers of the Liverpool Latin Seminar* 3 (1981) 343–61, at 355–8. For the possibility that it was Ælfric himself who initiated this practice of explaining the gospel pericope during mass, see Milton McC. Gatch, 'The Achievement of Ælfric and his Colleagues in European Perspective', in *Old English Homily and its Background*, ed. Szarmach and Huppé, pp. 43–73; Mary Clayton, 'Homiliaries and Preaching in Anglo-Saxon England',

Se massepreost sceal secgan Sunnandagum and mæssedagum þæs godspelles angyt on Englisc þam folce. And be þam Pater Nostre and be þam Credan eac, swa he oftost mage, þam mannum to onbryrdnysse, þæt hi cunnon geleafan and heora Cristendom gehealdan. Warnige se lareow wið þæt, þe se witega cwæð: *Canes muti non possunt latrare*, 'þa dumban hundas ne magon beorcan.' We sceolon beorcan and bodigan þam læwedum, þe læs hy for larlyste losian sceoldan. Crist cwæð on his Godspelle, be unsnoterum lareowum: *Cecus si ceco ducatum prestet, ambo in foueam cadunt*, 'Gif se blinda mann bið þæs oðres blindan latteow, þonne befeallað hy begen on sumne blindne seað.' Blind bið se lareow, gif git he þa boclare ne cann and beswicð þa læwedan mid his larleaste.[95]

[The masspriest must explain the meaning of the gospel on Sundays and massdays in English to the people. And also the Pater Noster and the Creed, as often as he can, to inspire the people, so that they might know how to believe and to keep their Christian faith. The teacher warns against that, as the prophet said: *Canes muti non possunt latrare*, 'the dumb hounds cannot bark.' We must bark and preach to the unlearned, lest they should be lost for lack of instruction. Christ said in his gospel, concerning unwise teachers: *Cecus si ceco ducatum prestet, ambo in foueam cadunt*, 'If the blind lead the blind, then they will both fall into a hidden ditch'. The teacher is blind, if he does not know book-learning and deceives the unlearned with his lack of instruction.]

In the late tenth century, Ælfric provided these same masspriests with the materials they needed to interpret the gospel for the unlearned through his two series of *Sermones Catholici*, now commonly known as the *Catholic Homilies*.[96] Each series comprises forty homilies arranged in sequence to follow the feast days of the liturgical calendar for use in alternating years. The survival of a large number of manuscript witnesses from the late

---

Peritia 4 (1985), 207–42, repr. in *Old English Prose: Basic Readings*, ed. Paul E. Szarmach, with the assistance of Deborah A. Oosterhouse, Basic Readings in Anglo-Saxon England 5 (New York: Garland, 2000), pp. 151–98.

[95] Bernhard Fehr, ed. *Die Hirtenbriefe Ælfrics*, Bibliothek der angelsäschsischen Prosa IX (Hamburg, 1914), reprinted with a supplementary introduction by Peter A. M. Clemoes (Darmstadt, 1964), 14, 64; I have modified punctuation and capitalisation and added italics. For discussion of the letter, see Joyce Hill, 'Wulfsige of Sherborne's Reforming Text', in *Leaders of the Anglo-Saxon Church: From Bede to Stigand*, ed. Alexander R. Rumble, Publications of the Manchester Centre for Anglo-Saxon Studies 12 (Woodbridge: Boydell, 2012), pp. 147–64.

[96] See James Hurt, *Ælfric*, Twayne's English Authors Series (New York: Twayne, 1972), pp. 42–59; Milton McC. Gatch, *Preaching and Theology in Anglo-Saxon England: Ælfric and Wulfstan* (Toronto: University of Toronto Press, 1977), esp. pp. 40–59. Aaron J Kleist dates the first series to 989–91, and the second to 991–92 (*The Chronology and Canon of Ælfric of Eynsham*, Anglo-Saxon Studies 37 [Cambridge: D. S. Brewer, 2019], pp. 71, 78).

tenth to the thirteenth centuries attests to the immense popularity of the *Catholic Homilies* over a long period.[97] Moreover, as Wilcox notes, the use of the *Catholic Homilies* in 'virtually every church, minster and monastery throughout England' constitutes 'the beginning of a form of mass communication that must have played a significant part in defining a sense of English identity at the turn of the millennium'.[98] While roughly a third of the items across the two series are narratives, such as saints' lives or biblical paraphrases, or sermons on more general themes, the remaining two thirds are homiletic in the sense in that they focus on the exegesis of a gospel pericope, that is the gospel reading excerpted for use in the mass.[99] The primary purpose of the *Catholic Homilies* was thus to ensure the orthodox interpretation of the Gospels throughout the *Angelcynn* and the avoidance of error or heresy (*gedwyld*), as he explains in the Old English Preface to the first series:[100]

---

[97] See Elaine Treharne, 'Making their Presence Felt: Readers of Ælfric, c. 1050–1350', in *A Companion to Ælfric*, ed. Hugh Magennis and Mary Swan, Brill Companions to the Christian Tradition 18 (Leiden: Brill, 2009), pp. 399–422, at 399–400. The earliest witness to the first series is London, British Library, Royal MS 7 C XII (Ker §257), from c. 990, with corrections in Ælfric's own hand; this is the text used by Clemoes for his edition. Both series are included in Cambridge University Library Gg.3.28 (1493) (Ker §15), c. 1000, which serves as the base text for the editions of Liuzza (*CH* I) and Godden (*CH* II) cited here (with some modifications of spelling and punctuation), and before them Benjamin Thorpe, ed. and trans., *The Homilies of the Anglo-Saxon Church: The First Part, Containing the Sermones Catholici or Homilies of Ælfric in the Original Anglo-Saxon, with an English Version*, 2 vols (London: The Ælfric Society, 1844).

[98] Jonathan Wilcox, 'Ælfric in Dorset and the Landscape of Pastoral Care', in *Pastoral Care in Late Anglo-Saxon England*, ed. Francesca Tinti, Anglo-Saxon Studies 6 (Woodbridge: Boydell, 2005), pp. 52–62, at 62. On the connection between biblical translation and national identity, see above, pp. 20–1, and below, pp. 150, 244–53.

[99] Gospel translations in Ælfric's homilies are printed in Pope, *Biblical Quotations*, pp. 137–226.

[100] Malcolm Godden argues that Ælfric uses the term *gedwyld* here to refer to 'sensational narratives which were clearly fictitious and in some cases of dubious morality' found in anonymous homilies, examples of which are preserved in the Blickling and Vercelli collections: 'Ælfric and the Vernacular Prose Tradition', in *Old English Homily and its Background*, ed. Szarmach and Huppé, pp. 99–117, at 102. Mary Clayton suggests that Ælfric disapproved of such texts because prior authorities had dismissed them as spurious: *Cult of the Virgin Mary*, p. 262. Scott DeGregorio comments that in Ælfric's biblical translations, 'the question of *gedwyld* goes beyond issues of sensationalism and authority to encompass the spiritual and cultural impact texts could have on the audiences that would have received them': '*Þegenlic* or *Flæsclic*: The Old English Prose Legends of St. Andrew', *JEGP* 102 (2003), 449–64, at 462.

Þa bearn me on mode – ic truwige ðurh Godes gife – þæt ic ðas boc of Ledenum gereorde to Engliscre spræce awende, na þurh gebylde mycelre lare, ac forðan ðe ic geseah and gehyrde *mycel gedwyld* on manegum Engliscum bocum, ðe ungelærede menn ðurh heora bilewitnysse to micclum wisdome tealdon, and me ofhreow þæt hi ne cuðon ne næfdon ða godspellican lare on heora gewritum, buton ðam mannum anum ðe þæt Leden cuðon, and buton þam bocum ðe Ælfred cyning snoterlice awende of Ledene on Englisc, ða synd to hæbbene.

For ðisum antimbre ic gedyrstlæhte, on Gode truwiende, þæt ic ðas gesetnysse undergann, and eac forðam ðe menn behofiað godre lare, swiðost on þisum timan þe is geendung þyssere worulde, and beoð fela frecednyssa on mancynne ærðan þe se ende becume […].

[Then it came to my mind – I trust through God's grace – that I should translate this book from the Latin language into English speech, not from the presumption of great learning, but because I saw and heard *great error* in many English books, which unlearned people in their simplicity have taken for great wisdom, and I regretted that they did not know or did not have the gospel teaching among their writings, except only for those who knew Latin, and except for those books which King Alfred wisely translated from Latin to English, which are available.

For this reason, I presumed, trusting in God, to undertake this task, and also because people need good instruction, especially at this time which is the ending of this world, and there will be many perils among humanity before the end comes […].][101] (Emphasis added).

Although Ælfric composed his *Catholic Homilies* primarily for priests to read aloud to the laity, as Malcolm Godden comments, he also expected them to be read and studied by 'more learned' individuals, including members of the laity who could read English as well as his fellow monks and nuns, some of whom would have had a poor command of Latin.[102]

Ælfric's main source for this ambitious project was Paul the Deacon's *Homiliary*, a collection of some 250 Latin homilies by patristic authors including Augustine, Gregory and Bede, commissioned by Charlemagne and completed *c*. 797.[103] However, as James Hurt notes, Ælfric's collection

---

[101] *CH*, I, pp. 6–7.
[102] Godden, ed. *Introduction, Commentary and Glossary*, pp. xxi–xxix.
[103] Ælfric's use of Paul the Deacon's *Homiliary* was first noted by Cyril L. Smetana, 'Aelfric and the Early Medieval Homiliary', *Traditio* 15 (1959), 163–204. In the Latin Preface to the first series, Ælfric acknowledges his debt to Augustine, Jerome, Bede and Gregory, as well as the Carolingian writers Smaragdus and Haymo. For a discussion of Ælfric's exegetical approach to Scripture in the *Catholic Homilies* as a means for instructing the laity in the basic tenets of faith focusing on his Lenten homilies, see Robert K. Upchurch, 'Catechetic

differs from Paul's *Homiliary* in two crucial areas: first, in the remarkable freedom he took in rearranging, excerpting and paraphrasing material from Paul's collected homilies; and second, in his use of the vernacular.[104] As Ælfric explains in the Latin Preface to the first series, he made these choices because he wanted to provide a body of orthodox preaching materials 'for the edification of the unlearned' (*ob ædificationem simplicium*).[105] In order to achieve this goal, Ælfric favours the use of 'plain English' (*simplicem Anglicam*) rather than the deliberately complex 'hermeneutic style' that had recently come into vogue for the writing of both Latin and the vernacular.[106]

In the Old English Preface to the first series, Ælfric seems to imply that there were no scriptural translations available in English at the time of writing except for those which had been commissioned by Alfred:[107]

and me ofhreow þæt hi ne cuðon ne næfdon ða godspellican lare on heora gewritum, buton ðam mannum anum ðe þæt Leden cuðon, and buton þam bocum ðe Ælfred cyning snoterlice awende of Ledene on Englisc, ða synd to hæbbene.[108]

Homiletics: Ælfric's Preaching and Teaching During Lent', in *Companion to Ælfric*, ed. Magennis and Swan, pp. 217–46.

[104] Hurt, *Ælfric*, p. 46. For detailed discussion of the sources of the *Catholic Homilies*, see Malcolm Godden, ed., *Ælfric's Catholic Homilies: Introduction, Commentary and Glossary*, EETS s.s. 18 (Oxford: Oxford University Press, 2000), pp. xxxviii–lxii. On Ælfric's use of his sources more generally, see Joyce Hill, 'Authority and Intertextuality in the Works of Ælfric', *Proceedings of the British Academy* 131 (2005), 157–81.

[105] CH I, Latin Preface, p. 173.

[106] CH I, Latin Preface, p. 173. In his Latin Preface to his Life of St Æthelwold, Ælfric makes a similar commitment to write *breui quidem narratione meatim sed et rustica* ('after my own manner in a brief and unpolished narrative') (text from Michael Lapidge and M. Winterbottom, eds, *Wulfstan of Winchester: The Life of St Æthelwold* [Oxford: Oxford University Press, 1991], *Ælfric's Vita S. Æthelwoldi*, ch. 1, p. 71; translation from Jonathan Wilcox, *Ælfric's Prefaces*, Durham Medieval Texts 9 [Durham: University of Durham, 1994], p. 132). On Ælfric's avoidance of the hermeneutic style in his Latin writings, see Christopher A. Jones, '*Meatim sed et rustica*: Ælfric of Eynsham as a Medieval Latin Author', *The Journal of Medieval Latin* 8 (1998), 1–57; Rebecca Stephenson, 'Ælfric of Eynsham and Hermeneutic Latin: *Meatim Sed et Rustica* Reconsidered', *The Journal of Medieval Latin* 16 (2006), 111–41; Stephenson, *Politics of Language*, pp. 135–87. See also Ann Eljenholm Nichols, 'Ælfric and the Brief Style', *JEGP* 70 (1971), 1–12.

[107] On the translation of Scripture into English in the age of Alfred, see above, Chapters 1 and 2. On Alfred's reputation as a biblical translator after the Norman Conquest, see Conclusion, pp. 249–51.

[108] CH I, Old English Preface, p. 174.

[and I regretted that they did not know nor had the evangelical doctrines among their writings, except for those people who knew Latin, and except for those books which King Alfred wisely translated from Latin into English, which are to be had.]

Non-Alfredian vernacular versions of the Gospels were in fact in circulation, as we have seen, in the form of the *Wessex Gospels* and the corpus of anonymous homilies which included (often inaccurate) translations of pericopes. Like the *Wessex Gospels*, the anonymous homilies tend to lack any substantial exegetical framework to guide the laity in the interpretation of the Gospels.[109] With his *Catholic Homilies*, Ælfric provided a series of accurate translations of gospel pericopes accompanied by authoritative exegesis, effectively replacing the need for rival translations. Ælfric signals his selective approach to gospel translation in the Latin Preface:

> Nec tamen omnia euangelia tangimus per circulum anni, sed illa tantummodo quibus speramus sufficere posse simplicibus ad animarum emendationem, quia saeculares omnia nequeunt capere, quamvis ex ore doctorum audiant.[110]

> [Yet we have not touched on all the gospels throughout the year, but only those which we hope will be sufficient for the improvement of the souls of simple people, because laypeople cannot understand everything, even if they hear it from the mouth of teachers.]

In summarising the content of the Gospels in his later *Treatise on the Old and New Testaments*, Ælfric would point the reader who wishes to gain greater understanding of this text to the *Catholic Homilies*:[111]

> Ic secge þis sceortlice, forðan þe ic gesett hæbbe of þisum feower bocum wel feowertig larspella on Engliscum gereorde, and sumne eacan ðærto. Þa þu miht rædan be þissere race on maran andgite ðonne ic her secge.[112]

> [I say this briefly, because I have written about these four books around forty homilies in the English language, or a little more. There you may read about this story with greater understanding than I might provide here.]

---

[109] Cf. Godden, 'Ælfric and the Vernacular Prose Tradition', pp. 108–9: 'Biblical exegesis figures little in other Old English homilies: there is a little in the Blickling collection but virtually none in the Vercelli Book (except for XVI and XVII) or other anonymous homilies.'
[110] *CH* I, Latin Preface, p. 4.
[111] On the *Treatise*, see Chapter Five.
[112] Marsden, ed. *Heptateuch*, I, pp. 220–1, ll. 579–82.

Evidently, Ælfric saw the *Catholic Homilies* as a more suitable means of conveying the meaning of the Gospels for laypeople than either the more comprehensive *Wessex Gospels* or the less reliable efforts of rival homilists.

Ælfric's Homily on 'The Annunciation of St Mary'

Ælfric's highly selective and exegetical approach to the Gospels is well represented by his homily on 'The Annunciation of St Mary' (*CH* I.13), which revolves around the pericope of Matthew 1.18–25, on the Virgin Birth. This is the same passage discussed above in relation to the Lindisfarne and Rushworth glosses, the *Wessex Gospels* and the *Gospel of Pseudo-Matthew*, allowing us to compare the translation strategies employed by each author.[113] Drawing on two homilies by Bede included in Paul the Deacon's *Homiliary*, one on Luke 1.26–38 (Homily 1.3) and the other on Matthew 1.18–25 (Homily 1.5),[114] as well as a range of other sources, Ælfric uses here the technique known as the 'continuous gloss', a form of exegesis where the gloss is interspersed with the text on which it is based. The Vulgate text describes how Mary was found to be with child before her marriage to Joseph (Mt. 1.18), his intention to keep the matter secret (Mt. 1.19), and the angel's revelation that the child is conceived of the Holy Ghost (Mt. 20–1). This miracle is then interpreted by Matthew as the fulfilment of the messianic prophecies of the Old Testament (Mt. 1.22–3). Ælfric simplifies this complex chronology and begins instead with a careful and thorough exposition of how God, the *ælmihtiga scyppend* ('almighty creator', l. 2), out of pity for the Fall, made known through signs and prophecies his intention to redeem mankind by sending his own son.[115] In order to establish an Old Testament context for the gospel pericope, Ælfric then provides a typological interpretation of Isaiah's prophecy (Is. 7.14), which is itself cited in Mt. 1.23:

> 'Efne sceal mæden geeacnian on hire innoðe and acennan sunu, and his nama bið geciged *Emmanuhel*,' þæt is gereht on urum geðeode, 'God is mid us.'

---

[113] *CH* I.13, pp. 230–47.

[114] For the Latin text, see David Hurst and Jean Fraipont, eds, *Beda Venerabilis: Opera homiletica. Opera rhythmica*, CCSL 122 (Turnhout: Brepols, 1955), 'Homeliarum euangelii libri ii', CPL 1367; for translations, see *Bede the Venerable: Homilies on the Gospels, Book One: Advent to Lent*, trans. Lawrence T. Martin and Dom David Hurst OSB, with contributions by Sister Benedicta Ward SLG (Piscataway, NJ: Gorgias Press, 2010), pp. 19–29, 44–51. For full discussion of the sources of Ælfric's homily on the Annunciation of Mary, see Godden, ed. *Introduction, Commentary and Glossary*, pp. 101–9.

[115] *CH* I.13, pp. 230–2. The *fontes* database notes that Ælfric may have made use of Alcuin's commentary *In Genesim* in this section.

['Behold, a virgin shall conceive in her womb and bring forth a son, and his name shall be *Emmanuel*,' that is interpreted in our language, 'God is with us'.][116]

Ælfric clarifies the meaning of the angel's statement to Joseph that 'all this was done so that it might be fulfilled which the Lord spoke by the prophet' (*ut adimpleretur id quod dictum est a Domino per prophetam*, Mt. 1.22) by introducing Ezekiel's prophecy of the closed gate in the house of God (Ez. 44.2). This typological interpretation of the paradox of the Virgin Birth is then made intelligible to Ælfric's 'unlearned' audience through simple and plain expository language, revolving around a series of clauses beginning *that signifies/that is*:[117]

> Þæt beclysede geat on Godes huse *getacnode* þone halgan mæigðhad þære eadigan Marian. Se Hlaford, ealra hlaforda Hlaford, *þæt is* Crist, becom on hire innoð, and ðurh hi on menniscnysse wearð acenned, and þæt geat bið belocen on ecnysse; *þæt is*, þæt Maria wæs mæden ær ðære cenninge, and mæden on ðære cenninge, and mæden æfter ðære cenninge.

> [*That* closed gate in God's house *signified* the holy virginity of the blessed Mary. The Lord, Lord of all lords, *that is*, Christ, entered her womb, and through her was brought forth in human nature, and that gate is shut for eternity; *that is*, that Mary was a virgin before the birth, a virgin at the birth, and a virgin after the birth.][118] (Emphases added).

Deepening this typological reading of Matthew, Ælfric then gestures to many other prophecies of the Virgin Birth that appear in the *ealdan æ* ('Old Law', i.e. the Old Testament) before turning to other books of the New Testament, citing St Paul's statement that God sent his son in the fulness of time for the redemption of mankind (Galatians 4.4–5) and paraphrasing the Gospel of Luke 1.26–38, from which he derives the name of the angel sent by God to Joseph. At this juncture, Ælfric paraphrases Bede's Homily on Luke 1.26–38, explaining that God sent the angel to Mary as recompense for the Fall – *Us becom ða dead and forwyrd þurh wif, and us becom eft lif and hredding þurh wimman* ('Death and destruction came to us through a woman, and later, life and salvation came to us through a woman') – as well as clarifying the meaning of the angel's name, *þæt is gereht "Godes strengð"* ('which is interpreted, "God's strength"').[119] Still following Bede's

---

[116] *CH* I.13, pp. 232–3.
[117] According to *fontes*, Ælfric probably draws this interpretation of Ezekiel from a sermon by Pseudo-Augustine.
[118] *CH* I.13, pp. 232–3.
[119] *CH* I.13, pp. 234–7.

homily on Luke, this reference to God's strength prompts Ælfric to make yet another link back to the Old Testament, this time in the form of a psalm citation:

> þe se sealmsceop mid þisum wordum herede: 'Drihten is strang and mihtig on gefeohte' (Ps. 23.8) – on ðam gefeohte, butan tweon, þe se Hælend deofol oferwann, and middangeard him ætbræd.

> [which the psalmist praised with these words: 'The Lord is strong and mighty in battle' (Ps. 23.8) – no doubt in the battle in which the Saviour overcame the devil, and took the world from him.][120]

This rich interpretive context is absent from Matthew's Gospel, which, as we have seen, does not name the angel or provide any detailed exposition of the relationship between the Virgin Birth and the Fall, save for the angel's declaration to Joseph, *enim salvum faciet populum suum a peccatis eorum* ('For he shall save his people from their sins', Mt. 1.21). Nor does Matthew offer an interpretation of the miracle of the Virgin Birth as a manifestation of God's strength. By bringing a wealth of references to other parts of the Bible to bear on the gospel pericope from Matthew, as well as Bede's homily on Luke, Ælfric is thus able to spell out the full spiritual significance of the biblical account of the Virgin Birth for his 'unlearned' audience.

Only now, having carefully positioned Matthew's account of the Virgin Birth within the wider context of salvation history, does Ælfric finally return to the gospel pericope itself. A brief citation from the gospel reading, however, immediately prompts a long exegetical passage which moves from an account of Jewish law (the historical or literal level of exegesis) to a meditation on the Holy Trinity (the spiritual):

> "Maria wæs beweddod Iosepe ðam rihtwisan" (Mt. 1.18–19). Hwi wolde God beon acenned of beweddodan mædene? For micclum gesceade, and eac for neode. Þæt Iudeisce folc heold Godes æ on þam timan; seo æ tæhte, þæt man sceolde ælcne wimman þe cild hæfde butan rihtre æwe stænan. Nu ðonne, gif Maria unbeweddod wære and cild hæfde, þonne wolde þæt Iudeisce folc, æfter Godes æ, mid stanum hi oftorfian. Ða wæs heo, ðurh Godes foresceawunge, þam rihtwisan were beweddod, and gehwa wende þæt he ðæs cildes fæder wære, ac he næs. Ac ða ða Ioseph undergeat þæt Maria mid cilde wæs þa wearð he dreorig, and nolde hire genealæcan, ac ðohte þæt he wolde hi diglice forlætan (Mt. 1.19). Þa ða Ioseph þis smeade, þa com him to Godes engel and bebead him þæt he sceolde habban gymene ægðer ge ðære meder ge þæs cildes,

---

[120] *CH* I.13, pp. 236–7, with modifications of punctuation and capitalisation; biblical citation supplied.

and cwæð þæt þæt cild nære of nanum men gestryned, ac wære of þam Halgan Gaste (Mt. 1.20). Nis na hwæðere se Halga Gast Cristes fæder, ac he is genemned to ðære fremminge Cristes menniscnysse forðan ðe he is willa and lufu þæs Fæder and þæs Suna. Nu wearð seo menniscnys þurh þone micclan willan gefremmed, and is ðeah hwæðere heora ðreora weorc untodæledlic. Hi sind þry on hadum, Fæder, and Sunu, and Halig Gast, and an God untodæledlic on anre godcundnysse. Ioseph ða, swa swa him se engel bebead, hæfde gymene ægðer ge Marian ge ðæs cildes (cf. Mt. 1.24), and wæs hyre gewita þæt heo mæden wæs, and wæs Cristes fostorfæder, and mid his fultume and frofre on gehwilcum ðingum him ðenode on ðære menniscnysse.

[*"Mary was betrothed to the righteous Joseph" (Mt. 1.18–19).* Why would God be born of a betrothed virgin? For a great reason, and also of necessity. The Jewish people held God's law at that time; the law directed that any woman who had a child out of lawful wedlock should be stoned. Now, therefore, if Mary had been unmarried and had a child, the Jewish people, according to God's law, would have killed her with stones. And so she was, by God's providence, betrothed to that righteous man, and everyone thought that he was the child's father, but he was not. *When Joseph understood that Mary was with child he became sad, and would not approach her, but thought that he would privately abandon her (Mt. 1.19).* While Joseph was considering this, God's angel came to him and commanded him to take care of both the mother and the child, and said that *the child was not begotten by a man, but by the Holy Spirit (Mt. 1.20)*. Yet the Holy Spirit is not Christ's father, but he is named as the maker of Christ's humanity because he is the will and love of the Father and the Son. Now his humanity was made through the great will, and yet it is the indivisible work of the three of them. They are three in persons, Father, and Son, and Holy Spirit, and one indivisible God in one divine nature. *Joseph then, as the angel had commanded him, took care both of Mary and the child (cf. Mt. 1.24)*, and was her witness that she was a virgin, and was Christ's foster father and, with his support and comfort in all things, served him in his human state.][121]

In keeping with his declared intention to translate only those parts of the Gospels that are required for 'the edification of the simple', Ælfric condenses two gospel verses into one, omitting any material that he felt might confuse the audience of the homily (material translated from the Latin is provided in italics):

---

[121] *CH* I.13, pp. 236–7; biblical citations supplied.

Studying, Reading and Preaching the Gospels

Vulgate	Ælfric
Mt.1.18 Christi autem generatio sic erat cum *esset desponsata* mater eius *Maria Ioseph* antequam convenirent inventa est in utero habens de Spiritu Sancto. ¹⁹ Ioseph autem *vir* eius cum esset *iustus* et nollet eam traducere voluit occulte dimittere eam.	Maria wæs beweddod Iosepe ðam rihtwisan
[¹·¹⁸ Now the generation of Christ was in this wise. When as his mother *Mary was espoused to Joseph*, before they came together, she was found with child, of the Holy Ghost. ¹⁹ Whereupon Joseph her husband, being *a just man*, and not willing publicly to expose her, was minded to put her away privately.]	[Mary was betrothed to the righteous Joseph.]

The contrast with the Lindisfarne and Rushworth glosses, wherein every individual element of the Latin verses is faithfully translated, and the *Wessex Gospels*, which render both verses into idiomatic English, could not be more striking. As a compensatory measure, in place of the word-for-word translation method followed by these earlier authors, Ælfric supplies an extensive commentary on the gospel passage, carefully drawing out its full spiritual meaning and clarifying many points of detail which otherwise might cause confusion. As we have seen, the glossators prevaricated over how best to translate *desponsata*, offering a range of options to their monastic readers. With the unlearned auditors of his homilies in mind, Ælfric can afford no such ambiguity, and therefore opts for absolute clarity first in translating *desponsata* as *beweddod* (the first option provided by both Aldred and Farman and the same term used in the *Wessex Gospels*) and then in providing a detailed explanation for this paradoxical statement that God was born of a wedded virgin. As we shall see, in his *Preface to Genesis* Ælfric would voice his concern that foolish (*dysig*) and unlearned (*ungelæred*) readers of scriptural translations, such as poorly educated priests and lay readers, not knowing the difference between the Old Law (*æ*) and the New, might be misled into believing that it is permissible to have multiple wives on the grounds that the patriarchs did the same.[122] For such readers, the story of the Virgin Birth presents even greater potential for misunderstanding and confusion. In his exegesis of

---

[122] See below, pp. 158–60. On Ælfric's disapproval of marriage among the secular clergy more generally, see Stephenson, *Politics of Language*, pp. 140–2.

Matthew's account of the annunciation, Ælfric therefore carefully explains how the Old Law relates to and is superseded by the New, moving from a succinct summary of Jewish law concerning the punishment for unmarried women derived from Bede's homily on Matthew 1.18–25 to an exposition of the Holy Trinity which has no known source.[123] Ælfric then returns to the gospel pericope, paraphrasing Mt. 1.24 again with reference to Bede's homily. Ælfric continues in this vein for the remainder of the homily, marshalling a wide range of scriptural citations and patristic authorities to provide a rich interpretive context for Matthew's account of the Virgin Birth. This movement from the literal-historical interpretation of Scripture to the spiritual is entirely typical of Ælfric's *Catholic Homilies*, in which the aim is always to provide clear exposition of the Gospels rather than word-for-word or sense-for-sense translation.

Two Palm Sunday Homilies: A Comparison

We find the same interpretive process at work in Ælfric's homily for Palm Sunday ('On the Lord's Passion', *CH* II.14), which contains an abbreviated translation and exegesis of Matthew's account of the crucifixion, the passage discussed above in relation to its treatment in the *Wessex Gospels* (Mt. 27.35–54).[124] As Christopher A. Jones notes, readings from Matthew 26–7 are conventionally assigned for Palm Sunday in the Roman lectionary, while Luke 22–3 and John 18–19 comprise the readings for Good Friday.[125] In order to illustrate Ælfric's exegetical method, this section will compare his Palm Sunday homily with an anonymous homily for the same day, HomS 18 (Cameron no. B.3.2.18), which provides a much closer translation of Matthew 26–7 with only occasional use of John 18–19.[126]

---

[123] For comparison with Ælfric's exegesis of the Holy Trinity in 'De Initio Creaturae' (*CH* I.I), and its reworking in his *Treatise*, see below, pp. 226–35. All of Ælfric's writing on the Trinity is deeply indebted to Augustine's *De Trinitate*.

[124] See above, pp. 100–3.

[125] Jones, 'Early English Homiletic Treatments of Christ's Passion', p. 241. See further Ursula Lenker, *Die westsächsische Evangelienversion und die Perikopenordnungen im angelsächsischen England*, Texte und Untersuchungen zur Englischen Philologie 20 (Munich: Wilhelm Fink, 1997); Godden, ed. *Introduction, Commentary and Glossary*, p. 109.

[126] HomS 18 is attested in three manuscripts: Cambridge Corpus Christi College MS 198 (eleventh/twelfth century), which is the most complete version and forms the basis for the edition cited here (Ker §48); Oxford Bodley 340 and 342 (early eleventh century) (Ker §309); and Cambridge Corpus Christi College MS 162 (early eleventh century) (Ker §38). For the texts, see Kenneth Gordon Schaefer, ed., 'An Edition of Five Old English Homilies for Palm Sunday, Holy Saturday, and Easter Sunday' (unpublished doctoral dissertation, Columbia University, 1972). This homily, together with six other anonymous Palm Sunday homilies,

Don Scragg observes that this anonymous text is one of a group of Easter homilies associated with Canterbury, each of which relates the events of the Easter period 'almost verbatim' and in which 'homiletic comment is sparse'.[127] Indeed, as Aidan Conti notes, HomS 18 'lacks any exegetical treatment of its subject, and thereby violates the pastoral directive' of Ælfric and Wulfsige that priests should explicate the *angyt* ('meaning') of the gospel on Sundays and massdays.[128] Hence, in rendering Matthew 27.39–42, the anonymous homilist sticks closely to the Vulgate source:

> and ða forðbigferendan hi yfelsacodon on hine and hrysedon heora heafod and cwædon, 'Uah! Ær ðu towurpe Godes templ and æfter þreora daga fæce eft getimbrodest; gif ðu sy Godes Sunu, hæl þe sylfne and astig of þisse rode and we gelefað on þe.' And gelice hi on bismer cwædon, 'Manige oðre he hale gedyde, and hine sylfne he ne mæg gehælen. Gif ðu si Cyning Iudea, astih nu of þisse rode.'[129]

> [and those passing by blasphemed on him and shook their heads and said, 'Look! Before you destroyed God's temple and after three days you rebuilt it; if you are God's Son, save yourself and come down from this cross and we will believe in you." And similarly they said in mockery, 'He saved many others, and he cannot save himself. If you are the King of the Jews, come down now from this cross.']

---

is now available in an online edition together with manuscript images via Winfried Rudolf, Thomas N. Hall, *et al.*, eds, *ECHOE Online: Electronic Corpus of Anonymous Homilies in Old English*, https://echoe.uni-goettingen.de, accessed 2 November 2024. The most detailed study of the homilist's translation technique is R. D. Fulk, 'The Refashioning of Christ's Passion in an Anonymous Old English Homily for Palm Sunday (HomS 18)', *JEGP* 116 (2017), 415–37.

[127] Donald G. Scragg, ed., *The Vercelli Homilies*, EETS o.s. 300 (Oxford: Oxford University Press, 1992), p. 1. Another of the homilies in this group is Vercelli Homily I, which translates the gospel pericope for Good Friday, John 18–19, while incorporating material from Matthew 26–7 as well as the other gospels. As Scragg comments, the homily termed 'Vercelli I' is attested in two versions, one (in the late tenth-century Vercelli Book) sticks closely to the Vulgate text of John 18–19, the other, attested in the eleventh-century manuscript Bodley 340/342 (where it is appears as a supplement for Ælfric's Palm Sunday Homily, as he did not provide a homily for Good Friday) as well as two other manuscripts, 'moves away from a literal translation to give a more fluent rendering, substituting indirect for direct speech and modernizing the language' (*Vercelli Homilies*, p. 1); for the text and commentary, see Scragg, ed., *Vercelli Homilies*, pp. 1–47.

[128] Aidan Conti, 'An Anonymous Homily for Palm Sunday, *The Dream of the Rood*, and the Progress of Ælfric's Reform', *N&Q* n.s. 48 (2001), 377–80, at 377.

[129] Schaefer, p. 30, ll. 168–74.

Although the anonymous homilist also omits Matthew's reference to the chief priests, scribes and moneylenders (27.41), on the whole, HomS 18 presents a close rendering of the gospel pericope in idiomatic Old English, with small but regular modifications of syntax and occasional omissions. Certainly, the approach of the anonymous homilist is much more faithful to the biblical source than the sense-for sense, functional equivalence approach taken by Ælfric, who as we shall see below compresses the two mocking speeches addressed to Christ into one. Moreover, in marked contrast to Ælfric's learned deployment of patristic authorities in his strictly orthodox exegesis of Matthew 27–9, the anonymous homilist appears to have supplemented their (often imperfect) knowledge of the scriptural narrative by borrowing certain imagery and phrasing from the popular Old English poem *The Dream of the Rood*.[130] Although the precise dating of the anonymous homily is unknown, linguistic evidence certainly places it before Ælfric, possibly in ninth-century Mercia.[131] Table 2 below compares the anonymous homilist's translation of Matthew 27.35–42 with the more faithful rendering of the same passage in the *Wessex Gospels*:

While the *Wessex Gospels* provide a complete translation of Matthew 27.35–42, the anonymous homilist freely edits his source, omitting, for example, the reference to Jesus in verse 37. The homilist also opts for a plainer prose style, lacking stylistic flourishes such as the repeated front-placement of *Soðlice/Witodlice* that we noted above in the *Wessex Gospels* (e.g. Mt. 27.35, 39). On the other hand, the homilist does include the Latin text of Isaiah's prophecy before providing the translation in verse 35, whereas the *Wessex Gospels* only supplies the translation. As previously noted, the *Wessex Gospels* appear to have been prepared for a reader who did not need access to the Latin. The presence of the Latin quotation in the anonymous homily, by contrast, reflects how this text served as a supplement to the liturgical reading of the Latin gospel pericope. By supplying the Latin quotation, the homilist anchors the translation in the scriptural source, underlining its status as an adjunct to the Vulgate text used in the liturgy. Although the anonymous homilist occasionally misconstrues the

---

[130] Two passages absent from the gospel accounts, namely an account of the cross bowing down to Joseph and Nicodemus and the carving out of tomb from *beorhtan stane* ('bright stone') for Christ, have direct parallels in *The Dream of the Rood* and it has been suggested that the homilist drew on this popular poem as a source: see Dorothy Horgan, 'The Dream of the Rood and a Homily for Palm Sunday', *N&Q* n.s. 29 (1982), 388–91; Conti, 'An Anonymous Homily for Palm Sunday'; and Fulk, 'Refashioning of Christ's Passion', 427–33.

[131] Schaefer, p. 47; Paul E. Szarmach, 'The Earlier Homily: *De Parasceve*', in *Studies in Earlier Old English Prose*, ed. Szarmach, pp. 381–99, at 382; Fulk, 'Refashioning of Christ's Passion', 416–19; Jones, 'Early English Homiletic Treatments of Christ's Passion', p. 243.

Table 2. Comparison of Matthew 27.35–42 in Vulgate, Wessex Gospels and HomS18.

Vulgate	Wessex Gospels	HomS 18
35 Postquam autem crucifixerunt eum, diviserunt vestimenta eius, sortem mittentes: ut impleretur quod dictum est per prophetam dicentem: 'Diviserunt sibi vestimenta mea, et super vestem meam miserunt sortem.' [And after they had crucified him, they divided his garments, casting lots; that it might be fulfilled which was spoken by the prophet, saying: 'They divided my garments among them; and upon my vesture they cast lots.']	35 Soþlice æfter þam þe hig hyne on rode ahengon hig todældon hys reaf: and wurpon hlot þærofer þæt wære gefylled þæt ðe gecweden wæs þurh ðone witegan and þus cwæð: 'Hig todældon heom mine reaf, and ofer mine reaf hig wurpon hlot.' [Truly after they had hanged him on a cross they divided his garments, and they cast lots thereover that it might be fulfilled that which was spoken by the prophet, and thus said: 'They divided my garments among them, and upon my garments they cast lots.']	35 Þa he ahangen wæs, þa wæs se cwide gefulled þe wæs þurh þa witegan gecweden, 'Diuiserunt sibi uestimenta mea, et super uestem meam miserunt sortem: Hi todældon him mine reaf, and ofer min hrægl hi sændon hlyt.' [When he was hanged, then the prophecy was fulfilled that was spoken by the prophet, 'Diuiserunt sibi uestimenta mea, et super uestem meam miserunt sorten: They divided my garments among them, and upon my garments they cast lots.']
36 Et sedentes servabant eum. [And they sat and watched him.]	36 And hig beheoldon hyne sittende: [And they beheld him sitting.]	36 And hi þær sæton and hine heoldon, [And they sat there and beheld him.]
37 Et imposuerunt super caput eius causam ipsius scriptam: 'Hic est Iesus Rex Iudaeorum.' [And they put over his head his cause written: 'This is Jesus the King of the Jews.']	37 and hig asetton ofer hys heafod hys gylt þus awritene: 'Ðis ys se Haelynd Iudea Cyning.' [And they put over his head his charge thus written: 'This is the Saviour, King of the Jews.']	37 and setton ofer his heafod on bismer, 'Þis is Cyning Iudea. [And they put over his head in mockery, 'This is the King of the Jews.']
38 Tunc crucifixi sunt cum eo duo latrones: unus a dextris, et unus a sinistris. [Then were crucified with him two thieves: one on the right hand, and one on the left.]	38 Ða wæron ahangen mid him twegen sceaþan, an on þa swiðran healfe and oðer on þa wynstran. [Then were hanged with him two thieves, one on the right side and the other on the left.]	38 And hi ða ahengon mid him twegen sceaðan, oðerne on þa swiðran healfe, oðerne on ða wynstran healfe. [And then they hanged with him two thieves, one on the right side, the other on the left side.]

³⁹ Witodlice þa wegferendan hyne bysmeredon and cwehton heora heafod	³⁹ Praetereuntes autem blasphemabant eum moventes capita sua,	³⁹ And þa forðbigferendan hi yfelsacodon on hine and hrysedon heora heafod
[Indeed, those that passed by mocked him and shook their heads]	[And they that passed by, blasphemed him, wagging their heads,]	[And those passing by blasphemed on him and shook their heads]
⁴⁰ and cwædon: 'Wa! þæt ðes towyrpð godes templ, and on prim dagum hyt eft getimbrað. Gehael nu þe sylfne: gyf þe sy Godes Sunu, ga nyþer of þære rode.'	⁴⁰ et dicentes: 'Vah! qui destruis templum Dei, et in triduo illud reaedificas: salva temetipsum: si Filius Dei es, descende de cruce.'	⁴⁰ and cwædon, 'Uah! Ær ðu towurpe Godes templ 7 æfter þreora daga fæce eft getimbrodest; gif ðu sy Godes Sunu, hæl þe sylfne 7 astig of þisse rode 7 we gelefað on þe.'
[and they said: 'Look! You that destroy God's temple, and in three days afterwards rebuild it, now save yourself: if you are God's son, come down from the cross.']	[And saying: Vah, you who destroyed the temple of God, and in three days rebuilt it: save your own self: if you are the Son of God, come down from the cross.]	[and said, 'Look! Before you destroyed God's temple and after three days you rebuilt it; if you are God's Son, save yourself and come down from this cross and we will believe in you.']
⁴¹ Eac sacerda ealdras hyne bysmerdon mid þam bocerum and mid þam ealdrum and cwædun:	⁴¹ Similiter et principes sacerdotum illudentes cum scribis et senioribus dicebant:	⁴¹ And gelice hi on bismer cwædon,
[Also the chief priests mocked him, with the scribes and the ancients, and said:]	[In like manner also the chief priests, with the scribes and ancients, mocking, said:]	[And they mocked him in the same way saying,]
⁴² 'Oþere he gehælde. and hyne sylfne gehælan ne mæg. Gyf he Israhela Cyning sy ga nu nyþer of þære rode and we gelyfað hym.'	⁴² 'Alios salvos fecit, seipsum salvum facere: si Rex Israel est, descendat nunc de cruce, et credimus ei.'	⁴² 'Manige oðre he hale gedyde, and hine sylfne he ne mæg gehælen. Gif ðu si Cyning Iudea, astih nu of þisse rode.'
[He saved others, and he cannot save himself. If he be the king of Israel, let him now come down from the cross, and we will believe him.']	[He saved others; himself he cannot save. If he is the king of Israel, come down from the cross and we will believe him.']	[He saved many others, and he cannot save himself. If you are the King of the Jews, come down now from this cross.']

Latin source, for the most part the remainder of the pericope is faithfully translated up to the end of Matthew 27.66, the final verse in the chapter, which describes the placement of Christ's body in a sepulchre which is to be guarded for three days.[132] The homily is then rounded off with a brief doxology, a conventional expression of praise used to end a hymn or sermon, typically devoted to the Trinity, as is the case here:

> [27.66] and him þærofer gesæton and hæfdon þæron gebroht þæs Hælendes lichaman, þe nu leofað and rixað mid Fæder and mid Sunu and mid ðam Halgum Gaste, a in ealra worulda woruld soðlice buton ende. Amen.[133]
>
> [and they placed him thereover and they had brought therein the Saviour's body, *who now rules with the Father and with the Son and with the Holy Ghost, eternally throughout all the world of worlds, truly without end. Amen.*] (Emphases added).

This brief passage is the nearest the anonymous homilist comes to a spiritual exegesis of the Passion, though as Fulk notes, the statement that Christ rules *mid Sunu* ('with the Son') is 'nonsensical', reflecting the author's limited training in the study of the Gospels.[134]

Following his directive for priests to clarify the gospel reading during Mass, and in sharp contrast to the anonymous homily, Ælfric's extensive Palm Sunday homily weaves together various passages from Matthew 26–7 with extracts from all four gospels, creating a unified 'gospel harmony.' This synthesis is further enriched by extensive references to Bede's Commentaries on Mark and Luke, along with works by Smaragdus and Haymo.[135] In the opening words of his homily, Ælfric signals his goal of providing priests with a single, condensed version of the Passion together with an interpretation of its spiritual meaning in plain language:

---

[132] Schaefer, p. 44, notes that in Mt. 27.64 the homilist mistakes the Latin *fors* ('chance') as a form of the noun *fortis* ('strength'), producing the reading *þaet nane strange ne cuman* ('that none should come forcefully'); see also Conti, 'An Anonymous Homily for Palm Sunday', 378; Fulk, 'Refashioning of Christ's Passion', 420–3.

[133] Schaefer, p. 33, ll. 212–15. Vercelli Homily I concludes with a similar doxology, though here the homilist directly addresses the audience with an exhortation to *men ða leofestan* ('most beloved people') (Scragg, ed., *Vercelli Homilies*, pp. 40–3).

[134] Fulk, 'Refashioning of Christ's Passion', 424–5.

[135] *Fontes* notes that Jerome's Commentary on Matthew and Augustine's Tractates on John lie behind these sources and suggests that both may have been used by Ælfric.

Drihtnes ðrowunge we willað *gedafenlice* eow secgan on Engliscum gereorde, *and ða gerynu samod. Na swa ðeah to langsumlice*, gif we hit swa gelogian magon.[136]

[We will *suitably* relate to you the Lord's Passion in English speech, *and the mysteries together. Not, however, at too great a length*, if we can arrange it.] (Emphases added).

Ælfric meets the challenge of relating Christ's Passion in a fittingly brief manner through combining or arranging (*gelogian*) a translation of elements of all four gospels into a single, coherent paraphrase, a practice to which he will return in his treatments of Joshua, Judges and other parts of the Bible.[137] For example, the Vulgate text of Matthew 17.1–5 describes how Jesus took Peter, James and John with him into a high mountain (17.1), where he was transfigured, his face shining like the sun and his garments as white as snow (17.2), and the prophets Moses and Elias stood talking with him (17.3), before Peter asks Jesus if he wishes them to make three temples, for him and the two prophets (17.4); while Peter was speaking, a bright cloud overshadows them and a voice says: *hic est Filius meus dilectus, in quo mihi bene conplacuit: ipsum audite* ('This is my beloved Son, in whom I am well pleased: hear ye him') (17.5).[138] In Ælfric's homily, these five biblical verses are condensed into a short passage which provides the key elements of the scriptural source in terms that are easily understood:

Moyses and Elias eac swilce sædon his ðrowunge on ær uppon anre dune ðe se Hælend astah mid ðrim leorningcnihtum, and his ansyn ætforan him eal scean swa swa sunne, and his gewæda scinon on snawes hwitnysse. Þa wolde Petrus slean sona ðreo geteld, for ðære gesihðe, ac ðær swegde ða stemn ðæs Heofonlican Fæder healice of wolcne: 'Ðes is min leofa sunu, on ðam me wel licað: gehyrað hine.'[139]

[Moses and Elias also previously spoke about his passion up on a mountain which the Saviour ascended with three disciples, and his countenance shone before them as the sun, and his clothes shone with the whiteness of snow. Then Peter wished to pitch three tents because of that vision, but the voice of the Heavenly Father sounded then from a cloud on high, 'This is my beloved son, with whom I am well pleased: obey him.']

---

[136] *CH* II.14, p. 137.

[137] See below, Chapter Five.

[138] Ælfric may also have had in mind here the equivalent passage in Luke 9.30–5, which shares many details with Matthew.

[139] *CH* II.14, p. 137 (with modifications).

By beginning his account of the Transfiguration with the Old Testament prophets, Moses and Elias, rather than Christ's ascent of the mountain, Ælfric emphasises the typological significance of this event. The names of the three disciples are omitted for the sake of concision, though Peter's name is subsequently supplied at the moment when he moves to make the three temples, rendered as *geteld* ('tents') in Ælfric's domesticating translation. The shift from paraphrase into a word-for-word translation of God the Father's direction to obey his son (Mt. 17.15) reflects the doctrinal importance of this biblical phrase. As we shall see, this theme of obedience – a moral lesson which Ælfric wishes to convey to his audience – will emerge as a key concern in the translation of the Heptateuch in which Ælfric would play a major role soon after he completed his two series of homilies.

Subsequent biblical passages from all four gospels are similarly abbreviated as Ælfric moves briskly through the story of the Passion by combining the accounts of Luke 22.1–5, Matthew 26.15 and Mark 14.11, which variously describe how the Jewish elders deliberated on how they might slay Jesus Christ and how Satan then entered into Judas Iscariot, who accepted their money to betray him. In paraphrasing Matthew 26.20 (*vespere autem facto discumbebat cum duodecim discipulis*, 'But when it was evening, he sat down with his twelve disciples'), Ælfric further domesticates his source by clarifying that these events took place *on ðam fiftan dæge, ðe ge ðunres hatað* ('on the fifth day, that you call Thursday').[140] The following passage, which describes how Christ washed the feet of his disciples, combines elements of Matthew 26.2 and John 13.4–5 and 12–15, to which Ælfric appends his own exegesis, again moving from the literal explanation that 'externally' (*wiðutan*) Christ cleaned the mud from their feet, to the spiritual interpretation that Christ purged them 'within [...] of the dirt of deadly sin' (*wiðinnan* [...] *fram eallum horwum healicra leahtra*).[141] A moral interpretation then completes the exegesis, as Ælfric describes how Christ commanded the disciples to wash each other's sins and 'to manifest humility with kind service to brothers' (*eadmodnysse cyðan mid geswære ðenunge symle gebroðrum*).

Having carefully explained to his audience how they should apply the lesson of this biblical episode to their own lives, Ælfric returns to his paraphrase of the four gospels, synthesising their respective accounts of how each of the disciples asked Christ which of them will betray him, and of how he blessed bread and wine signifying his body and blood and offered it to them. At this juncture, Ælfric again interrupts the biblical summary to provide another exegetical passage, this time derived from

---

[140] *CH* II.14, p. 138.
[141] *CH* II.14, p. 138.

Jerome's Commentary on Matthew, in order to clarify that Jesus' statement that it would have been better for whoever should betray him to have not been born (Matthew 26.24) does not mean that such a man had been anywhere before he was born, but simply 'that it were better for him that he had never been, than that he should be evil' (*þæt him betere wære þæt he næfre nære, ðonne he yfele wære*).[142] Ælfric then draws a moral lesson from Haymo of Auxerre, who explained that those who imitate Judas in betraying truth for money will share his fate in the torments of hell. Through frequent moralising interjections such as this, Ælfric continually ensures that his 'unlearned' audience is made fully aware of the relevance of the gospel story to their own spiritual lives.

Further deepening the exegetical framework for the gospel narrative, Ælfric then turns to Smaragdus, from whom he draws the following typological interpretation:

> Æfter gereorde Crist bletsode husel, for ðan ðe he wolde *ða Ealdan Æ* ær gefyllan, and siððan ða *Niwan Gecyðnysse* halwendlice ongunnon.[143]

> [After the meal Christ blessed the Eucharist, because he first wished to fulfil *the Old Law*, and afterwards to begin *the New Covenant* in a salutary way.] (Emphases added).

As we shall see in the next chapter, Ælfric was greatly concerned that priests and their parishioners should know the essential difference between the Old and New Law. Throughout his *Catholic Homilies*, Ælfric constantly emphasises this difference by carefully explaining how individual gospel verses fulfil the prophecies of the Old Testament.

Returning to the scriptural narrative of the Last Supper, Ælfric provides a close, word-for-word translation of Matthew 26.31–5, Christ's warning to Peter that he will deny him three times before the cock crows, before paraphrasing further passages from Matthew, John and Luke to produce a succinct account of Judas' betrayal of Christ in the Garden of Gethsemane. Christ's reproval of Peter, in which he states that he could have summoned twelve legions of angels to protect him, leads Ælfric into another exegetical passage, which quotes from Jerome's Commentary on Matthew on the precise number of angels implied, and possibly Candidus Fuldensis' *Opusculum de passione Domini* on how Christ did not desire the death of his disciples, but preserved them as teachers to all the nations. In the same manner, Ælfric continues to paraphrase the combined gospel accounts, with further reference to patristic and Carolingian exegetes, as the narrative progresses towards

---

[142] *CH* II.14, p. 139.
[143] *CH* II.14, p. 139 (with modifications).

the climactic moment of the crucifixion itself. From Bede's Commentary on Mark, Ælfric derives the interpretation of the soldiers' mockery of Christ as signifying that they held him in scorn, that the red robe signified the blood of Christ's death and that the sin of Adam is now forgiven because of Christ's thorny crown. For the account of the crucifixion itself, Ælfric first paraphrases Mark 15.22–3, in which the soldiers offer Christ a bitter drink, to which he adds an interpretation derived from Jerome that the drink signified the bitterness of his death, which he quickly cast away with his resurrection. He then continues with John 19.18–20 and 23–4, describing the crucifixion of the two thieves alongside Christ while probably drawing on Sedulius' interpretation of the four nails as signifying Christ's redemption of the four regions of the earth.[144]

Up until this point, Ælfric's Palm Sunday homily has comprised short, translated excerpts from various gospels and paraphrases interspersed with homiletic exegesis. It is only at this advanced point in the homily that we encounter the first sustained passage of gospel translation, a substantial part of Matthew 27.39–42, which bears comparison with the equivalent section of the *Wessex Gospels* (Table 3).[145]

As is evident from Table 3, Ælfric has considerably condensed these four verses from Matthew, omitting details deemed extraneous such as the Jews' shaking of their heads (27.39), the repetition of their accusation that he had saved others (27.42) and the inclusion of the chief priests, scribes and ancients among his accusers (27.41). Further potentially confusing information, such as the Jews' reference to Christ's prior destruction and rebuilding of the temple (27.40), is similarly glossed over, resulting in a much more streamlined narrative that caters to the needs of an unlearned audience listening to a homily being read aloud in church.

By contrast with the anonymous homilist discussed above, Ælfric supplements his paraphrase of Matthew's account of the mocking of Christ with a translation of Luke 23.39–43, in which one of the thieves asks Christ to prove his nature by saving him, only to be reproved by the second, who asks Christ to remember him when he comes into his kingdom. Following Jerome, Ælfric interprets the anagogical significance of this passage from Luke, explaining that the second thief passed happily to heaven and *se oðer gewende wælhreaw to helle* ('the other went bloodthirsty to hell'), while the two thieves together *getacnode* ('signified') on the one hand the Jewish people, who would not believe in Christ and mocked him on the gallows, and on the other the heathens, who believed in him and reproved the

---

[144] *Carmen paschale* 5, ll. 188–95.
[145] Cf. Luke 23.34, 39–43, which may have served as another source for this passage, though Matthew seems the more likely given Ælfric's use in the same passage of Jerome's Commentary on Matthew.

Table 3. Comparison of Matthew 27.39–42 in Vulgate, *Wessex Gospels* and Ælfric's Palm Sunday Homily.

Vulgate	Wessex Gospels	Ælfric
[39] Praetereuntes autem blasphemabant eum moventes capita sua,	[39] Witodlice þa wegferendan hyne bysmeredon and cwehton heora heafod	[39] Ða reðan iudei beheoldon feorran.
[[39] And they that passed by, blasphemed him, wagging their heads,]	[Indeed, those that passed by mocked him and shook their heads]	[Then the hateful Jews beheld at a distance.]
[40] et dicentes: Vah! qui destruis templum Dei, et in triduo illud reaedificas: salva temetipsum: si Filius Dei es, descende de cruce.	[40] and cwædon: "Wa! þæt ðes towyrpð godes templ and on þrim dagum hyt eft getimbrað. Gehæl nu þe sylfne. Gyf þe sy Godes Sunu, ga nyþer of þære rode;	and mid hospe clypodon to Hælendum Criste: "Gif ðu Godes Sunu sy, ga of ðære rode.
[40] And saying: Vah, you who destroyed the temple of God, and in three days rebuilt it: save your own self: if you are the Son of God, come down from the cross.]	[and they said, 'Alas! You that destroy God's temple, and in three days afterwards rebuild it, now save yourself: if you are God's Son, come down from the cross.]	[and with contempt shouted to the Saviour Christ: "If you are God's Son, come from the cross.]
[41] Similiter et principes sacerdotum illudentes cum scribis et senioribus dicebant:	[41] Eac sacerda ealdras hyne bysmerdon mid þam bocerum and mid þam ealdrum and cwædun:	
[[41] In like manner also the chief priests, with the scribes and ancients, mocking, said:]	[Also the chief priests mocked him, with the scribes and the ancients, and said:]	

[42] Alios salvos fecit, seipsum non potest salvum facere: si Rex Israel est, descendat nunc de cruce, et credimus ei:

[[42] He saved others; himself he cannot save. If he be the King of Israel, let him now come down from the cross, and we will believe him.]

[42] Oþere he gehælde, and hyne sylfne ne mæg. Gyf he Israhela Cyning sy, ga nu nyþer of þære rode and we gelyfað hym." and we siððan swa on ðe gelyfað."*

[[42] He saved others, and he cannot save himself. If he is the King of Israel, come down from the cross and we will believe him.] [and then we will believe in you."]

* *CH* II.14, pp. 145–46.

others *mid geleafan* ('with faith').[146] Drawing on the authority of the Church Fathers and the Gospel of Luke, Ælfric thus presents a simple and clear moral lesson for the unlearned on the rewards of faith and the punishments of unbelief.

For the remainder of his Palm Sunday Homily, Ælfric takes the same eclectic approach to the exposition of the pericope from Matthew, freely paraphrasing and translating passages from the three other gospels and interspersing these translations with exegesis derived from Jerome, Smaragdus, Bede, Candidus Fuldensis, Augustine and Haymo. Indeed, the pericope of the day, Mt. 26–7, is not directly cited again in the homily until the closing lines, where Ælfric paraphrases Mt. 27.62–6, before adding his own Christological conclusion (indicated below in italics) and Trinitarian doxology:

> Hwæt ða Iudei eodon to Pilate, bædon þæt he bude ða byrgene besettan mid wacelum weardum, þæt he ne wurde forstolen, and ðam folce gesæd þæt he sylf aryse. Þa geðafode Pilatus þæt hi hine besæton mid ymtrymincge, and ða ðruh geinnsegelodon; *ac Crist aras swa ðeah, of ðam deaðe gesund, on ðam ðriddan dæge æfter his ðrowunge, oferswiððum deaðe.* Sy him a wuldor mid his Heofonlican Fæder and ðam Halgan Gaste, on anre godcudnysse on ecere worulde. Amen.[147]

> [Whereupon the Jews went to Pilate, asking that he would command the sepulchre to be beset with watchful guards, so that he might not be stolen, and it be said to the people that he had arisen himself. Then Pilate permitted them that they might watch him with a guard, and to seal up the sepulchre; *but Christ arose, nevertheless, sound on the third day after his Passion, having overcome death.* Glory be to him with his Heavenly Father and that Holy Ghost, in one Godhead for eternity. Amen.]

Whereas the anonymous homilist simply tacks on the Trinitarian doxology to the final verse of Matthew 27, Ælfric bridges the gap between the sealing up of Christ's body in the tomb and him ruling in eternity by adding the crucial detail that Christ rose on the third day, defeating death.[148] With this intervention, Ælfric achieves the goal he had set for

---

[146] *CH* II.14, p. 146.
[147] *CH* II.14, p. 149.
[148] Ælfric may have had in mind various scriptural passages here, including Luke 24.7: *quia oportet Filium hominis tradi in manus hominum peccatorum et crucifigi et die tertia resurgere* ('The Son of man must be delivered into the hands of sinful men and be crucified and the third day rise again'), I Corinthians 15.4: *et quia sepultus est et quia resurrexit tertia die secundum scripturas* ('And that he was buried: and that he rose again on the third day according to the Scriptures'); and I Corinthians 15.54–7: *cum autem mortale hoc induerit inmortalitatem tunc fiet sermo qui scriptus est: absorta est mors in victoria. Ubi est mors victoria tua. Ubi*

himself in the opening of the Palm Sunday homily, to relate the essential mystery (*gerynu*) of Matthew's narrative of the Passion in plain English, leaving the laity in no doubt as to the full spiritual meaning (*angyt*) of the gospel reading for the day.

Ælfric's project

Comparison of Ælfric's Palm Sunday Homily with the anonymous homily for the same occasion, as well as the corresponding passages in the *Wessex Gospels*, reveals a good deal about the variety of approaches taken to the translation, adaptation and interpretation of the Gospels in the late Old English period. The various errors and misunderstandings in the anonymous homily, as well as its use of vernacular poetry, provides a window onto the world of popular piety beyond the immediate influence of the Benedictine Reform, in which a priest might produce his own – at times faulty – translation of scriptural passages used in the liturgy in order to meet his own pastoral needs. Indeed, Ælfric set out to compose his two series of *Catholic Homilies* to correct the *mycel gedwyld* ('great error') contained in such English writings, supplying priests with a set of more accurate scriptural translations supplemented by orthodox interpretations. Equipped with such carefully constructed homilies, English priests should now be able 'to bark and preach to the unlearned' (*beorcan and bodigan þam læwedum*) in precisely the manner recommended by Ælfric and Bishop Wulfsige. In their exegetical approach, the *Catholic Homilies* anticipate Ælfric's paraphrases of the first two historical books of the Old Testament, Joshua and Judges, as well as his *Treatise on the Old and New Testaments* discussed in the next two chapters.

Conclusion

This chapter has highlighted the diversity of approaches to the translation, adaptation and interpretation of the Gospels in tenth-century England. The form of each Old English rendering of the Gospels is determined by its purpose: the formal-equivalence interlinear glosses were added to Latin Gospel books to guide monastic readers in understanding the Latin text

---

est mors stimulus tuus. Stimulus autem mortis peccatum est virtus vero peccati lex. Deo autem gratias qui dedit nobis victoriam per Dominum nostrum Iesum Christum ('And when this mortal has put on immortality, then shall come to pass the saying that is written: Death is swallowed up in victory. O death, where is your victory? O death, where is your sting? Now the sting of death is sin: and the power of sin is the law. But thanks be to God, who has given us the victory through our Lord Jesus Christ.')

and to aid them in the practice of *lectio divina*; the functional equivalence *Wessex Gospels* were probably originally intended for private reading, perhaps by a lay patron or priest, though they were later repurposed for liturgical use; and the anonymous and Ælfrician homilies were designed for the use of priests and for the edification of the unlearned laity.[149]

In the prayer appended to the second series of *Catholic Homilies*, Ælfric reflected on how this project would benefit the *Angelcynn*, before announcing that he had no intention to produce any further translations of the Gospels or homilies:

> Ic ðancige þam Ælmihtigum Scyppende mid ealre heortan, þæt he me synfullum þæs geuðe, þæt *ic* ðas twa bec him to lofe and to wurðmynte *Angelcynne onwreah ðam ungelæredum*; ða gelæredan ne beðurfon þyssera boca, for ðan ðe him mæg heora agen lar genihtsumian. *Ic cweðe nu þæt ic næfre heononforð ne awende godspel oþþe godspeltrahtas of Ledene on Englisc.* Gif hwa ma awendan wille, ðonne bidde ic hine for Godes lufon þæt he gesette his boc onsundron fram ðam twam bocum ðe we awend habbað we truwiað þurh Godes diht. Sy him a wuldor on ecnysse.[150]

> [I thank the Almighty Creator with all my heart, that he has granted me, a sinner, that, to his praise and honour, *I have disclosed to the English race* these two books, *for the unlearned*; the learned have no need of these books, because their own learning may suffice them. *I say now that I never henceforth will translate gospel or gospel-expositions from Latin into English.* If anyone wishes to translate more, then I will pray him, for love of God, that he set his book apart from the two books that we have translated, we trust through God's direction. Be to him ever glory to eternity.] (Emphases added).

By urging future Gospel translators and interpreters to differentiate their efforts from his own work, Ælfric positions his *Catholic Homilies* as the authoritative source of biblical interpretation in English. Although he would never devote as much attention to the Gospels again, Ælfric's career as a biblical translator was nevertheless far from over. In the next chapter, we will see how Ælfric's abiding concern with the correct understanding (*angyt*) of Scripture, and his reservations about making Old Testament material available to the laity in English, would determine the course of his involvement in the Old English Heptateuch.

---

[149] As we shall see in the Conclusion, pp. 247–52, the *Wessex Gospels* and *Catholic Homilies* in particular enjoyed long afterlives, continuing to attract readers and influence English translations of the Bible into the late medieval and early modern periods.

[150] *CH* II.40, p. 345 (with modifications).

4

A Perilous Task: Making the Old English Heptateuch

By the end of the tenth century, Old English prose translations and paraphrases of key biblical texts including the Psalms, the Old and New Testament Laws and Gospels were already in circulation. It was around this time that a team of scholars in the south of England embarked on an ambitious series of prose translations of the Pentateuch, the first five books of the Old Testament.[1] The remarkable success of this project is attested by the large number of surviving manuscript witnesses dating from the first half of the eleventh century to the twelfth.[2] The two major extant manuscripts are Oxford, Bodleian Library, MS Laud Misc. 509 (MS L) (*c.* 1050–1100) and London, British Library, Cotton MS Claudius B. IV (MS B) (*c.* 1000–1050). MS L contains increasingly abbreviated translations of the books of the Pentateuch (Genesis, Exodus, Leviticus, Numbers and Deuteronomy), to which were appended Ælfric's paraphrases of the first two historical books (Joshua and Judges).[3] These seven biblical translations and paraphrases which form the core of MS L were therefore given the collective title 'Heptateuch' by Edward Thwaites in his seventeenth-century edition, though it is unclear whether they were ever conceived of

---

[1] For an overview, see Morrell, *Manual of Old English Biblical Materials*, pp. 3–13.
[2] On the continuing interest in the Heptateuch after the Norman Conquest, see Conclusion, pp. 244–52.
[3] Laud Misc. 509 (MS L; Ker §344) is the basis of Marsden's edition, from which all citations are taken. The contents are: Ælfric's *Preface to Genesis* (fols 1^r–3^r); *Genesis* (fols 3^r–37^r); *Exodus* (fols 37^r–65^v); *Leviticus* (65^v–72^r); *Numbers* (72^r–82^v); *Deuteronomy* (fols 82^v–98^v); *Joshua* (fols 98^v–107^r); *Judges* (fols 108^v–115^v); Ælfric's *Letter to Wulfgeat* (fols 115^v–120^v); and Ælfric's *Treatise on the Old and New Testaments* (*Letter to Sigeweard*) (fols 120^v–141^v). The main text is the work of a single late eleventh-century scribe, perhaps working at Christ Church Canterbury. Much of the text is heavily glossed in a Latin hand of the late eleventh to early twelfth century; on the gloss as a reassertion of the Latin text of the Vulgate, see Richard A. Marsden, 'Latin in the Ascendant: The Interlinear Gloss of Oxford, Bodleian Library, Laud Misc. 509', in *Latin Learning and English Lore: Studies in Anglo-Saxon Literature for Michael Lapidge*, ed. Katherine O'Brien O'Keeffe and Andy Orchard, 2 vols (Toronto: University of Toronto Press, 2005), II, pp. 132–52. See further below, pp. 162–3, 185, 247–8. The manuscript is fully digitised at https://digital.bodleian.ox.ac.uk/objects/c7c1517d-3014-4a3d-9038-f678cf4969b4/.

as such at the time of its compilation.[4] The biblical translations copied in MS L are framed by three works by Ælfric on biblical themes: his *Preface to Genesis*, in which he dedicates the translation of the first book of the Old Testament to the West-Saxon ealdorman Æthelweard; and two exegetical letters addressed to members of the English gentry, Wulfgeat and Sigeweard. As we shall see, all three works reveal the thirst for biblical translations among the English nobility in this period. MS B, on the other hand, contains only Ælfric's *Preface to Genesis* followed by the first six biblical books – the Pentateuch and Joshua. The Old Testament translations in MS B are accompanied by a series of lavish colour illustrations, and this codex is therefore referred to as the Old English Illustrated Hexateuch.[5]

In manuscripts L and B, rubrics introduce each of the first five biblical books, providing their Hebrew, Greek, Latin and English. While the

---

[4] Edward Thwaites, ed., *Heptateuchus, Liber Job, et Euangelium Nicdemi: Anglo-Saxonice; Historiæ Judith Fragmentum: Dano-Saxonice, edidit nunc primum ex MMS codicibus* (Oxford: Oxford Sheldonian Theatre, 1698).

[5] Cotton Claudius B. IV (MS B; Ker §142) contains Ælfric's *Preface to Genesis*, missing its beginning (fols 1ʳ–1ᵛ), followed by the Old English prose *Genesis* (fols 1ᵛ–72ᵛ), *Exodus* (fols 72ᵛ–105ʳ), *Leviticus* (105ᵛ–10ᵛ), *Numbers* (111ʳ–28ʳ), *Deuteronomy* (128ᵛ–39ʳ) and *Joshua* (fols 140ᵛ–55ᵛ). For a facsimile, see Dodwell and Clemoes, eds, *The Old English Illustrated Hexateuch*. MS B was used as the foundation of S. J. Crawford, ed., *The Old English Version of the Heptateuch, Ælfric's Treatise on the Old and New Testament, and his Preface to Genesis*, EETS o.s. 160 (London: Oxford University Press, 1922), which also presents the corresponding Latin Vulgate text. A new edition of the Heptateuch, with the *Preface to Genesis* and Letters to Wulfgeat and Sigeweard, based mainly on Crawford's transcription of B but with some material supplied from L and other manuscripts, has recently been published by John J. Gallagher and Michael Everson, eds, *The Old English Bible I: The Heptateuch (Genesis to Judges)*, Corpus Textuum Anglicorum 1 (Dundee: Evertype, 2024). The other main manuscript is Cambridge University Library Ii.1.33 (MS C) (*c*. 1150–1200) (Ker §18), which despite its late date is probably closest to the original; this MS only contains Ælfric's *Preface to Genesis* and the translation of Genesis 1–24.22 (with some passages, notably Gen. 4–5.31 and 10–11, differing substantially from MSS B and L), followed by excerpts from his *Catholic Homilies* and *Lives of Saints* and other works of moral instruction. Fragments of other parts of the Heptateuch are found in eight further manuscripts, while an excerpt of the translation of Genesis (chapters 37–50) is preserved in Cambridge Corpus Christi 201 (pp. 151–60) (Ker §49), a collection of Wulfstanian materials that also includes the Old English *Apollonius of Tyre* and a sequence of devotional poems; on the position of the Old English *Genesis* excerpt in this manuscript, see Daniel Anlezark, 'Reading "The Story of Joseph" in MS Cambridge Corpus Christi College 201', in *The Power of Words: Anglo-Saxon Studies Presented to Donald G. Scragg on his Seventieth Birthday*, ed. Hugh Magennis and Jonathan Wilcox (Morgantown: West Virginia University Press, 2006), pp. 61–94.

rubric for the Old English prose *Genesis* in MSS L, B and C simply reads *INCIPIT LIBER. GENESIS ANGLICE*, the rubrics for the other four books explain the meaning of each one's name for the benefit of readers unable to understand Latin:

> 'Ellesmoth' on Hebreisc, 'Exodus' on Grecisc, 'Exitus' on Lyden, 'Utfæreld' on Englisc.[6]

> ['Ellesmoth' in Hebrew', 'Exodus' in Greek, 'Exitus' in Latin, 'Out going' in English.]

> Her onginneð seo þridde boc, þe ys genemned on Ebreisc 'Vaiecra' and 'Leuiticus' on Grecisc and 'Ministerialis' on Lyden, þæt is 'þenungboc' on Englisc, for þam þara sacerda þenunga sind þar awritene.[7]

> [Here begins the third book, that is called in Hebrew 'Vaiecra' and 'Leviticus' in Greek and 'Ministerialis' in Latin, that is 'service book' in English, because the services of those priests are written therein.]

> Her ongind seo boc þe ys genemned on Ebreisc 'Vagedaber', þæt ys on Lyden 'Numerus' and on Englisc 'getel', for þam þe Israhela bearn wæron on þære getealde.[8]

> [Here begins the book that is called in Hebrew 'Vagedaber', that is in Latin 'Numerus' and in English 'number', because the children of the Israelites were numbered in there.]

> Her ongind seo boc þe is genemned on Ebreisc 'Helleadabarim' and on Grecisc 'Deuteronomium' and on Lyden 'Secunda lex' and on Englisc 'seo æftre æ'.[9]

> [Here begins the book that is called in Hebrew 'Helleadabarim' and in Greek 'Deuteronomy' and in Latin 'Secunda lex' and in English 'the second law'.]

The rubrics reflect the common medieval understanding of the Vulgate Bible itself as part of a chain of translations, echoing Alfred's statement in the Prose Preface to the *Pastoral Care* that the æ ('law') was first written in Hebrew before the Greeks, Romans and other Christian nations all turned it into their own languages.[10]

---

[6] Marsden, ed., *Heptateuch*, I, p. 89.
[7] Marsden, ed., *Heptateuch*, I, p. 129.
[8] Marsden, ed., *Heptateuch*, I, p. 138.
[9] Marsden, ed., *Heptateuch*, I, p. 154.
[10] See above, pp. 3–4.

The translations and paraphrases that comprise the Heptateuch were done in several stages by Ælfric and a group of anonymous translators working separately, as well as one or more compilers.[11] Although doubts remain as to the authorship of certain sections, the division of labour can be tentatively tabulated as follows on the basis of shifts in vocabulary, syntax and style:

Genesis 1–24.22	Ælfric
Genesis 4–5.31	Anonymous
Genesis 10–11	Anonymous
Genesis 12–24.26	Ælfric
Genesis 24.61–50.25	Anonymous
Exodus	Anonymous
Leviticus	Anonymous
Numbers 1–12	Anonymous
Numbers 13–26	Ælfric
Deuteronomy	Anonymous
Joshua	Ælfric
Judges	Ælfric

The translators worked from a version of the Vulgate, though a few isolated readings are closer to the *Vetus Latina* ('Old Latin') Bible.[12] Aaron Kleist dates Ælfric's *Preface* and his section of the Old English *Genesis* and his *Joshua* to c. 993–8, placing his contribution to *Numbers* and his para-

---

[11] See esp. Richard Marsden, 'Translation by Committee? The "Anonymous" Text of the Old English Hexateuch', in *The Old English Hexateuch: Aspects and Approaches*, ed. Rebecca Barnhouse and Benjamin C. Withers (Kalamazoo, MI: Western Michigan University/Medieval Institute Publications, 2000), pp. 41–89, who builds on, among others, Karl Jost, 'Unechte Ælfrictexte', *Anglia* 51 (1927), 81–103, 177–219; Josef Raith, 'Ælfric's Share in the Old English Pentateuch', *RES* 3 (1952), 305–14; and Peter A. M. Clemoes, 'The Composition of the Old English Text', in *The Old English Illustrated Hexateuch: British Museum Cotton Claudius B. IV*, ed. C. R. Dodwell and P. A. M. Clemoes, Early English Manuscripts in Facsimile 18 (Copenhagen: Rosenkilde and Bagger, 1974), pp. 42–53.

[12] See Richard Marsden, 'Old Latin Intervention in the Old English Heptateuch', *ASE* 23 (1994), 229–64; Marsden, *Text of the Old Testament*, pp. 402–37. Marsden notes that whenever an Old Latin reading appears to lie behind the translation choice, this is probably due to the translator's familiarity with a patristic source which itself used this version rather than the Vulgate, though some may be due to intervention in the exemplar, either in the form of glosses or annotations (*Text of the Old Testament*, p. 409).

phrase of *Judges c.* 998–1002.[13] The anonymous contributions are thought to have been completed by *c.* 1020.

In terms of sheer scale, this project dwarfs the Alfredian translations of the Psalms and Laws and bears comparison only with the *Wessex Gospels*; Marsden has therefore described both works as constituting 'the first sustained effort to translate Latin Scripture into English'.[14] Yet the idea of creating a Heptateuch is without clear precedent in biblical tradition, and it is possible therefore that the original goal may only have extended as far as the translation of the Pentateuch, the traditional division of the first five books of the Old Testament containing the laws of Moses. As we shall see below, in his *Preface to Genesis* Ælfric reveals that efforts to translate the book of Genesis were already underway prior to his involvement in the project. Marsden argues that the non-Ælfrician translations of Exodus, Leviticus, Deuteronomy and the first part of Numbers are the work of an independent team of later authors who 'hijacked the available work of Ælfric and supplied the rest in a joint endeavour'.[15] However, some years after he had translated the beginning of Genesis, Ælfric would state in his *Treatise on the Old and New Testaments* that *we habbað awend witodlice on Englisc* ('we have translated faithfully into English') the books of Exodus, Leviticus, Numbers and Deuteronomy, suggesting that he may have had some oversight of the whole project, or at least approved of it.[16]

The separateness of Ælfric's paraphrases of the first two historical books, Joshua and Judges, from the rest of the project is indicated by their lack of introductory rubrics, and the motivation behind the inclusion of both texts in MS L (and Ælfric's *Joshua* in MS B) is unclear. A noble patron may simply have wanted a volume containing as much Old Testament reading material in the vernacular as was available. Another possibility is that the compilation in MS L was designed to tell the history of the Israelites up until the time of the monarchy, which begins with the anointing of Saul in I Samuel (= I Kings).[17] Indeed, as we shall see below, the final book in the compilation, Ælfric's paraphrase of Judges, ends with a meditation on the origins of Judeo-Christian kingship, which connects the biblical judges who ruled Israel before the monarchical era with present-day English kings. Such a collection might have appealed to an English nobleman interested in the responsibilities of earthly rulers. As Malcolm Godden comments:

---

[13] Kleist, *Chronology and Canon*, p. 132.
[14] Marsden, 'Translation by Committee?, p. 85.
[15] Marsden, 'Translation by Committee?', p. 84.
[16] Marsden, ed., *Heptateuch*, I, p. 209, ll. 218–20.
[17] In the Christian Old Testament, the Historical Books begin with Joshua, Judges and Ruth, followed by I and II Samuel, I and II Kings, I and II Chronicles, Ezra, Nehemiah and Esther.

For the Anglo-Saxons the Old Testament was a veiled way of talking about their own situation. Sometimes it was a matter of explaining how things came to be as they are in the world. Sometimes it provided a figurative framework for analysing the Church and the clergy. But most often the Old Testament offered them a means of considering and articulating the ways in which kingship, politics and warfare related to the rule of God. Despite Ælfric's insistence that the old law had been replaced by the new, at least in its literal sense, in many ways the old retained its power for the Anglo-Saxons, and gave them a way of thinking about themselves as nations.[18]

The combination of the translations of the books of the Pentateuch with Ælfric's *Joshua* and *Judges* in MS L provided the English nobility with a wealth of examples of heroic military and national leaders. The translation and compilation of these materials invites such readers to reflect on how God's chosen people were consistently afflicted by foreign enemies when they turned away from his laws but enjoyed his favour when they were obedient to them. Together with the other Old English biblical prose texts discussed in this book, the Old English Heptateuch may therefore have contributed to the emergence of English national identity in this formative period.[19] As prominent patrons of the Benedictine Reform, pious noblemen such as Æthelweard and his son, Æthelmær, sought access to the monastic reading materials used in the Divine Office, which included the Heptateuch.[20] Lower-ranking members of the nobility, such as Wulfgeat

---

[18] Godden, 'Old Testament', p. 232.

[19] See above, p. 20–1.

[20] Marsden notes that the Heptateuch was prescribed reading in the pre-Lenten and Lenten monastic night office ('Cain's Face and Other Problems', p. 34). See further Milton McC. Gatch, 'The Office in Late Anglo-Saxon Monasticism', in *Learning and Literature in Anglo-Saxon England: Studies Presented to Peter Clemoes on the Occasion of his Sixty-Fifth Birthday*, ed. Michael Lapidge and Helmut Gneuss (Cambridge: Cambridge University Press, 1985), pp. 341–62, at 360–1. Gatch comments that while Ælfric would probably have found the biblical translations in the Heptateuch/Hexateuch 'too ample for the laity in general' (p. 361), the compiler may have had in mind 'the needs of monolingual monastic novices or schoolboys and of secular clergy on whom the canonical obligation of participating in the Office was being imposed' (p. 361 n. 73). Helen Gittos demonstrates that Ælfric's dedications of his works to lay patrons in prefaces are indebted to rhetorical convention and cautions that these statements should not be taken at face value ('The Audience for Old English Texts'). For a discussion of lay readership of the *Lives of Saints*, see E. Gordon Whatley, 'Pearls before Swine: Ælfric, Vernacular Hagiography, and the Lay Reader', in *Via Crucis: Essays on Early Medieval Sources and Ideas in Memory of J. E. Cross*, ed. Thomas D. Hill, Charles D. Wright and Thomas N. Hall (Morgantown, 2002), pp. 158–84.

and Sigeweard, appear to have shared this enthusiasm for biblical translations and other religious reading materials.[21] In response to their requests, Ælfric produced his *Lives of the Saints* and his contributions to the Heptateuch, as well as various sermon-like letters containing summaries of biblical material. Moreover, Daniel Anlezark has argued that an abbreviated version of the Benedictine Office, containing Latin and Old English psalms and prayers, was produced for members of the lay nobility in this period.[22] The Old English Heptateuch also seems to have been produced to meet this burgeoning demand among the laity for reading materials that had previously been available only to those in monastic orders.

While the Heptateuch was probably designed mainly for readers who could not access the Bible in Latin, Ælfric appears to have envisaged that at least some readers of the work were Latinate. Hence, in the copy of his translation of Genesis 24.15–60 preserved in MS L he recommends that the reader consult a Latin version of the text should they wish to find the full account of how Abraham's reeve secured a wife for Isaac: *swa hit þære Ledenbec awriten ys: ræde þær se þe wylle* ('thus it is written in the Latin book: he who wishes can read it there').[23] A small number of lay readers certainly could read Latin in this period, not least Æthelweard himself, who is credited with translating the Anglo-Saxon Chronicle into Latin.[24] Readers of the Heptateuch may also have included those same *ungelæredan preostas* ('unlearned priests') whom Ælfric criticises in his *Preface to Genesis*, as well perhaps as oblates, monks or nuns who were still learning Latin.[25] Yet as Benjamin C. Withers comments, the distinction

---

[21] See further Catherine Cubitt, 'Ælfric's Lay Patrons', in *Companion to Ælfric*, ed. Magennis and Swan, pp. 165–92.

[22] Daniel Anlezark, 'The Psalms in the Old English Office of Prime', in *Psalms and Medieval English*, ed. Atkin and Leneghan, pp. 198–217.

[23] Marsden, ed., *Heptateuch*, I, p. 50.

[24] Æthelweard's *Chronicon* is composed in the complex 'hermeneutic style' in fashion at the time; see Lapidge, *Anglo-Latin Literature*, pp. 105, 135–9. On Æthelweard's education as atypical for noblemen of his day, see Wormald, 'Anglo-Saxon Society and its Literature', p. 18. See further above, p. 57. On Æthelweard's relationship with Ælfric, and the possibility that there may have been other laymen who had some knowledge of Latin in this period, see Mechthild Gretsch, 'Historiography and Literary Patronage in late Anglo-Saxon England: The Evidence of Æthelweard's *Chronicon*', ASE 41 (2012), 205–48.

[25] See Joyce Hill, 'Monastic Reform and the Secular Church: Ælfric's Pastoral Letters in Context', in *England in the Eleventh Century: Proceedings of the 1990 Harlaxton Symposium*, ed. Carola Hicks, Harlaxton Medieval Studies 2 (Stamford: Paul Watkins, 1992), pp. 103–17. For a particularly negative view of the Latinity of the tenth-century English clergy and the possibility that even reformed monks required translations, see C. E. Hohler, 'Some Service Books of the Later Saxon Church', in *Tenth-Century Studies: Essays in Commemoration*

between a 'clerical' and 'lay' audience for such a project begins to break down when we consider that 'monks, priests, and nuns more often than not belonged to the same families or at least the same strata of society as potential lay readers.'[26] The prose translation of the Heptateuch could thus have served multiple purposes, making the key books of the Old Law accessible to a very wide audience of English men and women.

The provision of 394 colour illustrations in the manuscript copy of the Hexateuch (MS B) made these Old Testament narratives accessible even to those who could not read written English – that is, those who possessed only 'pragmatic literacy'.[27] Commenting on the 'workmanlike' quality of these illustrations, Marsden argues that the Hexateuch codex was probably not commissioned by a royal patron but for a wealthy member of the nobility.[28] Given the book's large size, Withers suggests that no more than three or four adults could be gathered around to view the images at any one time: 'Someone read while others listened and looked'.[29] Despite their modest artistic talents, the illustrators succeed in domesticating Old Testament scenes, making them more intelligible to the book's first users

---

of the Millennium of the Council of Winchester and 'Regularis Concordia, ed. David Parsons (London: Phillimore, 1975), pp. 60–83 and 217–27. In a recent study, Ondřej Fúsik argues that the translation of Genesis was aimed at 'male monks', on the grounds of perceived 'masculinisation' of female characters in the Latin source: 'Referencing Female Characters in the Old English *Heptateuch* Translation of Genesis: Evidence against Translation Automatisms', in *Translation Automatisms in the Vernacular Texts of the Middle Ages and the Early Modern Period*, ed. Vladimir Agrigoroaei and Ileana Sasu (Turnhout: Brepols, 2023), pp. 156–61. Stephenson, *Politics of Language*, pp. 147–52, emphasises that monks, as well as secular clerics, constitute a major element of the readership of Ælfric's vernacular writings despite the fact that he tends to dedicate such works to lay patrons.

[26] Benjamin C. Withers, *The Illustrated Old English Hexateuch, Cotton Claudius B. iv: The Frontier of Seeing and Reading in Anglo-Saxon England* (Toronto: University of Toronto Press, 2007), p. 178.

[27] See Withers, *Old English Hexateuch*, pp. 159–82.

[28] Marsden, 'Cain's Face and Other Problems', p. 34.

[29] Withers, *Old English Illustrated Hexateuch*, p. 176. David F. Johnson proposes that the illustrated Hexateuch was designed to be consulted by laymen when visiting a monastery or for older members of the laity who had retired into a monastery: 'A Program of Illumination in the Old English Illustrated Hexateuch: Visual Typology', in *Old English Hexateuch*, ed. Barnhouse and Withers, pp. 165–99. For discussion of how some of the illustrations are aimed at 'unsophisticated audiences', see Rebecca Barnhouse, 'Pictorial Exegesis in the Illustrated Old English Hexateuch', *Publications of the Medieval Association of the Midwest* 6 (1999), 109–32. For comparison with other illustrated manuscripts that were probably made for lay readers in this period, see Raw, 'The probable derivation of most of the illustrations in Junius 11 from an illustrated Old Saxon Genesis', 135–6.

and providing modern readers with an invaluable window onto daily life in early to mid-eleventh-century England.[30] For example, in the depiction of Pharaoh hanging the baker (Gen. 40.22) (fig. 9), the Egyptian ruler is presented in the centre of the page dressed in the style of a contemporary English king, crowned and surrounded by his *witan*, while the hanging scene on the right of the page, in which the gallows are fitted with steps for the executioner to climb and attach the noose, probably reflects present-day English practice. The conical hats that look like Phrygian caps worn by the members of the king's *witan*, on the other hand, provide a rare foreignising detail, perhaps copied from an exemplar that the artist used as a model:[31]

Elsewhere in the Hexateuch manuscript, biblical cities are modelled on contemporary English architecture, while depictions of farming techniques and other scenes of everyday life in biblical times probably reflect those known to the audience.

While the Hexateuch has attracted a good deal of scholarly attention on account of its illustrations, the prose translations themselves remain relatively neglected. In this chapter, I concentrate on the Heptateuch manuscript, MS L, exploring how its makers employed a range of translation strategies in order to bring the meaning of these key books of the Old Testament across to readers, ranging from word-for-word (formal equivalence) and sense-for-sense (functional equivalence) translation to homiletic paraphrase. As we shall see, the varying approaches to biblical translation utilised in this project reflect the authors' sensitivity to the risks involved in widening access to the Old Testament to readers who might lack the educational skills to unlock its spiritual meaning.

Ælfric's Preface to Genesis

Like many of Ælfric's major works, his translation of Genesis is furnished with an epistolary preface in which the author addresses his patron and implied reader, in this case the prominent West Saxon ealdorman

---

[30] On the extent to which such illustrations reflect real life and their debt to earlier models, see M. O. H. Carver, 'Contemporary Artefacts Illustrated in Late Saxon Manuscripts', *Archaeologia* 108 (1986), 117–45.

[31] On depictions of hanging in Ælfric and other early medieval English sources, see Susan Irvine, 'Hanging by a Thread: Ælfric's Saints' Lives and the *Hengen*', in *Hagiography in Anglo-Saxon England: Adopting and Adapting Saints' Lives into Old English Prose (c. 950–1150)*, ed. Loredana Lazzari, Patrizia Lendinara and Claudia Di Sciacca, Textes et études du Moyen Âge 73 (Barcelona-Madrid: Fédération Internationale des Instituts d'Etudes Médiévales, 2014), pp. 67–94. On hats and crowns in English art of this period, see Gale R. Owen-Crocker, *Dress in Anglo-Saxon England* (Woodbridge: Boydell, 2004), pp. 263–4.

Figure 9. London, British Library, Cotton MS Claudius B. IV, fol. 59ᵛ, 'Old English Illustrated Hexateuch: Pharaoh has his baker hanged (Gen. 40.22)'.

Æthelweard, and explains the rationale behind the work that follows.[32] Although this preface may originally have been intended to precede only the portion of the Genesis translation for which Ælfric was responsible (up to the story of Abraham and Isaac, Gen. 24), judging from its presence in all three major manuscripts (L, B and C) it appears to have come to serve as a preface for the entire Old English Heptateuch.[33] The preface is a key document in the history of Old English biblical prose, providing a detailed exposition of Ælfric's theory of scriptural translation. In MS B, the opening of the preface is missing, but the complete text is preserved in L (fig. 10):

Following a conventional greeting in which Ælfric addresses Æthelweard in the third person, the letter shifts into the first person as the author expresses his deep misgivings about translating Genesis for readers untrained in biblical exegesis:[34]

> Ælfric munuc gret Æðelwærd ealdormann eadmodlice. Þu bæde me leof þæt ic sceolde ðe awendan of Lydene on Englisc þa boc Genesis. Ða þuhte me *hefigtime* þe to tiþiene þæs, and þu cwæde þa þæt ic ne þorfte na mare awendan þære bec, buton to Isaace, Abrahames suna, for þam þe sum oðer man þe hæfde awend fram Isaace þa boc oþ ende.
>
> Nu þincð me, leof, þæt *þæt weorc is swiðe pleolic me oððe ænigum men to underbeginnenne*, for þan þe ic ondræde gif sum dysig man ðas boc ræt,

---

[32] Æthelweard and his son, Æthelmær, are the addressees of the Old English preface to Ælfric's *Lives of Saints*. For discussion of the *Preface to Genesis*, as well as Ælfric's overall approach to translating Genesis, see Hurt, *Ælfric*, pp. 100–3. On Ælfric's contribution to the Heptateuch, as well as the *Preface to Genesis* and *Treatise*, see Stanton, *Culture of Translation*, pp. 131–41.

[33] For the manuscripts, see above, p. 146 n. 5. For discussion of the relevance of Ælfric's preface to the entire project, see Melinda J. Menzer, 'The Preface as Admonition: Ælfric's Preface to Genesis', in *Old English Hexateuch*, ed. Barnhouse and Withers, pp. 15–39, at 15–19. Mark Griffith has highlighted how Ælfric draws here on a wide range of biblical and patristic sources, including Jerome's preface to his translation of Genesis in the Vulgate and *Letter to Pammachius*, as well as Pseudo-Jerome's *Breviarum in Psalmos* and Alcuin's *Quaestiones in Genesim* (*Interrogationes Sigewulfi*): 'Ælfric's Use of Sources in the Preface to Genesis, together with a Conspectus of Biblical and Patristic Sources and Analogues', *Florilegium* 17 (2000), 127–54. On the Preface's sophisticated structure and debt to classical models of letter-writing, see Mark Griffith, 'Ælfric's Preface to Genesis: Genre, Rhetoric and the Origins of the *ars dictaminis*', *ASE* 29 (2000), 215–34.

[34] This shift from the third to first person echoes the style of Alfred's epistolary prefaces. On Ælfric's knowledge of Alfredian works, see Malcolm R. Godden, 'Ælfric and The Alfredian Precedents', in *Companion to Ælfric*, ed. Magennis and Swan, pp. 139–63; and his 'Ælfric and the Vernacular Prose Tradition'. On Ælfric's complex attitude to the translation of the Bible, see Major 'Rebuilding the Tower of Babel'.

Figure 10. Oxford, Bodleian Library, MS Laud Misc. 509, fol. 1ʳ, 'Ælfric's *Preface to Genesis*'.

oððe rædan gehyrþ, þæ he wille wenan þæ he mote lybban nu on þære niwan æ swa swa þa ealdan fæderas leofodon, þa on þære tide ær þan þe seo ealde æ gesett wære, oþþe swa swa men leofodon under Moyses æ.³⁵

[Ælfric the monk humbly greets Ealdorman Æthelweard. You bade me, dear sir, that I should turn the book of Genesis for you from Latin into English. Then it seemed *difficult* to me to grant you that, and you then said that I need not translate more of the book except as far as Isaac, the son of Abraham, because some other person had translated the book for you from Isaac until the end.

Now it seems to me, dear sir, that *that work is very perilous for me or any man to undertake*, because I fear, if some foolish person reads this book or hears it read, that he will think that he may live now in the New Law just as the patriarchs lived then in that time before the Old Law was appointed, or just as men lived under the law of Moses.] (Emphases added).

Evidently work on a translation of Genesis – and perhaps other parts of the Old Testament – was already underway at the time of writing. As Melinda J. Menzer notes, while Ælfric typically gives voice to his reservations about translation at the end of his prefaces, in the *Preface to Genesis* he foregrounds his reluctance to undertake this 'perilous' (*pleolic*) task in the opening lines, and does so much more forcefully than in other instances.³⁶ Indeed, Menzer argues that the preface's unusually disjointed and confusing nature is itself a ploy by Ælfric to underline the complexity of the job which Æthelweard has requested of him.³⁷ Ælfric would have known that lay readers such as Æthelweard already had access to vernacular translations and adaptations

---

³⁵ Marsden, ed., *Heptateuch*, I, p. 3, ll. 2–13.
³⁶ Menzer, 'The Preface as Admonition', pp. 19–21. For example, in the prayer at the end of his second series of *Catholic Homilies*, Ælfric states: *Ic cweðe nu þæt ic næfre heonon-forð ne awende godspel oþþe godspel-trahtas of Ledene on Englisc* ('I declare now that henceforth I will never translate the gospel or gospel homilies from Latin into English'): *CH* II, p. 357; on this passage and Ælfric's presentation of himself as a reluctant translator of Scripture, see above, p. 144. On Ælfric's seeming disapproval of translations such as the *Wessex Gospels*, see above, pp. 123–5. In describing biblical translation as perilous, Ælfric echoes Jerome's preface to the Pentateuch translation in the Vulgate: *Periculosum opus certe, obtrectatorum latratibus patens, qui me adserunt in Septuaginta interpretum suggillationem nova pro veteribus cudere, ita ingenium quasi vinum probantes* ('Certainly a dangerous work, open to the barkings of detractors, who accuse me of insult to the Seventy [i.e. the Septuagint] to prepare a new interpretation from the old ones, thus approving ability like wine'). On Ælfric's familiarity with Jerome's prefaces, see Griffith, 'Ælfric's Use of Sources', 127–9.
³⁷ Menzer, 'The Preface as Admonition', p. 34.

of the Gospels as well, perhaps, as parts of the Old Testament.[38] Yet in Ælfric's view, such readers lack the training in biblical exegesis required to distinguish between the Old and the New Law (æ). As Ælfric explains to Æthelweard, such ignorance of the true interpretation of Scripture is unsurprising given that even some priests also lack this ability to read beyond the literal wording of the Old Testament:

> Hwilon ic wiste þæt sum mæssepreost, se þe min magister wæs on þam timan, hæfde þa boc Genesis and he cuðe be dæle Lyden understandan. Þa cwæþ he be þam heahfædere Iacobe þæt he hæfde feower wif: twa geswustra and heora twa þinena. Ful soð he sæde, ac he nyste, ne ic þa git, hu micel todal ys betweohx þære ealdan æ and þære niwan.[39]

> [Once I knew that a certain masspriest, who was my teacher at the time, owned the book of Genesis, and he could understand Latin a little; then he said about the patriarch Jacob, that he had four wives, two sisters and their two handmaidens. What he said was completely true, but he did not know, as I did not at that time, how great a difference there is between the Old Law and the New.]

In Ælfric's view, however, it is the duty of priests to explain the hidden, spiritual (*gastlic*) meaning of Scripture to lay people (*læwedum folce*):[40]

> Preostas sindon gesette to lareowum þam læwedum folce. Nu gedafnode him þæt hig cuþon þa ealdan æ gastlice understandan and hwæt Crist silf tæhte, and his apostolas, on þære niwan gecyðnisse, þæt hig mihton þam folce wel wissian to Godes geleafan and wel bisnian to godum weorcum.[41]

---

[38] For the possibility that the collection of Old English biblical verse in MS Junius 11 was compiled for a noble lay patron in this period, see Daniel Anlezark, 'Lay Reading, Patronage, and Power in Bodleian Library Junius 11', in *Ambition and Anxiety: Courts and Courtly Discourse, c. 700–1600*, ed. Giles E. M. Gasper and John McKinnell, Durham Medieval and Renaissance Monographs and Essays 3 (Toronto: Pontifical Institute of Medieval Studies, 2014), pp. 76–97.

[39] Marsden, ed., *Heptateuch*, I, p. 3, ll. 13–18.

[40] Katherine O'Brien O'Keeffe describes this process of reading beyond the surface or literal sense as 'symptomatic reading': 'Who Reads Now? The Anxieties of Millennial Reading: The 2019 Morton W. Bloomfield Lecture', in *The Practice and Politics of Reading, 650–1500*, ed. Daniel Donoghue, James Simpson, Nicholas Watson and Anna Wilson (Cambridge: D. S. Brewer, 2022), pp. 161–80, at 162. On Ælfric's emphasis on the duties of religious teachers in the *Treatise*, see below pp. 222–4. For his instruction that priests should explain the meaning of the gospel reading used in the mass in the *Letter for Wulfsige*, see above, pp. 119–20.

[41] Marsden, ed., *Heptateuch*, I, p. 4, ll. 38–42.

A Perilous Task: Making the Old English Heptateuch

[Priests are set up as teachers for lay people. Now it has become fitting for them that they know how to understand the Old Law spiritually, and what Christ himself taught and his apostles in the New Testament, so that they could guide the people properly to God's faith and set an example properly in good deeds.]

Ælfric knew Jerome's dictum that in translating Scripture, the best approach is to stick as closely as possible to the wording of the source.[42] Yet he was also aware that lay readers and poorly educated priests were ill-equipped to understand Genesis without a robust interpretive framework. In the *Catholic Homilies*, he had been able to circumvent the problem of translating the Bible for lay readers by supplying a wealth of authoritative patristic exegesis and biblical citation to accompany each gospel excerpt.[43] However, exegesis of this sort had no place in the sort of free-standing translation of Scripture requested by Æthelweard.

Weighing up these difficulties, Ælfric declares that while he will supply nothing more than the naked (*nacedan*) or plain narrative in his translation of Genesis, his readers should not be so foolish (*dysig*) as to read it only in the literal sense:[44]

> We secgað eac foran to, þæt seo boc is swiþe deop gastlice to understandenne and we ne writaþ ne mare buton þa nacedan gerecednisse. Þonne þincþ þam ungelæredum þæt eall þæt andgit beo belocen on þære anfealdan gerecednisse ac hit ys swiþe feor þam.[45]

[We also say in advance that the book is very profound to understand spiritually, and we are not writing anything more than the naked narrative. Then it may seem to the unlearned that all the sense is enclosed in the simple narrative, but it is very far from that.]

---

[42] For Jerome's *Letter to Pammachius*, see above, p. 33.

[43] See Chapter Three, pp. 119–43.

[44] Stanton argues that in presenting only the 'naked narrative', Ælfric was offering the unlearned an encounter with Scripture in simple language 'untroubled by rhetorical figures, allegory, typology, or any other features of human interpretative machinery', through which 'the faithful can experience the presence of God without beginning to understand its meaning (*Culture of Translation*, p. 134). For an exploration of the contrast between the vigorous promotion of vernacular reading in the Alfredian reform with Ælfric's more cautious approach, see O'Brien O'Keeffe, 'Who Reads Now?'. O'Brien O'Keeffe argues that the model of reading Alfred advocated in the Prose Preface to the *Pastoral Care* 'was simply an act of decoding words on a page', whereas for Ælfric reading 'was a composite set of highly fraught activities' (pp. 161–2).

[45] Marsden, ed., *Heptateuch*, I, p. 4, ll. 43–6.

In order to illustrate the complexity of the Book of Genesis to Æthelweard and other readers, he provides an exegetical interpretation of the spiritual meaning of the opening verses:

> Heo onginð þus: 'In principio creauit Deus celum et terram.' Þæt ys on Englisc, 'on anginne gesceop God heofenan and eorþan.' Hit wæs soðlice swa gedon þæt God ælmihtig geworhte on anginne, þa þa he wolde, gesceafta. Ac swa þeah, æfter gastlicum andgite, þæt anginn ys Crist, swa swa he sylf cwæþ to þam Iudeiscum: 'Ic eom angin þe to eow sprece.' Þurh þis angin worhte God fæder heofenan and eorþan, for þan he gesceop ealle gesceafta þurh þone sunu, se þe was æfre of him accened, wisdom of þam wisan fæder.[46]

> [It begins thus: 'In principio creauit Deus celum et terram.' That is in English, 'in the beginning God made heaven and earth.' It was truly done in this way that God Almighty made creation in the beginning, as he intended to. But also, in the spiritual sense, that meaning is Christ, just as he himself said to the Jews: 'I say to you, I am the beginning.' Through this beginning God the Father made heaven and earth, because he made all creation through that son, who was always born from him, wisdom from the wise father.]

As Jonathan Wilcox comments, the sheer length of the exegesis provided for this single biblical verse 'dramatizes the extent to which interpretation is necessary.'[47] The elaborate and sophisticated rhetoric of the *Preface* thus serves to underline Ælfric's point about the perils of translating the Old Testament for lay readers and poorly educated clerics. On the one hand, the words of Scripture should not be added to in the course of translation, yet the 'naked' text of the Old Testament is too complex for such readers to understand without accompanying exegesis.[48]

---

[46] Marsden, ed., *Heptateuch*, I, p. 5, ll. 49–57.
[47] Wilcox, *Ælfric's Prefaces*, p. 39.
[48] Wilcox, *Ælfric's Prefaces*, pp. 39–40. Ælfric did provide extensive exegesis of the Book of Genesis elsewhere in his writings, notably in his *Interrogationes Sigewulfi* ('Sigewulf's questions'), a translation of Alcuin's influential *Quaestiones in Genesim* ('Questions on Genesis') (*c.* 796), probably composed around the same time as the *Preface to Genesis*. Sigewulf is the name of Alcuin's student, who in the course of the work asks him 281 questions about the Book of Genesis. Clemoes argues that Ælfric composed his translation of this work 'precisely to clothe *þa nacedan gerecedinnse*' of his translation of Genesis ('The Chronology of Ælfric's Works', in *The Anglo-Saxons: Studies in Some Aspects of Their History and Culture Presented to Bruce Dickins*, ed. Peter Clemoes [London: Bowes & Bowes, 1959], pp. 212–47, repr. in *Old English Prose: Basic Readings*, ed. Szarmach, pp. 29–72, at 40). However, Griffith suggests on the basis of verbal parallels that Ælfric was in fact working on his version of the *Interrogationes* around the same time as the *Preface to Genesis* ('Ælfric's Use of Sources', 139–40). Fox argues

A Perilous Task: Making the Old English Heptateuch

Another issue which the biblical translator must tackle is syntax. We have seen how the Old English glosses added to Latin psalters and gospel books typically adhere to the word order of the source text, as their goal was to aid the reader in understanding the Latin. Ælfric's readers, on the other hand, have now requested a vernacular version of Genesis which can be read independently of the Latin source. In the *Letter to Pammachius*, Jerome had insisted that the word order of Scripture is sacred and must therefore be preserved, though in his preface to his translation of the Book of Job in the Vulgate he acknowledged that it was impossible to do so, recommending instead a flexible approach: *vel verbum e verbo, vel sensum e sensu, vel en utroque commixtum* ('sometimes word for word, sometimes sense for sense, sometimes a mixture of the two').[49] In the *Preface*, Ælfric similarly explains that while his translation of Genesis will not add anything to the source in terms of wording, it will make no attempt to replicate its syntax (*endebirdnisse*), as to follow the word order of the Latin would result in unidiomatic English:[50]

> Nu is seo foresæde boc on manegum stowum swiþe nearolice gesett, and þeah swiðe deoplice on þam gastlicum andgite. And heo is swa geendebyrd swa swa God silf hig gedihte þam writere Moise, and we ne durron na mare awritan on Englisc þonne þæt Liden hæfþ, ne þa endebirdnisse awendan, buton þam anum þæt þæt Leden and þæt Englisc nabbað na ane wisan on þære spræce fadunge. Æfre se þe awent oþþe se þe tæcþ of Ledene on Englisc, æfre he sceal gefadian hit swa þæt þæt Englisc hæbbe his agene wisan, elles hit biþ swiþe gedwolsum to rædenne, þam þe þæs Ledenes wisan ne can.[51]

> [Now the aforesaid book is in many places very obscurely written, and also very profoundly composed in the spiritual sense. And the word order is as if God himself had dictated it to the writer Moses, and we dare not write any more in English than the Latin has, nor change the word order, except that Latin and English do not have the same way of ordering speech. If anyone should wish to translate or to teach from Latin into English, he must always arrange it so that the English has its

---

that Ælfric transformed Alcuin's work into 'a much more basic exegetical primer', noting that he translates only 69 of Sigewulf's 281 questions ('Ælfric's *Interrogationes Sigewulfi*', pp. 33–4). On the *Interrogationes*, see further below, p. 176.

[49] On Jerome's *Letter to Pammachius*, see above, p. 33.

[50] As Stanton notes, Ælfric establishes his credentials here as a faithful translator as distinct from the prophetic or miraculous type represented by Cædmon (*Culture of Translation*, p. 136).

[51] Marsden, ed., *Heptateuch*, I, pp. 6–7, ll. 95–102.

own style, otherwise it will be very erroneous to read, for those who do not know the Latin.]

In the translation of Genesis that follows, although Ælfric briefly experiments with following the syntax of the Latin source, he quickly abandons this scheme and opts instead for a more natural, English prose style suitable for conveying the meaning of the source text to the reader. As we shall see, however, Ælfric's commitment to providing nothing more than the naked narrative of Genesis is often challenged by the nature of the source text itself, which contains a good deal of material deemed unsuitable or too challenging for poorly educated readers.

Genesis

Having reluctantly accepted his patron's request to supply him with a free-standing translation of Genesis ('affirmation' in Steiner's terminology), Ælfric proceeds to weigh up the meaning of each word in his Latin source at the level of grammar and syntax ('aggression'), evaluating which parts to bring over into the target language ('incorporation') before finally adapting the source in various ways to make it appealing and comprehensible to readers ('compensation').[52] In MS L, the Genesis translation begins immediately after the Preface at the bottom of fol. 3ʳ. The Old English text of Genesis has been heavily glossed in Latin by a hand dated to the late eleventh or twelfth century (fig. 11), demonstrating the continuing scholarly interest in the Heptateuch in this period.[53]

Comparison with the Vulgate source demonstrates Ælfric's largely formal-equivalence, word-for-word approach at this early stage in the translation:

| [1.1] In principio, creavit Deus caelum et terram. [1.2] Terra autem erat inanis et vacua, et tenebrae super faciem abyssi, et spiritus Dei ferebatur super aquas. [1.3] Dixitque Deus, "Fiat lux." Et facta est lux. | On anginne gesceop God heofenan and eorþan. [1.2] Seo eorðe soþlice wæs ydel and æmtig and þeostru wæron ofer þære niwelnisse brandnisse, and Godes gast wæs geferod ofer wateru. [1.3] God cwæþ þa: 'Geweorðe leoht', and leoht wearþ geworht.[54] |

---

[52] For Steiner's theory of translation, see above, p. xiii.
[53] See above, 145 n. 3, and below, pp. 247–8.
[54] Marsden, ed., *Heptateuch*, I, p. 8. Marsden's edition is based on MS Laud Misc. 509 (L), copied in the second half of the eleventh century, with some readings supplied from other manuscripts.

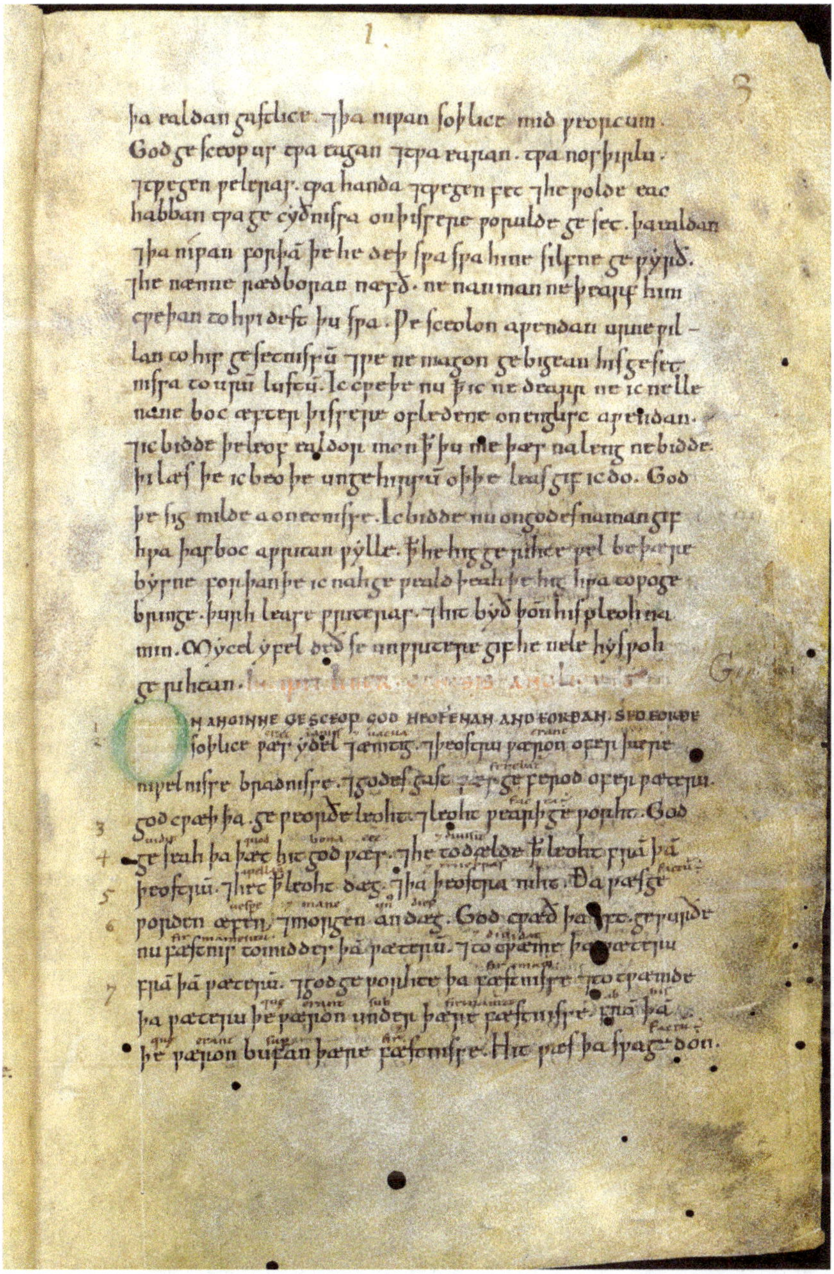

Figure 11. Oxford, Bodleian Library, MS Laud Misc. 509, fol. 3ʳ, 'Old English Heptateuch: End of Ælfric's *Preface to Genesis*/opening of Ælfric's translation of Genesis'.

[In the beginning God created heaven and earth. And the earth was void and empty, and darkness was upon the face of the deep; and the spirit of God moved over the waters. And God said: 'Be light made. And light was made.']

[In the beginning God created heaven and earth. And the earth was void and empty, and darkness was upon the face of the deep; and the spirit of God moved over the waters. God said then: 'Be light made. And light was made.']

Ælfric sticks remarkably closely here to the Latin source, both at the level of diction (e.g. *In principio* > *On anginne*; *caelum et terram* > *heofenan and eorþan*) and syntax (e.g. *creavit Deus* > *gesceop God*), leading some scholars to criticise his approach to biblical translation for being so literal that it borders on becoming incomprehensible.[55] Yet even in this short passage, Ælfric nevertheless makes small concessions to vernacular grammar (e.g. *Terra* > *Seo eorðe*) and word order (*Et facta est lux* > *and leoht wearþ geworht*). Although alliteration is not used consistently as it would be in his later rhythmical prose, there are occasional flashes (e.g. *ydel and æmtig*; *Godes gast*), and in one phrase Ælfric picks up on sound patterning in the Latin source and matches it, rendering **Dixitque Deus, "Fiat lux." Et facta est lux** with an elegant, chiasmic structure as *God cwæþ þa: 'Geweorðe leoht', and leoht wearþ geworht*.

In keeping with his stated intention to provide only the 'naked' narrative of the Bible, and in striking contrast with the elaborate exegesis showcased in the Preface, Ælfric's translation of Genesis adds very little to the wording of the text by way of explanation or interpretation. However, as Marsden has demonstrated, Ælfric not only alters syntax and wording to achieve smooth, idiomatic English prose, but he also frequently paraphrases, edits or simplifies his source so as not to mislead his relatively unlearned readers, especially from Ch. 7.[56] Particularly striking is Ælfric's consistent omission or downplaying of references to the misconduct of the patriarchs and matriarchs, an approach that is also adopted by the anonymous translators throughout the Heptateuch. For example, an anonymous translator omits the verse in which Rachel lies to Laban claiming that she cannot stand up *nequeo quia iuxta consuetudinem feminarum nunc accidit mihi* ('because it has now happened to me, according to the custom of women',

---

[55] Stanley Greenfield and Daniel G. Calder, *A New Critical History of Old English Literature*, with a survey of the Anglo-Latin Background by Michael Lapidge (New York: NYU Press, 1986), p. 85.

[56] Richard Marsden, 'Ælfric as Translator: The Old English Prose *Genesis*', *Anglia* 109 (2009), 319–58. For an overview of Ælfric's approach to translating Genesis as well as that of the anonymous translators of other parts of the Heptateuch, see also Rebecca Barnhouse, 'Shaping the Hexateuch', in *Old English Hexateuch*, ed. Barnhouse and Withers, pp. 91–108.

Gen. 31.35). References to concubinage among the patriarchs are similarly downplayed by Ælfric and his fellow translators, lest uneducated readers might be misled into believing that the Church condoned this practice.[57] Hence Ælfric cuts a verse which describes how Sarah took her Egyptian handmaiden, Hagar, and gave her to her husband, Abraham, as a wife (Gen. 16.3),[58] while the anonymous translator has excised the entire story of Abraham's second marriage to the concubine Cetura and his division of property among her offspring (Gen. 25.1–4, 6).[59] Passages which are deemed irrelevant or potentially boring are likewise cut, notably the long genealogies of the descendants of Noah.[60]

On rare occasions, however, Ælfric's concern that his readers might misinterpret the Old Testament overrides his stated intention to add nothing to the wording of the Latin source, causing him to insert exegetical comments more typical of a homily than a translation in the strict sense. One such

---

[57] On ecclesiastical condemnation of concubinage and polygamy among the English aristocracy and monarchy, as well as the unreformed clergy, see Margaret Clunies Ross, 'Concubinage in Anglo-Saxon England', *Past & Present* 108 (1985), 3–34, repr. in *Anglo-Saxon History: Basic Readings*, ed. David A. E. Pelteret, Basic Readings in Anglo-Saxon England 6 (New York: Routledge, 2000), pp. 251–88.

[58] On Ælfric's treatment of this story and other accounts in early medieval English art and literature, see Catherine E. Karkov, 'Hagar and Ishmael: The Uncanny and The Exile', in *Imagining the Jew in Anglo-Saxon Literature and Culture*, ed. Samantha Zacher, Toronto Anglo-Saxon Studies Series 21 (Toronto: University of Toronto Press, 2016), pp. 197–218.

[59] For the argument that the omission of Tamar's second marriage, to Onan who 'spilled his seed in the ground' (*sui semen fundebat in terram*) (Gen. 38.8–10), similarly reflects the translators' general avoidance of sexual topics throughout the Old English Heptateuch, see Mary C. Olson, 'Genesis and Narratology: The Challenge of Medieval Illustrated Texts', *Mosaic* 31 (1998), 1–24, at 14–21; Jonathan Wilcox, 'A Place to Weep: Joseph in the Beer-Room and Anglo-Saxon Gestures of Emotion', in *Saints and Scholars: New Perspectives on Anglo-Saxon Literature and Culture in Honour of Hugh Magennis*, ed. Stuart McWilliams (Cambridge: D. S. Brewer, 2012), pp. 14–32, at 17–22. For the recent suggestion that this same omission is more reflective of contemporary English concerns with widowhood, see A. Joseph McMullen and Chelsea Shields-Más, 'Tamar, Widowhood, and the Old English Prose Translation of Genesis', *Anglia* 138 (2020), 586–617. On the downplaying of sexual matters in Old English writing more generally, see Hugh Magennis, '"No Sex Please, We're Anglo-Saxons?": Attitudes towards Sexuality in Old English Prose and Poetry', *Leeds Studies in English* 26 (1995), 1–27.

[60] The genealogies of the descendants of Noah's sons, Shem, Ham and Japheth (Gen. 10.2–31) and the generations from Shem to Thare (Gen. 11.10–26) are missing from MSS L and B, thought to be the best witnesses to Ælfric's section. These sections are translated, however, in MS C, the work of one or more of the anonymous translators of the Heptateuch.

homiletic excursus occurs in Ælfric's treatment of the story of Lot and the angels in Sodom (Gen. 19.1–38).[61] The translation of the opening passage (Gen. 19.1–3) is typical of his approach to Genesis more generally (table 4); sections omitted in the Old English version are struck through, alterations to the Latin source are indicated by italics in both columns and wording original to Ælfric is underlined:

---

[61] On the treatment of homosexuality by Ælfric and other early medieval English authors more generally, see Malcolm R. Godden, 'The Trouble with Sodom: Literary Responses to Biblical Sexuality', *Bulletin of the John Rylands University Library of Manchester* 77 (1995), 96–119; David Clark, *Between Medieval Men: Male Friendship and Desire in Early Medieval English Literature* (Oxford: Oxford University Press, 2009).

Table 4. Comparison of Genesis 19.1–3 in Vulgate and Ælfric's Genesis

Vulgate	Ælfric's Genesis
Gen. 19.1 Veneruntque duo angeli Sodomam vespere, et sedente Lot in foribus civitatis. Qui cum vidisset eos, surrexit, et ivit obviam eis: adoravitque pronus in terram,	Comon þa on æfnunge twegen englas fram Gode asende to þære birig Sodoma. And Loth, Abrahames broðer sunu, sæt on ðære stræt and geseah hig. He aras þa sona and eode him togeanes and astrehte hyne ætforan þam englum
[And the two angels came to Sodom in the evening, and Lot was sitting in the gate of the city. And seeing them, he rose up and went to meet them: and worshipped prostrate to the ground,]	[Then two angels came in the evening sent from God to the city of Sodom. And Lot, Abraham's brother's son, sat on the street and saw them. He quickly arose then and went towards them and prostrated himself before those angels]
² et dixit: 'Obsecro, domini, declinate in domum pueri vestri, et manete ibi: lavate pedes vestros, et mane proficiscemini in viam vestram.' Qui dixerunt: 'Minime, sed in platea manebimus.'	and cwæð: 'Ic bidde eow, leof, þæt ge gecirron to minum huse and þær wunion nihtlanges, and þweað eowre fet þæt ge magon faran tomergen on eowerne weg.' Hig cwædon: 'Nateshwon, ac we wyllaþ wunian on þære stræt.'
[And said: 'I beseech you, my lords, turn in to the house of your servant, and lodge there: wash your feet, and in the morning you shall go on your way.' And they said: 'No, but we will abide in the street.']	[and said: I beseech you, beloved, that you turn in to my house and stay there for the night, and wash your feet so that you may go on your way in the morning.' They said: 'Not at all, for we wish to remain in the street.']
³ Compulit illos oppido ut diverterent ad eum: ingressisque domum illius fecit convivium, et coxit azyma, et comederunt.	Loth þa hig laþode geornlice oð þæt hig gecyrdon to his huse. He þa gearcode him gereord and hig æton.
[He pressed them very much to turn in unto him: and when they were come into his house, he made them a feast, and baked unleavened bread and they ate:]	[Lot earnestly pressed them until they turned into his house. He then prepared a meal for them and they ate.]

In translating these verses, Ælfric makes numerous small changes to the wording of the source, clarifying certain minor points of detail that might have confused his readers. For example, in the first verse he explains that the angels were sent by God, that Sodom was a city, and that Lot was Abraham's nephew (Gen. 19.1), while in 19.3 he omits the source's reference to *azyma* ('unleavened bread') as this would be unfamiliar to his readers. In Gen. 19.2, Ælfric makes a small lexical alteration, rendering the dative plural form *domini* ('lords'), which has a formal vocative function here, with the Old English formal term of address *leof* ('beloved'), thereby further domesticating the source text into English idiom.

Such minor alterations of wording, grammar and syntax in service of clarity and intelligibility are on display throughout Ælfric's translation of the story of Lot and the angels. For instance, the Vulgate's reference to the number of Lot's daughters (Gen. 19.15, 16) is dropped, as Ælfric had already clarified the number of his sons-in-law in verse 14, while a potentially confusing reference to Lot as *servus tuus* ('your servant') is replaced by the personal pronoun *me* (Gen. 19.19). Further modifications of wording and syntax may simply be a matter of personal choice and style: hence, for example, Ælfric reverses the word order of Gen. 19.23 *Sol egressus est super terram, et Lot ingressus est Segor* ('The sun was risen upon the earth, and Lot entered into Segor') to produce *Loth com þa to Segor, þa þa sunne upp eode* ('Then Lot came to Segor, when the sun came up').

Other small translation choices in Ælfric's rendering of the story of Lot are prompted by his abiding concern with theological orthodoxy. For example, the reference to the salvation of Lot's soul in Gen. 19.20, which might have perplexed a Christian reader given that Lot himself was not a Christian, is replaced with the simple statement that he wished to save his life, while ambiguity is further reduced with the substitution of the concluding rhetorical question with a simple statement of fact:

> est civitas haec iuxta, ad quam possum fugere, parva, et saluabor in ea: numquid non modica est, et **vivet anima mea**?

> [There is this city here at hand, to which I may flee, it is a little one, and I shall be saved in it: surely it is small enough **that my soul might live in it**?][62]

> Nu ys her gehende an gehwæde burh, to þære ic mæg fleon and **minum feore gebeorgan**.

> [Now there is a little city nearby, where I may flee and **save my life**.]

---

[62] Translation modified from Douay-Rheims, which has the overly literal: *is it not a little one, and my soul shall live.*

The Old English idiom 'to protect one's life' appears elsewhere in poetry but is rare in prose, though Ælfric uses it once in his *Life of St Edmund*.[63]

Ælfric's treatment of the story of Lot and Sodom is also noteworthy from a stylistic perspective, as it marks the introduction of Ælfric's late rhythmical prose style (at Gen. 19.19), characterised by the use of word pairs and two-stress phrases linked by alliteration.[64] This shift becomes more apparent if we present the prose in lineated layout, as has become the editorial convention for his *Lives*:

> [19.19] '[...] nu þu þine **m**ildheortnysse **m**e cyddest,
> for þan þe ic ne **m**æg on þam **m**unte **m**e gebeorgan,
> þe læs þe me þær gefo sum færlic yfel.
> [19.20] Nu ys her ge**h**ende an ge**h**wæde **b**urh,
> to þære ic mæg **f**leon and minum **f**eore gebeorgan.'
> [19.21] Him wæs þa geandwyrd þus: 'Ic **u**nderfeng þine **b**ene
> þæt ic þa **b**urh ne towende, nu ðu wylt þyder **b**ugan. [...].'

['[...] [19.19] Now you make known to me your mercy, because I cannot save my life on that mountain, lest some evil should quickly befall me there. [19.20] Now there is a little city nearby, where I may flee and save my life.' [19.21] He answered him thus: 'I received your prayer that I should not destroy the city, now you wish to return there. [...].']

In his rendering of the transformation of Lot's wife into a pillar of salt, Ælfric's lexical additions to the Latin enhance alliteration on *w* and *s*, as well as making the scene more dramatic; inserted words are underlined below and alliteration marked in bold:

---

[63] Ælfric's *Life of Edmund*: Clayton and Mullins, III.29, pp. 190–91, l. 59. For examples in poetry, see *Genesis A* (l. 1838a), *Beowulf* (ll. 1293a, 1548b, 2570b–71a, 2599a) and *The Battle of Maldon* (l. 194b).

[64] On Ælfric's rhythmical prose, see John C. Pope, *Homilies of Ælfric: A Supplementary Collection*, 2 vols, EETS o.s. 259 (London, Oxford University Press, 1967), I, pp. 105–36; Peter Clemoes, 'Ælfric', in *Continuations and Beginnings: Studies in Old English Literature*, ed. Eric G. Stanley (London: Nelson, 1966), pp. 176–209 (at pp. 203–4); Peter Clemoes, *Rhythm and Cosmic Order in Old English Christian Literature: An Inaugural Lecture* (Cambridge: Cambridge University Press, 1970); and Haruko Momma, 'Rhythm and Alliteration: Styles of Ælfric's Prose up to the *Lives of Saints*', in *Anglo-Saxon Styles*, ed. Karkov and Hardin Brown, pp. 253–70. On Ælfric's debt to the rhythmical prose style of earlier Old English homilies, see Bruce Mitchell, 'The Relation Between Old English Alliterative Verse and Ælfric's Alliterative Prose', in *Latin Learning and English Lore: Studies in Anglo-Saxon Literature for Michael Lapidge*, ed. Katherine O'Brien O'Keeffe and Andy Orchard, 2 vols (Toronto: University of Toronto Press, 2005), II, pp. 349–62. Stanton connects the development of rhythmical prose style with Ælfric's move towards a *sermo humilis* (plain style) (*Culture of Translation*, pp. 160–1).

| ^{19.26} Respiciensque uxor *eius* post se, versa est in statuam salis. | Ða beseah Lohtes wif <u>unwislice</u> underbæc and wearð <u>sona</u> awend to anum sealtstane, <u>na for wiglunge ac for gewisre getacnunge.</u> |
| [And *his* wife looking behind her, was turned into a statue of salt.] | [Then *Lot's* wife <u>unwisely</u> looked behind her and was <u>suddenly</u> turned into a stone of salt, <u>not for wilfulness but as a certain sign.</u>] |

However, on the whole Ælfric refrains from the ornate stylistic flourishes which appear with more consistency in his later works such as the *Lives of Saints*, opting instead for a plain, humble style mirroring that of his scriptural source.

It is in Ælfric's treatment of the actions of the Sodomites and Lot's daughters, however, that his homiletic instincts force him to temporarily abandon his principle of adding nothing to the wording of the source. Most strikingly, he excises all of Gen. 19.4–11, which describes how the men of Sodom attempted to 'know' Lot's houseguests, demanding that he bring them out of the house, only for Lot to offer them his daughters instead with the statement *abutimini eis sicut vobis placuerit* ('abuse you them as it shall please you'). [65] In place of this passage, Ælfric supplies a terse exegetical statement which has no basis in the biblical source:

Se leodscipe wæs swa bysmorfull þæt hig woldon fullice ongean gecynd heora galnysse gefyllan, na mid wimmannum ac swa fullice þæt us sceamað hyt openlice to secgenne, and þæt wæs heora hream þæt hig openlice heora fylþe gefremedon.

[The townspeople were so sinful that they wished to go completely against their nature to fall into lust, not with women but so completely that it shames us openly to say it, and that was their outcry that they openly performed their filth.]

As Malcolm Godden notes, while the sexuality of the Sodomites may have been only a minor element in the original biblical story, Ælfric is following a long tradition of exegesis in identifying homosexuality as the cause of

---

[65] On the debate surrounding whether the biblical narrative uses the term 'to know' in the sexual sense here or in the sense of simply to acquaint, see Godden, 'The Trouble with Sodom', 98. In the same article, Godden also discusses the common interpretation of Lot's offer of his daughters as an act of wisdom (110–11).

God's wrath.[66] Having made his own views on the sexual misconduct of the Sodomites clear to his readers, Ælfric emphasises the ferocity of God's wrath by adding intensifiers to the angels' words to Lot:

> [19.13] delebimus enim locum istum, eo quod increverit clamor eorum coram Domino, *qui* misit nos ut perdamus illos.
>
> [For we will destroy this place, because their cry is grown loud before the Lord, *who* has sent us to destroy them.]
>
> [19.13] We sceolon **soþlice** adiligan **ealle** þas stowe, for þam þe heora hream weox **to** swyþe ætforan Gode *and God us sende* þæt we hig fordon.
>
> [We must **truly** destroy **all** of this place, because their cry has grown **too** great before God, *and God sent us so* that we should destroy them.]

God's righteous anger is further emphasised in the expanded description of the destruction of the cities of Sodom and Gomorrah (Gen. 19.25) which features extensive alliteration on *g*, *w*, *b* and *ea(l)*; expansions are underlined and alliteration marked in bold:

[19.25] et *subvertit* civitates has, et omnem circa regionem, universos habitatores urbium, et cuncta terrae virentia.	**God** towearp þa swa <u>mid **g**raman</u> þa **b**urga and **eal**ne þone **ear**d endemes <u>towende</u> and **eal**le þa **b**urhwara <u>for**b**ærnde ætgædere</u>, and **eal**l þæt **g**rowende <u>**wæs** **wear**ð adilegod</u>.
[And *he destroyed* these cities, and all the country about, all the inhabitants of the cities, and all things that spring from the earth.]	[*God* thus destroyed those cities <u>with wrath</u> and likewise <u>overthrew</u> all the country about and <u>burned up</u> all the citizens <u>together</u>, and all that was growing <u>was blotted out</u>.]

Ælfric amplifies this biblical theme of divine wrath in his account of Lot in order to impress firmly upon his readers the dire consequences of sexual licentiousness, a topic with which he is much concerned elsewhere in his other writings for the laity. For example, in *De octo uitiis et de duodecim abusiuis gradus*, an adaptation of monastic treatises which seems to have

---

[66] Godden, 'The Trouble with Sodom', 98. Godden further notes that the poet of *Genesis A*, by contrast, was seemingly uninterested in the Sodomites' homosexuality, attributing the cause of the downfall of their city to the sins of drunkenness and rowdiness (109–13).

been aimed primarily at lay readers and which circulated as part of his *Lives of Saints*, Ælfric warns of the vice of lust:

> Se oðer leahter is forliger and ungemetgod galnyss. Se is gehaten *fornicatio*, and he befylð þone mannan, and macað of Cristes limum myltestrena lima ond and of Godes temple gramena wununge.

> [The second vice is adultery and intemperate lust. This is called *fornicatio* and it defiles a person and makes prostitutes' limbs out of Christ's limbs and a dwelling of fiends out of God's temple].[67]

Ælfric's condemnation of the Sodomites, and his concern that his readers should not be exposed to such material, again overrides his stated commitment to add nothing to the naked text of the Bible, steering him into further invective. Hence in Gen. 19.15, Ælfric renders the Vulgate's *scelere civitatis* ('the wickedness of the city') as *þisre scildigan burhware* ('these sinful citizens'), while he expands Gen. 19.24 by inserting his own damning assessment of how God punished them for their sins:

[19.24] Igitur Dominus pluit super Sodomam et Gomorrham sulphur et ignem a Domino de caelo.	And God sende to þam burgum eallbyrnende renscur mid swefle gemencged **and þa sceamleasan fordyde**.
[And the Lord rained upon Sodom and Gomorrha brimstone and fire from the Lord out of heaven.]	[And God sent to those cities a burning rain shower mingled with sulphur **and destroyed those shameless ones**.]

---

[67] Mary Clayton, ed. and trans., *Two Ælfric Texts: "The Twelve Abuses" and "The Vices and Virtues": An Edition and Translation of Ælfric's Old English Versions of "De duodecim abusivis" and "De octo vitiis et de duodecim abusivis"*, Anglo-Saxon Texts 11 (Cambridge: D. S. Brewer, 2013), pp. 144–5 (translation modified). Clayton identifies Ælfric's main sources for *De octo vitiis* as Alcuin's *De virtutibus et vitiis* (itself composed for Carolingian laity) and Cassian's monastic treatises, the *Conlationes* and *De institutis*. On Ælfric's adaptation of these sources for an English lay audience, see Clayton, esp. p. 106. Ælfric combined this work on the eight vices and virtues with an adaption of the Hiberno-Latin *De duodecim abusiuis gradus*.

A Perilous Task: Making the Old English Heptateuch

Just as Ælfric is willing to depart from the scriptural source in his eagerness to condemn the Sodomites, so in his rendering of Gen. 19.12 he expands on the Vulgate in placing extra emphasis on Lot's righteousness, inserting the epithet *se þe rihtlice leofode* ('the one who righteously believed') where the Latin had simply provided his name.

Ælfric's concern with the moral lives of his readers causes him to omit the Vulgate's description of how Lot's elder daughter told her sibling that she had lain with her father during the night after making him drunk (Gen. 19.34) and the reference to both daughters becoming pregnant *de patre suo* ('by their father') (Gen. 19.36).[68] The same reluctance to expose readers to the misconduct of the patriarchs lies behind the addition of the qualifying statement that Lot did not know if he had slept with his daughters *for þære/his druncenysse* ('because of the/his drunkenness') (Gen. 19.33, 35), a vice which Ælfric warns his lay readers of in his *Treatise on the Old and New Testaments* and his translation of Alcuin's *De virtutibus*.[69] In the Vulgate, Lot and his daughters, by contrast, commit incest because of the need for procreation.[70] In his own summary of the first age of the world in the *Treatise*, Ælfric would distinguish between the respective fates of the evil inhabitants of Sodom, who are damned because of their sinfulness, and Lot, who is spared because of his righteousness:

> And on þissere ylde þa yfelan leoda fif burhscira, ðæs fulan mennisces Sodomitisces eardes, mid sweflenum fyre færlice wurdon ealle forbærnde, and heora burga samod, buton Loþe anum þe God alædde þanon mid his ðrim hiwum for his rihtwisnisse.[71]

---

[68] Godden argues that Ælfric was less interested in the incest of Lot's daughters than the sin of the Sodomites, contrasting the 'matter-of-fact' style of this passage with his more polemical approach to the preceding episode ('The Trouble with Sodom', 103). On Ælfric's concern with sexual matters and voyeurism in his saints' lives, see Renée Trilling, 'Heavenly Bodies: Paradoxes of Female Martyrdom in Ælfric's *Lives of Saints*', in *Writing Women Saints in Anglo-Saxon England*, ed. Paul E. Szarmach (Toronto: University of Toronto Press, 2013), pp. 249–73.

[69] Ælfric makes a similar complaint about excessive drinking to another lay patron in his *Letter to Wulfgeat*, which is preserved in Laud Misc. 50 (MS L) along with the Heptateuch and *Treatise on the Old and New Testaments*. Cubitt (p. 184) places Wulfgeat in the same thegnly class as Sigeweard. See below, pp. 238–9. For the warning against drunkenness in the *Eight Vices*, see Clayton, ed., *Two Ælfric Texts*, pp. 142–5, 148–9.

[70] Indeed, medieval exegetes tended to view Lot's incest as a lesser sin than that of the Sodomites because it involved heterosexual intercourse: see Godden, 'The Trouble with Sodom'.

[71] Marsden, ed., *Heptateuch*, I, p. 206, ll. 145–8.

[And in this age the evil people of the five cities, the entire people of the land of the Sodomites, were all suddenly burned with sulphurous fire, and their city with them, except for Lot alone, whom God led out of there with his three relatives on account of his righteousness.]

While the *Treatise* makes no mention of Lot's incest with his daughters, in his translation of Genesis Ælfric's small twofold insertion of the explanatory phrase *for þære druncenysse* both excuses Lot's behaviour and serves as a warning to his lay readers of the terrible consequences that might befall them should they too indulge in excessive drinking.

Ælfric's cautious treatment of Lot and the Sodomites in his translation of Genesis can be contrasted with his more exegetical paraphrase of the same story in his sermon 'On the Prayer of Moses for Mid-Lent Sunday', an apocalyptic work included in his *Lives of the Saints* which reflects on how God has always punished sinners throughout history.[72] Following a brief summary of the fate of the rebel angels, the fall of Adam and the destruction of fornicators in the Great Flood, Ælfric delivers an abbreviated account of the destruction of Sodom and the flight of Lot and his family. Paraphrasing Gen. 18.22–33, Ælfric describes how Abraham pleaded with God on behalf of any righteous citizens who might be dwelling in Sodom:

> Eft ða God wolde wrecan mid fyre
> þa fulan forligeras þæs fracodostan mennisces,
> Sodomitiscra ðeoda, þa sæde he hit Abrahame.
> Habraham þa bæd þone Ælmihtigan ðus:
> "Þu Drihten, þe demst eallum deadlicum flæsce,
> ne scealt ðu þone rihtwisan ofslean mid þam arleasan.
> Gif ðær beoð fiftig wera wunigende on þam earde,
> rihtwise ætforan ðe, ara him eallum."
> Ða cwæð God him to eft: "Ic arige him eallum
> gif ic ðær finde fiftig rihtwisra."
> Þa began Abraham eft biddan God georne
> þæt he hi ne fordyde gif ðær feowertig wæron
> rihtwisra wera wunigende on ðære leode.
> God him ðæs getiþode and he began git biddan
> oðþæt he becom to tyn mannum, and him tiðode ða God
> þæt he nolde hi fordon gif he funde ðær tyn
> rihtwisra manna, and he wende ða him fram.

---

[72] For discussion of this text and its interpretation of the Viking invasions as a sign of God's wrath, see Malcolm Godden, 'Apocalypse and Invasion in Late Anglo-Saxon England', in *From Anglo-Saxon to Early Middle English*, ed. Eric G. Stanley, Malcolm Godden, Douglas Gray and Terry Hoad (Oxford: Oxford University Press, 1994), pp. 130–62.

[Likewise when God intended to punish by fire the foul fornicators of that most wicked people, the people of Sodom, then he told this to Abraham. Abraham then prayed to the Almighty thus: "You Lord, you who judge all mortal flesh, you ought not to kill the just person with the impious person. If there are fifty people living in this region, just in your judgement, spare them all." Then God spoke to him again: "I will spare them all if I find fifty just people there." Then Abraham began to entreat God urgently not to destroy them if there were forty just men living among that people. God granted him that and he began to entreat again until he came to ten people, and God granted him then that he would not destroy them if he found there ten just people, and then he went away from him.][73]

Whereas alliteration and other stylistic effects were used sparingly in the earlier translation of Genesis, 'On the Prayer of Moses' is representative of Ælfric's late, rhythmical prose style. In this passage, alliteration is used effectively to link sound and sense, underlining Ælfric's disgust at the conduct of the Sodomites (*þa fulan forligeras þæs fracodostan mennisces*, 'the foul fornicators of that most wicked people'). However, those same features of the story which had given him so much concern in his translation of Genesis – in particular the Sodomites' surrounding of Lot's house and their attempted rape of the angels – are now completely excised, as is the troublesome story of the incest of Lot and his daughters. In their place, Ælfric offers a moral interpretation of the significance of God's sparing of Lot:

God sende ða sona to ðam sceandlicum mannum
twegen englas on æfen and hi Abrahames broðor sunu,
Loth, mid his hiwum, alæddon of ðære byrig
and ðær næs na ma þe manful nære gemet.
God sende ða fyr on merigen and fulne swefel him to
and forbærnde hi ealle mid egeslicum fyre,
and ðær is nu ful wæter ðær ða fulan wunodon.
And Loth se rihtwisa wearð ahred ðurh God.
Be ðysum man mæg tocnawan þæt micclum fremiað
þam læwedum mannum þa gelæredan Godes ðeowas,
þæt hi mid heora ðeowdome him ðingian to Gode,
nu God wolde arian eallum ðam synfullum
gif he þær gemette tyn rihtwise menn.

[God immediately sent two angels in the evening to the shameful people, and they took Abraham's brother's son Lot, with his family, out of the city, and no more were found there who were not evil. Then in the

---

[73] Clayton and Mullins, II.12, pp. 38–41, ll. 190–206/190–207; translations adapted from this edition to UK spelling.

morning God sent fire and foul sulphur to them and burned them all up and destroyed their cities and all that region with a terrifying fire, and now there is foul water where the foul ones lived. And Lot the just man was saved by God. From this it can be known that the learned servants of God greatly benefit lay people, in that they intercede for them with God by their service, since God was willing to spare all the sinful people if he found ten just people there.][74]

In marked contrast to the Genesis translation, in which he strove to provide only the 'naked' narrative, Ælfric is now able to deliver a clear doctrinal message to his unlearned lay readers (*læwedum mannum*) in this homiletic paraphrase: if they avoid the sins of the Sodomites and imitate the righteousness of Lot, as well as receiving the intercession (*ðingian*) of learned (*gelæredan*) clergymen such as himself, they too will be spared God's wrath. Ælfric's description of the foul water which still marks the desolation of Sodom in this passage echoes his earlier *Interrogationes Sigewulfi*, in which he had contrasted the gentler, watery punishment of Noah's Flood with the devastating fiery wrath unleashed upon the Sodomites:

> On Noes flode wæs seo eorðe afeormað and eft geedcucod and on þæra Sodomitiscra gewitnunge forbarn seo eorþe and bið æfre unwæstmbære and mid fulum wætere ofergan.[75]

> [In Noah's Flood the earth was cleansed and afterwards revived, and in the punishment of the Sodomites the earth was completely burned and will forever be unfruitful and covered with foul water.]

By contrast with the generally conservative translation of Genesis, Ælfric was free in these and other homiletic works to guide his readers in their response to the often complex narratives of the Old and New Testaments.

At the end of the *Preface to Genesis*, Ælfric had stated his intention to translate no more Latin books after his version of Genesis, echoing his earlier statement at the end of the second series of *Catholic Homilies* that he would not translate any more Gospels or gospel-expositions:[76]

---

[74] Clayton and Mullins, II.12, pp. 40–1, ll. 207–20/207–20.

[75] George E. MacLean, ed., 'Ælfric's Anglo-Saxon Version of *Alcuini Interrogationes Sigewulfi in Genesin*', *Anglia* 6 (1883), 425–73, and *Anglia* 7 (1884), 1–59, at 48. On the equation of Ælfric and Alcuin in the thirteenth-century poem *The First Worcester Fragment*, perhaps on account of his translation of this work, see below, p. 246 n. 6. On the relationship between Ælfric's *Interrogationes* and his *Preface to Genesis*, see above, pp. 160–1 n. 48.

[76] For the debates surrounding Ælfric's reluctance to translate, see Wilcox, *Ælfric's Prefaces*, pp. 40–4; see further above, pp. 157–8.

Ic cweþe nu þæt ic ne dearr, ne ic nelle, nane boc æfter þissere of Ledene on Englisc awendan. And ic bidde þe, leof ealdorman, þæt þu me þæs na leng ne bidde, þi læs þe ic beo þe ungehirsum, oþþe leas gif ic do.[77]

[I say now that I do not dare, nor do I wish, to translate any other book after this from Latin into English. And I ask you, dear ealdorman, that you do not request this of me any longer, lest that I should be disobedient to you, or false if I do.]

Ælfric would in fact go on to translate and adapt several further biblical books, including the second half of Numbers and the paraphrases of Joshua and Judges. However, in these later renderings of the Old Testament, he would increasingly move away from word-for-word translation towards interpretive, homiletic exegesis, a process that would culminate in his summary of the entire Bible in the form of the *Treatise on the Old and New Testaments*.[78]

Exodus

The Old English prose *Exodus* was produced by two anonymous translators, with the changeover taking place around Ex. 17.[79] For the most part, these translators follow the functional equivalence approach employed throughout most of the Old English *Genesis*, whereby the meaning of the source text is brought over to the reader in the idiom and syntax of the target language. However, whereas all fifty of Genesis' chapters were translated, the approach to Exodus is considerably more selective: Chs 1–35.3 are rendered faithfully, with some abridgement, but the final four and a half chapters (35.4–40), in which Moses reiterates the commandments God had issued to him on Mount Sinai, are all cut.[80] As we shall see, this tendency towards abridgement becomes more pronounced as we move through the remaining books of the Heptateuch, reflecting the team's sensitivity to the needs of their readers.

The economical style of the prose *Exodus* is well represented in the first translator's selective treatment of the Israelites' crossing of the Red Sea (Ex. 14). In stark contrast to the poetic *Exodus*, which transforms this episode into a dramatic set piece covering over two hundred lines (ll. 447–590),[81] the prose version compresses the episode to its bare essen-

---

[77] Marsden, ed., *Heptateuch*, I, p. 7, ll. 115–18.
[78] On the *Treatise*, see Chapter Five.
[79] Marsden reaches this conclusion from analysis of variant readings based on Vulgate and Old Latin sources: *Text of the Old Testament*, pp. 420–9.
[80] On the treatment of Exodus in the Mosaic Prologue, see above, Chapter Two, pp. 54–67.
[81] *Exodus* was probably composed early in the Old English period (c. 700–850),

tials. Artistic flourishes are generally kept to a minimum, though there are occasional instances of alliteration (in bold) and balanced phrasing (underlined) suggestive of a conscious prose stylist:

> 14.15 'Sege Israhela **f**olce þæt hig **f**aron to þære Readan Sæ, 16 and aðene þine girde ofer þa sæ and todæl hig, þæt Israhelisce folc ga drium fotum innan þa sæ. 17 And ic ahyrde Pharaones **h**eortan and his folces þæt hig **f**arað æfter eow innan þa sæ, þæt ic beo gemærsod on Pharaone <u>and on eallum his here and on eallum his cratum</u> 18 and þa Egiptiscan witon þæt ic eom Drihten eower God.' 21 Þa Moises aþeonde his hand ofer þa sæ, þa sende Drihten micelne wind ealle þa niht and gewende þa sæ to drium, <u>and þæt wæter wearð on **tw**a todæled</u> and læg an **d**rie stræt þurh þa sæ, 22 <u>and þæt wæter stod on **tw**a healfa</u> þære stræt, swilce **tw**egen **h**ege weallas. Þa for eall Israhela folc þurh þa sæ on þone weg þe Drihten him geworhte and comon hale and gesunde þurh þa sæ, swa Drihten him behet. 23 Ða Pharao com to þære sæ, and eall his here, þa for he on þone ylcan weg æfter Israhela folce on dægred, <u>mid eallum his folce and mid eallum his wæpnum</u>. 26 Þa cwæð Drihten to Moise: 'Aþena þine hand <u>ofer þa sæ and ofer Pharaon and ofer ealne his here</u>.' 27 And he ahefde up his **h**and and seo sæ **s**loh togædere and ahwylfde Pharaones cratu 28 and adrencte hine sylfne and eall his **f**olc, þæt þar ne wearð furðon to laue an þe lif gebyrode. 29 Soðlice Moises and Israhela **f**olc foron þurh þæ sæ **d**rium fotum. 30 And **D**rihten alysde on þam **d**æge Israhela folc of þara Egiptiscan handum 31 and hig gesawon þa Egiptiscan deade, upp to lande aworpene, þa hira ær ehton on ðam lande þe hig þa to cumene wæron, and þæt Israhelisce folc on**d**redon him **D**rihten and hyrdon Gode and Moise his þeowe.[82]

> [15 'Say to the people of Israel that they should go to the Red Sea, 16 and lift up your rod over that sea and divide it, so that the Israelite people can go on dry land through the sea. 17 And I will harden Pharaoh's heart and his people's so that they follow after you into that sea, so that I will be glorified in Pharaoh and in all of his army and in all his chariots, 18 and the Egyptians will know that I am the Lord your God.' 21 Then Moses lifted his hand over the sea, then the Lord sent a great wind all that night and turned the sea into dry land, and that water was divided in two and a dry path lay through the sea, 22 and that water stood on both sides of the path, like two high walls. Then all the people of Israel went through that sea on the route that the Lord made for them and they came safe and sound through the sea, just as

---

but its sole manuscript witness is MS Junius 11, copied close to the time of the composition of the Heptateuch (c. 960–970).

[82] Marsden, ed., *Heptateuch*, I, pp. 109–10.

the Lord had promised them. ²³ Then Pharaoh came to that sea, and all his army, then he went on that same route after the people of Israel in the dawn, with all his people and with all his weapons. ²⁶ Then the Lord said to Moses: 'Lift your hand over the sea and over Pharaoh and over all his army.' ²⁷ And he raised up his hand and the sea struck together and covered over Pharaoh's chariots ²⁸ and drowned him and all his people, so that there remained not one of them alive. ²⁹ Truly Moses and the people of Israel went through the sea on dry land. ³⁰ And the Lord saved the people of Israel on that day from the hands of the Egyptians ³¹ and they saw the Egyptians dead, thrown up onto the shore, who before had pursued them on that land when they were come to them, and that Israelite people feared the Lord and obeyed God and Moses his messenger.]

Extraneous details in the Vulgate source are passed over, including God's question to Moses (Ex. 14.15: *quid clamas ad me*, 'why do you cry unto me?') and God's instruction that Moses should extend his hand (Ex. 14.16: *et extende manum*) over the water. Similarly, the repetition of Pharaoh's host, chariots and horsemen (Ex. 14.17: *in curribus et in equitibus illius*; Ex. 14.18: *atque in equitibus eius*) is reduced to a single reference to *his folces* ('his people') in verse 17 and an abbreviated reference to his army and chariots in verse 18. Other verses are cut entirely, such as Ex. 14.19–20, which describes the angel of God and the pillar of cloud standing between the Israelites and the pursuing army of Pharaoh, and Ex. 19.24–5, in which the Lord flings the Egyptians from their chariots as they realise the Lord is fighting on the side of the Israelites. Alert to the fact that readers of the Heptateuch might find the biblical motif of the pillars of cloud and fire confusing, the translator explains that the 'pillar of cloud' (*columna nubis*) was in fact a 'clear sign' (*swert tacen*) in 'the likeness' (*on [...] gelicynsse*) of a pillar (Ex. 13.21–2) (alliteration in bold):

[21] Dominus autem praecedebat eos ad ostendendam viam per diem in columna nubis, et per noctem in columna ignis, ut dux esset itineris utroque tempore. [22] Numquam defuit columna nubis per diem, nec columna ignis per noctem, coram populo.	And Drihten for beforan him and **swu**telode him þone weg on *dæg þurh swert tacn, on sweres gelicynsse*, and on niht **swi**lce an byrnende **sw**er him for beforan, [22] and symle him gelæste *þæt sweorte tacn* on dæg and þæt fyrene on niht.[83]
[And the Lord went before them to show the way, by day in a pillar of a cloud, and by night in a pillar of fire, that he might be the guide of their journey at both times. [22] There never failed the pillar of the cloud by day, nor the pillar of fire by night, before the people.]	[And the Lord went before them to show them the way by day *through a clear sign, in the likeness of a pillar*, and by night also a burning pillar went before them, [22] and *that clear sign* always served them by day and that fire by night.] (Emphases added).

Again, comparison with the poetic version is instructive: in the verse *Exodus*, the description of the pillars of cloud and fire takes up over thirty verse lines (ll. 72b–97), as the poet invites the learned (and probably monastic) reader to meditate on the miraculous image of the *halige seglas, / lyft-wundor leoht* ('holy sails, bright sky-wonder', ll. 89b–90a);[84] the prose version, by comparison, is truncated and simplified, to cater to readers untrained in the monastic practice of meditative reading.

A rare expansion to the Vulgate source occurs in Ex. 14.22, where the first translator rearranges the syntax, placing the comparison between the divided sea and walls first, before providing a brief explanation of the Lord's role in the Israelites' salvation (expansion in italics):

---

[83] Marsden, ed., *Heptateuch*, I, p. 110.
[84] For discussion of the complex imagery at work in this celebrated poetic passage, see Miranda Wilcox, 'Creating the cloud-tent-ship conceit in *Exodus*', *ASE* 40 (2012), 103–50.

¹⁴·²² et ingressi sunt filii Israhel per medium maris sicci erat enim aqua quasi murus a dextra eorum et leva.	and þæt wæter stod on twa healfa þære stræte, swilce twegen hege weallas. Þa for eall Irahela folc þurh þa sæ on þone weg þe Drihten him geworhte and comon hale and gesunde þurh þa sæ, swa Drihten him behet.
[And the children of Israel went in through the midst of the sea dried up; for the water was as a wall on their right hand and on their left.]	[and that water stood on both sides of the path, like two high walls. Then all the people of Israel went through that sea on the route *that the Lord made for them and they came safe and sound through the sea, just as the Lord had promised them.*]

While placing greater emphasis on God's covenant with his Chosen People, the introduction of the idiomatic English expression *hale and gesunde* ('safe and sound') also serves to further domesticate this key moment in the scriptural narrative.[85]

Leviticus

The irrelevance of many of the Judaic laws contained in Leviticus to contemporary English readers results in this book being even more severely edited in the Old English Heptateuch than either Genesis or Exodus, with many chapters reduced to a mere handful of verses. Although all seventeen verses of Chapter 1 are faithfully rendered, including instructions given by God to Moses from the tabernacle on the correct manner of offering animals as sacrifice, in Chapter 2 the translator begins to make extensive cuts, reducing the number of verses from sixteen to eight (Lev. 2.1, 2, 3, 4, 6, 11, 12 and 13). This drastic abbreviation continues throughout the translation of Leviticus. The omission of many minor details, such as instructions on the correct manner of preparing an oblation in a frying pan (Lev. 2.5) or gridiron (Lev. 2.7–10), allows for greater emphasis on the core theme of the biblical source text, namely that the Israelites were given strict instructions from God via Moses on how to make sacrifices.[86] Indeed, injunctions to fear the Lord God and keep his laws (e.g. Lev. 19.14, 32, 37; 19.19; 23.1; 25.17, 18) are not only retained but reinforced by a series

---

[85] *DOE Corpus* records four instances of the phrase in Old English prose.

[86] As we saw in Chapter Two of this volume, the Mosaic Prologue to the *Domboc* takes a similarly selective approach omitting long scriptural lists of outmoded Jewish practices now superseded by Christian laws; see pp. 62–6. For a recent study of supersessionist attitudes in the Heptateuch and other Old English biblical writing, see Mo Pareles, *Nothing Pure: Jewish Law, Christian Supersession, and Bible Translation in Old English* (Toronto: University of Toronto Press, 2024).

of variations on the statement *Ic eom Drihten [eowre God]* (e.g. Lev. 18.30; 19.12, 18–19, 36–7; 26.1, 13). This theme of obedience is most forcefully brought home in the conclusion to the Old English version. While the final chapter of the Vulgate source (Ch. 27) lists the reckoning of prices to be paid for various offences against God, the translator brings the vernacular version to a close with a relatively faithful translation of Chapter 26, concerning the terrible punishments which God will unleash on those who disobey his laws. In a departure from the periphrastic approach taken to most preceding chapters of Leviticus, now the translator makes extensive use of alliteration (in bold) and balanced phrasing (underlined), producing a powerful piece of rhythmical prose reminiscent of Ælfric's late style:

> 26.14 '[…] Gif ge me <u>ne **g**ehirað</u> and <u>mine **g**ebodu for**h**ogiað</u>, 15 and <u>mine æ</u> and <u>mine **d**omas forseð</u> and ne **d**oð <u>min **w**edd</u> for naht, 16 <u>ic **g**edo</u> eow þas þing. <u>Ic sende</u> hrædlice **f**yr and **g**ewirce eow to **w**ædlan. […] 17 <u>Ic wiðstande</u> ongen eow and ge **f**eallað be**f**oran eowrum **f**eondum and **g**ehirað þam þe eow **h**atiað. Ge **f**leoð, þeah eow man ne **d**rife. 18 <u>Ic eow **d**o</u> seofonfealdne ege, 19 and <u>ic **f**orbrece</u> eowre o**f**ermodignisse **h**eardnysse, and <u>ic **g**edo</u> þæt eow bið æ**g**þer **h**eard, ge **h**eofone ge eorðe. 20 And eall eower **g**eswinc bið idel; ne brin**g**ð eorðe eow nane wæstmas. 22 And <u>ic sende</u> on eow wildeor þæt forspillon eow and eowre **n**ytenu. 23 Gif ge **n**ellað onfon mine lare and **g**að ongean me, 24 <u>ic **g**a ongen eow</u> and slea eow. 25 And þonne ge fleoð fram byrig to byrig, ic sende cwealm on eow […]. 28 And <u>ic witnige eow</u> seofon witon, swa þæt ge etað eowre suna and eowre dohtra flæsc. 30 And <u>ic towurpe eowre</u> **h**eagan getimbru and eowre **h**earga ic tobrece, and ge feallað betwix eowrum deofolgildum. […] 41 And <u>ic **g**a ongen eow</u> and <u>**g**elæde eow</u> on feonda land, oþ eowre ly**þ**re mod a**b**lisige. Þonne **g**ebidde ge for eowrum arleasnissum, 42 and <u>ic **g**yme</u> min **w**edd þe ic **b**ehet Abrahame and Isaace and Iacobe. <u>Ic **g**ime</u> þæs landes; 43 þonne ge hit forlætað, hit licað me þeah hit weste sig. 44 <u>Ic eom</u> Drihten eowre God 45 þe eow ut alædde of Egipta lande beforan ealles folces gesihþe.'
>
> Ðis synd þa gebodu and domas and laga þe Drihten gesette betwyx him and Israhela folc on Sinai dune.[87]

['[…] 14 If you do not obey me and ignore my commandments, 15 and scorn my laws and do not keep my covenant at all, 16 I will do these things to you. I will send terrible fire and reduce you to poverty. […] 17 I will set my face against you and you will fall before your enemies and obey those whom you hate. You will flee, although men do not drive you. 18 I will deliver sevenfold terror on you, 19 and I will break your proud hardness, and I will make it so that you are always hard,

---

[87] Marsden, ed., *Heptateuch*, I, pp. 136–7.

and everything will be hard for you, either in heaven or on earth. [20] And all your work will be idle; the earth will not bring forth for you any fruits. [22] And I will send to you wild animals that will kill you and your cattle. [23] If you do not wish to receive my teaching, and go against me, [24] I will go against you and kill you. [25] And when you flee from city to city, I will send death to you [...]. [28] I will punish you with seven afflictions, so that you will eat your sons' and your daughters' flesh. [30] And I will topple you from your high towers and I will break your shrines, and you will fall amidst your devil-worship. [...] [41] And I will go against you and lead you into the land of enemies, unless your vile mind is ashamed. Then you will pray for your wickednesses, [42] and I will take care of my covenant that I promised to Abraham and Isaac and Jacob. I will take care of the land [43] when you abandoned it, it pleases me although it is waste. [44] I am the Lord your God [45] that led you out of the land of Egypt before the sight of all the people.'

These are the commandments and judgements and laws that the Lord established between himself and the people of Israel on Mount Sinai.]

The use of a range of literary and rhetorical devices, including homeoteleuton (e.g. *ne gehirað [...] forhogiað [...] forseð [...] ne doð*) and parallelism (e.g. *mine gebodu [...] and mine æ and mine domas [...] min wedd [...] mine æ and mine domas*), lends rhythm and structure to this passage. Most striking is the insistent anaphoric front-placement of the personal pronoun *ic* (underlined) followed by a series of present indicative verbs with future sense (*gedo, sende, wiðstande, forbrece, witnige, towurpe, tobrece, gyme*) culminating in the emphatic declaration: *Ic eom Drihten eowre God*.[88] By electing to end the Old English *Leviticus* by foregrounding the theme of divine wrath, rather than with the source text's list of prices for offences, the translator leaves contemporary English readers in no doubt of the dire consequences of failing to obey God's *æ* ('law').[89]

---

[88] In the equivalent passage in the Latin source, the first person singular personal pronoun *ego* appears relatively infrequently (Lev. 26.16: *ego quoque haec faciam vobis*; Lev. 26.24: *ego quoque contra vos adversus incedam*; Lev. 26.28: *et ego incedam adversum vos in furore contrario*; Lev. 26.41: *ambulabo igitur et ego contra eos*; Lev. 26.44: *ego enim sum Dominus Deus eorum*; Lev. 26.45: Lev. 26.45: *ego Dominus Deus*) as the subject is usually indicated by the verb.

[89] As Peter Clemoes notes, Ælfric's preoccupation with obedience to God inspired him to include homiletic paraphrases of certain Old Testament books in his *Catholic Homilies, Lives of Saints* and other writings: 'Chronology', p. 53. Job is included in the *Catholic Homilies*; Esther and Judith are Assmann 8 and 9, respectively; Kings and Maccabees are in the *Lives*. For an online edition of

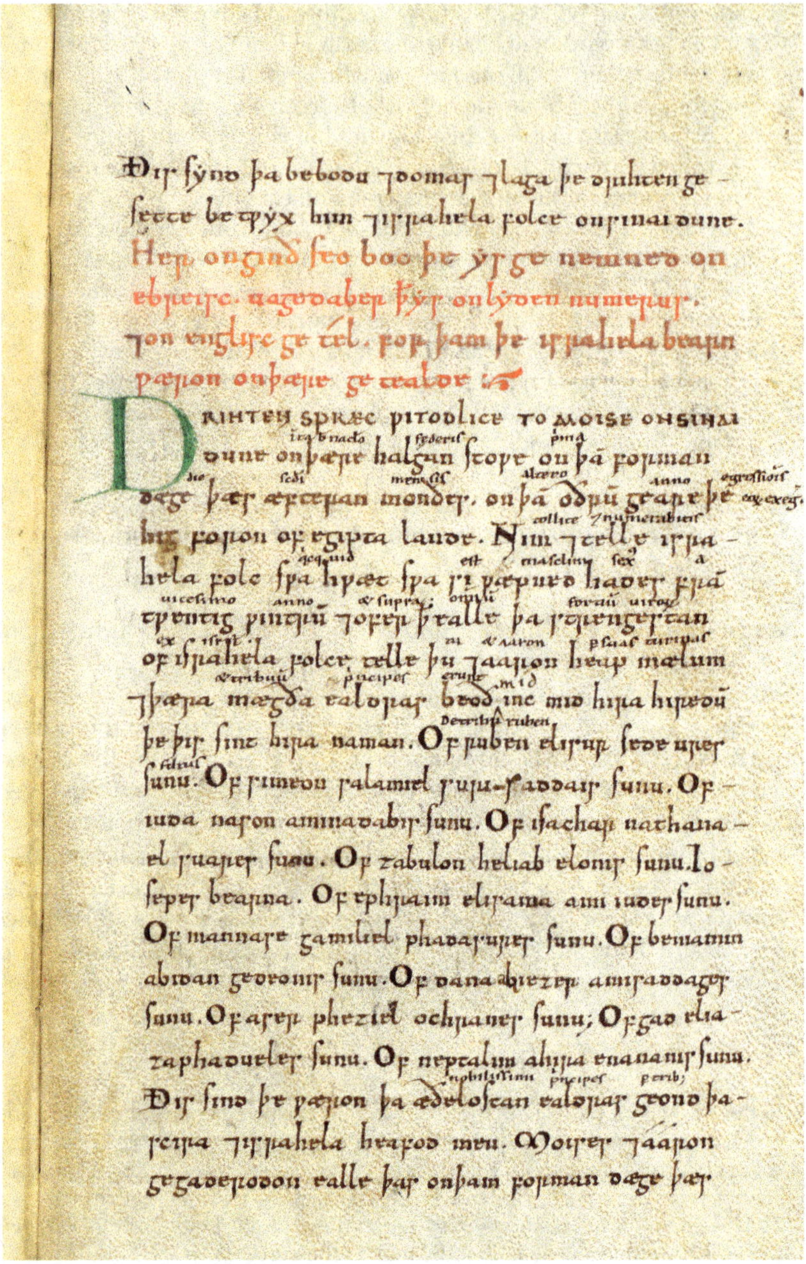

Figure 12. Oxford, Bodleian Library, MS Laud Misc. 509, fol. 72ʳ, 'Old English Heptateuch: end of *Leviticus*, opening of *Numbers*'.

Numbers

The Book of Numbers recounts the final phase of the wanderings of the Israelites in the desert under the leadership of Moses and Aaron, bookended by two censuses in which men of fighting age are enumerated. At the heart of this narrative are a series of episodes in which the Israelites incur God's wrath by lamenting their miserable condition in the desert and complaining that they should never have left Egypt. In addition to a large volume of legal material, including details of sacrifices and rules concerning the priestly tribe of Levites, Numbers also narrates the story of the twelve spies sent by Moses and Aaron to inspect the Promised Land, ten of whom are destroyed by God for claiming it is inhabited by giants. Moses and Aaron themselves incur God's wrath in the story of the waters of contradiction. There follows a series of military victories for Israel and the story of Balaam, a messenger sent to curse Israel who instead delivers blessings and oracles. With the defeat of the Midianites, the Israelites now settle in Moab, close to the promised land of Canaan, and at this point the Book of Numbers reaches its conclusion.

In MS L, the Old English *Numbers* begins immediately after the conclusion to the Old English *Leviticus* on fol. 72^r; again, extensive late eleventh- or twelfth-century Latin glosses are visible in the opening verse (fig. 12).[90] Chapters 1–25, containing the first census of the tribes of Israel, their wanderings in the desert and disobedience to God, are substantially truncated, while the final ten chapters (26–36), which include a second census, accounts of battles between Israel and the kings, various laws and the settlement of the Israelites in Moab, are cut in their entirety. The omission of this final section effectively reorients the entire book: whereas the main focus of the narrative in the Vulgate is the Israelites' wanderings and their arrival on the border of Canaan, the Old English *Numbers* instead presents a series of examples of the consequences of disobeying God set against a backdrop of military mobilisation.

Chapters 1–12 are thought to be the work of an anonymous translator, while Ælfric was responsible for chapters 13–26. Both translators foreground those parts of the biblical narrative that speak most directly to the spiritual and political concerns of the work's readers. In particular, the description of the gathering of the Israelite armies, the census and the appointment of military leaders in the opening section of Numbers would have had special resonance for readers such as Æthelweard, who were responsible for organising English wartime defences:

---

three of these works, see Stuart D. Lee, *Ælfric's Homilies on Judith, Esther and The Maccabees* (Oxford, 1999): https://users.ox.ac.uk/~stuart/kings/.

[90] For discussion of how these glosses reveal post-Conquest interest in the text, see above, p. 145 n. 3, and below, pp. 247–8.

Old English Biblical Prose

[1.1] Drihten spræc witodlice to Moise on Sinai dune on þære halgan stowe, on þam forman dæge þæs ætferan monðes, on þam oðrum geare þe hig foron of Egipta lande:
[2] 'Nim and telle Israhela folc swa hwæt swa si *wæpnedhades*, [3] fram twentig wintrum and ofer, þæt ealle þa strengestan of Israhela folc telle þu and Aaron *heapmælum*. [4] And þæra *mægða ealdras* beoð mid inc mid hira *hiredum*, [5] þe þis sint hira naman: Of Ruben, Elisur, Sedeures sunu. [6] Of Simeon, Salamiel, Surisaddais sunu. [7] Of Iuda, Nason, Aminadabis sunu. [8] Of Isachar, Nathanael, Suares sunu. [9] Of Zabulon, Heliab, Elonis sunu. [10] Iosepes bearna: Of Ephraim, Elisama, Amiiudes sunu. Of Mannase, Gamiliel, Phadasures sunu. [11] Of Beniamin, Abidan, Gedeonis sunu. [12] Of Dan, Abiezer, Amisaddages sunu. [13] Of Aser, Pheziel, Ochranes sunu. [14] Of Gad, Eliazapha, Dueles sunu. [15] Of Neptalim, Ahira, Enananis sunu.' [16] Ðis sind þe wæron þa *æðelostan ealdras* geond þa *scira* and Israhela *heafodmen*. [17] Moises and Aaron gegaderodon ealle þas [18] on þam forman dæge þæs æftran monðes, and demdon him [19] swa Drihten bebead Moise, and hig man tealde on Sinai westene.[91]

[[1.1] The Lord spoke truly to Moses on Mount Sinai in that holy place, on the first day of the second month, in the second year after they went out of Egypt:
[2] 'Take and count the people of Israel *all of those who are male*, [3] from twenty years upwards, count all those that are the strongest of the people of Israel by their *troops*, you and Aaron. [4] And *the princes of the tribes* will be with you with their *retainers*. [5] These are their names: Of Ruben, Elisur the son of Sedeur. [6] Of Simeon, Salamiel the son of Surisaddai. [7] Of Juda, Nason, son of Aminadab. [8] Of Isachar, Nathaniel, son of Suar. [9] Of Zabulon, Heliab, son of Elon. [10] Joseph's sons: Of Ephraim, Elisama, son of Amiiud. Of Mannase, Gamiliel, son of Phadasur. [11] Of Beniamin, Abidan, son of Gedeon. [12] Of Dan, Abiezer, son of Amisaddag. [13] Of Aser, Pheziel, son of Ochran. [14] Of Gad, Eliazapha, son of Duel. [15] Of Neptalim, Ahira, son of Enanan.' [16] These are the *noblest princes of the shires and the chief men* of the Israelites. [17] Moses and Aaron gathered all of these [18] on the first day of the second month and counted them [19] as the Lord had instructed Moses, and they were numbered in the desert of Sinai.] (Emphases added)

The translator makes the biblical narrative of the census directly relevant to such readers by using a range of English military terms: *turmas > heapmælum*; *domorum in cognationibus suis > hiredum* ('retainers'); *nobilissimi principes multitudinis per tribus et cognationes suas et capita exercitus Israhel > þa æðelostan ealdras geond þa scira and Israhela heafodmen*. The copy of the Old English

---

[91] Marsden, ed., *Heptateuch*, I, p. 138.

Numbers in the Hexateuch is further domesticated in the accompanying illustrations which depict the large-scale mustering of troops, a scenario that would have been familiar to contemporary readers (Cotton Claudius B. IV, fols 112^v–113^r). The Anglo-Saxon Chronicle, for example, records how Alfred gathered troops from various *sciras* ('shires') in preparation for the Battle of Eddington (MS A 878),[92] and later divided his army in two so that one part was always on active service while the other was stood down (MS A 893).[93] The failure of certain ealdormen to mobilise their troops effectively against the Danes was a source of recurring frustration for the author of the Anglo-Saxon Chronicle entries for the 990s and early 1000s.[94] Bucking the trend was the East Saxon ealdorman Byrhtnoth (d. 991), whose heroic organisation of his *fyrd* ('army', l. 221a) and *hiredmen* ('retainers', l. 261a) for battle against *hæðene scealcas* ('heathen attackers', l. 181b) is celebrated in the Old English poem *The Battle of Maldon*.[95] As we shall see below, Ælfric

---

[92] John Baker and Stuart Brookes, 'Explaining Anglo-Saxon Military Efficiency: The Landscape of Mobilization', *ASE* 44 (2015), 221–58, at 222. See further, Ryan Lavelle, *Alfred's Wars: Sources and Interpretations of Anglo-Saxon Warfare in the Viking Age*, Warfare in History 30 (Woodbridge: Boydell, 2010). Cf. Janet M. Bately, ed., *The Anglo-Saxon Chronicle: A Collaborative Edition, Volume 3, MS A* (Cambridge: D. S. Brewer, 1986), pp. 50–1.

[93] On Alfred's development of a system of fortified defences (*burhs*) each containing a garrison from which he could conscript men of fighting age, as witnessed by the document known as the Burghal Hidage, see David Hill and Alexander R. Rumble, eds, *The Defence of Wessex: The Burghal Hidage and Anglo-Saxon Fortifications* (Manchester: Manchester University Press, 1996); Georgina Pitt, 'Alfredian military reform: the materialization of ideology and the social practice of garrisoning', *Early Medieval Europe* 30 (2022), 408–36.

[94] See esp. ASC MS C 992, 993, 1003. See further John Scattergood, 'The Battle of Maldon and History', in *Literature and Learning in Medieval and Renaissance England: Essays Presented to Fitzroy Pyle*, ed. John Scattergood (Blackrock, Co. Dublin: Irish Academic Press, 1984), pp. 11–24.

[95] The biblical resonance of Byrhtnoth's actions were not lost on the author of the Latin *Life of Saint Oswald* (c. 1000), attributed to Byrhtferth of Ramsey, who evokes the Old Testament figures of Aaron and Hur, the warriors who supported Moses' hand in battle against Amalek (Ex. 17.10–12) (*Stabat ipse statura procerus, eminens super ceteros; cuius manum non Aaron et Hur sustentabant, sed multimoda pietas Domini fulciebat, quoniam ipse dignus er*, 'He himself was tall of stature, standing above the rest; Aaron and Hur did not stay his hands: it was the Lord's manifold mercy which sustained them, because he was worthy of it'). The *Life of Saint Oswald* also depicts Byrhtnoth defending himself to left and right in a manner which, as Michael Lapidge notes, echoes 1 Macc. 6.45 (*interficiens a dextris et a sinistris*) and 2 Cor. 6.7 (*exhibeamus nosmet ipsos [...] per arma iustitiae a dextris et a sinistris*): Michael Lapidge, ed., *Oxford Medieval Texts: Byrhtferth of Ramsey: The Lives of St Oswald and St Ecgwine* (Oxford: Oxford University Press, 2009), Vita S. Oswaldi IV.58, pp. 157–9; see also Michael Allen and Daniel Calder, eds and trans., *Sources and Analogues of Old English Poetry, Vol. 1: The Major Latin Texts*

would connect those English kings who had bravely protected their people by fighting against heathen invaders with their Old Testament forebears in his homiletic paraphrase of Judges. Like Ælfric, the anonymous translator of the first half of Numbers was thus alert to the contemporary political resonances of this section of the biblical source text.

In keeping with the pragmatic editorial principles established in the preceding rendering of Leviticus, the anonymous translator decided that long passages enumerating the fighting men of each tribe and their princes as reckoned by Moses and Aaron (Num. 1.19–44, 2.1–31) were otiose and therefore cut them entirely. Significantly, however, the Old English version retains God's instruction that Moses and Aaron should not number the priests among those preparing for battle:

> [1.45] Ðus fela wæs þæra manna þe Moises and Aaron and þa twelf Israhela ealdras getealdon fram twentigum wintrum and bufan, þam þæra þe to gefeohte faran mihton: six hund þusenda and þreo þusenda and fif hundred and fiftig. [47] Ða sacerdas mid hira hirede næron getealde mid him, [48] for þam þe Drihten bebead Moyse: 'Ne telle þu Leuies mægðe, ne sete þu hig mid Israhela folce, [50] ac sette hig to þære halgan stowe and to þingum þe þærto belimpað.' [54] Israhela bearn didon neah eallon þam þingum þe Drihten bebead þurh Moisen. [2.32] And ealles hira heres wæs, þa he todæled wæs, six hund þusenda and þreo þusenda and fif hundrydo and fiftig. [34] Hig foron floccmælum mid hira hiredum.[96]

> [[45] This was the number of those men that Moses and Aaron and the twelve princes of Israel counted from twenty years old and above, and those that were able to go to war: six hundred thousand and three thousand and five hundred and fifty. [47] The priests with their troops were not counted with them, [48] because the Lord instructed Moses: 'Do not count the kindred of Levi, nor place them with the people of Israel, [50] but put them in the holy place and to those things that belong thereto.' [54] The children of Israel performed all the things that the Lord instructed through Moses. [2.32] And all of their army was, when he separated them, six hundred thousand and three thousand and five hundred and fifty. [34] They went in companies with their troops.]

---

in Translation (Cambridge: D. S. Brewer, 1976), pp. 188–9. Aaron is also credited with organising the Israelite armies with Moses in Numbers.

[96] Marsden, ed., *Heptateuch*, I, pp. 138–9.

Although Ælfric certainly accepted the use of violence in the service of God and the concept of the Just War,[97] he was of the firm belief that monks should not take any part in worldly battles, a point he makes clear in his treatise on the Three Orders of Society, that is *laboratores, oratores, bellatores* ('those who work, those who pray, those who fight'):[98]

> Is nu forþy mare þæra muneca gewinn
> wið þa ungesewenlican deofla þe syrwiað embe us
> þonne sy þæra woruld-manna þe winnað wiþ ða flæsclican
> and wið þa gesewenlican gesewenlice feohtað.
> Nu ne sceolon þa woruld-cempan to woruldlicum gefeohte
> þa Godes þeowan neadian fram þam gastlican gewinne,
> forðan þe him fremað swiðor þæt þa ungesewenlican fynd
> beon oferswyðde þonne ða gesewenlican,
> and hit bið swyðe derigendlic þæt hi Drihtnes þeowdom forlætan
> and to woruld-gewinne bugan, þe him naht to ne gebryiað.

[The fight of the monks against the invisible devils who lay traps around us is greater now, therefore, than that of the men of the

---

[97] See James Cross, 'The Ethics of War in Old English', in *England before the Conquest: Studies in Primary Sources Presented to Dorothy Whitelock*, ed. Peter Clemoes and Kathleen Hughes (Cambridge: Cambridge University Press, 1971), pp. 269–82; James W. Earl, 'Violence and Non-Violence in Anglo-Saxon England: Ælfric's *Passion of St Edmund*', *PQ* 78 (1999), 125–49; E. Gordon Whatley, 'Hagiography and Violence: Military Men in Ælfric's *Lives of Saints*', in *Source of Wisdom: Old English and Early Medieval Latin Studies in Honour of Thomas D. Hill*, ed. Charles D. Wright, Frederick M. Biggs and Thomas N. Hall (Toronto: University of Toronto Press, 2007), pp. 217–38; and Ben Snook, 'Just War in Anglo-Saxon England: Transmission and Reception', in *Handbook of Medieval Culture: Fundamental Aspects and Conditions of the European Middle Ages*, ed. Albrecht Classen (Berlin: De Gruyter, 2015), pp. 99–120.

[98] The treatise forms the final part of Ælfric's paraphrase of the Book of Maccabees in his *Lives of the Saints*. See further Andrei Crișan, 'The Concept of the Three Orders of Society in Late Old English Prose', *Studia Universitatis Babes-Bolyai, Philologia* 3 (2024), 189–206. On the contemporary political and theological resonance of Ælfric's Maccabees and Three Orders, see further Godden, 'Apocalypse and Invasion', p. 141; Andrew Scheil, *The Footsteps of Israel: Understanding Jews in Anglo-Saxon England* (Ann Arbor, MI: University of Michigan Press, 2004), pp. 313–30; Samantha Zacher, 'Anglo-Saxon Maccabees: Political Theology in Ælfric's *Lives of Saints*', in *Old English Lexicology and Lexicography: Essays in Honor of Antonette diPaolo Healey*, ed. Maren Clegg Hyer, Haruko Momma and Samantha Zacher, Anglo-Saxon Studies 40 (Cambridge: D. S. Brewer, 2020), pp. 143–58; S. I. Rubinstein, 'The Politics of Ælfric's *Maccabees*', *RES* 74 (2023), 589–604. On the Three Orders more generally in this period, see Timothy E. Powell, 'The "Three Orders of Society" in Anglo-Saxon England', *ASE* 23 (1994), 103–32.

world who fight against human enemies and fight visibly against
the visible. Now worldly soldiers should not force the servants of
God away from the spiritual battle to the worldly battle, because it
will serve them better that invisible enemies are overcome rather
than the visible, and it would be very harmful for them to neglect
their service of the Lord and to turn to the worldly fight, which in
no way concerns them.][99]

The anonymous translator's selective rendering of Numbers 2 provides biblical support for Ælfric's dictum that a monk's place is in the cloister and not on the battlefield.

The transition from the anonymous translator to Ælfric at Numbers 13 is signalled by a brief recapitulation of the preceding biblical narrative, linking Numbers with Exodus, and the return of his distinctive rhythmical prose style which last appeared in his stint of the Old English *Genesis* from Ch. 19.19:[100]

> Anonymous author: [12.13] Moises þa clipode to Drihtne and cwæð: 'Drihten God, ic bidde þe, hæl hig.' [14] Drihten him andswarode and cwæð: 'Gif hire fæder spigette on hire nebb, hu ne sceolde hire, huru, þinga sceamian seofon dagas? Beo heo asindrod seofon dagas fram oðrum mannum and clipige hig mann siþþan ongen.' [15] Maria wæs belocen seofon dagas butan þære wicstowe and þæt folc ne stirode hwæder, ær þam þe Maria wearð hal geworden.[101]

> [[12.13] Moses then spoke to the Lord and said: 'Lord God, I pray to you, save her.' [14] The Lord answered him and said: 'If her father spat on her face, ought she not, indeed, be ashamed of this thing for seven days? Let her be separated for seven days from other people and people may call her back again.' [15] Mary was put out of the camp for seven days and that people did not move until Mary was called again.]

> Ælfric:[13.1] Æfter þam þe Moises se mæra heretoga mid Israhela folce, swa swa him bebead God, ofer þa Readan Sæ ferde and Pharo adrenced wæs, and siþþan se ælmihtiga God him æ gesette hæfde,

---

[99] Clayton and Mullins, II.23, pp. 334–7. On Ælfric's treatment of the different responsibilities of the three orders of society in his *Treatise*, see pp. 221–3.

[100] See further Marsden, 'Translation by Committee?', p. 45. Raith argues that Ælfric's sections of Numbers are derived from one of his homilies ('Ælfric's Share in the Old English Pentateuch', 314).

[101] Marsden, ed., *Heptateuch*, I, p. 143,

A Perilous Task: Making the Old English Heptateuch

þa þa seo fyrd com to Foran þam westene, ² ða cwæð se heofonlica God to þam halgan Moise: ³ 'Ceos þa menn þæt magon sceawigean þone eard Chanaan landes, þe ic Israhela folce forgifan wille to hira gewealde, and asend twelf heafodmenn of þam twelf mægðum.'[102]

[[13.1] Afterwards Moses the famous battle-chief among the people of Israel, just as God instructed him, went across the Red Sea and Pharaoh was drowned, and after the Almighty God had given him the Law, then the army came to the desert of Pharan ² then the heavenly God said to the holy Moses: ³ 'Choose the men that might examine that place, the land of Chanaan, which I will give to the people of Israel as their dominion, and send twelve chief-men from those twelve tribes.]

The anonymous author produces a very faithful but nevertheless idiomatic rendering of the Vulgate's account of the expulsion of Mary from the tribe for seven days on account of her leprosy.[103] Where alliteration does occur, it appears to be accidental and does not form any clear pattern or contribute to the rhythm of the passage. In striking contrast, Ælfric introduces a succinct summary of the key events of Exodus (the issuing of the law on Mount Sinai and the crossing of the Red Sea) and expands considerably on Num. 13.2 (*ibi locutus est Dominus ad Moysen dicens*, 'And there the Lord spoke to Moses, saying') by introducing epithets which create alliteration and rhythm: *Moise se mæra heretoga; cwæð se heofonlica God to þam halgan Moise*.[104]

---

[102] Marsden, ed., *Heptateuch*, I, p. 144.

[103] The final verse of Num. 12, verse 16 (*profectus est de Aseroth fixis tentoriis in deserto Pharan*, 'And the people marched from Haseroth, and pitched their tents in the desert of Pharan') is omitted, though it is unclear whether this was the decision of the anonymous translator or Ælfric.

[104] As we shall see, Ælfric will again use the heroic epithet *se mæra heretoga* to describe Moses in the opening of his homiletic paraphrase of Judges and in his *Treatise*; see pp. 206–7, 233. In his homily on 'The Circumcision', Ælfric refers to Moses as simply *se heretoga* (*CH* I.6, p. 112). He also uses the term once in his stint of *Genesis* (17.20) to describe the twelve princes (Lat. *duces*) who will proceed from Ishmael. Andy Orchard records three instances of the compound *here-toga* ('army-leader') in verse, once in *Gifts of Men* l. 76b, where it is used in the universal sense to refer to a good leader of armies, and twice in the *Metres of Boethius*, for the Roman consuls Boethius and Brutus, noting that it occurs 'more than 170 times in prose': *Word-Hord: A Lexicon of Old English Verse with Particular Focus on the Distribution of Nominal and Adjectival Compounds*, CLASP Ancillary Publications 1 (Oxford: CLASP, 2022), p. 159. Moses is described as *folc-toga* in the poetic *Exodus* (ll. 14a, 254a). For a survey of depictions of Moses as lawgiver, leader and writer in Anglo-Latin writing and Old English verse, see Gernot Wieland, 'Legifer, Dux, Scriptor: Moses in Anglo-Saxon Literature', in *Illuminating Moses: A History of Reception from Exodus to the Renaissance*, ed.

Ælfric's rhythmical prose style remains in use for most of the remaining part of Numbers, though it is temporarily suspended for practical reasons during various long lists of names (e.g. Num. 13.5–16). All of Chapter 13 and most of Chapter 14 are faithfully rendered, before Ælfric begins to make larger cuts to the remaining chapters, providing a foretaste of the 'brief style' he will employ in his paraphrases of Joshua and Judges and, in even more extreme form, in the *Treatise*.[105] All forty-one verses of Chapter 15, for example, are reduced to a terse summary: *God gesette þa Moyse menigfealde beboda*[106] ('God then established many commandments to Moses').

In keeping with the Heptateuch's tendency to downplay the misconduct of the patriarchs, Ælfric radically alters the biblical account of how Moses incurred God's wrath on account of his disobedience when striking the rock (Num. 20). In the Vulgate, the Israelites complain to Moses and Aaron that they have no water in the desert, saying that they wish that they had remained in captivity in Egypt (Num. 20.1–5); Moses and Aaron then go into the tabernacle and prostrate themselves before God, asking for his help (Num. 20.6). God speaks to Moses instructing him to take the rod and assemble the people with Aaron, and speak to the rock, which will yield water (Num. 20.8); Moses then takes the rod and gathers the people, asking them if the rock will bring forth water (Num. 20.9–10). Lifting up his hand, Moses twice strikes the rock with the result that water comes forth and the people drink (Num. 20.11). God then speaks to Moses and Aaron, criticising them for their disobedience and warning them of the punishment to come:

> [20.12] Quia non credidistis mihi, ut sanctificaretis me coram filiis Israhel, non introducetis hos populos in terram, quam dabo eis. [13] Haec est aqua contradictionis, ubi iurgati sunt filii Israhel contra Dominum, et sanctificatus est in eis.

> [[20.12] Because you have not believed me, to sanctify me before the children of Israel, you shall not bring these people into the land, which I will give them. [13] This is the water of contradiction, where the children of Israel strove with words against the Lord, and he was sanctified in them.]

Ælfric omits this passage as well as two further references detailing God's chastisement of Moses and Aaron (Num. 20.24, 17.14), while abridging other verses in this episode which cast Moses in a negative light:

> [20.1] Æfter þisum comon Israhela bearn to þam westene Sin, and þær

---

Jane Beal, *Commentaria* 4 (Leiden: Brill, 2013), pp. 185–209; Wieland does not discuss references to Moses in Old English prose.

[105] See further Nichols, 'Ælfric and the Brief Style'.
[106] Marsden, ed., *Heptateuch*, I, p. 147.

A Perilous Task: Making the Old English Heptateuch

sweolt Maria, Aarones swuster, and ys þær bebirged. ² Ða næs þær nan wæter on þam westene þam folce ³ and hig þa ciddon swiþe wið Moisen. ⁶ He clipode þa to Gode ⁷ and God cwæð him to: ⁸ 'Gang þu and Aaron and gegaderiað þis folc geond to þam stane and se stan eow slyþ wæter.' ¹⁰ Hig comon to þam flinte ¹¹ and he ætforan him eallum sloh mid þære girde tuwa þone flint and þær fleow sona of þam flinte wæter, swa genihtsumlice þæt heora nytena druncon, and eall Israela folc, of þære anre riðe. ¹⁴ Ða sende Moyses ærendrecan to Edom þam cyninge, ¹⁷ bæd þat he moste faran forð ofer his land be rihtum wege and ne hreppan his nan þing.[107]

[²⁰·¹ After the children of Israel came to the desert of Sin, and there Mary died, Aaron's sister, and is buried there. ² Then there was no water in the desert for that people ³ and they lamented greatly to Moses. ⁶ He called then to God ⁷ and God said to him: ⁸ 'Go you and Aaron and gather this people around that stone and the stone will give you water.' ¹⁰ They came to that rock ¹¹ and he before them all struck twice the rock with the rod and there suddenly water sprang out of the rock, so abundantly that their animals drank, and all the people of Israel, from that single stream. ¹⁴ Then Moses sent messengers to the king of Edom, ¹⁷ requesting that he might travel through his land by the correct way and not touch anything of his.]

The cumulative result of these omissions is that the entire biblical episode with Moses and the rock is recast as another instance of the prophet's faithfulness to God. As we shall see, however, Ælfric's decision to gloss over the incident at the waters of contradiction in Numbers will have unforeseen consequences in the translation of Deuteronomy which follows.[108]

The Old English *Numbers* thus demonstrates how English prose authors in the late tenth century drew on the Old Testament 'as a veiled way of talking about their own situation', as Godden puts it.[109] The abridgement of the censuses allows the vernacular version to resonate with the lived experience of kings and ealdormen who were responsible for mustering troops in this period. Similarly, the retention of the detail concerning the division of the priestly tribe of Levi from the fighting men in a passage otherwise heavily abbreviated speaks to contemporary concerns about monks participating in physical battle against the Danes. Above all, the Old English *Numbers* provides ample evidence for contemporary readers

---

[107] Marsden, ed., *Heptateuch,* I, pp. 148–9.
[108] See below, pp. 196–8. For Ælfric's brief treatment of Numbers and Deuteronomy in the *Treatise on the Old and New Testaments,* in which Moses' disobedience and punishment are similarly glossed over, see below, Chapter Five, p. 224
[109] Godden, 'Old Testament', p. 232.

that all three orders of society must obey God's laws during a time of national crisis.

Deuteronomy

With the translation of Deuteronomy, we witness something of a return to the more faithful translation style of the Old English prose *Genesis* and *Exodus*. The anonymous translator includes at least some material from most of the source text's thirty-four chapters, though much is nevertheless abridged. Those chapters which are cut in their entirety (Deut. 2 and 26) comprise Moses' extended account of the wanderings of the Israelites in the desert and the end of the Deuteronomic Code respectively – two passages that were evidently deemed repetitive and therefore extraneous. Other major and minor cuts similarly serve to streamline the text, again foregrounding the Heptateuch's central theme of obedience to God's laws. In Chapter 16, for example, verses 1–17 (instructions about the correct observance of the Passover feast and other festivals) and 21–2 (against planting a grove or tree near the altar of the Lord, and setting up a statue to oneself) are left out, while the verses that remain from this section, 18–20, contain material more relevant to contemporary readers on the appointment of judges and magistrates, the importance of not accepting bribes, and the necessity of adhering to justice in order to prove oneself worthy of inheriting God's Promised Land.

By contrast to this general abbreviating tendency, two chapters are translated in full: Chapter 5, a recapitulation of the Decalogue, and Chapter 34, which closes the book with an account of Moses' death. The fact that only these two chapters are rendered in full indicates that the main aim of the translation was to provide readers with basic instruction in the key tenets of the Old Law and the major historical events of the Old Testament.

Turning to the style of the translation, Deuteronomy is rendered into a confident, fluent Old English prose. On isolated occasions, such as the opening of the Song of Moses, we find balanced phrasing and even lyrical language:[110]

> 32.1 Audite, caeli, quae loquor audiat, terra verba oris mei. ² Concrescat in pluvia doctrina mea fluat ut ros eloquium meum quasi imber super herbam et quasi stillae super gramina. ³ Quia nomen Domini invocabo: date magnificentiam Deo nostro ⁴ Dei perfecta sunt opera, et omnes viae eius iudicia: Deus fidelis et absque ulla iniquitate iustus et rectus

---

[110] Marsden notes the possible influence of Old Latin readings on the translation of the 'Song of Moses', pointing to the use of this text in liturgical contexts (*Text of the Old Testament*, p. 435).

A Perilous Task: Making the Old English Heptateuch

[³²·¹ Hear, O you heavens, the things I speak, let the earth give ear to the words of my mouth. ²Let my doctrine gather as the rain, let my speech distil as the dew, as a shower upon the herb, and as drops upon the grass. ³Because I will invoke the name of the Lord: may you give magnificence to our God. ⁴The works of God are perfect, and all his ways are judgments: God is faithful and without any iniquity, he is just and right.]

³²·¹ 'Gehiraþ heofenas þa þing þe ic sprece and gehire eorþe min word. ² Weaxe min lar swa ren. Flowe min spræc swa deaw and swa smilte ren swa dropan ofer gærsa ciþas, ³ for þam þe ic clipie Drihtnes naman. Sillaþ mærþe urum Gode. ⁴ Godes weorc sint fullfremede and ealle his wegas sint domas. God ys getreowe and, butan ælcre unrihtwisnisse, rihtwis. [...].'¹¹¹

[³²·¹ Let the heavens hear the things about which I speak and let the earth hear my word. ²Let my teaching grow as the rain. Let my speech flow like the dew and like calm rain which drops over sprigs of herbs, ³because I will call out the Lord's name. Give magnificence to our God. ⁴God's works are perfected and all his ways are judgements. God is faithful and, without any unrighteousness, righteous.]

Front-placement of verbs (*Gehiraþ*; *gehire*; *Weaxe*; *Flowe*; *Sillaþ*), syntactical parallelism (*Gehiraþ heofenas* [...] *gehire eorþe*; *Weaxe min* [...] *Flowe min*), a fourfold *swa* construction, light alliteration on *h*, *w*, *s* and *d*, and the insertion of the adjective *smilte* ('calm') to modify the noun *ren* ('rain'), where the Latin simply has *imber*, all combine to provide rhythm, structure and texture to this polished piece of Old English prose.

Other relatively minor alterations to Deuteronomy occur at the level of syntax. For example, in Chapter 12 verses 1–31, commandments on the treatment of defeated enemies, the offering of sacrifices and prohibitions on the consumption of food and drink are all omitted, leaving only the core injunction of obedience to God's law:

¹²·³² Quod praecipio tibi, hoc tantum facito Domino: nec addas quicquam nec minuas.	'Wirceað ealle þa þing þe Drihten eow bebead and ne ice ge nan þing þærto, ne ne waniað. [...].'¹¹²
[What I command you, you must do only that to the Lord: neither add anything, nor diminish.]	[Do all the things which God instructed you and do not add anything to that, nor diminish it.]

---

[111] Marsden, ed., *Heptateuch*, I, p. 173.
[112] Marsden, ed., *Heptateuch*, I, p. 163.

Reversing the syntax, so that the substantive clause (*þe Drihten eow bebead*) comes after the imperative (*wirceað ealle þa þing*), allows the translator to begin the injunction with an imperative verb (*wirceað*), thus integrating this verse into a powerful sequence of front-placed jussives:

> [11.1] *Lufiað* Drihten eowerne God and *wircað* his bebodu and his æ and his domas on ælcne timan. ² *Oncnawað* todæg þa þing þe eowre bearn nyton, þa þe ne gehirdon Drihtenes lare eowres Godes [...]. ⁵ And *gumunað* hwæt he eow dide on þam westene [...]. [12.32] *Wirceað* ealle þa þing þe Drihten eow bebead and *ne ice* ge nan þing þærto, ne ne *waniað* [...]. [13.4] *Filigeað* Drihtne eowrum Gode and *ondrædað* hine and *healdaþ* his bebodu and *gehirað* hine and *þeawiað* him.[113]

> [[11.1] *Love* the Lord your God and *follow* his commandments and his law and his judgements at all times. ² *Know* today the thing that your children do not, when they did not hear the law of the Lord your God. [...] ⁵ And *remember* what he did for you in that desert [...]. [12.32] *Do* all the things which God instructed you and *do not add* anything to that, nor *diminish* it [...]. [13.4] *Follow* the Lord your God and *fear* him and *keep* his commandments and *obey* him and *serve* him.] (Emphases added).

In the Latin source, the imperative verb sometimes appears in clause-initial position (1.1: *ama itaque Dominum Deum tuum et observa praecepta eius*; 1.2 *cognoscite*), though the Old English verb *gumunað* ('remember', 1.5) has no equivalent in the Vulgate. Within the same sequence, the translator once more rearranges the DIRECT OBJECT + IMPERATIVE VERB structure of the first clause of 13.4 (*Dominum Deum vestrum sequimini et ipsum timete mandata illius custodite*) to sustain the pattern of opening each injunction with a jussive. Through small but consistent choices such as these, the translator produces a trimmed-down, communicative version of the final book of the Pentateuch, reiterating and elaborating the key elements of Mosaic law first outlined in Exodus.

Like the translator of Leviticus, the author of the Old English *Deuteronomy* had a strong sense of an ending, bringing the vernacular version of the biblical book to a stirring conclusion in a manner which differs substantially from the source. Following a recapitulation of the Decalogue and the Deuteronomic Code (Deut. 12–30), the Vulgate source concludes with four chapters comprising the Song of Moses (Deut. 32.1–43), the Blessing of Moses (Deut. 33.1–25) and an account of the prophet's death and burial (Deut. 34). The Old English translator renders all the individual verses of the Song of Moses and the account of the patriarch's death, but reduces the Blessing of Moses (Deut. 33.1–29)

---

[113] Marsden, ed., *Heptateuch*, I, p. 162.

A Perilous Task: Making the Old English Heptateuch

to a single, introductory verse (Deut. 33.1: *Moyses þa gebletsode ær his deaþe Israhela bearn, þa twelf mægða, ælc mid sindrigre bletsunge*), thereby foregrounding the key narrative elements of Moses' vision of the Promised Land, God's prevention of him from entering it on account of his sin at the rock (Num. 20) and the patriarch's subsequent death. The scribe of MS L indicates the final section of the text with a line of capitals two lines up from the bottom of fol. 97[v]:

> [32.48] DRIHTEN WÆS ÐA SPRECENDE[114] TO MOISE, þus cweðende: [49] 'Astih to me on þisne munt Abarim, þe ys on Nebo dune on þam lande Moab, ongean Iericho, and geseoh Chanaan land, þe ic forgife Israhela bearnum to agenne, and swelt on þam munte. [50] And þu bist beþeod to þinum folcum, swa swa Aaron þin broþur wæs dead on þære dune Or and wæs gelogod to his folcum, [51] for þam þe git agilton ætforan me on Israhela bearnum middan, æt þæs wiðersæces wæterum on Chades on þam westene Sin, and ge ne wurðedon me onmang Israhela bearnum. [52] Ðu scealt geseon þæt land and þu ne cymst þæron.'
> [33.1] Moyses þa gebletsode ær his deaþe Israhela bearn, þa twelf mægða, ælc mid sindrigre bletsunge, [34.1] and astah siþþan uppan þone munt Nebo on Fasgan cnæp, ongean þa burh Iericho, and Drihten him æteowode eall Galaad land oð Dan, [2] and eall Neptalim land and Effraim and Mannassen and eall þæt land oð þa itemistan sæ, [3] and þone suððæl and þa rumnisse Iericho feldes and palmtreowa birig, oð Segor.[115]

[[32.48] The Lord was speaking then to Moses, saying thus: [49] 'Go up into this mount Abarim, that is on Nebo hill in the land of Moab, over against Jericho, and see the land of Chanaan, which I will deliver to the children of Israel to possess, and die in that mountain. [50] And you will be gathered to your people, just as Aaron your brother was dead on that Mount Or and was gathered to his people, [51] because you trespassed against me in the midst of the children of Israel, at the waters of contradiction in Cades in the desert of Sin and you did not worship me among the children of Israel. [52] You shall see that land and you will not come therein.'
[33.1] Moses then blessed before his death the children of Israel, those twelve tribes, each with a separate blessing, [34.1] and went up then into that Mount Nebo to the peak of Phasga, over against the city of Jericho, and the Lord showed him all the land of Galaad as far as Dan, [2] and all the land of Nephtali and Ephraim and

---

[114] On the use of the past continuous construction in the opening of the Mosaic Prologue to the *Domboc*, see Chapter Two, pp. 59–62.
[115] Marsden, ed., *Heptateuch*, I, pp. 175–6.

Manasses and all that land as far as the furthermost sea, ³ and the southern part and breadth of the plan of Jericho and the city of palm trees, as far as Segor.]

As we have seen, in his translation of Numbers 20 Ælfric omitted those verses in which God criticised Moses for disobeying his instruction, in keeping with the Heptateuch's general tendency to downplay the misconduct of the patriarchs. A reader working their way through the Heptateuch sequentially would therefore be surprised by the reference in the translation of Deuteronomy to Moses' trespass *æt þæs wiðersæces wæterum on Chades on þam westene Sin*[116] ('at the waters of contradiction in Cad in the desert of sin', Deut. 32.51). Such inconsistencies between different parts of the Heptateuch highlight the complex and seemingly protracted circumstances of its creation. In the remainder of this chapter, I will explore how in the final two books of the Heptateuch Ælfric sought to resolve such issues by moving away from both formal- and functional equivalence translation towards paraphrase and homiletic exegesis.

Joshua

The Book of Joshua relates how Moses' appointed successor led the people of Israel, focusing on his wars and eventual conquest of the land of Canaan, ending with his death and burial. In the *Treatise*, Ælfric explains that he translated this book for Æthelweard, just as he had with Genesis. As a heroic military leader, Joshua has an obvious appeal for such readers.[117] Although scholars have grouped Ælfric's *Joshua* and *Judges* together as 'paraphrases' in order to distinguish them from the more faithful translation style of the preceding five books, the first of these two works in fact follows the functional equivalence approach taken in the preceding translations of the Pentateuch. Indeed, the rendering of Joshua is generally more faithful to its Vulgate source than the preceding translations of Leviticus, Numbers or Deuteronomy, in which far more biblical material is excised. From Chapter 5 onwards, Ælfric begins to merge two or more biblical verses into one, with larger alterations tending to cluster around the end of chapters. Hence, on several occasions Ælfric either merges the last or near-to-last verses (e.g. Jos. 1, 8, 9, and 12) or drops the final or penultimate verse entirely (e.g. Jos. 2, 10, 11 and 23).

---

[116] Marsden, ed., *Heptateuch*, I, p. 175.

[117] For analysis of the illustrations accompanying Ælfric's *Joshua* in the Hexateuch and its relationship to earlier illustrated bibles, see George Henderson, 'The Joshua Cycle in B.M. Cotton MS. Claudius B. IV', *Journal of the British Archaeological Association* 31 (1968), 38–59.

A Perilous Task: Making the Old English Heptateuch

Ælfric's economical approach to Joshua is on clear display in his treatment of Chapter 9. He begins by translating the first seven verses, with some abbreviation. For example, in verses 1–2, where the Vulgate provides a long list of the regions in which the various kings ruling beyond the Jordan dwelt, Ælfric provides only the basic outline of the story:

[9.1] Quibus auditis cuncti, reges trans Iordanem, qui versabantur in montanis, et in campestribus, in maritimis ac litore maris Magni hii quoque qui habitabant iuxta Libanum Hettheus et Amorreus et Chananeus Ferezeus et Eveus et Iebuseus [9.2] congregati sunt pariter ut pugnarent contra Iosue et Israhel uno animo eademque sententia.	[9.1] þes hlisa wearð þa cuð þære leoda cynegum þe begeondan Iordane eardiende wæron, [9.2] and gesamndon hi ealle anmodlice to gefeohte togeanes Iosue and Israhela bearnum.[118]
[[9.1] Now when these things were heard of, all the kings beyond the Jordan, that dwelt in the mountains, and in the plains, in the places near the sea, and on the coasts of the great sea, they also that dwell by Libanus, the Hethite, and the Amorrhite, the Chanaanite, the Pherezite, and the Hevite, and the Jebusite [9.2] gathered themselves together, to fight against Joshua and Israel with one mind, and one resolution.]	[[9.1] These things were heard of by the kings of the peoples who were dwelling beyond the Jordan, [9.2] and they all joined together with one mind to fight against Joshua and the children of Israel.]

By omitting the names of places and peoples, as well as compressing the Latin doublet *uno animo eademque sententia* into the single adverb *anmodlice*, Ælfric produces a more focused narrative that is more likely to hold a reader's attention.

The account of the siege of Gabaon that follows, in which Joshua is cast as the saviour of the city, has close parallels with the various descriptions of Danish attacks on English cities in the Anglo-Saxon Chronicle.[119] Table 5 shows how Ælfric employs alliteration in this passage to heighten the drama of the scene, while consistently abbreviating verses to maintain movement (alliteration is indicated in bold; omitted sections are struck out; alterations of wording are indicated by italics):

---

[118] Marsden, ed., *Heptateuch*, I, p. 184.
[119] See, for example, ASC MS A's descriptions of the sieges of York (867), Nottingham (868), Reading (871), Exeter (877, 894), Rochester (885) and London (994, 1013, 1016).

Table 5. Comparison of Joshua 10.5–10 in Vulgate and Ælfric's *Joshua*.

Vulgate	Ælfric's *Joshua*
Jos. 10. 5 Congregati igitur ascenderunt quinque reges Amorreorum rex Hierusalem rex Hebron rex Hieremoth rex Lachis rex Eglon simul cum exercitibus suis et castrametati sunt circa Gabaon obpugnantes eam. [So the five kings of the Amorrhites being assembled together, went up: the king of Jerusalem, the king of Hebron, the king of Jerimoth, the king of Lachis, the king of Eglon, they and their armies, and camped about Gabaon, laying siege to it.]	Ða comon þa fif cynegas mid **firde** to Gabaon and **wicodon** þær onemn, woldon hi oferwinnan. [Then the five kings came with armies to Gabaon and camped alongside there, they wished to conquer it.]
6 Habitatores autem Gabaon urbis obsessae miserunt, ad Iosue qui tunc morabatur in castris apud Galgalam et dixerunt ei, 'Ne retrahas manus tuas ab auxilio servorum tuorum ascende cito; et libera nos, ferque praesidium convenerunt enim adversum nos omnes reges Amorreorum qui habitant in montanis.' [But the inhabitants of the city of Gabaon, which was besieged, sent to Joshua, who then abode in the camp at Galgal; and said to him: 'Withdraw not your hands from helping your servants: come up quickly, and save us, and bring us succour: for all the kings of the Amorrhites, who dwell in the mountains, are gathered together against us.']	Ða sende seo buruhwaru sona to Iosue, **biddende** þæt he come and þa burh geheolde. [Then the citizens sent quickly to Joshua, asking that he should come and rule the city.]

⁷ Ascenditque Iosue de Galgalis et omnis exercitus bellatorum cum eo, viri fortissimi:

[And Joshua went up from Galgal, and all the army of the warriors with him, most valiant men.]

Iosue þa ferde mid his fyrde biderweard,

[Joshua then went with his army there,]

⁸ Dixitque Dominus ad Iosue: 'Ne timeas eos in manus enim tuas tradidi illos nullus tibi ex eis resistere poterit.'

[But the Lord said to Joshua: 'Fear them not: for I have delivered them into your hands: none of them shall be able to stand against you.']

and Drihten *him* cwæð to: 'Ne ondræd þu *þe nan þing*: on þine **h**anda ic **h**i betæce. **N**e mæg **h**eora **n**an þe wiðstandan.'

[And the Lord said to him: 'Do not fear anything for yourself: I have delivered them into your hands. None of them will be able to withstand you.']

⁹ Inruit itaque Iosue super eos repente tota ascendens nocte de Galgalis.

[Sc Joshua going up from Galgal all the night, came upon them suddenly.]

Iosue him þa **f**eng on *mid gefeohte*,

[Joshua came upon them with battle]

¹⁰ Et conturbavit eos Dominus, a facie Israhel, contrivitque plaga magna, in Gabaon; ac persecutus est per viam ascensus Bethoron, et percussit usque Azeca et Maceda.

[And the Lord troubled them, with a great slaughter, in Gabaon, and pursued them by the way of the ascent to Bethoron, and cut them off all the way to Azeca and Maceda.]

and Drihten hig aflymde *fram Israhela bearnum*. Hi **f**eollon þa swiðe on þam fleame ofslagene.*

[and the Lord put them to flight from the sons of Israel. Many of them died then, slain in that pursuit.]

---

* Marsden, ed., *Heptateuch*, I, p. 185.

The insertion of the adverb *sona* in verse 6 supplies alliteration with *sende* and *seo*. Similarly, in the same verse Ælfric alters the direct object of the final clause so that instead of the inhabitants of Gabaon asking Joshua to save *them*, they implore him to save or rule the *burh*. This small but significant translation choice in turn provides further alliteration through the repetition of *burh* and *buruhwaras* and the added verb *biddende* while also emphasising the defence of the fortified city, a theme to which English audiences around the turn of the millennium could readily relate. The omission of the specific geographic details of the battle further increases this episode's relevance to the lived experience of the military leaders among Ælfric's readers, for whom Joshua's heroic exploits could serve as an inspirational model. As we shall see, Ælfric would make explicit the link between Old Testament leaders of the Israelites and English rulers who protected their people against the Danes in the conclusion to his paraphrase of Judges.

The most substantial omissions occur towards the end of the narrative. Notably, the long account of the division of the Promised Land by lot in Chapters 13–20 is cut in its entirety, save for Jos. 14.2, which is moved into Chapter 21. Similarly, in Chapter 23 several verses detailing the division by lots and inheritance of land (3–5) and the divine punishments that will befall the Israelites if they worship false gods (8–16) are omitted, while verses relating Joshua's old age and imminent death (1–2) and his instructions to the Israelites to take courage and observe the laws of Moses (6–7) are retained. These translation choices allow Ælfric once more to foreground the figure of Joshua as a model war leader for his readers to admire and perhaps emulate.

As is the case in some of the preceding books of the Heptateuch, the final section of Joshua (Chs 23–4) is given special treatment, as it is here that the central theme of obedience is made most clear. Whereas Chs 12–22 are cut in their entirety, in the penultimate chapter (23) Ælfric strips the narrative to its essential elements, bringing its doctrinal message of obedience to the fore. Alliteration (marked in bold) is again used in this passage for rhetorical force:

> [23.1] Ða æfter langum **f**yrste **s**iððan hig on **f**riþe wunodon and Iosue **eal**dode, ² þa het he cuman him to Israhela bearn and þa yldostan heafodmenn ⁶ and **m**anode hig georne þæt hig **M**oyses **æ** on **eal**lum þingum heoldon, swa swa se **æ**lmihtiga God him on **S**inai **d**une gesette and **d**ihte. ⁷ He **b**æd hig þa georne þat hig **b**ugan ne sceoldon fram Godes **b**igengum to þam **b**ysmorfullum hæþengilde, on þæs folces wisan þe þær wearð ofslagen.

> [²³·¹ When they had dwelt in peace for a long time since and Joseph had grown old, ² then he commanded the children of Israel to come to him and the oldest chief men, ⁶ and instructed them eagerly that they

should keep Moses' law in all things, just as the Almighty God had set it down for him on Mount Sinai and commanded. [7] He eagerly instructed that they should not turn from God's practices to shameful heathen idolatry, in the manner of those people that were slain.]

Ælfric has translated the first two verses of Jos. 23 fairly closely, only leaving out repetitious references to the nations being subdued and Joshua's advanced years, as well as a list of all the various elders of the Israelites whom he called to hear his speech. However, he then cuts all of verses 3–5, which comprise the opening section of Joshua's speech reminding the Israelites of all that God has done for them. In place of these details, Ælfric jumps ahead to verse 6, which contains the core injunction in which Joshua warns the Israelites to obey *Moyses æ* ('Moses' law'). In translating this verse, he omits the injunction *et non declinetis ab eis nec ad dextram nec ad sinistram* ('and turn not aside from them neither to the right hand nor to the left'), instead providing his readers with a simple, unequivocal command to obey the law of God. Verse 7, in which Joshua forbids the Israelites from turning to idolatry, is translated in full, though again Ælfric adds a final explanatory clause, *on þæs folces wisan þe þær wearð ofslagen* ('in the manner of those that were slain'), linking this injunction with Ex. 32.25–9 in which 3000 Israelites are slain by the Levites for worshipping the golden calf. The remaining parts of Jos. 23, verses 8–16, containing Joshua's instructions that the Israelites should cleave to the Lord, a list of the various punishments which God will mete out to enemies of Israel and warnings against entering into marriage or friendship with them, are deemed extraneous and therefore cut. Also omitted is the opening segment of the final chapter (Jos. 24.1–15), in which Joshua gathers the elders and makes another speech before them, reiterating many of the instructions he had issued in the previous chapter, as well as listing his achievements and reminding them how he had led them out of Egypt, defeated their enemies and delivered them into Canaan, before once more warning them against worshipping false gods.

By omitting the final part of Ch. 23 and the opening of Ch. 24, Ælfric deftly merges Joshua's two final speeches, presenting the Israelites' reply in 24.16 as if it were their response to his first speech. In verse 16, he again inserts the adverb *anmodlice*, creating alliteration with *ælmihtigan* as well as underscoring the Israelites' covenant with God:

^{24.16} Responditque populus et ait, 'Absit a nobis ut relinquamus Dominum et serviamus diis alienis.'

Hig þa *anmodlice* cwædon þæt hig þam ælmihtigan Gode æfre woldon þeowian *on eallum heora life* [...].

[And the people answered, and said, 'God forbid we should leave the Lord, and serve strange gods.']

[They then *in one mind* said that they would always serve the Almighty *for all of their lives* [...].]

In his rendering of verse 31, Ælfric further endeavours to bring across the spiritual meaning of Joshua to his readers by rendering the Vulgate's statement that God had done works (*opera*) for Israel (*in Israhel*) as a more universal reflection that God had performed miracles or wonders (*wundra*) for them (*on him*):

^{24.31} Servivitque *Israhel* Domino cunctis diebus Iosue et seniorum qui longo vixerunt tempore post Iosue et qui noverant omnia opera Domini quae fecerat *in Israhel*.

Hig **d**idon eac swa on Iosues **d**agum and on þæra ealdra **d**agum þe æfter him leofodon, þe þa wundra cuðon þe God worhte *on him*.

[And *Israel* served the Lord all the days of Joshua, and of the ancients that lived a long time after Joshua, and that had known all the works of the Lord which he had done *in Israel*.]

[*They* also did so in Joshua's days and in the days of their elders who lived after him, who knew those wonders that God had performed *for them*.]

Cumulatively, multiple small changes of this nature serve to universalise the underlying moral themes of the biblical narrative, encouraging readers to see beyond the literal sense and to understand that God has always performed wonders for those who abide by his teachings. In his *Treatise*, Ælfric would further clarify the spiritual meaning of his translation of Joshua, explaining that 'in it one may see God's great wonders performed with deeds' (*on þam man mæg sceawian Godes micclan wundra mid weorcum gefremode*) as well as offering a typological interpretation: *Iosue hæfde ðæs Hælendes getacnunge, mid þam þe he gelædde to þam lande þat folce þe him behaten wæs*[120] ('Joshua had the betokening of the Saviour, when he led that people to that land that was promised to them'). Although this spiritual significance of the Book of Joshua is

---

[120] Marsden, ed., *Heptateuch*, I, p. 209.

A Perilous Task: Making the Old English Heptateuch

never made explicit in the Heptateuch version, the reader is nonetheless guided towards it through the many major and minor alterations that Ælfric makes throughout his translation. However, Ælfric's dissatisfaction with this selective method of scriptural translation – occupying a position somewhere between word-for-word and sense-for-sense, with much material omitted but little by way of interpretation added – is suggested by his radically different approach to Judges.

Judges

The Book of Judges recounts how, following the death of Joshua, the Israelites repeatedly fell back into disobedience and idol worship. God justly punishes this disobedience by delivering the Israelites into the hands of their enemies, before showing his favour by appointing a series of judges to rule over them. Each judge leads the Israelites to victory before the pattern of backsliding begins again. As with all the books of the Heptateuch, many of the key themes of Judges would have had special resonance for the English nobility of Ælfric's day, who were themselves engaged in a 'holy war' against the Danes.

Unlike the other books in the Heptateuch, however, Ælfric's *Judges* is not a translation but a homiletic paraphrase closer to his treatments of Judith and Esther contained in his homilies and the abbreviated summaries of Kings and Maccabees in the *Lives of Saints*.[121] Whereas all the other biblical translations in MS L including Ælfric's *Joshua* are written continuously as if they were one text, the copy of Ælfric's *Judges* begins on a new folio with the preceding page left blank. Both *Judges* and the *Treatise* which follows it in MS L appear to be derived from a different exemplar than the translations of Genesis-Joshua, leading Marsden to conclude that neither was part of the original project.[122] Indeed, as we

---

[121] For a study of Ælfric's *Judges* as both homily and biblical translation, see Paul S. Langeslag, 'Reverse-Engineering the Old English *Book of Judges*', *Neophilologus* 100 (2016), 303–14. On this group of biblical paraphrases, see Rachel Anderson, 'The Old Testament Homily: Ælfric as Biblical Translator', in *The Old English Homily: Precedent, Practice, and Appropriation*, ed. Aaron J. Kleist, SEM 17 (Turnhout: Brepols, 2007), pp. 121–42. Anderson, 'The Old Testament Homily', 136, emphasises the separateness of *Judges* from the biblical translations of Genesis-Joshua that precede it in MS L.

[122] Marsden, ed., *Heptateuch*, I, pp. clx–clxi. Clemoes places Ælfric's *Joshua* in the period 992–1002, together with *Genesis* and its preface and the *Lives of Saints* (containing *Kings* and *Maccabees*), and dates *Numbers* and *Judges* 1002–5 ('Chronology of Ælfric's Works', pp. 55–6). Kleist dates *Joshua, Kings* and *Maccabees c.* 993–998 and *Esther, Judith, Numbers* and *Judges c.* 998–1002 (*Chronology*, pp. 131–4, 136–7). On the dates of the various parts of the Heptateuch, see above, pp. 148–9. Another copy of Ælfric's *Judges* is preserved on

shall see, while the rest of the Heptateuch was composed for lay readers and poorly educated secular clergy, the paraphrase of Judges, composed entirely in Ælfric's late, rhythmical style, was probably written with a monastic audience in mind.

In place of the opening three chapters of the biblical source, which relate the wars and conquests of Judah, the death of Joshua, the Israelites' return to idol worship and the first appointments of judges, Ælfric provides his own succinct introduction summarising these events and linking them to other parts of the Bible, as well as signalling the text's spiritual meaning. In style and approach, this opening section is thus more characteristic of a homiletic paraphrase than a translation in the conventional sense. In addition to regular alliteration (in bold), Ælfric makes use of extensive repetition and parallel phrasing (underlined), producing a polished piece of literary prose:

> Æfter ðam ðe **M**oyses se **m**ære heretoga þæt **G**odes **f**olc **g**elædde of **P**harones þeowette ofer ða Readan **S**æ and God him æ gesette, and æfter þam þe Iosue be Godes sylfes gewissunge þæt **m**ankyn gebrohte mid swiðe **m**icclum sige to þam behatenan earde and hi þæron wunedon, þa wurdon hig **e**alles to **o**ft on yfel awende and mid yfelum weorce þone ælmihtigan God þearle gegremedon. And God hi eac sona hæðenum leodum let to anwealde, swa þæt þa hæðenan hæfdon heora geweald swa oft swa hig abulgon þam ælmihtigan Gode, oð þæt hig eft oncneowon heora yfelan dæden and gebugon to Gode, biddende his miltse. Ða funde he him **s**ona **s**umne **f**ultum æfre and he hig ahredde of þam reðan þeowte þæra hæðenra leoda þe heora hæfdon geweald. Hig næfdon nanne cyning him gecoren ne þa git, for ðam þe God sylf was heora wissiend þa and gesette him **d**eman þe **d**emdon þam folce to swiþe langum **f**yrste, oð þæt hi sylfe gecuron **S**aul him to cyninge, swa swa us **s**ecgað bec, be Godes geþafunge on **S**amueles timan.[123]

[After Moses the famous war leader, who (had) led that people of God out of Pharaoh's servitude across the Red Sea and God (had) established the law for them, and after Joshua, who through God's own instruction (had) brought that people with very many victories to that promised land and they (had) remained there, then it happened that they all turned to evil too often and with evil deeds they greatly angered the Almighty God. And God also quickly delivered them into the power of heathen

---

fols 108ʳ–116ʳ Oxford, Bodleian Library, MS Hatton 115, a late eleventh-century collection of Ælfrician homiletic and instructional materials, where it follows his sermon *De populo Israhel*, a condensed version of Exodus and Numbers. For discussion of *De populo Israhel*, see Scheil, *Footsteps of Israel*, pp. 295–312.

[123] Marsden, ed., *Heptateuch*, I, p. 190, ll. 1–17. Marsden provides line numbers for Ælfric's *Judges* due to its homiletic style.

peoples, so that those heathens had power over them for as long as they angered that Almighty God, until afterwards they knew their evil deeds and turned to God, praying for his mercy. Then he quickly found some help for them always and he delivered them from the terrible servitude of those heathen peoples who had rule over them. They had not chosen any king for themselves yet, because God himself was their ruler then and established judges for them who judged that people for a very long time, until they chose for themselves Saul as a king, just as books tell us, by God's permission in the time of Samuel.]

While the opening sentence echoes the linking passage that Ælfric provides in his stint of Numbers, this prologue nevertheless marks a major departure from the rest of Heptateuch both in style and content.[124]

The homiletic method becomes more evident as the paraphrase proper begins, in which Ælfric uses terms of address suggestive of oral performance to introduce sections of biblical paraphrase, such as *We willað nu secgan swutelicor be þisum* ('We now wish to speak more clearly about this') (Jud. 3.5), and *Ðeos racu us secgð, þe we nu ær rædon* ('This narrative says to us, which we have now read before') (Jud. 6.1–4). Another striking departure from the generally conservative translation style on display throughout the rest of the Heptateuch is the inclusion of regular homiletic inserts which relate the Old Testament narrative to other parts of the Bible, in particular the Psalms, which are supplied in Latin and then translated and interpreted, as in the manner of the *Catholic Homilies*.[125] Hence, in between the paraphrase of Jud. 5.32 and 6.1–4, Ælfric uses the account of God's delivery of the Israelites from their enemies in Chs 4 and 5 as an opportunity to introduce the words of the Psalmist, combining two psalm verses (Ps. 82.3 and 82.10):

We secgað nu eac þæt we singað be þisum on urum sealmsange, swa swa hit sang Dauid þurh þone Halgan Gast, God heriende þus: '*Ecce inimici tui sonauerunt et qui oderunt te extollerunt capud.* [82.10] *Fac illis sicut Madian et Sisare sicut Iabin in torrente Cison*' (Ps. 82.3). Ðæt ys on urum gereorde, he cwæð to his Drihtene: 'Efne nu Drihten þine fynd hyldað and þa þe þe hatiað ahebbað heora heafda. Do him swa swa Madian and swa swa Sisaran and swa swa Iabin æt þam burnan Cyson.' Hwæt sind Godes fynd buton þa fulan hæðenan and þa leasan cristenan þe hyldað ongean God, and mid unrihtwisnisse þa earman ofsittað and Godes lima dreccað, Gode to forsewennysse, ahebbende heora heafda on healicre modignesse? Ac þe sealm us segð hu him sceal getiman, swa swa ðam

---

[124] See above, p. 190.
[125] For a notable exception to this rule in Ælfric's treatment of Lot and Sodom, see above, pp. 170–7.

eagran Sisaran and þam **a**rleasan Iabine, þæt hi beon **a**dilegode fram Drihtenes **h**algum mannum, þa þe hi huxlice **h**er on life gedrehton.[126]

[We say now just as we sing about this in our psalmody, just as David sang it through the Holy Spirit, praising God thus: '*Ecce inimici tui sonauerunt et qui oderunt te extollerunt capud.* [82.10] *Fac illis sicut Madian et Sisare sicut Iabin in torrente Cison*' (Ps. 82.3). That is in our language, he said to his Lord: '[Ps. 82.3] Behold Lord, now your enemies hold against you and those that hate you raise up their heads. [82.10] Do to them as (you did) to Madian and to Sisara and to Jabin and at the brook of Cisson.' What are God's enemies except those foul heathens and those false Christians who hold against God, and with unrighteousness oppress the wretched and torture God's limbs, in contempt of God, raising their heads in haughty pride? But this psalm says to us what will befall them, just as befell the evil Sisarans and the impious Jabins, so that they were destroyed through God's holy people, when they disgracefully oppressed them here in life.]

While the *Prose Psalms* had prioritised the historical level of interpretation before moving to moral and Christological interpretations, Ælfric works in reverse, proceeding from the moral interpretation (*We secgað*) to the historical, which he then connects with the Holy Spirit. This progression from the moral level to the historical is then repeated as Ælfric explains the moral application of the Psalm verse to the lives of his audience before concluding with the biblical context of the punishment meted out to the Sisarans and Jabins. The equation of the oppressors of the Israelites in Judges with the enemies of David and *þa fulan hæðenan* ('those foul heathens') encourages contemporary English readers to view themselves as God's chosen people, delivered from the hands of the Vikings – a theme to which he will return in the conclusion to the work. The psalm citation and ensuing exegesis also allow Ælfric to draw out a moral lesson from the narrative of Judges, warning the audience of the terrible punishments that will befall them should they become *leasan cristenan* ('false Christians') and succumb to pride.

Another psalmic interlude is added to the paraphrase of Judges 7–8, which describes the victory of Israel over Madian under the leadership of Gideon in heavily abridged form. This passage reports the deaths in battle of *twegen ealdormen* ('two ealdormen') (Jud. 7.25), described only as *duos viros* ('two men') in the Vulgate source, and of Madian, Oreb and Zeb, as well as the defeat of *twegen ciningas* ('two kings'), Zebee and Salmana. The mention of these leaders of the enemies of Israel in the Vulgate source again prompts Ælfric to cite Ps. 82, which in turn leads him into a homiletic exegesis on the moral and spiritual implications of the Judges narrative more generally:

---

[126] Marsden, ed., *Heptateuch*, I, pp. 192–93, ll. 91–104.

Be þisum we singað eac on þam foresædan sealme ongean Godes wiðer-
winna þe willað æfre þwyres, swa swa se Halga Gast us sæde þurch
Dauid: '*Pone principes eorum sicut Oreb, Zeb et Zebee et Psalmana*' (Ps.
82.12). Ðæt ys on Engliscre spræce, 'Sete ðu ure Drihten heora ealdormen swa swa Horeb and Zeb and swa swa Zebee and Salmana.' Ðæt is
on angite þæt þa yfelan heafodmen, Godes wiðerwinnan, wurdon þa
gescinde and swa swa þas ealdormen wurdon þa gescinde.[127]

[About this we sing in that aforesaid Psalm against God's adversaries
who always wish after evil, just as the Holy Spirit said to us through
David: '*Pone principes eorum sicut Oreb, Zeb et Zebee et Psalmana*' (Ps.
82.12). That is in English speech, 'Make their ealdormen, our Lord, like
Horeb and Zeb and Zebee and Salmana.' That is in the sense that the evil
chief men, God's adversaries, became ashamed just as those ealdormen
became ashamed.]

In homiletic interludes such as these, Ælfric adds his own spiritual exegesis
to the scriptural narrative in a manner which clearly distinguishes this work
from the rest of the Heptateuch. Indeed, whereas the other books appear
to have been made for private reading by members of the laity or poorly
educated secular clergy, as Stewart Brookes notes, the references to the
singing of psalms in *Judges* suggest it was composed for reading aloud in a
monastic refectory.[128]

Ælfric's sensitivity to the concerns of a monastic audience lies behind
the numerous alterations he makes to the final section of his paraphrase of
Judges, an extended summary of the story of Samson and Delilah (Jud. 16).
Elements which are deemed otiose or inappropriate for such an audience,
such as Samson's intercourse with a prostitute in Gaza (16.1) are silently
glossed over, while Ælfric's repeated blaming of Delilah for tempting
Samson recasts the biblical narrative to make it more relevant to monks and
nuns engaged in constant struggle against sin.[129] The paraphrase of the story
of Samson ends with an extended exegesis of its spiritual meaning which
has no precedent in the biblical source: here Ælfric explains that Samson
*hæfde getacnunge ures Hælendes Crist þe on his agenum deaðe þone deofol gewylde
and his mihte oferswiðde and hine mankynnes benæmde*[130] ('had the signification
of our Saviour Christ who through his own death had power over the
devil and conquered his might and took away mankind from him'), while

---

[127] Marsden, ed., *Heptateuch*, I, pp. 194–95, ll. 150–7.
[128] Stewart Brookes, 'Reading Between the Lines: The Liturgy and Ælfric's *Lives of Saints* and Homilies', *Leeds Studies in English* 42 (2011), 17–28, at 19–20.
[129] Marsden, ed., *Heptateuch*, I, pp. 196–97, ll. 217–18, 224–5. The Douay-Rheims retains the Latin spelling *Dalila*, which I have modified here to the more common English spelling *Delilah*.
[130] Marsden, ed., *Heptateuch*, I, p. 198, ll. 253–5.

his carrying of the doors from the gates of Gaza (Judg. 16.3) *to bysmore his feondum* ('to humiliate his enemies') betokens how the Jews who killed *urne Drihten* ('our Lord') quickly placed him in a sepulchre with a guard:

> ac he tobreac hellegatu mid his hefonlican mihte and of þam deofle genam þone dæl þe he wolde Adames ofspringes. And he eaðelice aras of ðam deaðe gesund on þam þriddan dæge and astah to heofenum and to his halgan fæder, gewunnenum sige, to wuldre him sylfum and his halgum þegnum, þam ðe he alysde. Nelle we secgan na swiðor be þisum buton þæt se Israhel þe we embe spræcon mislice ferde oð þæt hi fengon to ciningum, swa swa on Cininga Bocum ys full cuð be ðam.[131]

> [but he broke the gates of hell with his heavenly might and seized from the devil that portion that he wanted of Adam's offspring. And he easily arose alive from that death on the third day and ascended to heaven to his Holy Father, dwelling in victory, to the glory of himself and his holy servants, those that he saved. We do not wish to say any more about this except that the Israel about which we spoke fared diversely until they came to kingship, just as the Books of Kings makes clear concerning that.]

This reference to the Books of Kings leads Ælfric into a lengthy discourse on the history of Christian kingship with no known source: the Romans first 'had for themselves *consuls* whom we call *counsellors*' (*hæfdon him 'consulas' þæt we cweðað 'rædboran'*) and then '*cesares* over them that we call *emperors*' ('*cesares' ofer hig þæt we cweðað 'caseras'*) up until the time of Constantine, 'the first Caesar that turned to Christ, and books tell us that he was victorious through the Saviour Christ that he had chosen' (*se forma casere ðe to Criste beah, and us secgað bec þæt he sigefæst was þurh þone Hælend Crist þe he gecoren hæfde*).[132] Ælfric then charts the triumphs of Constantine's *æftergengan* ('successors'), who were equally victorious on account of their faith, and the subsequent flourishing of Christendom and decline of devil-worship. In particular, the Byzantine emperors Theodosius I (*r*. 379–395) and II (*r*. 402–450), are presented as model Christian rulers. To illustrate this point, Ælfric recounts an episode in which angels led Theodosius II's troops across a marsh to storm the Western Emperor John's fortress at Ravenna and rescued a captured *ealdorman*, comparing this event to Moses leading the Israelites across the Red Sea.[133] Through God's intervention,

---

[131] Marsden, ed., *Heptateuch*, I, p. 198, ll. 257–66.

[132] Marsden, ed., *Heptateuch*, I, pp. 198–99, ll. 267–86.

[133] The ultimate source for this passage is Socrates Scholasticus' *Church History* (*c*. 440), a work which was known to Ælfric via Cassiodorus' Latin translation in his *Tripartite Ecclesiastical History* (*c*. 550), together with the histories of Sozomen and Theodoret. For citations of this work in various Ælfrician homilies, see Lapidge, *Anglo-Saxon Library*, p. 264. On imperial themes in Socrates'

Theodosius II defeated the king of the Persians, drowning a great army of Saracens in the River Euphrates and slaughtering his 'immortals' until he 'turned to the will of the caesar' (*beah to þæs caseres willa*).[134] The clear resonance between Theodosius II's wars with the Huns and the ongoing wars between the English and the Vikings is underlined in Ælfric's comment that since that time 'those heathen adversaries' (*þa wiðerrædan hæðenan*) have occasionally attempted to go 'raiding' (*on heregoð*) within the Roman emperor's dominion (*anwealde*). Ælfric's account of the victories of these Byzantine emperors demonstrates that God has always favoured leaders who have faith in him.

In order to bring this message home, Ælfric's *Judges* – and the text of the Old English Heptateuch itself – concludes with an encomium on the glories of the three greatest Christian kings of the English, Alfred, Æthelstan and Edgar. Each of these rulers is praised for protecting their people against foreign attackers, just as the biblical judges and Byzantine emperors had done before them. As a key instigator of the Benedictine Reform, Edgar is singled out for special attention on account of his promotion of the religious life (alliteration is marked in bold):

> On Englalande **e**ac oft wæron cyningas sig**e**fæste þurh God, swa swa we **s**ecgan geh**y**rdon. Swa swa wæs Ælfred cining þe oft gefeaht wið Denan, oþ þæt he **s**ige gewann and b**e**werode his leode. Swa gelice Æðestan þe wið **A**nlaf gefeaht and his firde **o**fsloh and **a**flimde hine **s**ylfne and he on **s**ibbe wunude **s**iþþan mid his leode. **E**adgar se **æ**ðela and se **a**nræda cining **a**rærde Godes lof on his leode gehwær, **e**alra cininga swioðost ofer **E**ngla ðeode, and him God gewilde his wiðerwinnan **a**, **c**iningas and **e**orlas, þæt hi **c**omon him to buton ælcum gefeohte, friðes wilniende, him underþeodde to þam þe he wolde. And he was gewurðod **w**ide geond land.
>
> We endiað nu þisne cwide, þus þancience ðam Almihtigan ealra his godnissa, se ðe æfre rixað on ecnisse. AMEN.[135]

[There were also kings in England often victorious through God, just as we have heard said. So was King Alfred who often fought against the

---

work, see Luke Gardiner, 'The Imperial Subject: Theodosius II and Panegyric in Socrates' *Church History*', in *Theodosius II: Rethinking the Roman Empire in Late Antiquity*, ed. Christopher Kelly (Cambridge: Cambridge University Press, 2013), pp. 244–68. For discussion of Cassiodorus' version, see Désirée Scholten, 'Cassiodorus' *Historia tripartita* before the Earliest Extant Manuscripts', in *The Resources of the Past in Early Medieval Europe*, ed. Clemens Gantner, Rosamond McKitterick and Sven Meeder (Cambridge: Cambridge University Press, 2015), pp. 34–50.

[134] Marsden, ed., *Heptateuch*, I, p. 199, l. 317.
[135] Marsden, ed., *Heptateuch*, I, p. 200, ll. 327–38.

Danes until he achieved victory and protected his people. So also was Æthelstan who fought against Anlaf and slew his army and put him to flight and he dwelt in peace afterwards with his people. The noble and single-minded King Edgar raised up God's praise everywhere among his people, the greatest of all the kings of the English, and God gave him power over his adversaries always, kings and nobles, so that they came to him without battle, suing for peace, submitting themselves to him as he wished; and he was honoured far and wide throughout the land.

We end now this speech, thus thanking the Almighty for all of his goodnesses, he who rules forever in eternity. AMEN.]

Ælfric's positioning of these three West Saxon kings as heirs to Constantine implies a *translatio imperii* of Christian emperorship from Rome to Wessex, in keeping with the styling of English rulers as emperors of Britain in charters and coins of this period.[136] Moreover, Ælfric's identification of the Constantinian dynasty with Samson and the other judges connects these English kings with the biblical leaders chosen by God to defend Israel prior to the establishment of the monarchy. Whereas the preceding sections of the Heptateuch emphasise the duties of earthly leaders, the conclusion to Ælfric's *Judges* thereby encourages its primarily monastic audience to view themselves as members of a chosen people protected by *cyningas sigefæste þurh God* ('kings victorious through God').[137]

The incorporation of elements of this passage from Ælfric's *Judges* into the Anglo-Saxon Chronicle annal on the death of Eadwig and accession of Edgar (MSS D and E 959) demonstrates the alertness of at least one contemporary reader to the political implications of Ælfric's homily on Judges.[138]

---

[136] On imperial themes in West Saxon literature and political thought in the tenth and eleventh centuries and the import of the Old English translation of the Orosian world history, see Francis Leneghan, '*Translatio Imperii*: The Old English *Orosius* and the Rise of Wessex', *Anglia* 133 (2015), 656–705; Francis Leneghan, 'End of Empire? Reading *The Death of Edward* in MS Cotton Tiberius B I', in *Ideas of the World in Early Medieval English Literature*, ed. Mark Atherton, Kazutomo Karasawa and Francis Leneghan, SOEL 1 (Turnhout: Brepols, 2022), pp. 403–34; and Omar Khalaf, 'Ælfred *se casere*: Kingship and Imperial Legitimation in the Old English *Orosius*', in *Age of Alfred*, ed. Faulkner and Leneghan, pp. 457–75. For the expression of West Saxon imperialism in maps as well as literature, see Helen Appleton, 'The Northern World of the Anglo-Saxon Mappa Mundi', *ASE* 47 (2018), 275–305; and Helen Appleton, 'Mapping Empire: Two World Maps in Early Medieval England', in *Ideas of the World*, ed. Atherton, Karasawa and Leneghan, pp. 309–34.

[137] On Ælfric's conception of the Three Orders of Society, see above pp. 188–9 and below, pp. 221–4.

[138] For the argument that Wulfstan was the author of this passage as well as the poetic annals for 975 (*Death of Edgar*) and 979 (on the death of Edward the

The chronicle passage is sometimes printed as verse due to its rhythmical features; verbal parallels with *Judges* are in italics:[139]

> On his dagum hit godode georne, and God him geuðe
> þet he wunode on sibbe þa hwile þe he leofode,
> and he dyde swa him þearf wes, earnode þes georne.
> He *arerde Godes lof* wide and Godes lage lufode
> and folces *frið* bette *swiðost þara cyninga*
> þe ær him gewurde be manna gemynde.
> *And God him* eac fylste þet *cyningas and eorlas*
> georne him to bugon and wurden *underþeodde*
> *to þam þe wolde,* and *butan gefeohte*
> eal he *gewilde* þet he sylf wolde.
> *He wearð wide geond þeodland swiðe geweorðad,*
> forþam þe he weorðode Godes naman georne
> and Godes lage smeade oft and gelome
> and Godes lof rædde oftost a simle
> for Gode and for worulde eall his þeode.[140]

[In his (i.e. Edgar's) days things prospered readily, in that he dwelled in peace for as long as he lived. And he readily merited this, doing as was his duty. Far and wide *he exalted God's praise* and loved God's law and improved the people's *security much more than those kings* who were before him within the memory of men. And God helped him too, so that *kings and earls* readily submitted to him and *were subjected to that which he wanted*. And *without battle* he controlled all that he himself wanted. He became greatly *honoured widely throughout* the land of the nation, for he readily honoured God's name, and deliberated God's law over and over again, and promoted God's praise far and wide, and counselled all his nation wisely, very often, always continuously, for God and for the world.]

Complementing the two more widely recognised chronicle poems composed in honour of Edgar, *The Coronation of Edgar* (ASC 973 MSS ABC) and *The Death of Edgar* (ASC 975 MSS ABC),[141] this passage follows Ælfric

---

Martyr), see Daniel Anlezark, 'Wulfstan and the Anglo-Saxon Chronicle', in *Wulfstan of York*, ed. Andrew Rabin and Catherine Cubitt (forthcoming).

[139] For discussion of the textual links, see Marsden, ed., *Heptateuch*, I, p. clxii.

[140] Susan Irvine, ed., *The Anglo-Saxon Chronicle: A Collaborative Edition, Volume 7, MS E* (Cambridge: D. S. Brewer, 2004), p. 56.

[141] On these two Edgar poems, see Mercedes Salvador-Bello, 'The Edgar Panegyrics in the Anglo-Saxon Chronicle', in *Edgar, King of the English 959–975: New Interpretations*, ed. Donald Scragg, Publications of the Manchester Centre for Anglo-Saxon Studies 8 (Woodbridge: Boydell, 2008), pp. 252–72; Scott Thompson Smith, 'The Edgar Poems and the Poetics of Failure in the Anglo-Saxon Chronicle', *ASE* 39 (2011), 105–37. On the annal for 959, see Thomas

in casting the English king as a God-fearing ruler who promoted the church's mission and protected his nation (*þeod*), and who merited God's favour by obeying his law (*Godes lage*). In its incorporation of elements of Ælfric's *Judges*, this Chronicle passage thus provides strong evidence for how Old English biblical prose contributed to the development of ideas of nation and kingship in early medieval England.

Despite its separate origins and distinct audience, when read in the context of MS L, the concluding section of Ælfric's *Judges* makes plain the relevance of these Old Testament stories to the lives of a wide range of contemporary English readers, including the lay nobility and gentry and those in monastic orders whom they had a duty to protect.[142]

Conclusion

The Old English Heptateuch presents a variety of approaches to biblical translation, adaptation and interpretation, ranging from the faithful, almost interlinear approach taken by Ælfric in the opening of his translation of Genesis to the free paraphrase of his homily on Judges. Uniting all these approaches, however, is a thoroughly domesticating sensibility, in which obscure or exotic elements are consistently downplayed or omitted whereas those parts of the biblical narrative which resonate with contemporary concerns are retained and sometimes even amplified. The various translation styles on display are all broadly speaking communicative, and only on rare occasions creative. As Ælfric explains in his *Preface to Genesis*, any translation from Latin into English must rearrange the syntax of the source in order to be intelligible: the Heptateuch authors therefore adopt a functional equivalence approach to bring over the meaning of the source text rather than its form. In Steiner's terminology, the first stage in the production of the Heptateuch is 'affirmation':[143] although Ælfric himself had strong reservations about the project, the team accepted the task of translating the first books of the Old Testament into prose for an audience who were otherwise unable to access its teaching. The next step is 'aggression' (or 'plundering'), in which the translators analyse the vocabulary, syntax, grammar and meaning of the first seven books of the Bible, weighing up their options for rendering them into English. The third stage is 'incorporation', the process of adaptation into

---

A. Bredehoft, *Textual Histories: Readings in the Anglo-Saxon Chronicle* (Toronto: University of Toronto Press, 2001), pp. 85–7.

[142] Noting that the central lesson of Ælfric's *Judges* is that God's favour towards rulers depends on their service, Langeslag concludes: 'This lesson applied to all audiences, but it was especially pertinent to men of worldly power, such as ealdorman Æthelweard' ('Old English *Book of Judges*', 313).

[143] See above, p. xiii, for Steiner's theory of translation.

the target language: in bringing across the core elements of the first seven books of the Bible into English, the translators are relatively faithful to their source, though the tendency towards abbreviation increases dramatically from Exodus onwards, culminating in the heavily paraphrastic approach taken in the later books. As part of this process of 'incorporation', numerous biblical passages deemed too risqué or offensive, or too confusing or boring, are omitted, with the result that the Old English Heptateuch emerges as a much more accessible, coherent and readable text than its unwieldy and at times repetitious biblical source. Finally, we arrive at the stage of 'compensation': in rendering the Heptateuch into the vernacular, the translators favour an idiomatic English prose style throughout, while Ælfric employs a rhythmical and alliterative prose style designed to appeal to the tastes of audiences familiar with vernacular preaching and poetry. Paratextual materials, including incipits, colophons and, in one manuscript, a scheme of lavish illustrations, further contribute to making the first seven books of the Old Testament more accessible and meaningful to a wide audience of lay and clerical readers.

Stripped of potentially confusing episodes, tediously long genealogies and irrelevant geographic details, the Heptateuch provided the English ruling elite with inspirational examples of heroic military leadership, inviting them to draw parallels between their own wars with the Vikings and the existential struggles of the Israelites. In this streamlined form, the core teaching of the Heptateuch that God's laws must be obeyed if his people are to enjoy his favour and avoid his wrath is made all the more clear. Nevertheless, the project was not without its own difficulties. On occasion, the decision to abbreviate the biblical narrative in the manner outlined above led to inconsistencies, such as when Ælfric's omission of the story of Moses' disobedience at the rock in Numbers is flatly contradicted by the ending of Deuteronomy.[144] Ælfric's subsequent turn from translation to paraphrase, in which the author can exert far more control over which parts of the source text are made available to the audience as well as determining how the selected material is framed, may be partially explained by his growing dissatisfaction with a project to which he seems never to have been entirely committed. Yet the Old English Heptateuch nonetheless stands as a remarkable literary achievement, widening access to the Old Testament to a broad audience comprising both lay and clerical elements. It would not be until the fourteenth century with the production of the Wycliffe Bible, that such a concerted effort to translate Scripture into English would be attempted again.[145]

---

[144] See above, pp. 192–3, 197–8.
[145] See below, Conclusion, pp. 249–50.

5

A Book for Many: Ælfric's *Treatise on the Old and New Testaments*

THE *TREATISE on the Old and New Testaments*, also known as the *Letter to Sigeweard*, marks the culmination of Ælfric's long preoccupation with biblical translation, adaptation and interpretation.[1] In this lengthy epistolary work composed sometime after 1005, Ælfric draws on all his skills as a biblical translator, homilist and exegete to summarise the contents of the entire Bible and explain the spiritual (*gastlic*) relationship between the Old and New Testaments to uneducated readers. Although the *Treatise* has attracted little attention from modern readers, Geoffrey Shepherd has described it as 'the most important treatment in English' of the issue of translation of the Bible before the Purvey tracts, i.e. the General Prologue to the Revised Wycliffe Bible, written *c*. 1395,[2] while Hugh Magennis terms it as 'the earliest extended discussion of the Bible, considered as a whole, in a western vernacular language and […] one of the major discussions of the Bible in medieval English.'[3] In the previous chapter, we saw how Ælfric and his co-translators had struggled to make this spiritual sense of

---

[1] Quotations of the *Treatise* are taken from Marsden's edition of the Heptateuch, which is based on MS Laud Misc. 509 (Ker §344) with some readings supplied from Oxford, Bodleian Library, Bodley 343 (Ker §310), a late twelfth-century collection of homilies which preserves only the section of the *Treatise* on the Old Testament. See also Larry J. Swain, ed., *Ælfric of Eynsham's Letter to Sigeweard: An Edition, Translation and Commentary* (Chicago: University of Illinois at Chicago, 2009). For discussion of the *Treatise*, see Hurt, *Ælfric*, pp. 90–92; Wilcox, *Ælfric's Prefaces*, pp. 37–44; Major, 'Rebuilding the Tower of Babel'; Thomas N. Hall, 'Ælfric and the Epistle to the Laodiceans', in *Apocryphal Texts and Traditions*, ed. Powell and Scragg, pp. 65–83; and Hugh Magennis, 'Ælfric: Letter to Sigeweard', in *The Literary Encyclopedia, Volume 1.2.1.01: English Writing and Culture: Anglo-Saxon England, 500–1066*, ed. Richard Dance and Hugh Magennis (2005): https://www.litencyc.com. For a translation, see Hugh Magennis, 'Ælfric of Eynsham's Letter to Sigeweard (Treatise on the Old and New Testaments)', in *Metaphrastes, or, Gained in Translation: Essays and Translations in Honour of Robert H. Jordan*, ed. Margaret Mullett, Belfast Byzantine Texts and Translations 9 (Belfast: Belfast Byzantine Enterprises, 2004), pp. 210–35.
[2] Shepherd, 'English Versions of the Scriptures before Wyclif', p. 375.
[3] Magennis, 'Ælfric of Eynsham's *Letter to Sigeweard*', p. 210.

to freagþe, ⁊ ðe leofað ⁊ rixað a to populoe ƿæreſ.
Incipit libellus de utroþe testamento et nouo.
Ðis geƿrit ƿas to anu men geðiht ac hit mæg swa ðeah manegum fremian.

Ælfric abbod gret freondlice siðferð æt hase heolon. Ic secge þe to soðan þ ʀ biþ swiðe wis ʀese wið ƿeorulde geƿitnes. ⁊ se hæfð forþgang for gode. ⁊ for populoe seðe wið goðu ƿeorcum liwaþ wylsum ge deugð. ⁊ his swide ge swutelod on halgum gewrytmsu þ þa halgan witan þe god wrote be ruxon þ se pufdwulle ƿaron on his ʀese populow. ⁊ nu halige ƿutdon on heofenum wuteʀ miʀhðe þurh an ge mynd suþly punað nu ato populoe for heoʀa aƿmeruʀse. ⁊ heoʀa swyðe wið god. Ða guntleafan men þe heoʀa lif aðrugon on culfe iorbnʀse ⁊ ʀwa ge endodon heoʀa ge mynd is forgiten on halgum gewrytuʀ. buton þ ʀecgað þa ealdan gewrytmsa heoʀa yfelan dæda ⁊ þ lng for mæʀe ƿutdon. Dubeor me for oft ung-lysepa gewrytena. ⁊ ic þe nege edode wllos swa cwhcer an ðam þe þu mid ƿeorcum þæt ge pilwoorst æt me þaða þu me bæd for goðes lufan ge þwe ʀic þe æt ham æt ƿinu hare ge ʀwrace. ⁊ ðaða ƿwide mænorc þaʀa ic mid þe wæs ⁊ þu mme gewrita bigean ne wihcere nu wille ic ð þu habbe hnʀu his brede mðe ʀswom ge liead. ⁊ þu hine habban þile þ þu eallos ne beo mmʀa boca berbled. God lufað þa goðan people. ⁊ þe ʀwle ing habban æt ur. ⁊ hne yʀ appreen peodlice behm

prologus

propre þ di ario.

the Heptateuch clear, relying on the strict censoring of passages that might be read too literally and only very occasionally resorting to exegesis. With the *Treatise*, Ælfric abandons biblical translation entirely in favour of summary, homiletic exegesis and sermon-like moral instruction.

The complete text of the *Treatise* is now the last item in MS Laud Misc. 509 (MS L), fols 120ᵛ–141ᵛ, where it follows Ælfric's homily on *Judges* and *Letter to Wulfgeat* (fig. 13).[4] The Old English Prose Life of Guthlac which originally followed the *Treatise* was separated from the codex by Cotton and is now MS Cotton Vespasian D. XXI fols 18–40.

Contents, Structure and Theme

Following a conventional third-person epistolary greeting of Sigeweard, the letter then shifts into the first person as Ælfric foregrounds his central theme of good works in the manner of a sermon:

> Ælfric Abbod gret freondlice Sigwerd æt Eastheolon. Ic secge þe to soðan þæt se bið swiþe wis, se þe mid weorcum spricð, and se hæfð forþgang for Gode and for worulde, se ðe mid godum weorcum hine sylfne geglengð.[5]

> [Abbot Ælfric greets in a friendly way Sigeweard at Asthall. I say to you as a truth that he is very wise, the one who speaks with works, and who has success before God and in the world, he who adorns himself through good works.]

Ælfric had previously stressed how a deep knowledge of Scripture was the foundation for a life of good works in his homily for Easter Sunday:

> Us is twyfeald neod on boclicum gewriten: anfeald neod us is þæt we ða boclican lare mid carfullum mode smeagan; oðer þæt we hi to weorcum awendan.[6]

> [We have a twofold need for written Scriptures: one need is that we should study the written Scripture with an attentive mind; the other is that we should turn them into works.]

In the *Treatise* he provides a wealth of examples from Scripture demonstrating the rewards of good deeds and the punishments of bad ones:

---

[4] Kleist, *Chronology*, pp. 157–8. Ælfric refers to himself as an abbot in the opening of the letter, indicating that it was composed after 1005, when he became abbot of Eynsham. For a post-Conquest partial witness to the *Treatise*, see below, Conclusion, p. 248.

[5] Marsden, ed., *Heptateuch*, I, p. 201, ll. 1–7.

[6] CH II.16, p. 162.

And þæt is swiðe geswutelod on halgum gesetnissum þæt þa halgan weras þe gode weorc beeodon, þæt hi wurðfulle wæron on þissere worulde. And nu halige sindon on heofenan rices mirhþe and heora gemynd þurhwunað nu a to worulde for heora anrædnisse and heora trywðe wið God. Ða gimeleasan men þe heora lif adrugon on ealre idelnisse, and swa geeondodon, heora gemynd is forgiten on halgum gewritum, buton þæt secgað þa Ealdan Gesetnissa heora yfelan dæda and þæt þæt hig fordemde sindon.[7]

[And that is very clear in holy writings that those men who were diligent about good works, that they were honoured in this world and are now saints in the bliss of the kingdom of heaven and their memory remains now forever because of their steadfastness and their faith in God. Those careless men who passed their lives in complete idleness, and so ended, their memory is forgotten in holy books, except that the Old Testament tells of their evil deeds and that they are damned.]

The *Treatise* proper begins with a catechistic exposition of the Holy Trinity and the Creation of the Angels. Responding to Sigeweard's request for writings in English, Ælfric supplies brief summaries of the essential elements of each of the seventy-two canonical books of the Bible, as well as succinct and unambiguous explanations of their origins and role within the wider structure of the Bible as a whole. In summarising biblical history, he also takes the opportunity to clarify many points of doctrine, for example explaining that there were eight people saved on Noah's Ark (Noah and his wife, their three sons, Shem, Ham and Japheth, and their three wives).[8] As Daniel Anlezark has shown, this was a theological point that needed to be made to the West Saxon nobility as the version of King Æthelwulf's genealogy preserved in the Anglo-Saxon Chronicle annal for 855 (MSS ABC) states that Noah had a fourth son named Sceaf, who was born on the Ark.[9] Ælfric would doubtless have viewed this notion of Noah's fourth son as an error (*gedwyld*) that needed to be corrected.

Utilising the framework of the conventional scheme of the Six Ages of the World, Ælfric proceeds through the various stages of salvation history,

---

[7] Marsden, ed., *Heptateuch*, I, p. 201, ll. 7–14.
[8] Marsden, ed., *Heptateuch*, I, p. 204, ll. 104–11.
[9] Anlezark, 'Sceaf, Japheth and the Origins of the Anglo-Saxons', 40–1. As Anlezark notes, in the version of the West Saxon genealogy included in Æthelweard's *Chronicon*, the story of Sceaf's birth in Noah's Ark preserved in the Anglo-Saxon Chronicle is replaced by a legend in which Sceaf is a foundling who arrived in a boat among the Danes, who then accepted him as their king (19–21). For connections with the story of Scyld Scefing in *Beowulf*, see Francis Leneghan, *The Dynastic Drama of 'Beowulf'*, Anglo-Saxon Studies 39 (Cambridge: D. S. Brewer, 2020), pp. 143–51.

explaining the relationship between people and episodes in the Old and New Testaments.[10] Having summarised the basic elements of the Genesis narrative – Creation, the sin of Adam, the story of Cain and Abel, the Flood, and the repopulation of the world by Noah's three sons – Ælfric then supplies a Christological exegesis of this story's significance (*getacnunga*) when read in light of the New Testament:

> We secgað nu mid ofste þas endebirdnisse, for þan ðe we oft habbað ymbe þis awriten mid maran andgite þa þu miht sceawian, and eac ða getacnunga.
>
> Þæt Adam getacnude, þe on ðam sixtan dæge gesceapen wæs þurh God, urne Hælend Crist, þe com to þissere worulde and us geedniwode to his gelicnisse. Eua getacnode, þe of Adames sidan God silf geworhte, Godes gelaðunge þe of Cristes sidan wearð acenned. Abel slege soðlice getacnode ures Hælendes slege þe ða Iudeiscan ofslogon, yfele gebroðra swa swa Cain wæs. Seth, Adames sunu, ys gesæd ærist, and he gecatnode untwilice Crist, se þe of deaðe aras on ðam þriddan dæge.[11]

> [We will now briefly narrate this sequence because we have often written about this with more understanding than you might be able to see, and also the significance.
>
> That Adam, who on the sixth day was made by God, signifies our Saviour Christ, who came into this world and renewed us in his likeness. Eve, who God made out of Adam's side, signifies God's faithful who were born out of Christ's side. The murder of Abel truly signifies our Saviour's murder, whom those Jews killed, evil brothers just as Cain was. Seth, Adam's son, is said to be first, and he undoubtedly signifies Christ, he who arose from death on the third day.]

Without the self-imposed limitations of his biblical translations, he is now able to exert far more control over which portions of the text his lay readers can access. The more flexible format of the *Treatise* also allows him to guide these same readers in the spiritual (*gastlic*) interpretation of Scripture – in particular the Old Testament – and thereby prevent them from falling into error.

Because he is no longer engaged in translating but in paraphrasing the Bible, Ælfric is also now at liberty to add supplementary material that does not appear in the Vulgate, notably the account of the Fall of the Angels and material on the lives of the apostles. The longest of these sections is an

---

[10] Marsden, ed., *Heptateuch*, I, p. 3. On the Six-Ages scheme, see John Burrow, *The Ages of Man: A Study in Medieval Writing and Thought* (Oxford: Clarendon Press, 1986), pp. 80–92. See further Harriet Soper, *The Life Course in Old English Poetry* (Cambridge: Cambridge University Press, 2023).

[11] Marsden, ed., *Heptateuch*, I, pp. 204–5, ll. 111–21.

episode from the life of John the Apostle, derived from a Latin translation of Eusebius' *Ecclesiastical History*.[12] This narrative exemplifies the *Treatise*'s central theme of the value of good works in relating how the apostle rescued a wayward youth from a life of iniquity. Ælfric's portrait of John serves as a model of an ideal pastor, a theme that recurs throughout the *Treatise*. Once the persecutions of the Emperor Domitian have ceased, John is summoned back to Rome, travelling to neighbouring towns in order to preach and set up churches in regions where there were none, appointing ordained priests to serve in them as well as consecrating a bishop and instructing the people. John selects a youth for Christian instruction, charging the recently consecrated bishop to tutor him in the faith, but the youth becomes dissolute, succumbing to vice and drunkenness. John rescues the youth from a band of thieves and ordains him, and the story concludes with a moralising passage in which Ælfric explains that anyone can mend their ways and win salvation if they are resolute.[13]

After a reiteration of the unity of the Old and New Testaments, the *Treatise* returns to this theme of pastoral care with reflections on the responsibility of teachers (*lareowas*) to instil knowledge of the Bible's teachings in all levels of society. Those who are so foolish as to reject *Cristes gesetnysse* ('the Scriptures of Christ') will suffer *on egeslicum witum* ('in terrible torments') in hell.[14] Similarly, it is the duty of counsellors (*witan*) to reflect on the causes of evil in society and to repair whichever *stelena þæs cinestol* ('supports of the throne') are broken. There follows a brief discourse on the three orders of society (those who work, those who fight and those who pray), a concept that has its earliest iteration in the Alfredian *Boethius* and is, as we have seen, treated in the section appended to Ælfric's Maccabees.[15] Here the political significance of the *Treatise* comes to the fore as Ælfric emphasises to his readers that *se cynestol* ('the throne') rests on these three supports: should one of them become broken, the kingdom will fall. Those who wish to become God's ministers must therefore set an example to others, resisting the temptation of bribes, lest such evil should spread among the people. As his final example of the punishments which will befall those who fail to believe in Christ, Ælfric presents his readers with a detailed and graphic account of the miserable fate of the Jews after the passion of Christ. In order to punish the Jews for killing Christ and his apostles and for their refusal to repent for these deeds, God sends the Romans to besiege them, with the result that they suffer famine, *sceamlica*

---

[12] Magennis notes that although Ælfric attributes the translation of Eusebius to Jerome, it is now known to have been done by Rufinus ('Ælfric of Eynsham's Letter to Sigeweard', p. 212).
[13] Marsden, ed., *Heptateuch*, I, p. 223–7, ll. 668–814.
[14] Marsden, ed., *Heptateuch*, I, p. 228, ll. 855–65.
[15] See above, pp. 188–90.

morð[16] ('shameful abominations'), exile and damnation. Ælfric contrasts this negative exemplum of the perils of *yfelan dæda*[17] ('evil deeds') with the benefits of good works in the closing doxology:

> Nu miht þu wel witan þæt weorc sprecað swiþor þonne þa nacodan word, þe nabbað nane fremminge. Is swa þeah god weorc on þam godan wordum, þonne man oðerne lærð and to geleafan getrimð mid þære soþan lare and þonne mann wisdom sprecð manegum to þearfe and to rihtinge, þæt God si geherod se þe a rixað. Amen.[18]

> [Now you can well understand that works speak louder than plain words, which have no effect. There is nevertheless good work in those good words, when a person teaches another and strengthens them in faith with that true instruction and when a person speaks wisdom for the benefit and correction of the multitude, so that God may be praised, who reigns forever and ever. Amen.]

In this passage, Ælfric again reflects on the duties of religious teachers such as himself, while reminding his readers that they too have responsibilities to instruct and correct others. This lesson becomes more pointed in the final part of the letter where Ælfric directly criticises Sigeweard for inducing him to drink more than was his custom on his last visit, before issuing him with a stern warning of the moral and physical dangers of excessive drinking:[19]

> Ðu woldest me laðian, þa þa ic wæs mid þe, þæt ic swiðor drunce swilce for blisse ofer minum gewunan. Ac wite þu, leof man, þæt se þe oðerne neadað ofer his mihte to drincenne, þæt se mot aberan heora begra gilt, gif him ænig hearm of þære drence becymð. Ure Hælend Crist on his halgan godspelle forbead þone oferdrenc eallum gelyfedum mannum; healde se ðe wille his gesetnysse. And þa halgan lareowas æfter þam Hælende aledon þone unðeaw þurh heora lareowdom and tæhton þæt man drince swa swa him ne derede, for ðan þe se oferdrenc fordeð untwilice þæs mannes sawle and his gesundfullnyse. And unhæl becymð of þam drence.[20]

> [You wished to invite me, when I was with you, that I should drink excessively for pleasure more than I am used to. But you know, beloved man, that he who compels another to drink beyond his capacity, that

---

[16] Marsden, ed., *Heptateuch*, I, p. 229, l. 910.
[17] Marsden, ed., *Heptateuch*, I, p. 229, ll. 917–18.
[18] Marsden, ed., *Heptateuch*, I, p. 229, ll. 918–23.
[19] For Ælfric's focus on drunkenness as the cause of Lot's incest in the Old English prose *Genesis*, see above, p. 173.
[20] Marsden, ed., *Heptateuch*, I, pp. 229–30, ll. 924–30.

A Book for Many: Ælfric's Treatise on the Old and New Testaments

he must bear the guilt of both of them, if any harm comes upon him on account of that drink. Our Saviour Christ in his holy gospel forbade excessive drinking to all those people who believed; let he who wishes hold his doctrine. And those holy teachers after the Saviour established the vices through their teachings and instructed that a man should drink so as not to harm himself, because excessive drinking undoubtedly destroys a man's soul and his health. And illness comes from drinking.]

Echoing his earlier writings on the Three Orders of Society, in these concluding passages Ælfric thus reminds both the clergy (*oratores*) and laity (*bellatores*) of their responsibilities towards each other, and to those who depend on them for religious instruction and military protection: the workers (*laboratores*). The *Treatise* thus offers a coherent vision of England as a Christian nation which, like the biblical nation of Israel, derives its core moral values from a correct understanding of the Bible and the strict observance of its laws. Indeed, as Ælfric explains towards the end of the *Treatise*, it is not possible to avoid evil and commit to good works without a sound knowledge of Scripture:

Hu mæg se man wel faran ðe his mod awent fram eallum þisum bocum and bið him swa anwille þæt him leofre bið þæt he lybbe æfre be his agenum dihte, ascired fram þisum, swilce he ne cunne Cristes gesetnyssa?[21]

[How can a person do well who turns his mind away from all these books and is so stubborn that he would rather live by his own judgement, cut off from them, as if he did not know of Christ's Scriptures?]

In Ælfric's rhetoric, to lead a good life, all Christians require access to the teachings of the Bible, be they *oratores*, *bellatores* or *laboratores*. Yet as we have seen, Ælfric had serious reservations about the wisdom of providing translations of Genesis and other parts of the Old Testament for the laity. Together with the other translators of the Heptateuch, he therefore took various compensatory measures to ensure that such readers were not exposed to elements of the Old Testament which they might misinterpret.

In the *Treatise*, Ælfric evokes the figure of Moses in support of his argument that it is the responsibility of elders (*maiores*) to instruct others in the meaning of the Scriptures:

Moyses us lærde, se mære witega, on his gesetnissum, þus secgende eallum: '*Interroga patrem tuum et adnuntiabit tibi maiores tuos et dicent tibi*' (Deut. 32.7), *et cetera*. Ðæt ys on Englisc, 'Asca þinne fæder embe ðone soþan God and he þe kyð be him. Befrin þine yldran and hig þe secgað.'

---

[21] Marsden, ed., *Heptateuch*, I, p. 228, ll. 855–8.

Gif þu nelt witan and beon gewissod her, þu scealt leornian ðær, þe laþre bið on egeslicum witum, ðæt þu wite þonne hwænne þe forsawe and hwæs gesetnysse.²²

[Moses taught us, the famous prophet, in his writings, saying thus to all: 'Interroga patrem tuum et adnuntiabit tibi maiores tuos et dicent tibi', et cetera (Deut. 32.7). That is in English, 'Ask your father about the true God and he will inform you about him; enquire of your elders and they will tell you.' If you do not wish to know and be informed here, you will learn there, where the dreadful afflictions will be more painful to you, so that you will know then who it was that you rejected and whose Scriptures.]

Throughout his long career as a biblical translator and exegete, Ælfric himself assumes the role of such an 'elder', diligently teaching *embe ðone soþan God* ('about the true God') and providing detailed and accessible instruction in *Cristes gesetnyssa* ('Christ's Scriptures') to all levels of society.

In addition to these spiritual goals, Ælfric also used the *Treatise* for the more practical purpose of drawing attention to his other writings, inviting his readers to consult this vernacular library of core Christian doctrine should they require more extensive accounts of biblical narratives:²³

We secgað nu mid ofste þas endeberdnisse, for þan ðe we oft habbað ymbe þis awriten mid maran andgite þa þu miht sceawian, and eac ða getacnunga.²⁴

[We will now speak of this narrative (i.e. Genesis) in brief, for we have already often written about this in greater detail which you can look up, and also the significances].

And we hit habbað awend witodlice on Englisc, on þam mann mæg gehiran hu se heofonlica God spræc mid weorcum and mid wundrum him to.²⁵

[And we have faithfully translated these books (i.e. Exodus, Leviticus, Numbers and Deuteronomy) into English; in them one can hear how the heavenly God spoke to him (i.e. Moses) through his works and his wonders.]

---

[22] Marsden, ed., *Heptateuch*, I, p. 228, ll. 858–65.
[23] See Wilcox, *Ælfric's Prefaces*, p. 43.
[24] Marsden, ed., *Heptateuch*, I, p. 204, ll. 111–13. Ælfric may also have had in mind here the many references to Genesis in his homilies, given the mention of the book's *getacnunga* ('significances'), which are largely left unsaid in his contributions to the Heptateuch.
[25] Marsden, ed., *Heptateuch*, I, p. 209, ll. 218–20.

A Book for Many: Ælfric's Treatise on the Old and New Testaments

Ðis ic awende eac on Englisc hwilon Æþelwerde ealdormen, on þam man mæg sceawian Godes micclan wundra mid weorcum gefremode.²⁶

[This (i.e. Joshua) I also translated into English once, for ealdorman Æthelweard; in it one may see God's great wonders carried out with deeds.]

Ðis man mæg rædan, se þe his recð to gehirenne, on þære Engliscan bec þe ic awende be þisum. Ic þohte þæt ge woldon þurh ða wundorlican race eower mod awendan to Godes willan on eornost.²⁷

[People can read about this (i.e. Judges), if they are interested in hearing it, in the book in English which I translated concerning this. I thought that you would wish to turn your minds through this wondrous narrative to God's will in earnest.]

The retrospective tone of the *Treatise* echoes the list which Bede provides at the end of his *Ecclesiastical History* (Ch. 24), as well as Augustine's *Retractions*.²⁸ Ælfric thus appears to have viewed the *Treatise* not only as his final word on biblical translation but also as his last will and testament as a religious teacher who had dedicated his life to the exposition of Scripture.²⁹

Style and Sources

In addition to the Vulgate itself, Ælfric draws on a typically wide range of patristic and vernacular sources in the *Treatise*, ranging from Augustine to a number of his own homilies and sermons which he repurposes and adapts.³⁰ The opening section of the *Treatise*, up to the fall of Lucifer, is

---

²⁶ Marsden, ed., *Heptateuch*, I, p. 209, ll. 230–2.
²⁷ Marsden, ed., *Heptateuch*, I, p. 210, ll. 249–52.
²⁸ For citations of Augustine's *Retractions* in Bede and its multiple manuscript witnesses from the period, see Lapidge, *Anglo-Saxon Library*, pp. 203, 290.
²⁹ Ælfric's death is dated *c.* 1010, so roughly five years after the completion of the *Treatise*. For a list of Ælfric's works thought to have been composed after the *Treatise*, see Kleist, *Chronology*, pp. 285–9; the majority of these works are supplementary homilies not included in the two series of *Catholic Homilies*.
³⁰ The sources for the *Treatise* are yet to be included on the *fontesanglosaxonici* database. Swain identifies the following works as potential or probable sources for various parts of the *Treatise*: Augustine's *De Trinitate, De Civitate Dei, De Doctrina Christiana* and *Enarrationes*; Rufinus' translation of Eusebius' *Historia Ecclesiastica*; Jerome's *Liber quaestionum hebraicarum in Genesim, Liber de viris illustribus* and *Liber interpretationis hebraicorum nomin*; Quodvultdeus (pseudo-Augustine), *Contra Iudaeos, paganos, et Arianos*; Martin of Braga's *De correctione rusticorum*; Caesarius of Arles' sermon 212; Gregory the Great, *Moralia in Iob*; Isidore, *Etymologiae* and *Allegoriae quaedam sacrae scripturae*; and Bede's Homilies, *Retractiones* and *De Temporibus* (*Letter to Sigeweard*, pp. 79–83).

composed in the rhythmical style characteristic of Ælfric's later writings. All the typical features of this style are on display from the outset (alliteration in bold):

> Ælfric **A**bbod gret freondlice **S**igwerd æt **Ea**stheolon. Ic **s**ecge þe to **s**oðan þæt se bið **sw**iþe **w**is, se þe mid **w**eorcum **s**pricð, and se hæfð forðgang for **G**ode and for **w**orulde, se ðe mid **g**odum **w**eorcum hine sylfne ge**g**lengð. And þæt is **sw**iðe ge**sw**utelod on *halgum* ge**s**etnissum þæt þa **h**algan **w**eras þe gode **w**eorc beeodon, þæt hi wurðfulle wæron on þissere **w**orulde. And nu **h**alige sindon on **h**eofenan rices **m**irhþe and heora ge**m**ynd þurhwunað nu **a** to worulde for heora **a**nrædnisse and heora trywðe wið God.[31]

[Abbot Ælfric greets in a friendly way Sigeweard at Asthall. I say to you as a truth that he is very wise, the one who speaks with works, and who has success before God and in the world, he who adorns himself through good works. And that is very clear in holy writings that those men who were diligent about good works, that they were honoured in this world and are now saints in the bliss of the kingdom of heaven and their memory remains now for ever because of their steadfastness and their faith in God.]

This ornate opening passage features sustained alliteration on *s, w, sw-, g, h* and *m*, as well as word pairs (*swiþe wis* [...] *swiðe geswutelod; for Gode and for worulde; on heofenan rices mirhþe and heora gemynd; halgum gesetnissum* [...] *halgan weras*), polyptoton (*halgum, halgan, halige*), syntactical repetition (*þæt se bið swiþe wis* [...] *þæt is swiðe geswutelod; se þe mid weorcum spricð* [...] *se ðe mid godum weorcum hine sylfne geglengð; and heora gemynd* [...] *for heora anrædnisse and heora trywð*), and threefold repetition of the key noun *weorc* ('works').

The long exegetical section that follows, concerning the nature of the Trinity and its role in the act of Creation, is a radical reworking of the opening of the first sermon 'On the Beginning of Creation' (*De Initio Creaturae*) in Ælfric's First Series of *Catholic Homilies*, itself indebted to Augustine's *De Trinitate*.[32] In composing his *Treatise*, Ælfric transformed the relatively plain style of his earlier sermon into the rhythmical prose characteristic of his late style. I quote the passage from 'On the Beginning

---

[31] Marsden, ed., *Heptateuch*, I, p. 201, ll. 4–11.
[32] Another example of Ælfric repurposing material from his homilies elsewhere in the *Treatise* is the simile in which John the Baptist is said to prefigure Christ just as the daystar goes before the sun and the beadle before the judge (Marsden, ed., *Heptateuch*, I, p. 219, ll. 508–12), which also appears in his homily on the Nativity of John the Baptist (*Catholic Homilies* I.25). The simile is itself derived from a sermon by Pseudo-Augustine, though in this instance the passage is much altered and Ælfric does not transform it into rhythmical prose.

of Creation' first for comparison; alliteration is marked in bold, with word pairs and doublets underlined:

> An **a**ngin is ealra þinga, þæt is God Ælmihtig. He is ordfruma and ende – he is ordfruma, forði þe he wæs æfre; he is ende butan ælcere geendunge, forðan ðe he bið æfre ungeendod. He is ealra cyninga cyning and ealra hlaforda hlaford; he **h**ylt mid **h**is mi**h**te **h**eofonas and eorðan, and **e**alle **g**esceafta butan **g**eswince, and he be**sce**awað þa niwelnyssa ðe **u**nder þyssere **e**orðan sind. He aweċð **e**alle duna mid **a**nre h**a**nda, and **e**alle **e**orðan he belicð on his handa, and ne mæg nan þing his **w**illan **w**iðstandan. Ne mæg nan gesceaft fulfremedlice smeagan ne understandan ymbe God. Maran cyððe habbað englas to Gode þonne men, and þeahhweðere hi ne magon fulfremedlice understandan ymbe God. He **g**esceop **g**esceafta ða ða he wolde; þurh his **w**isdom he ge**w**orhte ealle ðing, and þurh his **w**illan he hi ealle geliffæste. Þeos Ðrynnys is an God, þæt is, se Fæder, and his Wisdom of him sylfum æfre acenned, and heora begra willa, þæt is, se Halga Gast. He nis na acenned, ac he gæð of ðam Fæder and of ðam Suna gelice. Þas ðry hadas sindon an Ælmihtig God, se geworhte heofenas and eorðan and ealle gesceafta.
>
> [There is one beginning of all things, which is God Almighty. He is the beginning and the end – he is the beginning, because he always was; he is the end without any ending, because he is forever unended. He is king of all kings and lord of all lords; he holds heavens and earth with his might, and all creation without effort, and he looks upon the abyss which is under the earth. He weighs all the mountains with his hands, and he encloses all the earth in his hands, and nothing can withstand his will. No creature can completely imagine or understand God. The angels have greater kinship to God than men, and yet they cannot completely understand God. He created creation just as he wanted; through his wisdom he made all things, and through his will he gave them all life. This Trinity is one God, that is, the Father, and his Wisdom eternally begotten of himself, and the will of both of them, that is, the Holy Spirit. He is not born, but he goes equally from the Father and from the Son. These three persons are one almighty God, who wrought the heavens and earth and all creation.][33]

In this opening section of the sermon, alliteration is largely limited to the opening passage, which also features syntactical and lexical repetition and variation (*He is ordfruma [...] he is ordfruma [...] he is ende*).[34] The

---

[33] *CH* I.1, pp. 14–15.
[34] For sensitive discussion of the style of this passage, and the manner in which it anticipates Ælfric's later, more elaborate style, see Gabriella Corona, 'Ælfric's

corresponding passage in the *Treatise*, by contrast, is considerably more stylised, with alliteration and balanced phrasing employed to great effect:

Se Ælmihtiga Scippend geswutelode hine sylfne þurh þa micclan weorc ðe he geworhte æt fruman and wolde þæt ða gesceafta gesawon his mærða and on wuldre mid him wunodon on ecnisse on his underþeodnisse, him æfre gehirsume, for ðam þe hit ys swiðe wolic þæt ða geworhtan gesceafta þam ne beon gehirsume þe hi gesceop and geworhte. Næs þeos woruld æt fruman, ac hi geworhte God silf, se þe æfre þurhwunode buton ælcum anginne on his miclan wuldre and on his mægenþrimnisse, <u>eall swa mihtig</u> swa he nu ys, <u>and eall swa micel</u> on his leohte, for ðan ðe he ys soð leoht and lif and soðfæstnisse. And se ræd wæs æfre on his rædfæstum geþance þæt he wircan wolde þa wundorlican gesceafta, be þan ðe he wolde þurh his micclan wisdom þa gesceafta gescippan, and þurh his soðan lufe hig liffæstan on þam life þe hig habbað. Her is seo halige þrinnis on þisum þrim mannum. Se Ælmihtiga Fæder of nanum oðrum gecumen, and se micla wisdom of þam wisan Fæder æfre of him anum butan anginne acenned, se þe us alisde of urum þeowte syððan mid þære menniscnisse þe he of Marian genam. Nu is heora begra lufu him bam æfre gemæne, þæt is se Halga Gast þe ealle þing geliffæst swa micel; and swa mihtig þæt he mid his gife ealle þa englas onliht þe eardiað on heofenum, and ealra manna heortan þe on middanearde libbað, þa þe rihtlice gelifað on þone lifiendan God. And ealra manna synna soðlice forgifð, þam þe heora synna silfwilles behreowsiað, and nis nan forgifenis buton þurh his gife. And he spræc þurh witegan þe witegodon ymbe Crist, for þan þe he ys se willa and witodlice lufu þæs Fæder and þæs Suna, swa swa we sædon ær. Seofonfealde gifa he gifð mancynne (git be þam ic awrat ær on sumum oðrum gewrite on Engliscre spræce), swa swa Isaias se witega hit on bec sette on his witegunge.[35]

[The Almighty Creator manifested himself by the great works which he performed in the beginning, and he wished that creation should see his glory and should dwell with him in eternity, always obedient to him in its service. For it is very wrong that creation should be disobedient to him who created it. This world did not exist at first, but God himself made it, who was ever without beginning in his great glory and who in his majesty was as mighty as he now is, and also as great in his light: for he is light itself, and life and truth. And the plan was always in his intended thought that he would make these wonderful creatures,

---

(Un)Changing Style: Continuity of Patterns from the *Catholic Homilies* to the *Lives of Saints*', *JEGP* 107 (2008), 169–89, at 181–5.

[35] Marsden, ed., *Heptateuch*, I, pp. 201–2, ll. 28–55.

A Book for Many: Ælfric's Treatise on the Old and New Testaments

because he wished through his great wisdom to create them, and by his true love to quicken them into life, which they now have.

The Holy Trinity is in these three persons: the almighty Father, who came from no other being; the great Wisdom ever begotten by that wise Father from him alone, without beginning, who redeemed us afterwards from our bondage with his incarnation, which he received from Mary; the love of both of them, which is ever common between them, is the Holy Spirit, who endows all things with life. He is so great and mighty that by his grace he gives light to all the angels who dwell in heaven and to the hearts of all the people living on earth who believe rightly in the living God; and truly he forgives the sins of all the people who freely repent of their sins, and there is no forgiveness except through his grace. He spoke through the prophets who made prophecies concerning Christ, for he is the will and truly the love of the Father and the Son, just as we said before. He gives yet a sevenfold gift to humankind, concerning which I have written already in a certain other treatise in English, just as the prophet Isaiah set it down in the book of his prophecy.]

In addition to regular alliteration of two-stress phrases, this passage features word pairs and anaphora (e.g. *on wuldre mid him wunedon on ecnisse on his underþeodnisse; on his miclan wuldre and on his mægenþrimnisse; eall swa mihtig [...] and eall swa micel*) and doublets (e.g. *hi gesceop and geworhte*). Key concepts such as 'work', 'life', 'prophecy' and 'grace' are emphasised through elaborate polyptoton (e.g. *weorc [...] geworhte [...] geworhtan [...] geworhte; geliffæst [...] libbað [...] gelifað [...] lifiendan; witegan [...] witegodon [...] witodlice [...] witega [...] witegunge; gifa [...] gifð*). The account of Creation in the *Treatise* also places considerably more emphasis on typology than the sermon on which it is based, linking, for example, the Creation with the Incarnation and Virgin Birth, while introducing the concepts of forgiveness through grace (*gife*) and the fulfillment of the Old Testament prophecy of Isaiah in Christ.

Further material from 'On the Beginning of Creation' is recycled in the next section of the *Treatise*, which presents a typological interpretation of the events which took place before Creation. The story of the expulsion of Lucifer and the rebel angels from heaven is, of course, absent from the Book of Genesis and therefore had no place in the translation of that book which Ælfric made for Æthelweard in the 990s.[36] However, the Fall of the Angels is alluded to elsewhere in the Bible, in particular Isaiah 14, Ezekiel 28 and Revelation 12, as well as in various patristic sources known in England.[37] The relevant passage in 'On the Beginning of Creation' is

---

[36] See above, pp. 153–77.
[37] On Ælfric's extensive writing on the angelic fall, see Michael Fox, 'Ælfric on the Creation and Fall of the Angels', *ASE* 31 (2002), 175–200. The Fall of the Angels

again composed in the relatively plain style more characteristic of Ælfric's earlier prose:

> He gesceop tyn engla werod, þæt sind, englas and heah-englas, *throni, dominationes, principatus, potestates, virtutes, cherubim, seraphim* [Col. 1.16]. Her sindon nigon engla werod; hi nabbað nænne lichaman, ac hi sindon ealle gastas, swiðe strange and mihtige and wlitige, on micelre fægernysse gesceapene <u>to lofe and to wurðmynte</u> heora scyppende. Þæt teoðe werod <u>abreað and awende</u> on yfel. God hi gesceop ealle gode and let hi habban agenne cyre, swa hi heora scyppend <u>lufedon and filigdon</u>, swa hi hine forleton. Þa wæs ðæs teoðan werodes ealdor swiðe <u>fæger and wlitig</u> gesceapen, swa þæt he wæs gehaten "Leohtberend." Ða began he to modigenne for ðære fægernysse þe he hæfde, and cwæð on his heortan þæt he wolde and eaðe mihte beon his scyppende gelic, and sittan on ðam norðdæle heofenan rices [cf. Is. 14.13] and habban andweald and rice ongean God Ælmihtigne. Þa gefæstnode he ðisne ræd wið þæt werod þe he bewiste, and hi ealle to ðam ræde gebugon. Ða ða hi ealle hæfdon ðysne ræd betwux him gefæstnod, þa becom Godes grama ofer hi ealle, and hi ealle wurdon awende of þam fægeran hiwe þe hi on gesceapene wæron to laðlicum deoflum. And swiðe rihtlice him swa getimode: ða ða he wolde mid modignysse beon betera þonne he gesceapen wæs, and cwæð þæt he mihte beon þam Ælmihtigum Gode gelic, þa wearð he and ealle his geferan <u>forcuþran and wyrsan</u> þonne ænig oðer gesceaft. And ða hwile ðe he smeade hu he mihte dælan rice wið God, þa hwile gearcode se Ælmihtiga Scyppend him and his geferum helle wite, and hi ealle adræfde of heofenan rices myrhðe and let befeallan on þæt ece fyr ðe him gegearcod wæs [cf. Matt. 25.41] for heora ofermettum.

> [He made ten hosts of angels, that is, angels and archangels, *thrones, dominions, principalities, powers, virtues, cherubim, seraphim*. Here are nine hosts of angels; they have no body, but they are all spirits, very

---

is also the subject of the opening section of the Old English poetic paraphrase *Genesis A* (ll. 1–102). For the influence of this tradition on Old English poetry and prose, see Thomas D. Hill, 'The Fall of Angels and Man in the Old English *Genesis B*', in *Anglo-Saxon Poetry: Essays in Appreciation, For John C. McGalliard*, ed. Lewis E. Nicholson and Dolores Warwick Frese (Notre Dame and London: University of Notre Dame Press, 1975), pp. 279–90; Thomas D. Hill, 'The Fall of Satan in the Old English *Christ and Satan*', *JEGP* 73 (1977), 315–25; David F. Johnson, 'The Fall of Lucifer in *Genesis A* and Two Anglo-Latin Royal Charters', *JEGP* 97 (1998), 500–21; Daniel Anlezark, 'The Fall of the Angels in *Solomon and Saturn II*', in *Apocryphal Texts and Traditions*, ed. Powell and Scragg, pp. 121–33; Jill Fitzgerald, *Rebel Angels: Space and Sovereignty in Anglo-Saxon England* (Manchester: Manchester University Press, 2019); and Leneghan, 'Beowulf, the Wrath of God and the Fall of the Angels'.

strong and mighty and lovely, created in great beauty for the praise and honour of their creator. The tenth host rebelled and turned to evil. God created them all good and let them have their own choice, either to love and follow their creator or forsake him. The leader of the tenth host was created very fair and beautiful, so that he was called "Lightbearer." Then because of his beauty he began to be proud, and said in his heart that he would and easily could be equal to his creator, and sit in the north part of the kingdom of heaven and have power and rule against God Almighty. Then he confirmed this plan with the host that he ruled, and they all agreed to that council. When they had all confirmed this council among themselves, God's anger came over them all, and they were all turned from the fair form in which they were created into loathsome devils. And quite rightly this happened to them: when in his pride he wanted to be better than he was created, and said that he might be equal to the Almighty God, then he and all his companions became more wicked and worse than any other creature. And while he was scheming how he might share the kingdom with God, the Almighty Creator was preparing the torments of hell for him and his companions, and drove them all from the joy of the kingdom of heaven and let them fall into the eternal fire that was prepared for them because of their arrogance.][38]

Alliteration is reserved for the description of God's wrath (*Godes grama*) and two other phrases (*wurdon awende; gearcode se Ælmihtiga Scyppend*), while doublets and word pairs are also used sparingly (*to lofe and to wurðmynte; abreað and awende; lufedon and filigdon; fæger and wlitig; forcuþran and wyrsan*). In adapting this passage for the *Treatise*, Ælfric produces a moving and highly stylised set-piece which again has all the hallmarks of his late style (alliteration is marked in bold; wordplay and polyptoton are italicised; balanced phrasing and doublets are underlined):

Se Ælmihtiga *scippend*, ða ða he englas *gesceop*, þa geworhte he þurh his wisdom tyn engla werod on þam forman dæge on micelre fægernisse, fela þusenda on ðam frumsceafte, þæt hi on his wuldre hine wurðedon, ealle lichamlease, leohte and strange, buton eallum synnum on gesælþe libbende, swa wlitiges gecindes swa we secgan ne magon. And nan yfel ðing næs on ðam englum þa git, ne nan yfel ne com ðurh Godes gesceapennisse, for ðan ðe he sylf ys **eall** *god* [cf. Matt. 19.17, Mark 10.18, Luke 18.19] and ælc *god* cimð of him [cf. Gen. 1.31], and ða englas þa *wunodon* on þam *wuldre* mid *Gode*.

Hwæt þa binnan six dagum þe se soða *God* þa *gesceafta gesceop* þe he *gescippan wolde, gesceawode* se **an engel**, þe þær ænlicost wæs, hu fæger he silf wæs and hu scinende on wuldre, and cunnode his mihte þæt he mihtig wæs gesceapen, and him wel gelicode his wurðfulniss þa.

---

[38] *CH* I.1, pp. 17–18.

Ðe hatte 'Lucifer' [cf. Is. 14.12], þæt ys 'leohtberend', for ðære miclan beorhtnisse his mæran hiwes. Ða þuhte him to huxlic þæt he hiran sceolde ænigum hlaforde, þa he swa ænlic wæs, and nolde wurðian þone þe hine geworhte and him þancian æfre ðæs þe he him forgeaf, and beon him underðeodd þæs ðe swiþor geornlice for þære micclan mærðe þe he hine *gemæðegode*. He nolde þa habban his scippend him to hlaforde, ne he nolde þurhwunian on ðære soþfæstnisse ðæs soðfæstan Godes sunu, þe hine gesceop fægerne, ac wolde mid *riccetere* him *rice* gewinnan and þurh modignisse hine macian to Gode, and nam him gegadan ongean Godes willan, to his unræde on eornost gefæstnod. Ða næfde he nan setl, hwær he sittan mihte, for ðan ðe nan heofon nolde hine aberan ne nan rice næs þe his mihte beon ongean Godes willan, þe geworhte ealle ðinc. Ða afunde se modiga hwilce his *mihta* wæron, þa þa his fet ne *mihton* furðon ahwar standan, ac he feoll ða adun, to deofle awend, and ealle his gegadan of ðam Godes hirede into helle wite be heora gewirhtum.[39]

[The Almighty Creator, when he created the angels, then created through his wisdom ten troops of angels on the first day in great beauty, many thousands at the creation, so that they dwelt with him in his glory, all bodiless, light and strong, without any sins living in blessedness, of such beautiful nature that we cannot speak of it. And no evil thing was in any of those angels yet, nor did any evil come through God's creation, because he himself is all good and all good proceeds from him, and those angels then dwelt in that glory with God.

Alas, then within six days the true God made the creation which he desired to make, one angel, he who was excellent, perceived how beautiful he himself was, and how shining in glory, and knew his might, that he was created mighty, and then he greatly liked his worthiness. He was named "Lucifer," that is "light-bearing," because of the mighty brightness of his great form. Then it seemed to him too unseemly that he should obey any lord, when he was so excellent, and he desired not to worship him who had made him, and not to thank him ever for what he had given him, and not to be subject to him very eagerly for the great glory with which he had honoured him. He did not wish not to have his Creator as his lord, nor did he wish to remain in faithfulness to the true Son of God, who created him beautiful, but he wished to win for himself a kingdom with power, and wished through pride to make himself God, and eagerly secured companions for himself against God's will, to his folly. Then he had no throne where he might sit, because heaven did not wish to suffer him, nor was there any kingdom that might be his against God's will, who made all things. Then the proud one found what his strengths were, when his feet might not even stand anywhere, but then

---

[39] Marsden, ed., *Heptateuch*, I, pp. 202-3, ll. 56-83.

he fell down, and he turned into the devil, and all his companions fell from God's household into the torments of hell because of their works.]

While 'On the Beginning of Creation' simply states that the leader of the rebel angels was *swiðe fæger and wlitig gesceapen, swa þæt he wæs gehaten Leohtberend*, the *Treatise* provides an exegetical interpretation of his name, first supplying the Latin form given in the Vulgate and then glossing its English translation: *Ðe hatte 'Lucifer', þæt ys 'leohtberend', for ðære miclan beorhtnisse his mæran hiwes* ('He was called 'Lucifer', 'that is 'Light-bearing one', because of the great brightness of his great form').[40] The opening phrase, *Se ælmihtiga scippend*, echoes the language used in the first part of the exposition of Creation in the *Treatise* cited above, as well as the variant *Se ælmihtiga fæder* used to introduce the preceding exposition of the Trinity. A panoply of rhetorical tropes and literary devices are on display in this *tour de force* of rhythmical prose, including *exclamatio* (*Hwæt*), word-play (e.g. *gode/God*; *an engel/ænlicost*; *mærðe/gemæðegode*; *riccetere/rice*; *mihta/ne mihton*), polyptoton (e.g. *scippend* [...] *gesceop* [...] *gesceapennisse* [...] *gesceop* [...] *gescippan wolde*), balanced phrasing and syntactical parallelism (e.g. *He nolde þa habban* [...] *he nolde þurhwunian*) and doublets (e.g. *for ðære miclan beorhtnisse his mæran hiwes*), while extensive, regular alliteration of two-stressed phrases provides rhythm and links key concepts (*scippend, gesceop; geworhte, wisdom, werod; forman, fægernisse fela, frumsceafte*).

Ælfric's rhythmical prose style becomes more visible when presented as lineated text, as is now the editorial norm for his *Lives of Saints* (/ indicates stressed sounds; | indicates the half-line break or caesura; alliteration in bold):

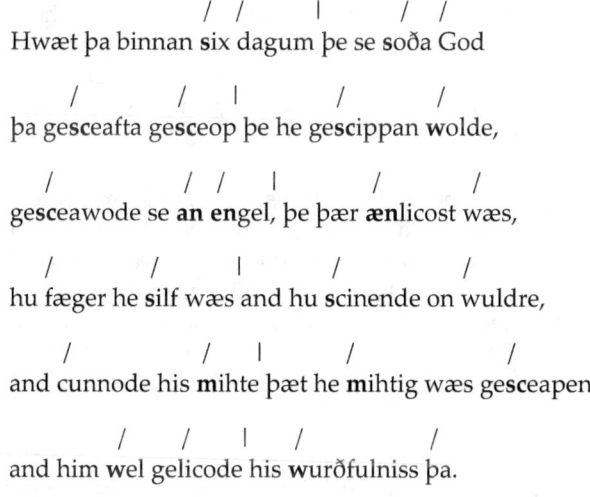

              / / | / /
Hwæt þa binnan six dagum þe se soða God

    /   / | /   /
þa gesceafta gesceop þe he gescippan wolde,

    /   / / | /   /
gesceawode se **an engel**, þe þær **æn**licost wæs,

   /   / | /   /
hu fæger he silf wæs and hu scinende on wuldre,

   /   / | /   /
and cunnode his **mi**hte þæt he **mi**htig wæs ge**sc**eapen,

    /   / | /   /
and him wel gelicode his **w**urðfulniss þa.

---

[40] Marsden, ed., *Heptateuch*, I, p. 203, ll. 68–9.

However, alliteration and rhythmical phrasing feature less frequently in the subsequent section of the *Treatise* describing the Fall of Adam and Eve and the composition of the Pentateuch by Moses:

> Ða on ðam sixtan dæge siþþan ðis gedon wæs, gesceop se Ælmihtiga God mannan of eorðan, Adam, mid his handum and him sawle forgeaf [Gen. 2.7], and Evan eft siþþan of Adames ribbe [Gen. 2.21-2], þæt hi sceoldon habban, and heora ofspring mid him, þa fægeran wununge þe se feond forleas, gif hi gehirsumedon heora scippende on riht. Ða beswac se deofol siððan eft þa men, þæt hi Godes bebod tobræcon forraþe and wurdon þa <u>deadlice and adræfde</u> butu of ðære myrhþe to ðisum middanearde <u>and on sorhge leofodon and on geswincum siþþan</u>, and eall heora ofsprinc þe him of com siððan, oþ þæt ure Hælend Crist ure yfel gebette, swa swa þeos racu æfter us segð.
>
> We nymað of þam bocum þas endebyrdnysse þe Moises awrat, se mæra heretoga, swa swa him God silf dihte on heora sunderspræce, þa þa he mid Gode wunode on þam munte Sinai feowertig daga on an and underfeng his lare, and he ætes ne gimde on eallum þam fyrste for ðære miclan bisnunge þæra boca lare. Fif bec he awrat mid wundorlicum dihte. Seo forme ys Genesis, þe befehð þas racu ærest fram frumsceafte and be Adames synne, and hu he leofode nigan hund geara and þrittig geara[41] on þære forman ylde þissere worulde and bearn gestrinde be his gebeddan Euan. And he siððan gewat mid sorge to helle.[42]

[Then on the sixth day after this was done, the almighty God created man from the earth, Adam, with his own hands, and gave him a soul, and also afterward Eve from Adam's rib, so that they and their offspring with them should have the fair dwelling that the fiend lost, if they obeyed their creator properly. Then afterwards the devil deceived these people, so that they quickly broke God's command, and they became mortal and he drove both of them out of that place of joy to this middle-earth, and they lived in sorrow and toil, and all their offspring who came from them afterward, until our Saviour Christ atoned for our evil, just as this account tells us after.

We begin with the series of books that Moses wrote, the famous war leader, just as God himself dictated in their private speech then, when he dwelled with God on Mount Sinai for forty days at once and received his teaching, and he had no concern for eating in all that time because of the great example of the teaching of the books. He wrote five books with wonderful composition. The first is Genesis, which includes the first account from creation and Adam's sin, and how he lived nine hundred

---

[41] *and þrittig geara* is omitted in MS L (Laud Misc. 509) but supplied from Bo. (Bodley 343)
[42] Marsden, ed., *Heptateuch*, I, pp. 203–4, ll. 84–103.

and thirty years in the first age of this world, and had children by his wife Eve. And afterwards he went with sorrow to hell.]

This plainer prose style, closer to that of Ælfric's earlier writings, remains in use for the rest of the *Treatise*, though there are occasional isolated examples of alliteration.[43] It is unclear why Ælfric chose to abandon the high style in the *Treatise* after his account of the Fall of the Angels. He may have used this elevated register in the opening section in order to grab his reader's attention before settling into a less ornate style for the challenging task of summarising the entire Bible.

Creating an English Bible

Debate about the contents of the biblical canon began in the early centuries of the Church.[44] However, as Larry Swain notes, although Ælfric was probably familiar with Jerome's *Prologus Galeatus* and Letter 53, which were often included in medieval bibles, and Isidore's *Proemia*, none of these works appear to have served as immediate sources for the *Treatise*. Rather, Ælfric's choice of canonical texts is largely determined by the contents of the Vulgate itself, as well as Jerome's various prefaces to individual books.[45] Many biblical books are given Ælfric's seal of approval either by virtue of the fact that he personally translated them or assisted in their translation, such as the books of the Pentateuch and Joshua, or because they are referred to as the subject of one his homilies, such as Judges, Kings, Job, Esther, Judith and Maccabees.[46] The canonicity of other Old Testament books which lie outside Ælfric's own body of writings, however, requires further explication; hence, for example, he explains that the Book of Ruth

---

[43] For example, in the introduction to the Three Orders of Society: *Witan sceoldon smeagan mid wislicum geþeahte, þonne on mancinne to micel yfel bið, hwilc þæra stelenna þæs cinestoles were tobrocen, and betan ðone sona. Se cinestol stynt on þisum þrim stelum* (Marsden, ed., *Heptateuch*, I, p. 228, ll. 867–9); and the criticism of the Jews: *Ic wolde secgan be þam ungesæligum folce, be þam Iudeiscum, þe urne Drihten ahengon, ac ic wolde ærest secgan þæt þæt ic gesæd hæbbe. Manega ðær gelyfdon of þam mancinne on Crist ac se mæsta dæl þæs mancinnes nolde on hine gelyfan and losodon forði* (Marsden, ed., *Heptateuch*, I, p. 229, ll. 879–92).

[44] For the patristic background to this topic, see Hans Freiherr von Campenhausen, *The Formation of the Christian Bible*, trans. J. A. Baker (Minneapolis: Fortress Press, 1972); Bruce M. Metzger, *The Canon of the New Testament* (Oxford: Clarendon Press, 1987); Lee M. McDonald and James A. Sanders, eds, *The Canon Debate* (Peabody, MA: Hendrickson Publishers, 2002); and van Liere, *Introduction to the Medieval Bible*, pp. 53–79.

[45] Swain, *Letter to Sigeweard*, pp. 69–79.

[46] For a helpful list indicating the location of these biblical materials in Ælfric's works, see Wilcox, *Ælfric's Prefaces*, pp. 41–3.

is geendebyrd on ure bibliothecan[47] ('is included in the canon of our Bible'), as are the three books which Solomon composed, Proverbs, Ecclesiastes and the Song of Songs: *þas bec standað nu on þære bibliotheca*[48] ('these books now have their place in the Bible'). Two further canonical Old Testament books, Wisdom and Ecclesiasticus, are traditionally attributed to Solomon on the grounds of their style and eloquence but, Ælfric explains, they are in fact the work of Jesus son of Sirach and are *swiðe micele bec, and man hig ræt on circan to micclum wisdome swiðe gewunelice*[49] ('very great books, and which by accepted custom are read in church for their great wisdom'). The books of the twelve prophets (*witega*), Hosea, Joel, Amos, Obadiah, Jonah, Micah, Nahum, Habbakuk, Zephaniah, Haggai, Zechariah and Malachi, are all given Ælfric's approval, while the Book of Ezra *ys geendebyrd on þissere gesetnysse mid deopum andgitte on diglum getacnungum*[50] ('is included in this Testament with profound meaning and hidden significances'). Another prophetic book included in the English *bibliotheca* is Tobit, which serves as a further example of good works: *And seo boc ys geteald to þisum getele, for ðan þe þæron ys eac swilce getacnung*[51] ('And that book is counted within this number, because within it there is also great significance'). Old Testament books excluded from both the Vulgate and Ælfric's English Bible, on the other hand, include the minor prophets Elijah and Elisha, despite the fact that they composed their works inspired by the true God: *heora bec ne synd na on ure gesetnissum on þære bibliopecan, swa swa þas oðre beoð*[52] ('their books are not in our canon of the Bible, as the others are').

In his brief summary of the New Testament, Ælfric follows Jerome in sanctioning the writings of the four evangelists, directing readers to his *Catholic Homilies* for an authoritative guide to their interpretation:[53]

> Ic secge þis sceortlice, for ðan þe ic gesett hæbbe of þisum feower bocum wel feowertig larspella on Engliscum gereorde, and sumne eacan ðærto. Þa þu miht rædan be þissere race on maran andgite ðonne ic her secge.[54]
>
> [I speak of this briefly, because I have composed around forty homilies, or just over, in the English language concerning these four books. There you can read about this story with greater understanding than I provide here.]

---

[47] Marsden, ed., *Heptateuch*, I, p. 210, l. 255.
[48] Marsden, ed., *Heptateuch*, I, p. 211, ll. 311.
[49] Marsden, ed., *Heptateuch*, I, p. 213, ll. 357–8.
[50] Marsden, ed., *Heptateuch*, I, p. 216, ll. 444–5.
[51] Marsden, ed., *Heptateuch*, I, p. 217, ll. 458–9.
[52] Marsden, ed., *Heptateuch*, I, p. 216, ll. 438–9.
[53] On the *Catholic Homilies*, see above, Chapter Three, pp. 119–44.
[54] Marsden, ed., *Heptateuch*, I, pp. 220–1, ll. 579–82.

A Book for Many: Ælfric's Treatise on the Old and New Testaments

By repeatedly emphasising the canonicity of the four gospels (e.g. *Feower Cristes bec sindon be Criste sylfum awriten*,[55] 'Four books of Christ are written about Christ himself'; *Ðas synd þa feower ean of anum wyllspringe þe gað of paradisum ofer Godes folc wide*,[56] 'These are the four streams from one wellspring which flows from paradise far over God's people') while remaining silent on the status of the Gospels of Nicodemus and Pseudo-Matthew and other popular works such as the *Vision of St Paul*, Ælfric excludes these apocryphal works from his vision of the English Bible.[57] Hence, the two epistles of Peter are accepted despite their great length: *Ac hig synd maran þonne man æt mæssan ræt and habbað langne tige to geleafan trimminge, and hig synd to bocum getelade on þære bibliothecan*[58] ('but they are larger than the sections read at mass and have a great effect in strengthening the faith, and they are counted as books in the Bible'), as are the epistles of James, John, Judas and Paul and the Acts of the Apostles. By referring to Revelation as *æftemyst on ðære bibliothecan*[59] ('the last in the Bible'), Ælfric allows for no further additions to the biblical canon.

We have seen how throughout his career as a biblical translator, Ælfric was concerned with distinguishing between the Old and New Law. In the *Treatise*, he illustrates the essential unity of the Old and New Testaments through the story of Isaiah's vision of two hosts of angels singing praise of God (Is. 6.3):

> Ða twa seraphin soðlice getacnodon þa Ealdan Gekyðnysse and eac þa Niwan, þe heriað mid wordum and mid weorcum æfre þone Ælmihtigan God, se þa ana rixað on anre Godgundnysse butan anginne and ende.[60]

> [These two seraphim truly signify the Old Testament and also the New, which praise that Almighty God forever with words and with works, he who alone reigns in one Godhead without beginning or end.]

In his *Preface to Genesis*, Ælfric expressed reservations about making the plain text of the Old Testament available to poorly educated readers who might be led astray by its contents, while at the same time providing his patron Æthelweard with examples of the complex nature of the exegesis involved in unlocking its spiritual meaning.[61] In the making of the Heptateuch, Ælfric and his fellow translators at

---

[55] Marsden, ed., *Heptateuch*, I, p. 219, l. 519.
[56] Marsden, ed., *Heptateuch*, I, p. 219, ll. 537–9.
[57] On Ælfric's disapproval of such apocryphal works, see Hall, 'Ælfric and the Epistle to the Laodiceans', pp. 65–6.
[58] Marsden, ed., *Heptateuch*, I, p. 221, ll. 587–9.
[59] Marsden, ed., *Heptateuch*, I, p. 223, ll. 672–3.
[60] Marsden, ed., *Heptateuch*, I, p. 227, ll. 822–5.
[61] See above, pp. 153–62.

times radically edited their Old Testament sources in order to make this material more palatable for the same unlearned readership. By dispensing with translation in favour of homiletic paraphrase and exegetical summary in the *Treatise*, Ælfric was now free to explain to lay readers how the key events of the Old Testament prefigure those in the New.

At the end of this exegetical summary of the Old and New Testaments, Ælfric states that there are seventy-two books in the Bible, though sometimes they are split in two in church on account of their length, just as the peoples were divided into the same number at the Tower of Babel and the same number of disciples were sent by Christ to preach his teachings.[62] Ælfric is careful in this final section to distinguish these seventy-two canonical books from other works composed by holy teachers which are cherished widely throughout Christendom to the glory of Christ.[63] The *Treatise* thereby not only paraphrases and explains the spiritual meaning of the entire Bible but also defines its parameters for readers who might otherwise be led into error by reading apocryphal or otherwise non-canonical books.

Audience

Following a Latin incipit, the text of the *Treatise* in MS L begins with the statement: *Ðis gewrit wæs to anum men gediht ac hit mæg swa ðeah manegum fremian*[64] ('This treatise was made for one person but it may serve many') (fig. 13). Although Sigeweard's identity is unknown, Catherine Cubitt places him along with two other named recipients of letters from Ælfric, Sigefryth and Wulfgeat, in 'a middle stratum of thegns; prosperous local figures who acted as surety for each other, witnessed each other's property transactions and regularly attended the hundred and shire courts'.[65] Ælfric's active involvement in the pastoral care of such laymen is made clear in the opening, epistolary section of *Treatise*, in which he recalls

---

[62] Thomas Hall suggests that Ælfric included Paul's Epistle to the Laodiceans as the fifteenth epistle despite Jerome's condemnation of this letter as apocryphal, because he wanted to make up a total of seventy-two books, a number whose symbolic association further confirms the unity of the Old and New Testaments ('Ælfric and the Epistle to the Laodiceans'). As Swain notes, other authorities known to Ælfric, including Augustine, Isidore and Cassiodorus, list only seventy-one books of the Bible (*Letter to Sigeweard*, pp. 76–7).

[63] Marsden, ed., *Heptateuch*, I, p. 227, ll. 836–45.

[64] Marsden, ed., *Heptateuch*, I, p. 201, ll. 2–3.

[65] Cubitt, 'Ælfric's Lay Patrons', pp. 186–7.

that Sigeweard had invited him to his house and requested a supply of English books:[66]

> Ælfric Abbod gret freondlice Sigwerd æt Eastheolon. [...] Ðu bæde me foroft Engliscra gewritena and ic þe ne getiðode ealles swa timlice, ær ðam þe þu mid weorcum þæs gewilnodest æt me, þa ða þu me bæde for Godes lufon georne þæt ic þe æt ham æt þinum huse gespræce. And þu ða swiðe mændest, þa þa ic mid þe wæs, þæt þu mine gewrita begitan ne mihtest. Nu wille ic þæt þu hæbbe huru þis litle, nu ðe wisdom gelicað. And þu hine habban wilt þæt þu ealles ne beo minra boca bedæled.[67]

> [Abbot Ælfric greets Sigeweard at Asthall in a friendly manner. [...] You requested from me very often for writings in English, and I did not grant it to you all too quickly, when you previously desired this from me with works, then you eagerly asked me, for the love of God, that I should speak with you at home at your house. And then you greatly complained, when I was with you, that you were unable to obtain my writings. Now I desire that you at least should have this little book, now that wisdom is pleasing to you. And you desire to have it so that you are not deprived of all of my books.]

The *Letter to Wulfgeat*, preserved between Ælfric's *Judges* and the *Treatise* in MS L, begins in a similar fashion, with the abbot again explaining how this layman had requested English books from him:

> Ic Ælfric abbod on ðisum Engliscum gewrite
> freondlice grete mid godes gretinge
> Wulfget æt Yimandune! Be þam þe wit nu her spræcon
> be ðam Engliscum gewritum, ðe ic þe alænde,
> þæt þe wel licode þære gewrita andgit,
> and ic sæde, þæt ic wolde þe sum asendan git.[68]

> [I Abbot Ælfric, in these English writings, greet in a friendly manner with God's greeting Wulfgeat at Yimandum. Concerning that about which we two recently spoke here, about those English writings which I lent you, that the understanding of the writings greatly pleased you, and I said that I desired to send you some more.]

It is clear from the content of the letters themselves that the 'English writings' requested in both cases were on biblical topics, whether in the

---

[66] See further Shannon O. Ambrose, 'The Theme of Lay *Clænnyss* in Ælfric's Letters to Sigeweard, Sigefryð, and Brother Edward', *Mediaevalia* 35 (2014), 5–21.
[67] Marsden, ed., *Heptateuch*, I, p. 201, ll. 4–5, 14–21.
[68] Assmann, ed., *Angelsaechsische Homilien und Heiligenleben*, I, p. 1, ll. 1–6.

shape of translations or homiletic paraphrases.[69] As men expected to play a role in the organisation of military defences, such men could take inspiration from biblical narratives such as the story of Judith, which as Ælfric explains in the *Treatise*, is written in English *eow mannum to bysne þæt ge eowerne eard mid wæpnum bewerian wið onwindendne here* ('for you men as an example, so that you eagerly defend the land with weapons against the attacking army').[70] Gentry such as Sigeweard might also have used the *Treatise* to provide basic biblical instruction to members of their households, perhaps with the assistance of a chaplain.[71] Viewed within such a domestic setting, the potential of the *Treatise* as a tool for wider pastoral care becomes clear.[72] Moreover, as Cubitt notes, 'local thegns' such as Sigeweard and Wulfgeat were also responsible for the administration of their local parish church, with duties including the appointment of priests, the foundation of churches and the provision of vessels, vestments and books.[73] Equipped with a copy of Ælfric's *Treatise*, such men would know precisely which books they should acquire for their priests.[74]

Secular priests themselves could also benefit from reading the *Treatise* by dipping into it as a source of exempla, as Wilcox suggests, or simply by using it as a refresher of key episodes in biblical history.[75] It is certainly with these priests in mind that Ælfric contrasts ignorant teachers

---

[69] Patrick Wormald comments: 'Ælfric actually addressed more of his works to laymen (mere "gentry", apart from Æthelweard and his son) than to clergy. They may not, in the modern sense, have read them. Equally, it splits hairs to insist that they could not: they still wished to own his books' ('Anglo-Saxon Society and its Literature', p. 18).

[70] Marsden, ed., *Heptateuch*, I, p. 217, ll. 465–7.

[71] See Gerald P. Dyson, *Priests and their Books in Later Anglo-Saxon England*, Anglo-Saxon Studies 34 (Cambridge: D. S. Brewer, 2019), pp. 24–5.

[72] On this topic more generally, see the essays in *Pastoral Care in Late Anglo-Saxon England*, ed. Francesca Tinti, Anglo-Saxon Studies 6 (Woodbridge: Boydell Press, 2005).

[73] See further Cubitt, 'Ælfric's Lay Patrons', pp. 186–7; Cubitt suggests that Sigeweard owned an estate near Ælfric's abbey at Eynsham. As Magennis notes, *Eastheolon* is probably Asthall, around eight miles from Eynsham ('Ælfric of Eynsham's *Letter to Sigeweard*', p. 211).

[74] For discussion of the reading materials used by English priests in this period, see Dyson, *Priests and their Books*. On the development of a system of self-contained local parishes in the English Church c. 850–1100, see John Blair, *The Church in Anglo-Saxon Society* (Oxford: Oxford University Press, 2005), pp. 426–504.

[75] Wilcox, *Ælfric's Prefaces*, p. 41. On the likelihood that secular clergy formed an important element of Ælfric's readership, despite his reluctance to dedicate works to them in his prefaces, see Stephenson, *Politics of Language*, pp. 135–46.

A Book for Many: Ælfric's Treatise on the Old and New Testaments

with those who know their Bible well and are therefore able to draw examples from both the Old and New Testaments:[76]

> Ða lareowas þe nellað heora lare nyman of þisum halgum bocum, ne heora gebysnunga, þa beoð swilce lareowas, swa swa Crist sylf sæde: 'Cecus si ceco ducatum prestet, ambo in foueam cadent' (cf. Mt. 15.14). 'Gif se blinda man byð þæs blindan latteow, þonne befeallað hi begen on sumne blindne seað.' Ða lareowas þe willað heora lare nyman of þisum halgum bocum, and heora gebysnunga, ge of þære Ealdan Gekiðnisse ge of ðære Niwan, þa beoð swilce lareowas, swa swa Crist eft sylf cwæð: 'Omnis scriba doctus in regno celorum similis est homini patri familias qui profert de thesauro suo noua et uetera' (Mt. 13.15). 'Ælc gelæred bocere on Godes gelaðunge ys gelic þam hlaforde þe forlæt simble of his agenum goldhorde ealde þing and niwe.'[77]

> [Those teachers who do not wish to take their instruction from these holy books, nor their examples, then those teachers are like those about whom Christ said: 'Cecus si ceco ducatum prestet, ambo in foueam cadent.' (cf. Mt. 15.14) 'If the blind man guides the blind man, then they will both fall into a blind pit.' Those teachers who wish to take their instruction from these holy books, and their examples, both from the Old Testament and the New, they are like those about whom Christ afterwards said: 'Omnis scriba doctus in regno celorum similis est homini patri familias qui profert de thesauro suo noua et uetera' (Mt. 13.15). 'Each learned scholar among God's faithful is like that lord who always gives from his own gold-hoard things old and new.']

We saw above how in the *Preface to Genesis* Ælfric had expressed his concerns about the poor levels of scriptural knowledge among English priests. With the *Treatise*, Ælfric took the matter into his own hands by supplying these same priests with the tools to understand the Old Law spiritually and to know the teachings of Christ and the Apostles. The *Treatise* was thus a true 'book for many', serving as a guide to the correct interpretation of Scripture for bookish members of the gentry and for priests whose duty was to explain the Bible to the ordinary people.

---

[76] For Ælfric's complaint that some priests are ignorant about the relationship between the Old and the New Testaments in his *Preface to Genesis*, see above, pp. 158–9. On the *Letter for Wulfsige*, see above, pp. 119–20.
[77] Marsden, ed., *Heptateuch*, I, p. 227, ll. 825–36.

Conclusion

Over a decade into his career as an at-times reluctant biblical translator, Ælfric had now produced an epistolary sermon which contained a succinct summary of the entire Bible as well as providing basic instruction in its meaning. Like the bulk of the Heptateuch before it, the *Treatise* was composed to meet the continuing demand for biblical translations among the unlearned, be they members of the laity or poorly educated secular clergy. However, while the translations included in the Heptateuch for the most part dealt with problematic passages in the Old Testament by simply leaving them out, the *Treatise* eschews translation in favour of brief summaries of key biblical figures and episodes. Indeed, in its preference for exegesis and paraphrase over the plain translation of the 'naked' text, the *Treatise* reflects Ælfric's own unease with the entire project of making biblical material available to the laity in Old English prose for private, unsupervised reading.[78] Supplementing the summary of the biblical narrative are a series of homiletic passages that explain core aspects of Christian doctrine, typological interpretations of the Old Testament and brief biographies of significant figures in biblical history. The *Treatise* could thus serve as a true 'book for many', a *Libellus* ('short book') providing an abbreviated account of the contents of the Bible together with the tools to unlock its hidden, spiritual meaning for *bellatores*, *laboratores* and *oratores* alike.

The *Treatise* provides a first glimpse of the idea, if not the reality, of an English Bible.[79] In Ælfric's vision, this project would not take the form of a single volume but rather, as the Old English word for 'Bible', *bibliotheca*, implies, a small library comprising essential biblical and exegetical works in English. Many of these books were composed by or associated with Ælfric himself, among them various biblical translations, homilies, sermons and paraphrases.[80] Despite their evident popularity, there could be no place for apocrypha such as the Gospels of Nicodemus

---

[78] Cf. Stanton, *Culture of Translation*, p. 141: 'his solution of freer scriptural translation acknowledged just how much of the writer is in the translation, recognized the impossibility of displacing all the interpretive function onto external institutional practices, and found a better way to integrate translation and interpretation into the text itself.'

[79] Another codex compiled in this period, MS Junius 11, appears to have been conceived as an abbreviated vernacular version of salvation history running from the Fall of the Angels to Judgement Day in Old English verse: in its present state the manuscript contains *Genesis A* (and *B*), *Exodus*, *Daniel* and *Christ and Satan*, though material has been lost after the text of *Daniel*. See above, pp. 15, 79 n. 8.

[80] Clemoes argues that Ælfric conceived of his own body of work as a carefully planned 'literary enterprise' carried out to completion, centred on 'universal

and Pseudo-Matthew in Ælfric's English *bibliotheca*: as the *Treatise* repeatedly emphasises, there are only four gospels. Ælfric's silence on the *Wessex Gospels* in the *Treatise*, as well as the work of anonymous homilies, indicates that he viewed his own *Catholic Homilies* as a more suitable summary of the Gospels for a broad audience. This small library of sanctioned biblical translations, adaptations and interpretations would ensure that English *oratores, bellatores* and *laboratores* would have access to *Cristes gesetynsse* ('Christ's Scripture') in their own language.[81]

---

history' and 'Christ's redemption of man' ('Chronology of Ælfric's Works', pp. 57–8).

[81] So comprehensive was this corpus of Old English biblical prose that Wulfstan does not appear to have felt the need to compose any free-standing biblical translations in all his prolific career as a writer. On Wulfstan's possible knowledge of Ælfric's *Judges*, see above, pp. 212–13. On the use of biblical excerpts in Wulfstan's homilies and those influenced by his writing, see Winfried Rudolf, 'Quoting the Bible in Times of Trouble: Wulfstan and the Story of Saul and Jonathan in Napier Homily xxxvi', in *Sermons, Saints, and Sources*, ed. Hall and Rudolf, pp. 137–70. On Wulfstan's appropriation of the voice of the Old Testament prophets, see Andy Orchard, 'Wulfstan as Reader, Writer, and Rewriter', in *The Old English Homily*, ed. Kleist, pp. 311–41, at 314–16. For a recent discussion of Wulfstan's use of biblical tropes in his writings, see Pareles, *Nothing Pure*, pp. 118–38. For discussion of Wulfstan's homilies more generally, see Gatch, *Preaching and Theology*, pp. 18–22, 105–28; and Joyce Tally Lionarons, *The Homiletic Writings of Archbishop Wulfstan*, Anglo-Saxon Studies 14 (Cambridge: D. S. Brewer, 2010).

Conclusion

Sanctus Beda was iboren her on Breotene mid us,
And he wisliche bec awende
Þet beo Englise leoden þurh weren ilerde.
And he þeo cnotten unwreih, þe questiuns hoteþ,
Þa derne diʒelnesse þe deorwurþe is.   5
Ælfric abbod, þe we Alquin hoteþ,
He was bocare, and þe fif bec wende:
Genesis, Exodus, Leuiticus, Numerus, Vtronomius.
Þurh þeos weren ilaerde ure leoden on Englisc.
[…]
Þeos laerden ure leodan on Englisc, naes deorc heore liht,
   ac hit faeire glod.
Nu is þeo leore forleten, and þet folc is forloren.
Nu beoþ oþre leoden þeo laereþ ure folc,
And feole of þen lorþeines losiæþ and þet folc forþ mid.
Nu saeiþ ure Drihten þus, *Sicut aquila prouocat pullos suos*   20
ad uolandum. et super eos uolitat.
This beoþ Godes word to worlde asende,
Þet we sceolen faeier feþ festen to Him.

[Saint Bede was born here in Britain with us,
And wisely he translated books
So that the English people were taught by them.
And he unravelled the problems, called the *Quæstiones*,
That obscure enigma which is precious.   5
Abbot Ælfric, whom we call Alcuin,
Was a writer and translated the five books:
Genesis, Exodus, Leviticus, Numbers, Deuteronomy
With these our people were taught in English.
[…]
These taught our people in English. Their light was not dim,
but shone brightly,
Now that teaching is forsaken, and the folk are lost.
Now there is another people which teaches our folk,
And many of our teachers are damned, and that folk with them.
Now our Lord speaks thus, "As an eagle stirs up her young   20
To fly, and hovers over them."

Conclusion

> This is the word of God, sent to the world
> That we shall fix a beautiful faith upon him.]¹

The late twelfth-century poem generally known as the *First Worcester Fragment* is typically read as a lament for the collapse of English learning in the years following the Norman Conquest of 1066.² What has not attracted comment is the poet's foregrounding of biblical translation and interpretation as the crowning achievement of pre-Conquest English learning. Strikingly, the Middle English poet makes no mention of Bede's most celebrated work, the *Historia ecclesiastica gentis Anglorum* (*Ecclesiastical History of the English People*), or any of his many important works of science, grammar or hagiography. Instead, the poem's opening asserts that Bede translated (*awende*) books so that they could be taught to the English (ll. 2–3). Bede does not mention any such translations in the list of his works appended to the *Historia Ecclesiastica*, yet we saw in the Introduction to this book that the monk Cuthbert credits him with translating the first part of the Gospel of John on his deathbed, while Bede himself states that he made versions of the Gloria and Creed available in the vernacular for the use of ignorant priests.³ The *Quæstiones* mentioned in ll. 4–5 probably refers to one of Bede's biblical commentaries, either *Thirty Questions on the Books of Kings* or another exegetical work which later came to be known as *On Eight Questions*.⁴ This post-Conquest poet, then, appears to have regarded Bede chiefly as a biblical translator and interpreter who *þeo*

---

1   Text and translation, with modifications, from S. K. Brehe, 'Reassembling the *First Worcester Fragment*', *Speculum* 65 (1990), 521–36. The poem, sometimes labelled *The Disuse of English*, *The Bede Fragment* or *Sanctus Beda*, is preserved in Worcester Cathedral F. 174 (Ker §398), a thirteenth-century manuscript containing copies of Ælfric's *Grammar* and *Glossary* and one other early Middle English poem, *The Soul's Address to the Body*, all written out by the Tremulous Hand of Worcester. This fabled figure, known for his distinctively shaky handwriting, provides an important witness to the ongoing interest in Old English writing in the thirteenth century: see esp. Christine Franzen, *The Tremulous Hand of Worcester: A Study of Old English in the Thirteenth Century* (Oxford: Oxford University Press, 1991).
2   See Treharne, 'Making their Presence Felt', pp. 401–5. Stephen M. Yeager, *From Lawmen to Plowmen: Anglo-Saxon Legal Tradition and the School of Langland* (Toronto: University of Toronto Press, 2014), pp. 99–120, emphasises that the poem does not refer to the Conquest directly and reflects a history of laments on the decline of English learning stretching back to Alfred and beyond. See also Seth Lerer, 'Old English and its Afterlife', in *The Cambridge History of Medieval English Literature*, ed. David Wallace (Cambridge: Cambridge University Press, 1999), pp. 7–34, at 22–6.
3   See above, pp. 16–17.
4   Both works are translated by Trent W. Foley and Arthur G. Holder in *Bede: A Biblical Miscellany* (Liverpool: Liverpool University Press), pp. 81–182.

cnotten unwreih ('unravelled the knots', l. 5) and *derne diȝelnesse* ('obscure enigma', l. 6) of Scripture for the *Englise leoden* ('English people', l. 3).

The *First Worcester Fragment* takes an equally selective view of Ælfric's career as a leading teacher of the English, again foregrounding his biblical writings rather than his (now) more celebrated *Lives of Saints* or *Catholic Homilies*. Joseph Hall suggested that in highlighting Ælfric's work on the Old English Pentateuch, the poet betrayed his ignorance of his other biblical translations.[5] S. K. Brehe, on the other hand, acknowledges that the Pentateuch's concern with 'the national and spiritual identity of Israel and its people's struggle against faithlessness and foreign oppression' fits well with the poem's own themes.[6] We have seen in Chapter Three that Ælfric did not, in fact, translate all of the Pentateuch, though he did make substantial contributions to the Old English *Genesis* and *Numbers*, as well as composing various other biblical paraphrases, homilies and summaries.[7] The presence of Ælfric's *Preface to Genesis* in the two major manuscripts of the Heptateuch (MS L) and Hexateuch (MS B) may have created the impression that he was responsible for the whole work.

The evidence presented in this book bears out the *First Worcester Fragment*'s claim that biblical translation and interpretation were key factors in the development of English national identity. From the diverse ethnicities of the multiple eighth-century English kingdoms, Bede drew on his profound knowledge of the Bible to envision a single *gens Anglorum* ('English people'), an 'imagined community' united by their common Germanic ancestry, language and faith under the rule of a single Archbishop at Canterbury.[8] In the late ninth century, King Alfred commissioned translations of the Psalms and parts of the Old and New Law to educate lay readers and thereby restore wisdom and prosperity to the *Angelcynn* after more than a century of Viking incursions.

---

[5] Joseph Hall, *Selections from Early Middle English, 1130–1250*, 2 vols (Oxford: Clarendon Press, 1920), II, p. 226.

[6] Brehe, 531–2. Brehe notes that in referring to Ælfric as *Alcuin*, the poet did not mistakenly conflate the two figures but rather sought to distinguish Ælfric from his various namesakes and to stress that he translated the Northumbrian-Carolingian scholar's *Quæstiones in Genesim* into English (531). Mark Faulkner suggests that this may explain the reference to Bede's *Quæstiones* in l. 6, with the poet confusing Bede, Ælfric and Alcuin: *A New Literary History of the Long Twelfth Century: Language and Literature between Old and Middle English* (Cambridge: Cambridge University Press, 2022), pp. 230–1.

[7] See above, p. 148

[8] Benedict Anderson coined this term to describe the nation as it developed in the nineteenth century in his influential *Imagined Communities*. For arguments that locate the development of the nation in the early medieval period, however, with England perhaps the earliest example, see, for example, Hastings, *The Construction of Nationhood*, and works cited above, p. 20 n. 74.

Conclusion

By the end of the tenth century, the production of a prose translation of the Gospels and the proliferation of vernacular homilies made the core teachings of the New Testament available both for private reading and preaching. Ælfric's *Catholic Homilies*, in particular, were designed to provide orthodox interpretation of the Gospels for the entire community of English Christians.[9] By the turn of the eleventh century, the Old English Heptateuch provided the ruling elite of what was now *Englaland* with models for understanding their role as protectors of a Christian nation subject to God's law. Finally, Ælfric's *Treatise* delivered a succinct overview of the entire Bible and a guide to its meaning for the benefit of a broad community of English lay and clerical readers.

Despite the *First Worcester Fragment* poet's claim that this rich corpus of vernacular biblical writing has been lost due to the arrival of 'another people' (*oþre leoden*, l. 13), recent scholarship has emphasised the continuing use of Old English texts after the Conquest.[10] Indeed, not only Ælfric's *Catholic Homilies* but also many of the other examples of Old English biblical prose discussed in this book remained in circulation long after 1066. For example, the twelfth-century Eadwine or Canterbury Psalter presents the text of all three of Jerome's Latin psalters (the Romanum, the Gallicanum and the Hebraicum), with interlinear glosses supplied in both Old English – following the tradition of the Vespasian and Cambridge psalters discussed in Chapter One – and Anglo-Norman, framed by the Latin *Glossa Ordinaria*.[11] As we have seen, several manuscripts of the *Wessex Gospels* date from the twelfth or thirteenth centuries, indicating ongoing scholarly interest in this major work of Old English biblical prose.[12] Moreover, the Old English 'Pentateuch' that the *First Worcester Fragment* poet attributes to Ælfric was itself read and studied well into the post-Conquest period: a twelfth-century interlinear Latin gloss appears in sections of Laud Misc. 509 ('the Heptateuch'), occasionally supplying

---

[9] See Wilcox, 'Ælfric in Dorset', p. 62; see further above, p. 121.

[10] On Old English after the Conquest in general, see Elaine Treharne, *Living Through Conquest: The Politics of Early English, 1020–1220* (Oxford: Oxford University Press, 2012); and Faulkner, *Long Twelfth Century*. On the continuing use and influence of the Old English biblical translations, see esp. Marsden, 'Cain's Face, and Other Problems'; and Elizabeth Solopova, 'From Bede to Wyclif: The Knowledge of Old English within the Context of Late Middle English Biblical Translation and Beyond', *RES* 71 (2020), 805–27.

[11] Cambridge, Trinity College MS R.17.1; see Mark Faulkner, 'The Eadwine Psalter and Twelfth-Century English Vernacular Literary Culture', in *Psalms and Medieval English*, ed. Atkin and Leneghan, pp. 72–106.

[12] See above, p. 91 n. 38. See further Roy M. Liuzza, 'Scribal Habit: The Evidence of the Old English Gospels', in *Rewriting Old English in the Twelfth Century*, ed. Mary Swan and Elaine M. Treharne, CSASE 30 (Cambridge: University of Cambridge Press, 2000), pp. 143–65.

the missing Latin text for biblical passages omitted or summarised in the Old English,[13] while more glosses were added to the codex by various thirteenth- or fourteenth-century readers, including the latter sections where the *Letter to Wulfgeat* and the *Treatise* are copied.[14] Finally, the post-Conquest use of Ælfric's *Treatise* is demonstrated by the survival of a truncated version, shorn of its epistolary opening and the New Testament summary, in Oxford, Bodleian Library, MS Bodley 343, an important collection of mostly Ælfrician and Wulfstanian homilies copied in the second half of the twelfth century.[15] Evidently, the *Treatise* was still regarded as a valuable guide to the Old Testament long after it had fulfilled its original purpose as an overview of the entire Bible for poorly educated early eleventh-century readers.[16]

The translation, adaptation and interpretation of Scripture into English continued in the centuries following the Conquest, though verse had once more become the medium of choice.[17] Notably, in the mid-twelfth-century, the Augustinian Friar Orm produced his *Ormulum*, a long series of verse homilies that follows the cycle of the liturgical calendar in the manner of Ælfric's *Catholic Homilies* and includes translations of gospel pericopes as well as parts of Acts.[18] The single manuscript copy of the *Ormulum*, Oxford Bodleian Library MS Junius 1, written in Orm's own hand, features a simplified spelling system designed for the use of Anglo-Norman

[13] See above, pp. 145 n. 3, 162–3.

[14] Solopova, 'From Bede to Wyclif', 814–15. Mark Faulkner has recently emphasised that excerpts from the Heptateuch were incorporated into twelfth- or thirteenth-century homiliaries (*Long Twelfth Century*, pp. 230–1). Faulkner notes that Ælfric's *Preface to Genesis* and his translation of Gen. 1–24.22 are copied in a twelfth-century homiliary, Cambridge, University Library, MS Ii. 1. 33, fols 2–24^v (Ker §18), while two apothegms from Deut. 18.11–12, possibly derived from the same source, are included in Cambridge, Trinity College, MS. R. 9. 17 (819), fol. 48^v (Ker §89) (*Long Twelfth Century*, p. 230 n. 15).

[15] For full description of the manuscript, see Susan Irvine, ed., *Old English Homilies from MS Bodley 343*, EETS o.s. 302 (Oxford: Oxford University Press, 1993); Irvine edits seven Old English homilies contained in this manuscript, four of them by Ælfric, but does not include the *Treatise* in her edition.

[16] Ker §310; the *Treatise* is copied on fols 129^r–132^r as the first item in section F, where it is succeeded by a sermon by Wulfstan on baptism. Susan Irvine describes the items in this section of the codex as 'a miscellany of religious pieces with no apparent pattern in their arrangement' (*Old English Homilies from MS Bodley 343*, p. xlvi). See further Susan Irvine, 'The Compilation and Use of Manuscripts containing Old English in the Twelfth Century', in *Rewriting Old English in the Twelfth Century*, ed. Swan and Treharne, pp. 55–60.

[17] On the preference for verse over prose as a medium for biblical translation in early Old English (i.e. before the age of Alfred), see above, pp. 13–16, 20

[18] Nils-Lennart Johannesson and Andrew Cooper, eds, *The Ormulum*, EETS o.s. 360, 361 (Oxford: Oxford University Press, 2022–3).

speaking priests who were required to preach to their congregations in English.[19]

It was not until the fourteenth century, with the appearance of first the Middle English *Glossed Prose Psalter* and Richard Rolle's *English Psalter* and then the Wycliffite Bible, the first complete English Bible, that English prose once more became a major vehicle for biblical translation.[20] Significantly, the authors of the General Prologue to the Wycliffite Bible invoke the figures of Bede and King Alfred as precedents for their project:

> Lord God, siþ at þe bigynnyng of feiþ so many men translatiden into Latyn and to greet profit of Latyn men, lat o symple creature of God translate into Englich for þe profit of Englisch men, for if worldli clerkis loken wel her cronyclis and bookis þei shulen fynde þat Bede translatide þe Bible and expownyde myche in Saxoyn, þat was Englisch or comune langage of þis lond in his tyme, and not oneli Bede but also kyng Alurede, þat foundide Oxenforde, translatide in his laste daies þe bigynnyng of þe Sauter into Saxoyn, and wolde more if he hadde lyued lengere.[21]

> [Lord God, since at the beginning of the faith so many men translated into Latin and to the great profit of the Romans, let a simple creature of God translate into English for the profit of English men, for if worldly clerks study their chronicles and books attentively they should discover that Bede translated the Bible and expounded much of it in Saxon (i.e. Old English), that was (the) English or common language of this land in his time, and not only Bede but also King Alfred, who founded Oxford, translated in his last days the beginning of the Psalter into Saxon, and would have done more if he had lived longer.]

We saw in the Introduction to this book how Alfred had himself used similar rhetoric in support of his plan to have the 'books most necessary for all people to know' translated into English, just as Otfrid had done

---

[19] Another important English verse translation of Scripture from this period is the Middle English Metrical Psalter (also known as the *Surtees Psalter*) (c. 1300). For this and other Middle English psalm translations and adaptations, see Francis Leneghan, 'Introduction: A Case Study of Psalm 50.1-3 in Old and Middle English', in *Psalms and Medieval English*, ed. Atkin and Leneghan, pp. 1–33, at 16–23. The impact of Old English biblical prose after the Conquest is also evident in the emergence of vernacular biblical writing in the French of England: the earliest French-language psalter is *The Oxford Psalter*, a prose translation of Jerome's Gallican Psalter made by the mid-twelfth century.

[20] See Annie Sutherland, *English Psalms in the Middle Ages, 1300–1450* (Oxford: Oxford University Press, 2015).

[21] Mary Dove, ed., *The Earliest Advocates of the English Bible: The Texts of the Medieval Debate* (Exeter: Liverpool University Press, 2010), p. 84.

before him when composing his Old High German gospel harmony.²² In addition to drawing inspiration from these earliest English translators of the Bible, the authors of the Wycliffite Bible appear to have consulted Old English biblical translations as a source for vocabulary, as noted by Marsden and Solopova: hence, for example, the Latin term *perizomata*, used in the Vulgate to describe the clothing Adam and Eve fashioned for themselves in Genesis 3.7, is rendered as *brechis* in both the Early and Late Versions of the Wycliffite Bible, a translation choice that can be traced back to Ælfric's portion of the Old English *Genesis*, where we find the term *wædbrec*.²³ These lexical connections provide further hints of the sustained scholarly interest in Old English biblical prose in the late Middle Ages.

The precedent of Old English biblical translation would again be invoked in the Tudor period, this time in support of the Protestant cause. In 1528, William Tyndale defended his translation of the Bible by claiming that King Æthelstan (r. 924–39), rather than his grandfather Alfred, *caused the holy scripture to be translated into the tongue that then was in England*, citing the evidence of unspecified chronicles.²⁴ Following Archbishop Parker's rediscovery of the *Wessex Gospels*, John Foxe presented Queen Elizabeth I with a printed edition of this work in 1571; the framing of the Old English text with the 1568 Bishop's Bible implies the continuity of English biblical translation over the centuries. Foxe explains in his preface that, contrary to the claims of some of his contemporaries who view it as *dangerous to haue them* [i.e. the Scriptures] *in our popular language translated*, there is ample proof that the Bible was translated into English *long before the Conquest*. Foxe cites the examples of Bede, who *did translate the whole Bible in the Saxon tongue*, and Alfred, who *translated both the olde Testament and the new into his own natiue language*.²⁵ Addressing his own royal patron,

---

[22] See above, pp. 10–11.

[23] Marsden, 'Cain's Face and Other Problems', pp. 41–2; Solopova, 'From Bede to Wyclif', 822–4. As Solopova demonstrates, the Wycliffite reading itself went on to influence the wording of the sixteenth-century Geneva Bible, which also has *breeches* (earning this Bible the nickname 'the breeches Bible'), before it gave way to *apruns* in Tyndale and Coverdale and *aprons* in the King James (823).

[24] William Tyndale, *The Obedience of a Christian Man* (1528), ed. David Daniell (Harmondsworth: Penguin, 2000), p. 19. See further Sarah Foot, *Æthelstan: The First King of England* (New Haven, CT: Yale University Press, 2011), pp. 233, 237. Tyndale may have had access to the lost life of Æthelstan that was known to William of Malmesbury; see Matthew Firth, 'Constructing a King: William of Malmesbury and the Life of Æthelstan', *Journal of the Australian Early Medieval Association* 13 (2017), 69–82.

[25] John Foxe, ed., *The Gospels of the fower Evangelistes translated in the olde Saxons tyme out of Latin into the vulgare toung of the Saxons, newly collected out of Auncient Monumentes of the sayd Saxons, and now published for testimonie of the same* (London: John Daye, 1571). Like William of Malmesbury, Foxe also attributes translations

Conclusion

Foxe credits King Alfred not only with the *Wessex Gospels* but with the translation of *aboue a large hundred of learned homelies* for regular use in the English church, seemingly conflating him with Ælfric:[26]

> As for the bokes of holy Scripture they were sorted by *Alfrede*, as by thys edition may appeare, to be read to the people, as the sonday or festiual day did them require, with certain daies in the weeke, for the better instruction of the people in their comon prayers: who also prouided that hys people should be instructed by those homelies red by the ministers of the those days, & vsed not onely to be openly red vnto the plaine people, but also to be red in the prestees Synodes and Conuocations, and were also vsed amongest the religious both men and women for their Collations (as they call them) so that neither the difficulties of the Scriptures, as is alleaged, nor yet the profunditie of the mysteries in the same, nor the basenesse of our language (as it is commonly slaundered) was any sufficient cause to hinder these good fathers of thys their diligent labours.[27]

Foxe claims that the printing of this book will stand as further proof that the religion presently taught in England *is no new reformation of things lately begonne [...] but rather a reduction of the Church to the Pristine state of olde conformitie, which once it had, and almost lost by discontinuaunce of a fewe later yeares*.[28] For Protestant reformers like Foxe, Old English biblical prose could thus serve as a beacon of the ancient independence of the English Church from Rome.

Old English biblical prose was continually cited by scholars in the post-Reformation period in support of claims for the antiquity of the English church and language. Hence, when William l'Isle printed Ælfric's *Treatise* in 1623, he described the work as *an ancient monument of the Church of England*,[29] while in 1715 Elizabeth Elstob defended the publication of her *Rudiments of Grammar for the English-Saxon Tongue*, the first modern English grammar of Old English, against the criticisms of scholars such as Jonathan Swift with the following rejoinder:

---

of Bede, Gregory and Orosius to Alfred. See further Hugh Magennis, 'Not Angles but Anglicans? Reformation and Post-Reformation Perspectives on the Anglo-Saxon Church, Part I: Bede, Ælfric and the Anglo-Saxon Church in Early Modern England', *ES* 96 (2015), 243–63.

[26] On Ælfric's *Catholic Homilies*, see above, pp. 119–44.
[27] Foxe, sig. Aiiij r.
[28] Foxe, sig. ¶ ij r.
[29] William L'Isle, ed., *A Saxon Treatise Concerning the Old and New Testament. Written about the Time of King Edgar (700 Yeares Agoe) by Ælfricus Abbas* (London: John Haviland, 1623).

> The *Gospels*, the *Psalms*, and a great part of the Bible are in *Saxon*, so are the *Laws* and *Ecclesiastical Canons*, and *Charters* of most of our *Saxon Kings*; these one wou'd think might deserve their Credit.[30]

In Elstob's view, the existence of biblical translations as well as other ecclesiastical and legal documents in Old English lends prestige to the language and makes it a subject worthy of scholarly investigation.

As this brief overview demonstrates, Old English biblical prose would continue to shape debates about the nature of the English language, Church and nation centuries after the Conquest. Although the fashion for translating the Bible into English prose that began under Alfred in the late ninth century had already begun to wane by the mid-eleventh century, the cultural memory of this practice endured and came to serve as an inspiration for subsequent generations. While it might be tempting to attribute this long hiatus in the production of English biblical prose entirely to the events of 1066, this book has argued that other factors were involved, notably the resistance of influential figures such as Ælfric to the entire project of making the Bible available to a wide swathe of English readers.

The works of Old English biblical prose discussed in this book served a variety of purposes which determined their shape and form. Though not strictly speaking prose, interlinear glosses provided an impetus to meditation and language acquisition for monastic readers, serving as a guide to the meaning of the Latin text of the Vulgate. Free-standing prose translations, such as the Alfredian *Prose Psalms* and Mosaic Prologue to the *Domboc*, the *Wessex Gospels* and Heptateuch, as well as the gospel pericopes translated (and in some cases interpreted) in homilies, made these key parts of the Bible accessible for groups of readers and listeners for whom English rather than Latin was the main language of literacy. By contrast with the glosses, in all these free-standing prose translations the vernacular serves as a substitute for the Latin, bringing the meaning of the scriptural source to the reader. Finally, Ælfric's eventual abandonment of word-for-word translation in favour of free homiletic paraphrase and summary reflects his lifelong commitment to ensuring that all members of English society had access to the contents of the Bible in their own language. In this common endeavour

---

[30] Elizabeth Elstob, *The Rudiments of Grammar for the English-Saxon Tongue, First Given in English: with an Apology for the Study of Northern Antiquities, Being Very Useful Towards the Understanding Our Ancient English Poets, and Other Writers* (London: W. Bowyer, 1715), p. 6. See Hugh Magennis, 'Not Angles but Anglicans? Reformation and Post-Reformation Perspectives on the Anglo-Saxon Church, Part II: Seventeenth and Eighteenth Centuries', *ES* 96 (2015), 363–78.

Conclusion

to make the Bible's teaching available to diverse audiences, the authors of Old English biblical prose would prove worthy successors to their illustrious forebears whom King Alfred had admiringly described as *wise wealhstodas* ('wise translators').[31]

---

[31] For the Prose Preface to the Old English *Pastoral Care*, see above, Introduction, pp. 3–4.

Bibliography

Digital Reproductions of Manuscripts

Cambridge Corpus Christi College MS 140 (*Wessex Gospels*): https://parker.stanford.edu/parker/catalog/ks656dq8163

Cambridge, University Library, MS Ff. 1. 23 (Cambridge Psalter): https://cudl.lib.cam.ac.uk/view/MS-FF-00001-00023/1

London, British Library, Cotton MS Claudius B. IV (Old English Illustrated Hexateuch):
https://www.bl.uk/research/digitised-manuscripts/ [currently unavailable]

London, British Library, Cotton MS Nero D. IV (Lindisfarne Gospels): https://iiif.bl.uk/uv/#?manifest=https://bl.digirati.io/manifests/ark:/81055/man_10000006.0x000001

London, British Library, MS Cotton Vespasian A. I (Vespasian Psalter): https://www.bl.uk/research/digitised-manuscripts/ [currently unavailable]

Oxford, Bodleian Library, MS Laud Misc. 509 (Old English Heptateuch): https://digital.bodleian.ox.ac.uk/objects/8bb9aff1-d6ab-4b6b-8322-09fa694d890f/

Oxford, Bodleian Library, MS Auct. D. 2. 19 (Rushworth Gospels): https://digital.bodleian.ox.ac.uk/objects/b708f563-b804-42b5-bd0f-2826dfaeb5cc/surfaces/f0fd9c40-0e3d-45b4-9a1d-19d092474ad4/

Paris, Bibliothèque nationale de France, MS Lat. 8824 (Paris Psalter): https://gallica.bnf.fr/ark:/12148/btv1b8451636f

Editions

Allen, Michael, and Daniel Calder, eds and trans. *Sources and Analogues of Old English Poetry, Vol. 1: The Major Latin Texts in Translation* (Cambridge: D. S. Brewer, 1976).

Assmann, Bruno, ed. *Angelsaechsische Homilien und Heiligenleben. Bibliothek der Angelsaechsischen Prosa*, 3 vols (Kassel: Wissenschaftliche Buchgesellschaft, 1889).

Bately, Janet, ed. *The Anglo-Saxon Chronicle: A Collaborative Edition, Volume 3, MS A* (Cambridge: D. S. Brewer, 1986).

Bintley, Michael D., and Richard North, eds. *Andreas: An Edition* (Liverpool: Liverpool University Press, 2016).

Bright, James W., and Robert L. Ramsay, eds *Liber Psalmorum: The West-Saxon Psalms, Being the Prose Portion, or the 'First Fifty', of the so-called Paris Psalter* (Boston: D. C. Heath & Co., 1907).

Cathey, James E., ed. *Hêliand: Text and Commentary*, Medieval European Studies II (Morganstown, WV: West Virginia University Press, 2002).

Challoner, Richard, ed. *The Holy Bible: Douay-Rheims Version, revised by the servant of God Bishop Richard Challoner A.D. 1749–1752* (London: Baronius Press, 2007).

Clayton, Mary, ed. and trans. *The Apocryphal Gospels of Mary in Anglo-Saxon England*, CSASE 26 (Cambridge: University of Cambridge Press, 1998).

———, *Two Ælfric Texts: "The Twelve Abuses" and "The Vices and Virtues": An Edition and Translation of Ælfric's Old English Versions of "De duodecim abusivis" and "De octo vitiis et de duodecim abusivis"*, Anglo-Saxon Texts 11 (Cambridge: D. S. Brewer, 2013).

Clayton, Mary, and Juliet Mullins, eds and trans. *Old English Lives of the Saints: Ælfric*, 3 vols, DOML 58, 59, 60 (Harvard MA: Harvard University Press, 2019).

Clemoes, Peter, ed. *Ælfric's Catholic Homilies: The First Series: Text*, EETS s.s. 17 (Oxford: Oxford University Press, 1997).

Cleveland Coxe, A., ed. and trans. *Expositions on the Book of Psalms by Saint Augustine of Hippo*, Nicene and Post-Nicene Fathers: First Series, Volume VIII (New York: 1888).

Colgrave, Bertram, and R. A. B. Mynors, eds and trans. *Bede's Ecclesiastical History of the English People*, rev. edn (Oxford: Clarendon Press, 1992).

Cook, Albert S., ed. *Biblical Quotations in Old English Prose Writers* (London: MacMillan and Co., 1898).

Crawford, S. J., ed. *The Old English Version of the Heptateuch, Ælfric's Treatise on the Old and New Testament, and his Preface to Genesis*, EETS o.s. 160 (London: Oxford University Press, 1922).

Cross, James E., ed. *Two Old English Apocrypha and Their Manuscript Source: 'The Gospel of Nichodemus' and 'The Avenging of the Saviour'*, CSASE 19 (Cambridge: Cambridge University Press, 1996).

diPaolo Healey, Antonette, ed. *The Old English Vision of St. Paul* (Cambridge, MA: Mediaeval Academy of America, 1978).

Doane, Alger N., ed. *The Saxon Genesis: An Edition of the West Saxon 'Genesis B' and the Old Saxon Vatican 'Genesis'* (Madison, WI: University of Wisconsin, 1991).

Dove, Mary, ed. *The Earliest Advocates of the English Bible: The Texts of the Medieval Debate* (Exeter: Liverpool University Press, 2010).

Dümmler, Ernst, ed. *Epistolae Karolini Aevi II*, MGH Epistolae 4 (Berlin: Weidmann, 1895).

Erdmann, Oskar, ed. *Otfrids Evangelienbuch*, Altdeutsche Textbibliothek 49 (Tübingen: Max Niemeyer, 1957).

Bibliography

Fehr, Bernhard, ed. *Die Hirtenbriefe Ælfrics*, Bibliothek der angelsäschsischen Prosa IX (Hamburg, 1914), reprinted with a supplementary introduction by Peter A. M. Clemoes (Darmstadt, 1964).

Foley, Trent W., and Arthur G. Holder, trans. *Bede: A Biblical Miscellany* (Liverpool: Liverpool University Press).

Foxe, John, ed. *The Gospels of the fower Evangelistes translated in the olde Saxons tyme out of Latin into the vulgare toung of the Saxons, newly collected out of Auncient Monumentes of the sayd Saxons, and now published for testimonie of the same* (London: John Daye, 1571).

Fulk, R. D., ed. and trans. *The Old English Pastoral Care*, DOML 72 (Cambridge, MA: Harvard University Press, 2021).

Gallagher, John J., and Michael Everson, eds. *The Old English Bible I: The Heptateuch (Genesis to Judges)*, Corpus Textuum Anglicorum 1 (Dundee: Evertype, 2024).

Godden, Malcolm, ed. *Ælfric's Catholic Homilies: The Second Series: Text*, EETS s.s. 5 (Oxford: Oxford University Press, 1979).

——, *Ælfric's Catholic Homilies: Introduction, Commentary and Glossary*, EETS s.s. 18 (Oxford: Oxford University Press, 2000).

Haddan, Arthur West, and William Stubbs, eds. *Councils and ecclesiastical documents relating to Great Britain and Ireland*, 3 vols (Oxford: Clarendon Press, 1869–78).

Hilberg, Isidor, ed. *Jerome: Epistulae*, CSEL 54 (Turnhout: Brepols, 2010).

Hurst, David, and Jean Fraipont, eds. *Beda Venerabilis: Opera homiletica. Opera rhythmica*, CCSL 122 (Turnhout: Brepols, 1955).

Irvine, Susan, ed. *Old English Homilies from MS Bodley 343*, EETS o.s. 302 (Oxford: Oxford University Press, 1993).

——, *The Anglo-Saxon Chronicle: A Collaborative Edition, Volume 7, MS E* (Cambridge: D. S. Brewer, 2004).

Johannesson, Nils-Lennart, and Andrew Cooper, eds. *The Ormulum*, EETS o.s. 360, 361 (Oxford: Oxford University Press, 2022–3).

Johnson, John, trans. *A collection of the laws and canons of the Church of England from its first foundation to the conquest, and from the conquest to the reign of King Henry VIII*, 2 vols (Oxford: John Henry Parker, 1850).

Jones, Christopher A., ed. and trans. *Old English Shorter Poems: Volume I: Religious and Didactic*, DOML 15 (Cambridge, MA: Harvard University Press, 2012).

Jurasinski, Stefan, and Lisi Oliver, eds and trans. *The Laws of Alfred: The Domboc and the Making of English Law* (Cambridge: Cambridge University Press, 2021).

Keynes, Simon, and Michael Lapidge, eds and trans. *Alfred the Great: Asser's 'Life of King Alfred' and Other Contemporary Sources* (Harmondsworth: Penguin, 1983).

Kotake, Tadashi, ed. *Rushworth One: An Edition of Farman's Old English Interlinear Gloss to the Rushworth Gospels*, Medium Ævum Monographs

44, new series (Oxford: The Society for the Study of Medieval Languages and Literature, 2023).

Kuhn, Sherman M., ed. *The Vespasian Psalter* (Ann Arbor: University of Michigan Press, 1967).

Lapidge, Michael, ed. *Oxford Medieval Texts: Byrhtferth of Ramsey: The Lives of St Oswald and St Ecgwine* (Oxford: Oxford University Press, 2009).

Lapidge, Michael, and M. Winterbottom, eds. *Oxford Medieval Texts: Wulfstan of Winchester: The Life of St Æthelwold* (Oxford: Oxford University Press, 1991).

Lee, Stuart D., ed. *Ælfric's Homilies on* Judith, Esther *and* The Maccabees (Oxford, 1999): https://users.ox.ac.uk/~stuart/kings/.

Liebermann, Felix, ed. *Die Gesetze der Angelsachsen*, 3 vols (Halle: Max Niemeyer, 1903–16).

L'Isle, William, ed. *A Saxon Treatise Concerning the Old and New Testament. Written about the Time of King Edgar (700 Yeares Agoe) by Ælfricus Abbas* (London: John Haviland, 1623).

Liuzza, Roy M., ed. *The Old English Version of the Gospels*, EETS o.s. 304, 314, 2 vols (Oxford: Oxford University Press, 1994, 2000).

——, ed. and trans. *The Old English Catholic Homilies: The First Series: Ælfric*, DOML 86 (Cambridge, MA: Harvard University Press, 2024).

Lockett, Leslie, ed. and trans. *Augustine's 'Soliloquies' in Old English and in Latin*, DOML 76 (Cambridge, MA: Harvard University Press, 2022).

MacLean, G. E., ed. 'Ælfric's Anglo-Saxon Version of *Alcuini Interrogationes Sigewulfi in Genesin*', *Anglia* 6 (1883), 425–73, and *Anglia* 7 (1884), 1–59.

Marsden, Richard, ed. *The Old English Heptateuch and Ælfric's 'Libellus de veteri testament et novo'*, 2 vols, EETS o.s. 330 (Oxford: Oxford University Press, 2008).

Martin, Lawrence T., and Dom David Hurst OSB, trans., with contributions by Sister Benedicta Ward SLG. *Bede the Venerable: Homilies on the Gospels, Book One: Advent to Lent* (Piscataway, NJ: Gorgias Press, 2010).

Meeder, Sven. 'The *Liber ex lege Moysi*: Notes and Text', *The Journal of Medieval Latin* 19 (2009), 173–218.

Murphy, G. Ronald, trans. *The Heliand: The Saxon Gospel: A Translation and Commentary* (Oxford: Oxford University Press, 1992).

O'Donnell, Daniel Paul, ed. *Cædmon's Hymn: A Multimedia Study, Edition and Archive* (Cambridge: D. S. Brewer, 2005).

O'Neill, Patrick P., ed. *King Alfred's Old English Prose Translation of the First Fifty Psalms*, Medieval Academy Books 104 (Cambridge, MA: Medieval Academy of America, 2001).

——, ed. and trans. *Old English Psalms*, DOML 42 (Cambridge, MA: Harvard University Press, 2016).

Orchard, Andy. *Word-Hord: A Lexicon of Old English Verse with Particular Focus on the Distribution of Nominal and Adjectival Compounds*, CLASP Ancillary Publications 1 (Oxford: CLASP, 2022).

Pope, John C., ed. *Homilies of Ælfric: A Supplementary Collection, being twenty-one full homilies of his middle and later career for the most part not previously edited with some shorter pieces mainly passages added to the second and third series*, 2 vols, EETS o.s. 259, 260 (London: Oxford University Press, 1967–8).

Riyeff, Jacob, trans. *The Old English Rule of Saint Benedict with Related Old English Texts* (Collegeville, MN: Cistercian Publications, 2017).

Rudolf, Winfried, Thomas N. Hall, et al., eds. *ECHOE Online: Electronic Corpus of Anonymous Homilies in Old English*, https://echoe.uni-goettingen.de, accessed 2 November 2024.

Schaefer, Kenneth Gordon, ed. 'An Edition of Five Old English Homilies for Palm Sunday, Holy Saturday, and Easter Sunday' (unpublished doctoral dissertation, Columbia University, 1972).

Scragg, Donald G., ed. *The Vercelli Homilies*, EETS o.s. 300 (Oxford: Oxford University Press, 1992).

Schröer, Arnold, ed. *Die angelsächsischen Prosabearbeitungen der Benediktinerregel*, Bibliothek der angelsächsischen Prosa 2 (Kassel: G. H. Wigand, 1885–88).

Skeat, Walter W., ed. *The Holy Gospels in Anglo-Saxon, Northumbrian, and Old Mercian Versions* (Cambridge: Cambridge University Press, 1871–87).

——, ed. and trans. *Ælfric's Lives of Saints: being a set of sermons on saint's days formerly observed by the English Church*, 2 volumes, EETS o.s. 76, 82 and 94, 114 (London: N. Trübner & Co., 1881–5, 1890–1900), repr. as 2 volumes, 1966.

Sievers, Eduard, ed. *Tatian: Lateinisch und altdeutsch mit ausführlichem Glossar* (Paderborn: Schöningh, 1872).

Sisam, Celia, and Kenneth Sisam, eds. *The Salisbury Psalter*, EETS o.s. 242 (London: Oxford University Press, 1959).

Stevenson, William H., ed. *Asser's Life of King Alfred*, with an article by Dorothy Whitelock (Oxford: Clarendon Press, 1957).

Streitberg, Wilhelm, ed. *Die Gotische Bibel*, 7th edn (Heidelberg: Universitätsverlag C. Winter, 2000).

Swain, Larry J., ed. *Ælfric of Eynsham's Letter to Sigeweard: An Edition, Translation and Commentary* (Chicago: University of Illinois at Chicago, 2009).

Sweet, Henry, ed. *The Oldest English Texts*, EETS o.s. 83 (London: Trübner and Co., 1885).

Tamoto, Kenichi, ed. *The MacRegol Gospels or The Rushworth Gospels: Edition of the Latin Text with the Old English Interlinear Gloss Transcribed from Oxford Bodleian Library, MS Auctarium D. 2. 19* (Amsterdam: John Benjamins, 2013).

Thorpe, Benjamin, ed. *The Homilies of the Anglo-Saxon Church: The First Part, Containing the Sermones Catholici or Homilies of Ælfric in the Original Anglo-Saxon, with an English Version*, 2 vols (London: The Ælfric Society, 1844).

Thwaites, Edward, ed. *Heptateuchus, Liber Job, et Euangelium Nicdemi: Anglo-Saxonice; Historiæ Judith Fragmentum: Dano-Saxonice, edidit nunc primum ex MMS codicibus* (Oxford: Oxford Sheldonian Theatre, 1698).

Turk, M. H., ed. *The Legal Code of Ælfred the Great* (Boston: Ginn and Company, 1893).

Tyndale, William. *The Obedience of a Christian Man* (1528), ed. David Daniell (Harmondsworth: Penguin, 2000).

von Tischendorf, Constantin, ed. *Evangelia Apocrypha* (Leipzig: Hermann Mendelsohn, 1853; 2nd edn, 1876).

Walker, Alexander, trans. *Apocryphal Gospels, Acts, and Revelations* (Edinburgh: T. & T. Clark, 1870).

Walsh, P. G., trans. *Cassiodorus: Explanation of the Psalms, Vol. 1* (New York: Paulist Press, 1990).

Weber, Dom Robert, ed. *Collectanea Biblica Latina x, Le Psautier Romain et les autres anciens psautiers latins* (Rome: Libreria Vaticana, 1953).

Weber, Robert, and Roger Gryson, eds *Biblia Sacra Vulgata*, fifth edn (Stuttgart: Württembergische Bibelanstalt, 2007).

Whitelock, Dorothy, Martin Brett and Christopher N. L. Brooke, eds. *Councils & Synods with other Documents relating to the English Church, I: A.D. 871–1204* (Oxford: Clarendon Press, 1981).

Wildhagen, Karl, ed. *Der Cambridger Psalter (Hs. Ff. 1.23 University Libr. Cambridge) zum ersten Male hrsg., mit besonderer Berücksichtigung des lateinischen Textes, von Karl Wildhagen: I. Text mit Erklärungen*, Bibliothek der angelsächsischen Prosa vol. 7 (Hamburg: H. Grand, 1910).

Wilkins, David, ed. *Concilia Magnae Britanniae et Hiberniae, ab Anno MCCCL ad Annum MDXLV. Volumen Tertium* (London: Davis, 1737).

William of Malmesbury: Gesta Regum Anglorum, ed. R. A. B. Mynors, R. M. Thomson and M. Winterbottom, Oxford Medieval Texts, 2 vols (Oxford: Oxford University Press, 1998–9).

Wright, D. H., ed. *Early English Manuscripts in Facsimile, XIV: The Vespasian Psalter, British Museum Cotton Vespasian A. I* (Copenhagen and London: Rosenkilde and Bagger, 1967).

Secondary Sources

Adair, Anya. 'A Troublesome Source: The *Liber Ex Lege Moysi* and the Mosaic Prologue to King Alfred's Domboc', *American Notes & Queries* 35 (2022), 212–17.

Ambrose, Shannon O. 'The Theme of Lay *Clænnyss* in Ælfric's Letters to Sigeweard, Sigefryð, and Brother Edward', *Mediaevalia* 35 (2014), 5–21.

Anderson, Benedict. *Imagined Communities: Reflections on the Origin and Spread of Nationalism* (New York: Verso, 1983; revised 1991).

Anderson, Rachel. 'The Old Testament Homily: Ælfric as Biblical Translator', in *The Old English Homily: Precedent, Practice, and Appropriation*, ed. Aaron J. Kleist, SEM 17 (Turnhout: Brepols, 2007), pp. 121–42.

Anlezark, Daniel. 'The Fall of the Angels in *Solomon and Saturn II*', in *Apocryphal Texts and Traditions in Anglo-Saxon England*, ed. Kathryn Powell and Donald G. Scragg, Publications of the Manchester Centre for Anglo-Saxon Studies 2 (Cambridge: D. S. Brewer, 2003), pp. 121–33.

——. 'Sceaf, Japheth and the Origins of the Anglo-Saxons', *ASE* 31 (2006), 13–46.

——. 'Reading "The Story of Joseph" in MS Cambridge Corpus Christi College 201', in *The Power of Words: Anglo-Saxon Studies Presented to Donald G. Scragg on his Seventieth Birthday*, ed. Hugh Magennis and Jonathan Wilcox (Morgantown: West Virginia University Press, 2006), pp. 61–94.

——. 'Lay Reading, Patronage, and Power in Bodleian Library Junius 11', in *Ambition and Anxiety: Courts and Courtly Discourse, c. 700–1600*, ed. Giles E. M. Gasper and John McKinnell, Durham Medieval and Renaissance Monographs and Essays 3 (Toronto: Pontifical Institute of Medieval Studies, 2014), pp. 76–97.

——. 'The Psalms in the Old English Office of Prime', in *The Psalms and Medieval English Literature: From the Conversion to the Reformation*, ed. Tamara Atkin and Francis Leneghan (Cambridge: D. S. Brewer, 2017), pp. 198–217.

——. 'The Trilingual *titulus crucis* Tradition in Oxford, Bodleian Library, Hatton 20', in *The Embroidered Bible: Studies in Biblical Apocrypha and Pseudepigrapha in Honour of Michael E. Stone*, ed. Lorenzo DiTommaso, Matthias Henze and William Adler, Studia in Veteris Testamenti Pseudepigrapha 26 (Leiden: Brill, 2017), pp. 64–78.

——. 'Which Books are "Most Necessary" to Know? The Old English *Pastoral Care* Preface and King Alfred's Educational Reform', *ES* 98 (2017), 759–80.

——. 'Wulfstan and the Anglo-Saxon Chronicle', in *Wulfstan of York*, ed. Andrew Rabin and Catherine Cubitt (forthcoming).

Appleton, Helen. 'The Northern World of the Anglo-Saxon Mappa Mundi', *ASE* 47 (2018), 275–305.

——. 'Mapping Empire: Two World Maps in Early Medieval England', in *Ideas of the World in Early Medieval English Literature*, ed. Mark Atherton, Kazutomo Karasawa and Francis Leneghan, SOEL 1 (Turnhout: Brepols, 2022), pp. 309–34.

Bibliography

Atherton, Mark. 'Quoting and Requoting: How the Use of Sources Affects Stylistic Choice in Old English Prose', *Studia Neophilologica* 72 (2000), 6–17.

——. *The Making of England: A New Literary History of the Anglo-Saxon World* (London: I. B. Tauris, 2017).

Atkin, Tamara, and Francis Leneghan, eds. *The Psalms and Medieval English Literature: From the Conversion to the Reformation* (Cambridge: D. S. Brewer, 2017).

Backhouse, Janet. *The Lindisfarne Gospels* (Ithaca, NY: Cornell University Press, 1981).

Baker, John, and Stuart Brookes. 'Explaining Anglo-Saxon Military Efficiency: The Landscape of Mobilization', *ASE* 44 (2015), 221–58.

Barker, James William. *Tatian's 'Diatessaron': Composition, Redaction, Recension, and Reception* (Oxford: Oxford University Press, 2021).

Bately, Janet M. 'Lexical Evidence for the Authorship of the *Prose Psalms* in the Paris Psalter', *ASE* 10 (1982), 69–95.

——. 'Old English Prose Before and During the Reign of Alfred', *ASE* 17 (1988), 93–138.

——. 'Did Alfred Actually Translate Anything? The Integrity of the Alfredian Canon Revisited', *MÆ* 78 (2009), 189–215.

——. 'Alfred as Author and Translator', in *A Companion to Alfred the Great*, ed. Nicole Discenza and Paul E. Szarmach, Brill Companions to the Christian Tradition 58 (Leiden: Brill, 2015), pp. 113–42.

Barnhouse, Rebecca. 'Pictorial Exegesis in the Illustrated Old English Hexateuch', *Publications of the Medieval Association of the Midwest* 6 (1999), 109–32.

——. 'Shaping the Hexateuch', in *The Old English Hexateuch: Aspects and Approaches*, ed. Rebecca Barnhouse and Benjamin C. Withers (Kalamazoo, MI: Western Michigan University/Medieval Institute Publications, 2000), pp. 91–108.

Barnhouse, Rebecca, and Benjamin C. Withers, eds. *The Old English Hexateuch: Aspects and Approaches* (Kalamazoo, MI: Western Michigan University/Medieval Institute Publications, 2000).

Barton, John. *The Word: On the Translation of the Bible* (London: Penguin, 2022).

Biggs, Frederick M., ed. *Sources of Anglo-Saxon Literary Culture: The Apocrypha*, Instrumenta Anglistica Medievalia 1 (Kalamazoo, MI: Medieval Institute Publications, 2007).

Blair, John. *The Church in Anglo-Saxon Society* (Oxford: Oxford University Press, 2005).

Blom, Alderik H. *Glossing the Psalms: The Emergence of the Written Vernaculars in Western Europe from the Seventh to the Twelfth Centuries* (Berlin: De Gruyter, 2017).

Boyle, Elizabeth. *History and Salvation in Early Ireland* (Abingdon: Routledge, 2021).

Bredehoft, Thomas A. *Textual Histories: Readings in the Anglo-Saxon Chronicle* (Toronto: University of Toronto Press, 2001).

——. *Authors, Audiences and Old English Verse* (Toronto: University of Toronto Press, 2009).

Brehe, S. K. 'Reassembling the *First Worcester Fragment*', *Speculum* 65 (1990), 521–36.

Brooks, Britton Elliott. *Restoring Creation: The Natural World in the Anglo-Saxon Saints' Lives of Cuthbert and Guthlac*, Nature and Environment in the Middle Ages 3 (Cambridge: D. S. Brewer, 2019).

Brookes, Stewart. 'Reading Between the Lines: The Liturgy and Ælfric's *Lives of Saints* and Homilies', *Leeds Studies in English* 42 (2011), 17–28.

Brown, Michelle P. *The Lindisfarne Gospels: Society, Spirituality and the Scribe* (Toronto: University of Toronto Press, 2003).

——. *Bede and the Theory of Everything* (London: Reaktion Books, 2023).

Burrow, John. *The Ages of Man: A Study in Medieval Writing and Thought* (Oxford: Clarendon Press, 1986).

Butler, Emily. 'Alfred and the Children of Israel in the Prose Psalms', *N&Q* 57 (2010), 10–17.

——. '"And Thus Did Hezekiah": Perspectives on Judaism in the Old English Prose Psalms', *RES* 67 (2016), 617–35.

——. 'Examining Dualities in the Old English *Prose Psalms*', in *The Age of Alfred: Rethinking English Literary Culture c. 850–950*, ed. Amy Faulkner and Francis Leneghan, SOEL 3 (Turnhout: Brepols, 2024), pp. 409–28.

Cain, Christopher M. 'The Apocryphal Legend of Abgar in Ælfric's *Lives of Saints*', *PQ* 89 (2010), 383–402.

Campbell, Jackson J. 'To Hell and Back: Latin Tradition and Literary Use of the *Descensus ad Infernos* in Old English', *Viator* 13 (1982), 107–58.

Campbell, James. *The Anglo-Saxon State* (London-New York: Hambledon and London, 2000).

Carella, Bryan. 'The Source of the Prologue to the Laws of Alfred', *Peritia* 19 (2005), 91–118.

——. 'Evidence for Hiberno-Latin Thought in the Prologue to the Laws of Alfred', *SP* 108 (2011), 1–26.

——. 'Asser's Bible and the Prologue to the Laws of Alfred', *Anglia* 130 (2012), 195–206.

Carver, M. O. H. 'Contemporary Artefacts Illustrated in Late Saxon Manuscripts', *Archaeologia* 108 (1986), 117–45.

Chase, Colin. 'God's Presence through Grace as the Theme of Cynewulf's *Christ II* and the Relationship of this Theme to *Christ I* and *Christ III*', *ASE* 3 (1974), 87–101.

Chazelle, Celia. *The Codex Amiatinus and Its Sister Bibles: Scripture, Liturgy, and Art in the Milieu of the Venerable Bede* (Leiden: Brill, 2019).

Clark, David. *Between Medieval Men: Male Friendship and Desire in Early Medieval English Literature* (Oxford: Oxford University Press, 2009).
Clayton, Mary. 'Homiliaries and Preaching in Anglo-Saxon England', *Peritia* 4 (1985), 207–42; reprinted in *Old English Prose: Basic Readings*, ed. Paul E. Szarmach, with the assistance of Deborah A. Oosterhouse, Basic Readings in Anglo-Saxon England 5 (New York: Garland, 2000), pp. 151–98.
——. 'Ælfric and the Nativity of the Blessed Virgin Mary', *Anglia* 104 (1986), 286–315.
——. *The Cult of the Virgin Mary in Anglo-Saxon England*, CSASE 2 (Cambridge: Cambridge University Press, 1990).
Clemoes, Peter A. M. 'The Chronology of Ælfric's Works', in *The Anglo-Saxons: Studies in Some Aspects of Their History and Culture Presented to Bruce Dickins*, ed. Peter Clemoes (London: Bowes & Bowes, 1959), pp. 212–47, repr. in *Old English Prose: Basic Readings*, ed. Paul E. Szarmach, with the assistance of Deborah A. Oosterhouse, Basic Readings in Anglo-Saxon England 5 (New York: Garland, 2000), pp. 29–72.
——. 'Ælfric', in *Continuations and Beginnings: Studies in Old English Literature*, ed. Eric G. Stanley (London: Nelson, 1966), pp. 176–209.
——. *Rhythm and Cosmic Order in Old English Christian Literature: An Inaugural Lecture* (Cambridge: Cambridge University Press, 1970).
——. 'The Composition of the Old English Text', in *The Old English Illustrated Hexateuch: British Museum Cotton Claudius B. IV*, ed. C. R. Dodwell and Peter A. M. Clemoes, Early English Manuscripts in Facsimile 18 (Copenhagen: Rosenkilde and Bagger, 1974), pp. 42–53.
Clunies Ross, Margaret. 'Concubinage in Anglo-Saxon England', *Past & Present* 108 (1985), 3–34, repr. in *Anglo-Saxon History: Basic Readings*, ed. David A. E. Pelteret, Basic Readings in Anglo-Saxon England 6 (New York: Routledge, 2000), pp. 251–88.
Coatsworth, Elizabeth. 'The Book of Enoch and Anglo-Saxon Art', in *Apocryphal Texts and Traditions in Anglo-Saxon England*, ed. Kathryn Powell and Donald Scragg, Publications of the Manchester Centre for Anglo-Saxon Studies 2 (Cambridge: D. S. Brewer, 2003), pp. 135–50.
Conti, Aidan. 'An Anonymous Homily for Palm Sunday, *The Dream of the Rood*, and the Progress of Ælfric's Reform', *N&Q* n.s. 48 (2001), 377–80.
Corona, Gabriella. 'Ælfric's (Un)Changing Style: Continuity of Patterns from the *Catholic Homilies* to the *Lives of Saints*', *JEGP* 107 (2008), 169–89.
Crépin, André. 'Bede and the Vernacular', in *Famulus Christi: Essays in Commemoration of the Thirteenth Centenary of the Birth of the Venerable Bede*, ed. Gerald Bonner (London: S.P.C.K., 1976), pp. 170–92.
Crişan, Andrei. 'The Concept of the Three Orders of Society in Late Old English Prose', *Studia Universitatis Babes-Bolyai, Philologia* 3 (2024), 189–206.

Cross, James E. 'The Ethics of War in Old English', in *England before the Conquest: Studies in Primary Sources Presented to Dorothy Whitelock*, ed. Peter Clemoes and Kathleen Hughes (Cambridge: Cambridge University Press, 1971), pp. 269–82.

Crowley, Joseph. 'Anglicized Word Order in Old English Continuous Interlinear Glosses in British Library, Royal 2.A.XX', *ASE* 29 (2000), 123–51.

Cubitt, Catherine. *Anglo-Saxon Church Councils, 650–850* (Leicester: Leicester University Press, 1995).

——. 'Ælfric's Lay Patrons', in *A Companion to Ælfric*, ed. Hugh Magennis and Mary Swan, Brill's Companions to the Christian Tradition 18 (Leiden: Brill, 2009), pp. 165–92.

Davis, Craig. R. 'Gothic *Beowulf*: King Alfred and the Northern Ethnography of the Nowell Codex', *Viator* 50 (2019), 99–129.

DeGregorio, Scott. '*Þegenlic* or *Flæsclic*: The Old English Prose Legends of St. Andrew', *JEGP* 102 (2003), 449–64.

de Waard, Jan, and Eugene Nida. *From One Language to Another: Functional Equivalence in Bible Translating* (Nashville: Nelson, 1986).

Dillon, Myles. 'Scél saltrach na rann', *Celtica* 4 (1958), 1–43.

diPaolo Healey, Antonette. 'Anglo-Saxon Use of the Apocryphal Gospel', in *The Anglo-Saxons: Synthesis and Achievement*, ed. J. Douglas Woods and David A. E. Pelteret (Waterloo, ON: Wilfrid Laurier University Press, 1986), pp. 93–104.

Doane, Alger N. 'The Transmission of *Genesis B*', in *Anglo-Saxon England and the Continent*, ed. Hans Sauer and Joanna Story, with the assistance of Gaby Waxenberger (Tempe, AZ: Arizona Center for Medieval and Renaissance Studies, 2011), pp. 63–81.

Dy, Oliver, and Wim François. 'Vernacular Translations of the Latin Bible', in *The Oxford Handbook of the Latin Bible*, ed. H. A. G. Houghton (Oxford: Oxford University Press, 2023), pp. 392–405.

Earl, James W. 'Violence and Non-Violence in Anglo-Saxon England: Ælfric's *Passion of St Edmund*', *PQ* 78 (1999), 125–49.

Elliott, Constance O., and Alan S. C. Ross. 'Aldrediana XXIV: The Linguistic Peculiarities of the Gloss to St John's Gospel', *English Philological Studies* 13 (1972), 49–72.

Elstob, Elizabeth. *The Rudiments of Grammar for the English-Saxon Tongue, First Given in English: with an Apology for the Study of Northern Antiquities, Being Very Useful Towards the Understanding Our Ancient English Poets, and Other Writers* (London: W. Bowyer, 1715).

Falluomini, Carla. *The Gothic Version of the Gospels and Pauline Epistles: Cultural Background, Transmission and Character* (Berlin: de Gruyter, 2015).

Faulkner, Amy. 'Royal Authority in the Biblical Quotations of the Old English *Pastoral Care*', *Neophilologus* 102 (2017), 125–40.

——. 'The Mind in the Old English *Prose Psalms*', *RES* 70 (2019), 597–617.

Faulkner, Amy, and Francis Leneghan. 'Introduction: Rethinking English Literary Culture *c.* 850–950', in *The Age of Alfred: Rethinking English Literary Culture c. 850–950*, ed. Amy Faulkner and Francis Leneghan, SOEL 3 (Turnhout: Brepols, 2024), pp. 17–48.

Faulkner, Mark. 'The Eadwine Psalter and Twelfth-Century English Vernacular Literary Culture', in *The Psalms and Medieval English Literature: From the Conversion to the Reformation*, ed. Tamara Atkin and Francis Leneghan (Cambridge: D. S. Brewer, 2017), pp. 72–106.

——. *A New Literary History of the Long Twelfth Century: Language and Literature between Old and Middle English* (Cambridge: Cambridge University Press, 2022).

Fernández Cuesta, Julia, and Sara M. Pons-Sanz, eds. *The Old English Gloss to the Lindisfarne Gospels: Language, Author and Context*, Anglia Book Series 51 (Berlin: De Gruyter, 2016).

Firth, Matthew. 'Constructing a King: William of Malmesbury and the Life of Æthelstan', *Journal of the Australian Early Medieval Association* 13 (2017), 69–82.

Fitzgerald, Jill. *Rebel Angels: Space and Sovereignty in Anglo-Saxon England* (Manchester: Manchester University Press, 2019).

Foot, Sarah. 'The Making of the *Angelcynn*: English Identity Before the Norman Conquest', *Transactions of the Royal Historical Society* 6 (1996), 25–49.

——. *Æthelstan: The First King of England* (New Haven, CT: Yale University Press, 2011).

——. 'The Historiography of the Anglo-Saxon "Nation-State"', in *Power and the Nation in European History*, ed. Len Scales and Oliver Zimmer (Cambridge: Cambridge University Press, 2005), pp. 125–42.

Fox, Michael. 'Ælfric on the Creation and Fall of the Angels', *ASE* 31 (2002), 175–200.

——. 'Ælfric's *Interrogationes Sigewulfi*', in *Old English Literature and the Old Testament*, ed. Michael Fox and Manish Sharma (Toronto: University of Toronto Press, 2012), pp. 25–63.

Frank, Roberta. 'Some Uses of Paronomasia in Old English Scriptural Verse', *Speculum* 47 (1972), 207–26.

——. 'Germanic Legend in Old English Literature', in *The Cambridge Companion to Old English Literature*, 2nd edn, ed. Malcolm Godden and Michael Lapidge (Cambridge: Cambridge University Press, 2013), pp. 82–100.

Frantzen, Allen J. *King Alfred*, Twayne's English Authors Series (Boston: Twayne Publishers, 1986).

Franzen, Christine. *The Tremulous Hand of Worcester: A Study of Old English in the Thirteenth Century* (Oxford: Oxford University Press, 1991).

Fulk, R. D. *A History of Old English Meter* (Philadelphia: University of Pennsylvania Press, 1992).

———. 'The Refashioning of Christ's Passion in an Anonymous Old English Homily for Palm Sunday (HomS 18)', *JEGP* 116 (2017), 415–37.

Fúsik, Ondřej. 'Referencing Female Characters in the Old English *Heptateuch* Translation of Genesis: Evidence against Translation Automatisms', in *Translation Automatisms in the Vernacular Texts of the Middle Ages and the Early Modern Period*, ed. Vladimir Agrigoroaei and Ileana Sasu (Turnhout: Brepols, 2023), pp. 156–61.

Gardiner, Luke. 'The Imperial Subject: Theodosius II and Panegyric in Socrates' *Church History*', in *Theodosius II: Rethinking the Roman Empire in Late Antiquity*, ed. Christopher Kelly (Cambridge: Cambridge University Press, 2013), pp. 244–68.

Gatch, Milton McC. *Preaching and Theology in Anglo-Saxon England: Ælfric and Wulfstan* (Toronto: University of Toronto Press, 1977).

———. 'The Achievement of Ælfric and his Colleagues in European Perspective', in *The Old English Homily and its Background*, ed. Paul E. Szarmach and Bernard F. Huppé (Albany, NY: State University of New York Press, 1978), pp. 43–73.

———. 'The Office in Late Anglo-Saxon Monasticism', in *Learning and Literature in Anglo-Saxon England: Studies presented to Peter Clemoes on the Occasion of his Sixty-Fifth Birthday*, ed. Michael Lapidge and Helmut Gneuss (Cambridge: Cambridge University Press, 1985), pp. 341–62.

Gates, Jay Paul. 'The Alfredian Prose Psalms and a Legal English Identity', in *Law, Literature, and Social Regulation in Early Medieval England*, ed. Andrew Rabin and Anya Adair, Anglo-Saxon Studies 47 (Cambridge: D. S. Brewer, 2023), pp. 31–53.

Gillespie, Vincent, and Kantik Ghosh, eds. *After Arundel: Religious Writing in Fifteenth-Century England* (Turnhout: Brepols, 2011).

Gillingham, Susan. *Psalms Through the Centuries: A Reception History Commentary on Psalms 1–72* (Chichester: Wiley-Blackwell, 2018).

Gittos, Helen. 'The Audience for Old English Texts: Ælfric, Rhetoric and "The Edification of the Simple"', *ASE* 43 (2014), 231–66.

Gneuss, Helmut. 'The Origin of Standard Old English and Æthelwold's School at Winchester', *ASE* 1 (1972), 63–83.

———. 'King Alfred and the History of Anglo-Saxon Libraries', in *Modes of Interpretation in Old English Literature: Essays in Honour of Stanley B. Greenfield*, ed. Phyllis Rugg Brown, Georgina Ronan Crampton and Fred C. Robinson (Toronto: University of Toronto Press, 1986), pp. 29–49.

Godden, Malcolm. 'Ælfric and the Vernacular Prose Tradition', in *The Old English Homily and its Background*, ed. Paul E. Szarmach and Bernard F. Huppé (Albany, NY: State University of New York Press, 1978), pp. 99–117.

———. 'Apocalypse and Invasion in Late Anglo-Saxon England', in *From Anglo-Saxon to Early Middle English*, ed. Eric G. Stanley, Malcolm

Godden, Douglas Gray and Terry Hoad (Oxford: Oxford University Press, 1994), pp. 130–62.

——. 'The Trouble with Sodom: Literary Responses to Biblical Sexuality', *Bulletin of the John Rylands University Library of Manchester* 77 (1995), 96–119.

——. 'The Anglo-Saxons and the Goths: Rewriting the Sack of Rome', *ASE* 31 (2002), 47–68.

——. 'King Alfred's Preface and the Teaching of Latin in Anglo-Saxon England', *English Historical Review* 117 (2002), 596–604.

——. 'Did King Alfred Write Anything?', *MÆ* 76 (2007), 1–23.

——. 'The Alfredian Project and its Aftermath: Rethinking the Literary History of the Ninth and Tenth Centuries', *Proceedings of the British Academy* 162 (2009), 93–12.

——. 'Ælfric and The Alfredian Precedents', in *A Companion to Ælfric*, ed. Hugh Magennis and Mary Swan, Brill Companions to the Christian Tradition 18 (Leiden: Brill, 2009), pp. 139–63.

——. 'Biblical Literature: The Old Testament', in *The Cambridge Companion to Old English Literature*, 2nd edn ed. Malcolm Godden and Michael Lapidge (Cambridge: Cambridge University Press, 2013), pp. 214–33.

——. 'Why did the Anglo-Saxons switch from Verse to Prose?', in *The Age of Alfred: Rethinking English Literary Culture, c. 850–950*, ed. Amy Faulkner and Francis Leneghan, SOEL 3 (Turnhout: Brepols, 2024), pp. 565–91.

Gow, Andrew Colin. 'The Bible in Germanic', in *The New Cambridge History of the Bible, vol. 2: From 600 to 1450*, ed. Richard Marsden and E. Ann Matter (Cambridge: Cambridge University Press, 2012), pp. 198–216.

Greenfield, Stanley B., and Daniel G. Calder, *A New Critical History of Old English Literature*, with a survey of the Anglo-Latin Background by Michael Lapidge (New York: NYU Press, 1986).

Gretsch, Mechthild. *The Intellectual Foundations of the English Benedictine Reform*, CSASE 25 (Cambridge: Cambridge University Press, 1999).

——. 'The Junius Psalter Gloss: Tradition and Innovation', in *Edward the Elder 899–924*, ed. N. J. Higham and David Hill (London: Routledge, 2001), pp. 280–91.

——. 'Winchester Vocabulary and Standard Old English: The Vernacular in Late Anglo-Saxon England', *Bulletin of the John Rylands Library* 83 (2001), 41–87.

——. 'Historiography and Literary Patronage in late Anglo-Saxon England: The Evidence of Æthelweard's *Chronicon*', *ASE* 41 (2012), 205–48.

Griffith, Mark. 'Ælfric's Use of Sources in the Preface to Genesis, together with a Conspectus of Biblical and Patristic Sources and Analogues', *Florilegium* 17 (2000), 127–54.

——. 'Ælfric's Preface to Genesis: Genre, Rhetoric and the Origins of the *ars dictaminis*', *ASE* 29 (2000), 215–34.

Grünberg, M., ed. *The West-Saxon Gospels: A Study of the Gospel of Saint Matthew with Text of the Four Gospels* (Amsterdam: Scheltema and Holkema, 1967).

Hall, Joseph. *Selections from Early Middle English, 1130–1250*, 2 vols (Oxford: Clarendon Press, 1920).

Hall, Thomas N. 'The *Euangelium Nichodemi* and *Vindicta Saluatoris* in Anglo-Saxon England', in *Two Old English Apocrypha and Their Manuscript Source: 'The Gospel of Nichodemus' and 'The Avenging of the Saviour'*, ed. J. E. Cross, CSASE 19 (Cambridge: Cambridge University Press, 1996), pp. 36–81.

——. 'Ælfric and the Epistle to the Laodiceans', in *Apocryphal Texts and Traditions in Anglo-Saxon England*, ed. Kathryn Powell and Donald Scragg, Publications of the Manchester Centre for Anglo-Saxon Studies 2 (Cambridge: D. S. Brewer, 2003), pp. 65–83.

Hargreaves, Henry. 'From Bede to Wyclif: Medieval English Bible Translations', *Bulletin of the John Rylands University Library* 48 (1965), 118–40.

Hastings, Adrian. *The Construction of Nationhood: Ethnicity, Religion and Nationalism* (Cambridge: Cambridge University Press, 1997).

Hawk, Brandon. *Preaching Apocrypha in Anglo-Saxon England* (Toronto: University of Toronto Press, 2018).

Henderson, George. 'The Joshua Cycle in B.M. Cotton MS. Claudius B. IV', *Journal of the British Archaeological Association* 31 (1968), 38–59.

Hill, David, and Alexander R. Rumble, eds. *The Defence of Wessex: The Burghal Hidage and Anglo-Saxon Fortifications* (Manchester: Manchester University Press, 1996).

Hill, Joyce. 'Monastic Reform and the Secular Church: Ælfric's Pastoral Letters in Context', in *England in the Eleventh Century: Proceedings of the 1990 Harlaxton Symposium*, ed. Carola Hicks, Harlaxton Medieval Studies 2 (Stamford: Paul Watkins, 1992), pp. 103–17.

——. 'Authority and Intertextuality in the Works of Ælfric', *Proceedings of the British Academy* 131 (2005), 157–81.

——. 'Wulfsige of Sherborne's Reforming Text', in *Leaders of the Anglo-Saxon Church: From Bede to Stigand*, ed. Alexander R. Rumble, Publications of the Manchester Centre for Anglo-Saxon Studies 12 (Woodbridge: Boydell, 2012), pp. 147–64.

Hill, Thomas D. 'Vision and Judgement in the Old English *Christ III*', *SP* 70 (1973), 233–42.

——. 'The Fall of Angels and Man in the Old English *Genesis B*', in *Anglo-Saxon Poetry: Essays in Appreciation, For John C. McGalliard*, ed. Lewis E. Nicholson and Dolores Warwick Frese (Notre Dame and London: University of Notre Dame Press, 1975), pp. 279–90.

———. 'The Fall of Satan in the Old English *Christ and Satan*', *JEGP* 73 (1977), 315–25.

———. 'Literary History and Old English Poetry: The Case of *Christ I, II, III*', in *Sources of Anglo-Saxon Culture*, ed. Paul E. Szarmach with the assistance of Virginia Darrow Oggins, Studies in Medieval Culture 20 (Kalamazoo, MI: Medieval Institute Publications, Western Michigan University, 1986), pp. 3–22.

———. 'The *Passio Andreae* and *The Dream of the Rood*', *ASE* 38 (2010), 1–10.

Hofstetter, Walter. 'Winchester and the Standardization of Old English Vocabulary', *ASE* 17 (1988), 139–68.

Hohler, C. E., 'Some Service Books of the Later Saxon Church', in *Tenth-Century Studies: Essays in Commemoration of the Millennium of the Council of Winchester and 'Regularis Concordia*, ed. David Parsons (London: Phillimore, 1975), pp. 60–83 and 217–27.

Hopkins, Stephen C. E. 'An Old English Fragment of the *Letter of Christ to Agbar*', *N&Q* 66 (2019), 173–6.

Horgan, Dorothy. '*The Dream of the Rood* and a Homily for Palm Sunday', *N&Q* n.s. 29 (1982), 388–91.

Hurley, Mary Kate. 'Alfredian Temporalities: Time and Translation in the Old English *Orosius*', *JEGP* 112 (2013), 405–32.

Hurt, James. *Ælfric*, Twayne's English Authors Series (New York: Twayne, 1972).

I'A Bromwich, John. 'Who Was the Translator of the Prose Portion of the Paris Psalter', in *The Early Cultures of North-West Europe*, ed. Cyril Fox and Bruce Dickins (Cambridge: Cambridge University Press, 1950), pp. 289–304.

Irvine, Susan. 'The Compilation and Use of Manuscripts containing Old English in the Twelfth Century', in *Rewriting Old English in the Twelfth Century*, ed. Mary Swan and Elaine M. Treharne, CSASE 30 (Cambridge: Cambridge University Press, 2000), pp. 55–60.

———. 'Hanging by a Thread: Ælfric's Saints' Lives and the *Hengen*', in *Hagiography in Anglo-Saxon England: Adopting and Adapting Saints' Lives into Old English Prose (c. 950–1150)*, ed. Loredana Lazzari, Patrizia Lendinara and Claudia Di Sciacca, Textes et études du Moyen Âge 73 (Barcelona-Madrid: Fédération Internationale des Instituts d'Etudes Médiévales, 2014), pp. 67–94.

Izydorczyk, Zbigniew, ed. *The Medieval Gospel of Nicodemus: Texts, Intertexts, and Contexts in Western Europe* (Tempe, AZ: Medieval and Renaissance Texts and Studies, 1997).

Jayatilaka, Rohini. 'The Old English Benedictine Rule: Writing for Women and Men', *ASE* 32 (2007), 147–87.

Johnson, David F. 'The Fall of Lucifer in *Genesis A* and Two Anglo-Latin Royal Charters', *JEGP* 97 (1998), 500–21.

——. 'A Program of Illumination in the Old English Illustrated Hexateuch: Visual Typology', in *The Old English Hexateuch: Aspects and Approaches*, Rebecca Barnhouse and Benjamin C. Withers (Kalamazoo, MI: Western Michigan University/Medieval Institute Publications, 2000), pp. 165–99.

Jolly, Karen Louise. *The Community of St. Cuthbert in the Late Tenth Century: The Chester-le-Street Additions to Durham Cathedral Library A.IV.19* (Columbus: Ohio State University Press, 2012).

Jones, Christopher A. '*Meatim sed et rustica*: Ælfric of Eynsham as a Medieval Latin Author', *The Journal of Medieval Latin* 8 (1998), 1–57.

——. 'Early English Homiletic Treatments of Christ's Passion: Generic and Liturgical Influences', in *Sermons, Saints, and Sources: Studies in the Homiletic and Hagiographic Literature of Early Medieval England*, ed. Thomas N. Hall and Winfried Rudolf, SOEL 6 (Turnhout: Brepols, 2025), pp. 241–63.

Jones, Jasmine. 'Vernacular Theology in the Old English *Advent Lyrics*: Monastic Devotion to Mary', *RES* 75 (2024), 1–16.

Jost, Karl. 'Unechte Ælfrictexte', *Anglia* 51 (1927), 81–103, 177–219.

Jurasinski, Stefan. 'The *Domboc* in the Laws of Edward the Elder', in *The Age of Alfred: Rethinking English Literary Culture c. 850–950*, ed. Amy Faulkner and Francis Leneghan, SOEL 3 (Turnhout: Brepols, 2024), pp. 523–46.

Jurkowski, Maureen. 'The Selective Censorship of the Wycliffite Bible', in *The Wycliffite Bible: Origin, History and Interpretation*, ed. Elizabeth Solopova (Leiden: Brill, 2016), pp. 371–88.

Kapteijn, J. M. N. 'Die Übersetzungstechnik der gotischen Bibel in den Paulinischen Briefen', *Indogermanische Forschungen* 29 (1911–12), 260–367.

Karkov, Catherine E. 'Hagar and Ishmael: The Uncanny and The Exile', in *Imagining the Jew in Anglo-Saxon Literature and Culture*, ed. Samantha Zacher, Toronto Anglo-Saxon Studies Series 21 (Toronto: University of Toronto Press, 2016), pp. 197–218.

Kaske, Robert E. '*Beowulf* and the Book of Enoch', *Speculum* 46 (1971), 421–31.

Kears, Carl. *MS Junius 11 and its Poetry* (York: York Medieval Press, 2023).

Keefer, Sarah Larratt, and David R. Burrows. 'Hebrew and the Hebraicum in late Anglo-Saxon England', *ASE* 19 (1990), 67–80.

Kelly, Susan. 'Anglo-Saxon Lay Society and the Written Word', in *The Uses of Literacy in Early Medieval Europe*, ed. Rosamond McKitterick (Cambridge: Cambridge University Press, 1990), pp. 36–62.

Keynes, Simon. 'Royal Government and the Written Word in Late Anglo-Saxon England', in *The Uses of Literacy in Early Medieval Europe*, ed. Rosamond McKitterick (Cambridge: Cambridge University Press, 1990), pp. 226–57.

——. *The Councils of 'Clofesho'* (Leicester: Leicester University Press, 1994).

——. 'Alfred the Great and the Kingdom of the Anglo-Saxons', in *A Companion to Alfred the Great*, ed. Nicole Discenza and Paul E. Szarmach, Brill Companions to the Christian Tradition 58 (Leiden: Brill, 2015), pp. 13–46.

Khalaf, Omar. '*Ælfred se casere*: Kingship and Imperial Legitimation in the Old English *Orosius*', in *The Age of Alfred: Rethinking English Literary Culture c. 850–950*, ed. Amy Faulkner and Francis Leneghan, SOEL 3 (Turnhout: Brepols, 2024), pp. 457–75.

Kleist, Aaron J. *The Chronology and Canon of Ælfric of Eynsham*, Anglo-Saxon Studies 37 (Cambridge: D. S. Brewer, 2019).

Knight Bostock, J. *A Handbook on Old High German Literature*, 2nd edn (Oxford: Clarendon Press, 1976).

Kuhn, Sherman M. 'The Vespasian Psalter Gloss: Original or Copy?', *PMLA* 74 (1959), 161–77.

Langeslag, Paul S. 'Reverse-Engineering the Old English *Book of Judges*', *Neophilologus* 100 (2016), 303–14.

Lapidge, Michael. *Anglo-Latin Literature, 600–899* (London: Hambledon Press, 1996).

——. 'Versifying the Bible in the Middle Ages', in *The Text in the Community: Essays on Medieval Works, Manuscripts, Authors, and Readers*, ed. Jill Mann and Maura Nolan (Notre Dame: University of Notre Dame Press, 2005), pp. 11–40.

——. *The Anglo-Saxon Library* (Oxford: Oxford University Press, 2006).

Lavelle, Ryan. *Alfred's Wars: Sources and Interpretations of Anglo-Saxon Warfare in the Viking Age*, Warfare in History 30 (Woodbridge: Boydell, 2010).

Lawton, David. *Voice in Later Medieval English Literature: Public Interiorities* (Oxford: Oxford University Press, 2016).

Leclerq, Jean. *The Love of Learning and the Desire for God*, trans. Catherine Misrahi (New York: Fordham University Press, 1961).

Leneghan, Francis. '*Translatio Imperii*: The Old English *Orosius* and the Rise of Wessex', *Anglia* 133 (2015), 656–705.

——. 'Introduction: A Case Study of Psalm 50.1–3 in Old and Middle English', in *The Psalms and Medieval English Literature: From the Conversion to the Reformation*, ed. Tamara Atkin and Francis Leneghan (Cambridge: D. S. Brewer, 2017), pp. 1–33.

——. 'Making the Psalter Sing: The Old English *Metrical Psalms*, Rhythm and *Ruminatio*', in *The Psalms and Medieval English Literature: From the Conversion to the Reformation*, ed. Tamara Atkin and Francis Leneghan (Cambridge: D. S. Brewer, 2017), pp. 173–97.

——. *The Dynastic Drama of 'Beowulf'*, Anglo-Saxon Studies 39 (Cambridge: D. S. Brewer, 2020).

———. 'End of Empire? Reading *The Death of Edward* in MS Cotton Tiberius B I', in *Ideas of the World in Early Medieval English Literature*, ed. Mark Atherton, Kazutomo Karasawa and Francis Leneghan, SOEL 1 (Turnhout: Brepols, 2022), pp. 403–34.

———. 'Beowulf, the Wrath of God and the Fall of the Angels', *ES* 105 (2024), 383–403.

Lenker, Ursula. *Die westsächsische Evangelienversion und die Perikopenordnungen im angelsächsischen England*, Texte und Untersuchungen zur Englischen Philologie 20 (Munich: Wilhelm Fink, 1997).

———. 'The West Saxon Gospels and the Gospel Lectionary in Anglo-Saxon England: Manuscript Evidence and Liturgical Practice', *ASE* 28 (1999), 141–78.

Lerer, Seth. 'Old English and its Afterlife', in *The Cambridge History of Medieval English Literature*, ed. David Wallace (Cambridge: Cambridge University Press, 1999), pp. 7–34.

Liebermann, Felix. 'King Alfred and Mosaic Law', *Transactions of the Jewish Historical Society* 6 (1912), 21–31.

Lindelöf, Uno. *Studien zu altenglischen Psalterglossen*, Bonner Beiträge zur Anglistik, Heft XIII (Bonn: P. Hanstein, 1904).

Lindstedt, Samira. 'Prayer as Performance, *c.* 1050–1250' (unpublished doctoral dissertation, University of Oxford, 2021).

Lionarons, Joyce Tally. *The Homiletic Writings of Archbishop Wulfstan*, Anglo-Saxon Studies 14 (Cambridge: D. S. Brewer, 2010).

Liuzza, Roy M., ed. *The Poems of MS Junius 11* (New York: Routledge, 2002).

———. 'Who Read the Gospels in Old English?', in *Words and Works: Studies in Medieval English Language and Literature in Honour of Fred C. Robinson*, ed. Peter S. Baker and Nicholas Howe (Toronto: University of Toronto Press, 1998), pp. 3–24.

———. 'Scribal Habit: The Evidence of the Old English Gospels', in *Rewriting Old English in the Twelfth Century*, ed. Mary Swan and Elaine M. Treharne, CSASE 30 (Cambridge: University of Cambridge Press, 2000), pp. 143–65.

———. 'Reconstructing a Lost Manuscript of the Old English Gospels', in *Medieval English and Dutch Literatures: The European Context: Essays in Honour of David F. Johnson*, ed. Larissa Tracy and Geert H. M. Claassens (Cambridge: D. S. Brewer, 2022), pp. 15–28.

Lockwood, W. B. 'Vernacular Scriptures in Germany and the Low Countries before 1500', in *The Cambridge History of the Bible, vol. 2: The West from the Fathers to the Reformation*, ed. G. W. H. Lampe (Cambridge: Cambridge University Press, 1969), pp. 428–34.

Magennis, Hugh. '"No Sex Please, We're Anglo-Saxons?": Attitudes towards Sexuality in Old English Prose and Poetry', *Leeds Studies in English* 26 (1995), 1–27.

——. 'Ælfric of Eynsham's *Letter to Sigeweard* (*Treatise on the Old and New Testaments*)', in *Metaphrastes, or, Gained in Translation: Essays and Translations in Honour of Robert H. Jordan*, ed. Margaret Mullett, Belfast Byzantine Texts and Translations 9 (Belfast: Belfast Byzantine Enterprises, 2004), pp. 210–35.

——. 'Ælfric: *Letter to Sigeweard*', in *The Literary Encyclopedia, Volume 1.2.1.01: English Writing and Culture: Anglo-Saxon England, 500–1066*, ed. Richard Dance and Hugh Magennis (2005): https://www.litencyc.com

——. 'Not Angles but Anglicans? Reformation and Post-Reformation Perspectives on the Anglo-Saxon Church, Part I: Bede, Ælfric and the Anglo-Saxon Church in Early Modern England', *ES* 96 (2015), 243–63.

——. 'Not Angles but Anglicans? Reformation and Post-Reformation Perspectives on the Anglo-Saxon Church, Part II: Seventeenth and Eighteenth Centuries', *ES* 96 (2015), 363–78.

Magoun Jr, Francis P. 'Otfrid's Ad Liutbertum', *PMLA* 58 (1943), 869–90.

Major, Tristan. 'Rebuilding the Tower of Babel: Ælfric and Bible Translation', *Florilegium* 23 (2006), 47–60.

——. '*Awriten on þreo geþeode*: The concept of Hebrew, Greek, and Latin in Old English and Anglo-Latin Literature', *JEGP* 120 (2021), 141–76.

Marsden, Richard A. 'Old Latin Intervention in the Old English Heptateuch', *ASE* 23 (1994), 229–64.

——. *The Text of the Old Testament in Anglo-Saxon England*, CSASE 15 (Cambridge: Cambridge University Press, 1995).

——. 'Cain's Face, and Other Problems: The Legacy of the Earliest English Bible Translations', *Reformation* 1 (1996), 29–51.

——. 'Translation by Committee? The "Anonymous" Text of the Old English Hexateuch', in *The Old English Hexateuch: Aspects and Approaches*, ed. Rebecca Barnhouse and Benjamin C. Withers (Kalamazoo, MI: Western Michigan University/Medieval Institute Publications, 2000), pp. 41–89.

——. 'Latin in the Ascendant: The Interlinear Gloss of Oxford, Bodleian Library, Laud Misc. 509', in *Latin Learning and English Lore: Studies in Anglo-Saxon Literature for Michael Lapidge*, ed. Katherine O'Brien O'Keeffe and Andy Orchard, 2 vols (Toronto: University of Toronto Press, 2005), II, pp. 132–52.

——. 'Ælfric as Translator: The Old English Prose *Genesis*', *Anglia* 109 (2009), 319–58.

——. 'The Bible in English', in *The New Cambridge History of the Bible, Volume 2: From 600 to 1450*, ed. Richard Marsden and E. Ann Matter (Cambridge: Cambridge University Press, 2012), pp. 217–38.

——. 'Biblical Literature: The New Testament', in *The Cambridge Companion to Old English Literature*, ed. Malcolm Godden and Michael Lapidge, 2nd edn (Cambridge: Cambridge University Press, 2013), pp. 234–50.

Marx, C. W. 'The *Gospel of Nicodemus* in Old English and Middle English', in *The Medieval Gospel of Nicodemus: Texts, Intertexts, and Contexts in Western Europe*, ed. Zbigniew Izydorczyk (Tempe, AZ: Medieval and Renaissance Texts and Studies, 1997), pp. 207–59.

McBrine, Patrick. *Biblical Epics in Late Antiquity and Anglo-Saxon England: Divina in Laude Voluntas* (Toronto: University of Toronto Press, 2017).

McDonald, Lee M., and James A. Sanders, eds. *The Canon Debate* (Peabody, MA: Hendrickson Publishers, 2002).

McGowen, Joseph P. 'On the "Red" Blickling Psalter Glosses', *N&Q* 54 (2007), 205–7.

McMullen, A. Joseph, and Chelsea Shields-Más. 'Tamar, Widowhood, and the Old English Prose Translation of Genesis', *Anglia* 138 (2020), 586–617.

McNamara, Martin. 'Psalter Text and Psalter Study in the Early Irish Church (A.D. 600–1200)', in his *The Psalms in the Early Irish Church*, Journal for the Study of the Old Testament Supplement Series 165 (Sheffield: Sheffield Academic Press, 2000), pp. 19–142.

——. *The Bible in the Early Irish Church 550–850* (Leiden: Brill, 2022).

Menzer, Melinda J. 'The Preface as Admonition: Ælfric's Preface to Genesis', in *The Old English Hexateuch: Aspects and Approaches*, ed. Rebecca Barnhouse and Benjamin C. Withers (Kalamazoo, MI: Western Michigan University/Medieval Institute Publications, 2000), pp. 15–39.

Michel, Laurence. '*Genesis A* and the *Praefatio*', *Modern Language Notes* 62 (1947), 545–50.

Mitchell, Bruce. *Old English Syntax* (Oxford: Clarendon Press, 1985).

——. 'The Relation Between Old English Alliterative Verse and Ælfric's Alliterative Prose', in *Latin Learning and English Lore: Studies in Anglo-Saxon Literature for Michael Lapidge*, ed. Katherine O'Brien O'Keeffe and Andy Orchard, 2 vols (Toronto: University of Toronto Press, 2005), II, pp. 349–62.

Molyneaux, George. *The Formation of the English Kingdom in the Tenth Century* (Oxford: Oxford University Press, 2015).

Momma, Haruko. 'Rhythm and Alliteration: Styles of Ælfric's Prose up to the *Lives of Saints*', in *Anglo-Saxon Styles*, ed. Catherine E. Karkov and George Hardin Brown (Albany, NY: State University of New York Press, 2003), pp. 253–70.

Morrell, Minnie Cate. *A Manual of Old English Biblical Materials* (Knoxville, TN: University of Tennessee Press, 1965).

Morrish, Jennifer. 'King Alfred's Letter as a Source on Learning in England', in *Studies in Earlier Old English Prose: Sixteen Original Contributions*, ed.

Paul E. Szarmach (Albany, NY: State University of New York Press, 1986), pp. 87–108.

Murdoch, Brian. 'An Early Irish Adam and Eve: *Saltair na Rann* and the Traditions of the Fall', *Mediaeval Studies* 35 (1973), 146–77.

Nagucka, Ruta. 'Glossal Translation in the Lindisfarne Gospel according to Saint Matthew', *Studia Anglica Posnaniensia* 31 (1997), 179–201.

Nichols, Ann Eljenholm. 'Ælfric and the Brief Style', *JEGP* 70 (1971), 1–12.

Niles, John D. 'The Myth of the Anglo-Saxon Oral Poet', *Western Folklore* 62 (2003), 7–61.

Norton, David. *A History of the English Bible as Literature* (Cambridge: Cambridge University Press, 2000).

O'Brien O'Keeffe, Katherine. 'Who Reads Now? The Anxieties of Millennial Reading: The 2019 Morton W. Bloomfield Lecture', in *The Practice and Politics of Reading, 650–1500*, ed. Daniel Donoghue, James Simpson, Nicholas Watson and Anna Wilson (Cambridge: D. S. Brewer, 2022), pp. 161–80.

Ó Carragáin, Éamonn. *Ritual and the Rood: Liturgical Images and the Old English Poems of the Dream of the Rood Tradition* (Toronto: University of Toronto Press, 2005).

Ó Fearghail, Fearghus. 'Translating the Bible into Irish 1565–1850', in *Ireland and the Reception of the Bible: Social and Cultural Perspectives*, ed. Bradford A. Anderson and Jonathan Kearney (London: T. & T. Clark, 2018), pp. 59–78.

Olson, Mary C. 'Genesis and Narratology: The Challenge of Medieval Illustrated Texts', *Mosaic* 31 (1998), 1–24.

O'Neill, Patrick P. 'The Prose Translation of Psalms 1–50', in *A Companion to Alfred the Great*, ed. Nicole Discenza and Paul E. Szarmach, Brill Companions to the Christian Tradition 58 (Leiden: Brill, 2015), pp. 256–81.

Orchard, Andy. 'The Style of the Texts and the Translation Strategy', in *Two Old English Apocrypha and Their Manuscript Source: 'The Gospel of Nichodemus' and 'The Avenging of the Saviour'*, ed. J. E. Cross, CSASE 19 (Cambridge: Cambridge University Press, 1996), pp. 105–30.

——. 'Wulfstan as Reader, Writer, and Rewriter', in *The Old English Homily: Precedent, Practice, and Appropriation*, ed. Aaron J. Kleist, SEM 17 (Turnhout: Brepols, 2007), pp. 311–41.

——. 'The Word Made Flesh: Christianity and Oral Culture in Anglo-Saxon Verse', *Oral Tradition* 24 (2009), 293–318.

——. 'Both Style and Substance: The Case for Cynewulf', in *Anglo-Saxon Styles*, ed. Catherine E. Karkov and George Hardin Brown (Binghampton, NY: SUNY Press, 2003), pp. 271–305.

——. 'Alcuin and Cynewulf: The Art and Craft of Anglo-Saxon Verse', *Journal of the British Academy* 8 (2020), 295–399.

Orton, Daniel. 'Royal Piety and Davidic Imitation: Cultivating Political Capital in the Alfredian Psalms', *Neophilologus* 98 (2014), 477–92.

Owen-Crocker, Gale R. *Dress in Anglo-Saxon England* (Woodbridge: Boydell, 2004).

Pagliarulo, Giuseppe. 'Word Order in the Lindisfarne Glosses?', *Neophilologus* 94 (2010), 625–35.

Pareles, Mo. *Nothing Pure: Jewish Law, Christian Supersession, and Bible Translation in Old English* (Toronto: University of Toronto Press, 2024).

Parkes, Malcolm. 'Rædan, areccan, smeagan: How the Anglo-Saxons read', *ASE* 26 (1997), 1–22.

Pitt, Georgina. 'Alfredian military reform: the materialization of ideology and the social practice of garrisoning', *Early Medieval Europe* 30 (2022), 408–36.

Porck, Thijs. 'Newly Discovered Pieces of an Old English Glossed Psalter: The Alkmaar Fragments of the N-Psalter', *ASE* 49 (2024), 1–66.

Powell, Timothy E. 'The "Three Orders of Society" in Anglo-Saxon England', *ASE* 23 (1994), 103–32.

Pulsiano, Phillip. 'The Originality of the Old English Gloss of the *Vespasian Psalter* and its Relation to the Gloss of the *Junius Psalter*', *ASE* 25 (1996), 37–62.

Pratt, David. *The Political Thought of King Alfred the Great* (Cambridge: Cambridge University Press, 2007).

——. 'The Illnesses of King Alfred the Great', *ASE* 30 (2001), 31–90.

——. 'The Voice of the King in "King Edgar's Establishment of Monasteries"', *ASE* 41 (2012), 145–204.

Raith, Josef. 'Ælfric's Share in the Old English Pentateuch', *RES* 3 (1952), 305–14.

Rauer, Christine. 'The Earliest English Prose', *Journal of Medieval History* 27 (221), 485–96.

——. Review of Michelle P. Brown, *Bede and the Theory of Everything*, *SELIM* 29 (2024), 142–5.

Raw, Barbara. 'The probable derivation of most of the illustrations in Junius II from an illustrated Old Saxon *Genesis*', *ASE* 5 (1976), 133–48.

Reiss, Katherine, and Hans J. Vermeer. *Towards a General Theory of Translational Action: Skopos Theory Explained*, trans. by Christiane Nord and Marina Dudenhöfer (London: Routledge Taylor & Francis Group, 2014).

Richards, Mary P. 'The Laws of Alfred and Ine', in *A Companion to Alfred the Great*, ed. Nicole Discenza and Paul E. Szarmach, Brill Companions to the Christian Tradition 58 (Leiden: Brill, 2015), pp. 282–309.

Roberts, Jane. 'Some Anglo-Saxon Psalters and their Glosses', in *The Psalms and Medieval English Literature: From the Conversion to the Reformation*, ed. Tamara Atkin and Francis Leneghan (Cambridge: D. S. Brewer, 2017), pp. 37–71.

Ross, Alan S. C. 'A Connection between Bede and the Anglo-Saxon Gloss to the Lindisfarne Gospels', *Journal of Theological Studies* 20 (1969), 482–94.

——. 'Supplementary Note to "A Connection between Bede and the Anglo-Saxon Gloss to the Lindisfarne Gospels?"', *Journal of Theological Studies* 24 (1973), 519–21.

Rubinstein, S. I. 'The Politics of Ælfric's *Maccabees*', *RES* 74 (2023), 589–604.

Rudolf, Winfried. 'A Fragment of the Old English Version of the Gospel of Mark in the Folger Shakespeare Library, Washington, DC', *The Library* 7 (2017), 405–17.

——. 'Quoting the Bible in Times of Trouble: Wulfstan and the Story of Saul and Jonathan in Napier Homily xxxvi', in *Sermons, Saints, and Sources: Studies in the Homiletic and Hagiographic Literature of Early Medieval England*, ed. Thomas N. Hall and Winfried Rudolf, SOEL 6 (Turnhout: Brepols, 2025), pp. 137–70.

Ryan, Salvador. 'The Bible and "the People" in Ireland, ca. 1100–ca. 1650', in *Ireland and the Reception of the Bible: Social and Cultural Perspectives*, ed. Bradford A. Anderson and Jonathan Kearney (London: T. & T. Clark, 2018), pp. 43–58.

Salvador-Bello, Mercedes. 'The Edgar Panegyrics in the Anglo-Saxon Chronicle', in *Edgar, King of the English 959–975: New Interpretations*, ed. Donald Scragg, Publications of the Manchester Centre for Anglo-Saxon Studies 8 (Woodbridge: Boydell, 2008), pp. 252–72.

——. 'Educating King and Court: The Exeter Book and the Transmission of Poetic Anthologies in the (Post-)Alfredian Period', *SELIM* 29, special edition on *New Readings in Alfredian Literature*, ed. Francis Leneghan (2024), 71–94.

Scales, Len, and Oliver Zimmer, eds. *Power and the Nation in European History* (Cambridge: Cambridge University Press, 2005).

Scattergood, John. 'The *Battle of Maldon* and History', in *Literature and Learning in Medieval and Renaissance England: Essays Presented to Fitzroy Pyle*, ed. John Scattergood (Blackrock, Co. Dublin: Irish Academic Press, 1984), pp. 11–24.

Scheil, Andrew. *The Footsteps of Israel: Understanding Jews in Anglo-Saxon England* (Ann Arbor, MI: University of Michigan Press, 2004).

Schleiermacher, F. D. E. 'Über die verschiedenen Methoden des Übersetzens', transl. Susan Bernovsky as 'On the Different Methods of Translating', in *The Translation Studies Reader*, ed. Lawrence Venuti (London: Routledge, 2004), pp. 43–63.

Scholten, Désirée. 'Cassiodorus' *Historia tripartita* before the Earliest Extant Manuscripts', in *The Resources of the Past in Early Medieval Europe*, ed. Clemens Gantner, Rosamond McKitterick and Sven Meeder (Cambridge: Cambridge University Press, 2015), pp. 34–50.

Scragg, Donald G. 'The Corpus of Vernacular Homilies and Prose Saints' Lives before Ælfric', *ASE* 8 (1979), 223–77.

——. 'The Corpus of Anonymous Lives and Their Manuscript Context', in *Holy Men and Holy Women: Old English Prose Saints' Lives and Their Contexts*, ed. Paul E. Szarmach (Albany, NY: State University of New York Press, 1996), pp. 209–30.

Shepherd, Geoffrey. 'English Versions of the Scriptures before Wyclif', in *The Cambridge History of the Bible, Volume 2: The West from the Fathers to the Reformation*, ed. G. W. H. Lampe (Cambridge: Cambridge University Press, 1969, repr. 2008), pp. 362–87.

Sisam, Kenneth. *Studies in the History of Old English Literature* (Oxford: Clarendon Press, 1953).

——. 'Canterbury, Lichfield, and the Vespasian Psalter', *RES* 7 (1956), 1–10.

Smalley, Beryl. *The Study of the Bible in the Middle Ages* (Oxford: Blackwell, 1952).

Smetana, Cyril L. 'Aelfric and the Early Medieval Homiliary', *Traditio* 15 (1959), 163–204.

Snook, Ben. 'Just War in Anglo-Saxon England: Transmission and Reception', in *Handbook of Medieval Culture: Fundamental Aspects and Conditions of the European Middle Ages*, ed. Albrecht Classen (Berlin: De Gruyter, 2015), pp. 99–120.

Solomonik-Pankrashova, Tatyana. 'Giving Voice to the Psalms in the Alfredian Metre 4 of Boethius', *Logos: A Journal, of Religion, Philosophy Comparative Cultural Studies & Art* 115 (2023), 140–9.

Solopova, Elizabeth, ed. *The Wycliffite Bible: Origin, History and Interpretation* (Leiden: Brill, 2017).

——. 'From Bede to Wyclif: The Knowledge of Old English within the Context of Late Middle English Biblical Translation and Beyond', *RES* 71 (2020), 805–27.

Soper, Harriet. *The Life Course in Old English Poetry* (Cambridge: Cambridge University Press, 2023).

Stanley, Eric G. 'New Formulas for Old: *Cædmon's Hymn*', in *Pagans and Christians: The Interplay between Christian Latin and Traditional Germanic Cultures in Early Medieval Europe*, ed. Tette Hofstra, L. A. J. R. Houwen and Alasdair A. MacDonald, Medievalia Groningana 16 (Groningen: Egbert Forsten, 1995), pp. 131–48.

——. 'The Lindisfarne Gospels: Aldred's Gloss For God and St Cuthbert and All the Saints Together Who are in the Island', in *The Lindisfarne Gospels: New Perspectives*, ed. Richard Gameson, Library of the Written Word 57 (Leiden: Brill, 2017), pp. 206–17.

Stanton, Robert. 'The (M)other Tongue: Translation Theory and Old English', in *Translation Theory and Practice in the Middle Ages*, ed. Jeanette Beer (Kalamazoo, MI: Medieval Institute Publications, 1997), pp. 33–46.

―――. *The Culture of Translation in Anglo-Saxon England* (Cambridge: D. S. Brewer, 2002).

Steiner, George. *After Babel: Aspects of Language and Translation*, 3rd edn (Oxford: Oxford University Press, 1998).

Stephenson, Rebecca. 'Ælfric of Eynsham and Hermeneutic Latin: *Meatim Sed et Rustica* Reconsidered', *The Journal of Medieval Latin* 16 (2006), 111–41.

―――. *The Politics of Language: Byrhtferth, Ælfric, and the Multilingual Identity of the Benedictine Reform* (Toronto: University of Toronto Press, 2015).

Stolzenburg, Hans. *Zur Übersetzungstechnik des Wulfila* (Halle a S.: Buchdruckerei des Waisenhauses, 1905).

Sutherland, Annie. *English Psalms in the Middle Ages, 1300–1450* (Oxford: Oxford University Press, 2015).

Szarmach, Paul E. 'The Earlier Homily: *De Parasceve*', in *Studies in Earlier Old English Prose: Sixteen Original Contributions*, ed. Paul E. Szarmach (Albany, NY: State University of New York Press, 1986), pp. 381–99

―――. 'Ælfric's Judith', in *Old English Literature and the Old Testament*, ed. Michael Fox and Manish Sharma (Toronto: University of Toronto Press, 2012), pp. 64–88.

Thompson Smith, Scott. 'The Edgar Poems and the Poetics of Failure in the Anglo-Saxon Chronicle', *ASE* 39 (2011), 105–37.

Tinti, Francesca, ed. *Pastoral Care in Late Anglo-Saxon England*, Anglo-Saxon Studies 6 (Woodbridge: Boydell, 2005).

Toswell, M. J. *The Anglo-Saxon Psalter* (Turnhout: Brepols, 2014).

―――. 'The Ninth-Century Psalter in England', in *The Age of Alfred: Rethinking English Literary Culture c. 850–950*, ed. Amy Faulkner and Francis Leneghan, SOEL 3 (Turnhout: Brepols, 2024), pp. 389–408

Treharne, Elaine. 'Making their Presence Felt: Readers of Ælfric, c. 1050–1350', in *A Companion to Ælfric*, ed. Hugh Magennis and Mary Swan, Brill Companions to the Christian Tradition 18 (Leiden: Brill, 2009), pp. 399–422.

―――. 'The Authority of English, 900–1150', in *The Cambridge History of Early Medieval English Literature*, ed. Clare A. Lees (Cambridge: University of Cambridge Press, 2013), pp. 554–78.

―――. *Living Through Conquest: The Politics of Early English, 1020–1220* (Oxford: Oxford University Press, 2012).

Treschow, Michael, Paramjit S. Gill, and Tim B. Swartz, 'King Alfred's Scholarly Writings and the Authorship of the First Fifty Prose Psalms', *Heroic Age* 12 (2009), http://www.heroicage.org/issues/12/treschow-gillswartz.php.

Treschow, Michael. 'The Prologue to Alfred's Law Code: Instruction in the Spirit of Mercy', *Florilegium* 13 (1994), 79–110.

―――. '*Godes Word* for *Vox Domini* in Psalm 28 of the Paris Psalter: Biblical Translation and Alfredian Politics', *Florilegium* 31 (2014), 165–80.

Trilling, Renée. 'Heavenly Bodies: Paradoxes of Female Martyrdom in Ælfric's *Lives of Saints*', in *Writing Women Saints in Anglo-Saxon England*, ed. Paul E. Szarmach (Toronto: University of Toronto Press, 2013), pp. 249–73.

Upchurch, Robert K. 'Catechetic Homiletics: Ælfric's Preaching and Teaching During Lent', in *A Companion to Ælfric*, ed. Hugh Magennis and Mary Swan, Brill Companions to the Christian Tradition 18 (Leiden: Brill, 2009), pp. 217–46.

van Liere, Frans. *An Introduction to the Medieval Bible* (Cambridge: Cambridge University Press, 2014)

Venuti, Lawrence. *The Translator's Invisibility* (New York: Routledge, 1995).

——. ed. *The Translation Studies Reader* (London: Routledge, 2012).

von Campenhausen, Hans Freiherr. *The Formation of the Christian Bible*, trans. J. A. Baker (Minneapolis: Fortress Press, 1972).

Watson, Nicholas. 'Censorship and Cultural Change in Late-Medieval England: Vernacular Theology, the Oxford Translation Debate, and Arundel's Constitutions of 1409', *Speculum* 70 (1995), 822–64.

——. *Balaam's Ass: Vernacular Theology Before the English Reformation, Volume 1: Frameworks, Arguments, English to 1250* (Philadelphia: University of Pennsylvania Press, 2022).

Whatley, E. Gordon. 'Hagiography and Violence: Military Men in Ælfric's *Lives of Saints*', in *Source of Wisdom: Old English and Early Medieval Latin Studies in Honour of Thomas D. Hill*, ed. Charles D. Wright, Frederick M. Biggs and Thomas N. Hall (Toronto: University of Toronto Press, 2007), pp. 217–38.

——. 'Pearls before Swine: Ælfric, Vernacular Hagiography, and the Lay Reader', in *Via Crucis: Essays on Early Medieval Sources and Ideas in Memory of J. E. Cross*, ed. Thomas D. Hill, Charles D. Wright and Thomas N. Hall (Morgantown, 2002), pp. 158–84.

Whitelock, Dorothy. 'The Prose of Alfred's Reign', in *Continuations and Beginnings: Studies in Old English Literature*, ed. Eric G. Stanley (London: Nelson, 1966), pp. 67–103.

Wieland, Gernot. '*Legifer, Dux, Scriptor*: Moses in Anglo-Saxon Literature', in *Illuminating Moses: A History of Reception from Exodus to the Renaissance*, ed. Jane Beal, Commentaria 4 (Leiden: Brill, 2013), pp. 185–209.

Wiesenekker, Evert. 'The Vespasian and Junius Psalters Compared: Glossary or Translation?', *Amsterdamer Beiträge zur älteren Germanistik* 40 (1994), 21–39.

——. *Word be Worde, Andgit of Andgite: Translation Performance in the Old English Interlinear Glosses of the Vespasian, Regius and Lambeth Psalters* (Huizen: Bout, 1991).

Wilcox, Johnathan. *Ælfric's Prefaces*, Durham Medieval Texts 9 (Durham: University of Durham, 1994).

———. 'Ælfric in Dorset and the Landscape of Pastoral Care', in *Pastoral Care in Late Anglo-Saxon England*, ed. Francesca Tinti, Anglo-Saxon Studies 6 (Woodbridge: Boydell, 2005), pp. 52–62.

———. 'A Place to Weep: Joseph in the Beer-Room and Anglo-Saxon Gestures of Emotion', in *Saints and Scholars: New Perspectives on Anglo-Saxon Literature and Culture in Honour of Hugh Magennis*, ed. Stuart McWilliams (Cambridge: D. S. Brewer, 2012), pp. 14–32.

Wilcox, Miranda. 'Creating the cloud-tent-ship conceit in *Exodus*', *ASE* 40 (2012), 103–50.

Withers, Benjamin C. *The Illustrated Old English Hexateuch, Cotton Claudius B. iv: The Frontier of Seeing and Reading in Anglo-Saxon England* (Toronto: University of Toronto Press, 2007).

Wormald, Patrick. 'The Uses of Literacy in Anglo-Saxon England and Its Neighbours', *Transactions of the Royal Historical Society*, 5th series, 27 (1977), 95–114.

———. 'Anglo-Saxon Society and its Literature', in *The Cambridge Companion to Old English Literature*, ed. Malcolm Godden and Michael Lapidge (Cambridge: Cambridge University Press, 1991), pp. 1–22.

———. '*Engla lond*: The Making of an Allegiance', *Journal of Historical Sociology* 1 (1994), 1–24

———. *The Making of English Law: King Alfred to the Twelfth Century, Vol. 1: Legislation and its Limits* (Oxford: Blackwell, 1999).

———. 'Germanic Power Structures: The Early English Experience', in *Power and the Nation in European History*, ed. Len Scales and Oliver Zimmer (Cambridge: Cambridge University Press, 2005), pp. 105–24.

Wright, Charles D. *The Irish Tradition in Old English Literature*, CSASE 6 (Cambridge: Cambridge University Press, 1993).

Wright, Roger. 'Late Latin and early Romance: Alcuin's *De Orthographia* and the Council of Tours (813 A.D.)', *Papers of the Liverpool Latin Seminar* 3 (1981), 343–61.

Yeager, Stephen M. *From Lawmen to Plowmen: Anglo-Saxon Legal Tradition and the School of Langland* (Toronto: University of Toronto Press, 2014).

Zacher, Samantha. *Rewriting the Old Testament in Anglo-Saxon Verse: Becoming the Chosen People* (London: Bloomsbury, 2013).

———. 'Circumscribing the Text: Views on Circumcision in Old English Literature', in *Old English Literature and the Old Testament*, ed. Michael Fox and Manish Sharma (Toronto: University of Toronto Press, 2012), pp. 89–118.

———. 'Anglo-Saxon Maccabees: Political Theology in Ælfric's *Lives of Saints*', in *Old English Lexicology and Lexicography: Essays in Honor of Antonette diPaolo Healey*, ed. Maren Clegg Hyer, Haruko Momma and Samantha Zacher, Anglo-Saxon Studies 40 (Cambridge: D. S. Brewer, 2020), pp. 143–58.

Index

Aaron 185–8, 192–3, 197–8
Abraham 15, 155, 157, 165, 174–5, 182–3
Acta Pilati 111
Acts of the Apostles 20–1, 51, 54, 58, 59, 69–70, 73, 79, 237, 248
Adam and Eve 113, 139, 174, 210, 220, 234–5, 250
Advent Lyrics (Christ I) 15, 78
Ælfric of Eynsham
 Catholic Homilies 22, 60 n. 27, 80, 86, 109, 119–44, 157 n. 36, 159, 176–7, 207, 226–8, 236, 243, 246, 247, 248
  Annunciation of St Mary (*Annunciatio S. Mariæ*) 94 n. 47, 125–30
  On the Beginning of Creation (*De Initio Creaturae*) 226–33
  Palm Sunday: On the Lord's Passion (*Sermo de Sacrificio in die Pascae*) 130–44
 Eight Vices and Twelve Abuses (De octo uitiis et de duodecim abusiuis gradus) 171–2, 173
 Esther 183 n. 89, 205
 Genesis 145 n. 3, 162–77, 224, 244, 246
 Interrogationes Sigewulfi 155 n. 33, 160–1 n. 48, 176
 Joshua 112, 136, 143, 145, 146, 148, 149, 150, 177, 192, 198–205, 225, 235
 Judges 112, 136, 143, 145 n. 3, 148, 149, 150, 177, 187, 190 n. 104, 191, 202, 205–14, 235, 240
 Judith 183 n. 89, 205, 235, 239
 Letter for Wulfsige 119–20, 131, 143
 Letter to Wulfgeat 145 n.3, 146, 150, 173 n. 69, 218, 238, 239–40, 248
 Lives of Saints

 Kings 183 n. 89, 205, 235
 Letter of Christ to Agbar 110
 Maccabees 183 n. 89, 188–90, 205, 221, 235
 On the Three Orders of Society 188–90, 235 n. 43
 On the Prayer of Moses 174–5
 readership of 150–1, 155 n. 32
 Numbers 145 n. 3, 146 n. 5, 148, 149, 177, 185–94, 198, 205 n. 122, 207, 215, 224, 244, 246
 post-Conquest reputation of 244–53
 Preface to Genesis 129, 145 n. 3, 146, 149, 151, 153–62, 176, 214, 237, 241, 246, 248 n. 14
 rhythmical prose style 169, 175, 190–92, 206–7, 215, 226, 233–5
 Treatise on the Old and New Testaments (Letter to Sigeweard) 22, 110, 124, 145 n. 3, 149, 173–4, 177, 192, 198, 204, 205, 216–43, 247, 248, 251
Æthelberht of Kent, King 56, 75
Æthelmær, Ealdorman 150, 155 n. 32
Æthelstan, King 211–12, 250
Ælfthryth 51
Æthelweard, Ealdorman 146, 150, 155 n. 32, 157–60, 155–60, 185, 198, 214 n. 142, 225, 229, 237, 240 n. 69
 Chronicon 151 n. 24, 219 n. 9
Æthelwold, Bishop 35 n. 35, 92–3, 123 n. 106
Æthelwulf, King 12 n. 43, 67, 219
Aidan, Bishop 6
Alcuin 16, 125 n. 115, 244, 246 n. 6
 De virtutibus et vitiis 172 n. 67, 173
 Quaestiones in Genesim 125 n. 115, 155 n. 33, 160–1 n. 48, 246 n. 6

Index

see also under Ælfric,
    Interrogationes Sigewulfi
Aldred
  see under Lindisfarne Gospels,
    Old English gloss on
Alfred, King
  Asser's *Life* of
    see under Asser's *Life of Alfred*
  Domboc
    see under *Domboc*
  educational reforms of 3–6,
    11–12, 19, 20, 22, 34–5, 39–42,
    50, 51, 52, 53, 65, 109, 122–3,
    246, 249–53
  involvement in legislation 56–8,
    75–7
  Prose Preface to Old English
    Pastoral Care 3–6, 11, 34–5,
    41, 50, 52, 57, 71, 76, 147, 159
    n. 44
  Prose Psalms
    see under *Prose Psalms*, Old
    English
  Soliloquies
    see under *Soliloquies*, Old
    English
  wars of 41, 187, 211–12
Andreas 79
Anglo-Saxon Chronicle 12 n. 41, 67,
  151, 187, 199, 212–13, 219
Apocrypha 15, 22, 79, 80, 109–19
  see also under *Avenging of the
    Saviour, Descensus ad infernos,
    Gospel of Nicodemus, Gospel of
    Pseudo-Matthew, Vision of St
    Paul*
Apostles 55, 58, 59, 69, 71–6, 159,
    220, 221, 237, 241
  see also under Acts of Apostles
Arator 11
Ascension (Christ II)
  see under Cynewulf
Asser's *Life of Alfred* 12 n. 41, 41, 50,
    51, 56–8
Augustine 122, 135, 142, 238
  De Trinitate 130 n. 123, 225, 226

Enarrationes in Psalmos 28, 225
    n. 30
  Retractions 225
Arundel, Thomas 2–4, 6
Avenging of the Saviour, Old
    English 110–15
  see also under *Vindicta Salvatoris*

Babel, Tower of 238
Bede 6, 20, 122, 125, 126–7, 130, 135,
    139, 142, 225
  Bede's Death Song 17, 79
  Ecclesiastical History 13–14, 245
    see also under *Bede*, Old English
  Letter to Ecgbert 16
  post-Conquest reputation
    of 244–6, 249–50
  translation of Gospel of
    John 16–19, 41, 80
Bede, Old English 5
Benedictine Reform 92–3, 143, 150,
    211
Beowulf 79 n. 7, 110 n. 67, 113, 169
    n. 63, 219 n. 9
Bishop's Bible (1568) 250
  see also under Foxe, John
Boethius, Old English 5, 39, 40 n. 44,
    62, 191 n. 104, 221
Byrhtnoth, Ealdorman 187

Caesarius of Arles 78, 225 n. 30
Cain and Abel 15, 220
Cambridge (Winchcombe)
    Psalter 35–8
Candidus Fuldensis 138, 142
Canterbury Psalter
  see under Eadwine (Canterbury)
    Psalter
Cassiodorus 39, 41 n. 53, 46, 48, 49
    n. 69, 210–11 n. 133, 238 n. 62
Cædmon's Hymn 1 n. 1, 13–16, 18,
    161 n. 50
Cetura 165
Christ in Judgement (Christ III) 20 n.
    73, 78
Codex Amiatinus 16
Codex Fuldensis 9

283

Collatio legum Mosaicarum et Romanorum 55
Cynewulf
   Ascension (*Christ II*) 78
   Fates of the Apostles 79

Daniel 15, 79 n. 8, 242 n. 79
David, King 26, 28–30, 40–1, 44, 45, 49, 51 n. 73, 53, 65, 67 n. 47, 97–9, 207–9
Decalogue 54, 59, 62–5, 193, 194, 196
Delilah 209
Descensus ad infernos 111
Deuteronomy, Book of 145, 223–4
   see also under Old English Heptateuch, *Deuteronomy*
Deuteronomy, Old English prose
   see under Old English Heptateuch
Dialogues, Old English 5 n. 11, 62
Domboc
   Mosaic Prologue 6, 21, 54–77, 93, 252
Dream of the Rood, The 15, 79, 111, 132

Eadwine (Canterbury) Psalter 27 n. 13, 247
Edward the Elder, King
   education of 51
Edgar, King 92, 211–14
   King Edgar's Establishment of Monasteries 93
Enoch, Book of (Enoch I) 109–10
Evangelienbuch
   see under Otfrid's *Evangelienbuch*
Euangelium Nichodemi 111–12
   see also under *Gospel of Nicodemus*, Old English
Exeter Book 12, 78, 79 n. 8, 80, 91 n. 38, 92
Exodus, Book of 15, 20, 21, 51, 54–5, 59–67, 73 n. 62, 190–1, 196, 206
   see also under Old English Heptateuch, *Exodus*
Exodus, Old English prose
   see under Old English Heptateuch

Exodus, Old English verse 15, 79 n. 8, 191 n. 104, 242 n. 79

Fall of the Angels 15, 110, 220, 229–35, 242 n. 79
Farman
   see under Rushworth (MacRegol) Gospels
First Worcester Fragment 244–7
Foxe, John 106 n. 58, 250–1
Fulk of Rheims, Archbishop 56 n. 11, 71–2

Genesis, Book of 6, 54, 234–5, 250
   see also under Old English Heptateuch, *Genesis*
Genesis A 15, 79 n. 8
Genesis B 6 n. 13, 12 n. 43
Genesis, Old English prose
   see under Old English Heptateuch
Geneva Bible 250 n. 23
Glossed Prose Psalter, Middle English 249
Gospel Harmonies 8–11, 79, 80, 135, 250
Gothic Bible
   see under Ulfilas (Wulfila)
Golden Rule 59, 70–1, 93
Gospel of Nicodemus 237, 242–3
   see also under *Gospel of Nicodemus*, Old English
Gospel of Nicodemus, Old English 80, 91 n. 38, 110–15
Gospel of Pseudo-Matthew 237, 242–3
   see also under *Gospel of Pseudo-Matthew*, Old English
Gospel of Pseudo-Matthew, Old English 115–19
Gregory the Great 5, 78, 122, 251 n. 25, 225 n. 30
   see also under *Dialogues*, Old English

Hagar 165
Haymo of Auxerre 122 n. 103, 135, 138, 142

Heliand 9, 12 n. 43, 94 n. 47
Heptateuch, Old English 6, 22,
    59–60, 92, 94, 97, 108, 109, 137,
    145–215, 216–18, 237–8, 242,
    246, 247–8, 252
  Genesis 145–9, 162–77, 246, 250
    see also under Ælfric
  Exodus 145–9, 177–81, 215, 224,
    244
  Leviticus 145–9, 181–3, 244
  Numbers 145–9, 185–94, 205 n.
    122, 207, 215, 224, 244, 246
    see also under Ælfric
  Deuteronomy 145–9, 193, 194–8,
    198, 215, 224, 244, 248 n. 14
  Joshua
    see under Ælfric
  Judges
    see under Ælfric
Hexateuch, Old English
  Illustrated 146, 152–4, 186–7,
    198 n. 117, 246
  see also under Manuscripts,
    London, British Library,
    Cotton MS Claudius B. IV
Hezekiah, King 40, 41, 45, 53, 65
Hincmar of Rheims 55, 68 n. 50

Ine, King 75
Isaiah 8, 125, 132, 229, 237

Jerome 4 n. 7, 25–6, 33, 85, 110, 115,
    122 n. 103, 135 n. 135, 137–8,
    139, 142, 155 n. 33, 157 n. 36,
    159, 161, 221 n. 12, 225 n. 30,
    235, 236, 238 n. 62, 247, 249
Joseph, father of Jesus 82, 85, 98–9,
    116–18, 125–9, 132 n. 130
John, Gospel of 9–10, 81, 92, 111,
    130, 131 n. 127, 137, 138, 139
  see also under Bede, translation of
    Gospel of John
Joshua, Old English prose
  see under Ælfric
Judges, Old English prose
  see under Ælfric
Junius Psalter 27 n. 13, 32

Juvencus 11, 17

King James Bible 1, 250 n. 23

Laban 164–5
Lambeth Psalter 35
Letter of Christ to Agbar
  see under Ælfric
Leviticus, Book of 54, 55, 73
  see also under Old English
    Heptateuch, *Leviticus*
Leviticus, Old English prose
  see under Old English Heptateuch
Liber ex Lege Moysi 54–5, 59 n. 23,
    65 n. 39
Lindisfarne Gospels 81
  Aldred's Old English gloss on 18
    n. 68, 21–2, 80, 81–7, 90–1, 94,
    95–6, 97 n. 49, 99, 100
l'Isle, William 251
Lord's Prayer, The 16, 17, 79 n. 8
Lot 165–76
Lucifer 225, 229, 232, 233
  see also under Fall of the Angels
Luke, Gospel of 70, 72, 111, 125–7,
    130, 135–9, 142 n. 148

MacRegol Gospels
  see under Rushworth Gospels
Maldon, The Battle of 169 n. 63, 187
Manuscripts
  Bibliothèque nationale de France,
    MS Latin 8824
    see under Paris Psalter
  Cambridge Corpus Christi
    College, MS 140 91 n. 38,
    103–6
  Cambridge, University Library,
    MS Ii.2.11 91 n. 38, 106, 110,
    112
  London, British Library, Cotton
    MS Claudius B. IV 145–6,
    153–4, 186–7, 197 n. 117
    see also under Hexateuch, Old
      English Illustrated
  Oxford, Bodleian Library, MS
    Hatton 114 116, 119

285

Oxford, Bodleian Library, MS
    Junius 11   1 n. 2, 12, 15, 79 n.
    8, 158 n. 38, 177–8 n. 81, 242
    n. 79
Oxford, Bodleian Library, MS
    Laud Misc. 509   145, 155–6,
    162–3, 217–18, 234 n. 41, 247–8
Oxford, Bodleian Library, MS
    Bodley 343   116 n. 86, 216 n.
    1, 234 n. 41, 248
Oxford, Bodleian Library, MS
    Bodley 441   91 n. 38, 106–7
Saint-Omer, Bibliothèque
    Municipale, 202   112, 113
Mary, mother of Jesus   115–19,
    125–30, 228–9
Matthew, Gospel of   16, 68, 82–91,
    92, 94, 97, 100–3, 106, 125–43
    see also under Lord's Prayer, The
Metrical Psalms   20 n. 73, 24 n. 3, 27
    n. 15, 42
Mosaic Prologue to *Domboc*
    see under *Domboc*
Moses   54, 55, 56, 59–69, 74, 76,
    136, 137, 149, 157, 161, 174–5,
    177–9, 181–98, 202–3, 206, 210,
    215, 223–4, 234

Noah   15, 67 n. 47, 165, 176, 219–20
Numbers, Book of   54, 55, 206 n. 122
    see also under Old English
    Heptateuch, *Numbers*
Numbers, Old English prose
    see under Old English Heptateuch

Offa, King   74 n. 64, 75
Old High German Tatian   9–10
Ormulum   248–9
Orosius, Old English   5, 48 n. 68, 62,
    251 n. 25
Oswald, Archbishop   92
Oswald, King   6
Otfrid's *Evangelienbuch*   10–11, 39,
    249–50
Oxford Psalter, The   249 n. 19
Owun
    see under Rushworth (MacRegol)
    Gospels
Palm Sunday Homily (HomS 18),
    Anonymous   130–43
Paul the Deacon   122, 125
Paris Psalter   24 n. 3, 40, 42–5, 90
    see also under *Prose Psalms*,
    Metrical Psalms
Peter, St   136–8
Pharaoh
    destruction of army in Red
    Sea   178–9, 190–1, 206–7
    hanging of baker   153–4
Priests   81, 86, 109, 143, 144, 147,
    152, 221, 240, 249
    duties of   119, 122, 131, 135, 138,
    159, 188–90
    ignorance of   129, 151, 159, 241,
    245
Prose Psalms   2 n. 3, 6, 21, 25, 38–53,
    62, 65, 67, 118 n. 91
Prudentius   11
Pseudo-Matthaei Evangelium
    see under *Gospel of Pseudo-
    Matthew*, Old English

Rachel   164–5
Revelation, Book of   229, 237
Rolle, Richard   1 n. 1, 249
Royal (Regius) Psalter   27 n. 13, 27
    n. 15, 35
Rushworth (MacRegol) Gospels   81
    Farman's Old English gloss
    on   87–91, 94, 95–6, 97 n. 49,
    99, 100

Samson   209, 212
Sarah   165
Saul, King   149, 206–7
Saxon Genesis   6 n. 13, 9 n. 27, 12 n.
    43
    see also under *Genesis B*
Sedulius   17, 78, 139
Septuagint   4 n. 7, 7, 33 n. 28, 157
    n. 36
Sigefryth   238

Index

Sigeweard   146, 151, 218, 222–3, 226, 238–40
  see also under Ælfric, *Treatise on the Old and New Testaments*
Smaragdus   122 n. 103, 135, 138, 142
Sodom and Gomorrah
  Ælfric's writings on   165–76
Soliloquies, Old English   5 n. 11, 39, 61 n. 28, 62
Solomon, King   56, 236

Tatian, *Diatessaron*   9
  see also under Gospel Harmonies
Theodore of Mopsuestia   38–40
Theodosius I, Emperor   210–11
Theodosius II, Emperor   210–11
Three Orders of Society   188–90, 193–4, 212 n. 137, 221, 223, 235 n. 43
Tyndale, William   1, 250

Ulfilas (Wulfila)
  Gothic Bible   7–8

Venuti, Lawrence   xii
Vespasian Psalter
  Old English gloss to   25–35, 36, 38, 46, 247
Vikings   41, 64, 81, 174 n. 72, 208, 211, 215, 246
Vindicta Salvatoris   111–12, 114–15
  see also under *Avenging of the Saviour*, Old English
Vision of St Paul   110, 237

West Saxon Gospels
  see under *Wessex Gospels*
Wessex Gospels   6, 22, 60 n. 28, 80, 81 n. 15, 91–109, 110, 112, 124–5, 129, 132–4, 139–41, 143–4, 149, 157 n. 36, 243, 247, 250–2
William of Malmesbury   5, 41, 250 n. 24
Winchcombe Psalter
  see under Cambridge Psalter
Wulfsige, Bishop of Sherborne
  see under Ælfric, *Letter for Wulfsige*
Wulfstan, Archbishop   146 n. 5, 212–13 n. 138, 243 n. 81, 248
Wycliffite Bible   1 n. 1, 46 n. 62, 215, 216, 249, 250

ANGLO-SAXON STUDIES

Details of ealier volumes can be found on the Boydell & Brewer website.

Volume 17: Writing Power in Anglo-Saxon England: Texts, Hierarchies, Economies, *Catherine A. M. Clarke*

Volume 18: Cognitive Approaches to Old English Poetry, *Antonina Harbus*

Volume 19: Environment, Society and Landscape in Early Medieval England: Time and Topography, *Tom Williamson*

Volume 20: Honour, Exchange and Violence in *Beowulf*, *Peter S. Baker*

Volume 21: *John the Baptist's Prayer* or *The Descent into Hell* from the Exeter Book: Text, Translation and Critical Study, *M. R. Rambaran-Olm*

Volume 22: Food, Eating and Identity in Early Medieval England, *Allen J. Frantzen*

Volume 23: Capital and Corporal Punishment in Anglo-Saxon England, *edited by Jay Paul Gates and Nicole Marafioti*

Volume 24: The Dating of *Beowulf*: A Reassessment, *edited by Leonard Neidorf*

Volume 25: The Cruciform Brooch and Anglo-Saxon England, *Toby F. Martin*

Volume 26: Trees in the Religions of Early Medieval England, *Michael D. J. Bintley*

Volume 27: The Peterborough Version of the Anglo-Saxon Chronicle: Rewriting Post-Conquest History, *Malasree Home*

Volume 28: The Anglo-Saxon Chancery: The History, Language and Production of Anglo-Saxon Charters from Alfred to Edgar, *Ben Snook*

Volume 29: Representing Beasts in Early Medieval England and Scandinavia, *edited by Michael D. J. Bintley and Thomas J. T. Williams*

Volume 30: Direct Speech in *Beowulf* and Other Old English Narrative Poems, *Elise Louviot*

Volume 31: Old English Philology: Studies in Honour of R. D. Fulk, *edited by Leonard Neidorf, Rafael J. Pascual and Tom Shippey*

Volume 32: 'Charms', Liturgies, and Secret Rites in Early Medieval England, *Ciaran Arthur*

Volume 33: Old Age in Early Medieval England: A Cultural History, *Thijs Porck*

Volume 34: Priests and their Books in Late Anglo-Saxon England, *Gerald P. Dyson*

Volume 35: Burial, Landscape and Identity in Early Medieval Wessex, *Kate Mees*

Volume 36: The Sword in Early Medieval Northern Europe: Experience, Identity, Representation, *Sue Brunning*

Volume 37: The Chronology and Canon of Ælfric of Eynsham, *Aaron J. Kleist*

Volume 38: Medical Texts in Anglo-Saxon Literary Culture, *Emily Kesling*

Volume 39: The Dynastic Drama of *Beowulf*, *Francis Leneghan*

Volume 40: Old English Lexicology and Lexicography: Essays in Honor of Antonette diPaolo Healey, *edited by Maren Clegg Hyer, Haruko Momma and Samantha Zacher*

Volume 41: Debating with Demons: Pedagogy and Materiality in Early English Literature, *Christina M. Heckman*

Volume 42: Textual Identities in Early Medieval England: Essays in Honour of Katherine O'Brien O'Keefe, *edited by Jacqueline Fay, Rebecca Stephenson and Renée R. Trilling*

Volume 43: Bishop Æthelwold, his Followers, and Saints' Cults in Early Medieval England: Power, Belief, and Religious Reform, *Alison Hudson*

Volume 44: Global Perspectives on Early Medieval England, *edited by Karen Louise Jolly and Britton Elliott Brooks*

Volume 45: Performance in *Beowulf* and Other Old English Poems, *Steven J. A. Breeze*

Volume 46: Wealth and the Material World in the Old English Alfredian Corpus, *Amy Faulkner*

Volume 47: Law, Literature, and Social Regulation in Early Medieval England, *edited by Anya Adair and Andrew Rabin*

Volume 48: The Reigns of Edmund, Eadred and Eadwig, 939–959: New Interpretations, *edited by Mary Elizabeth Blanchard and Christopher Riedel*

Volume 49: Emotional Practice in Old English Literature, *Alice Jorgensen*

Volume 50: Old English Studies and its Scandinavian Practitioners: Nationalism, Aesthetics and Spirituality in the Nordic Countries, 1733–2023, *Robert E. Bjork*

Volume 51: Remains of the Past in Old English Literature, *Jan-Peer Hartmann*

Volume 52: Constructing the Anglo-Saxon Chronicles, *Daniel Anlezark*

Volume 53: Cultural Connections between the Continent and Early Medieval England, *edited by Thijs Porck, Kees Dekker and László Sándor Chardonnens*

www.ingramcontent.com/pod-product-compliance
Lightning Source LLC
Chambersburg PA
CBHW051603230426
43668CB00013B/1959